...OVEL

From Far Away™

Vol. 4

Story and Art by
Kyoko Hikawa

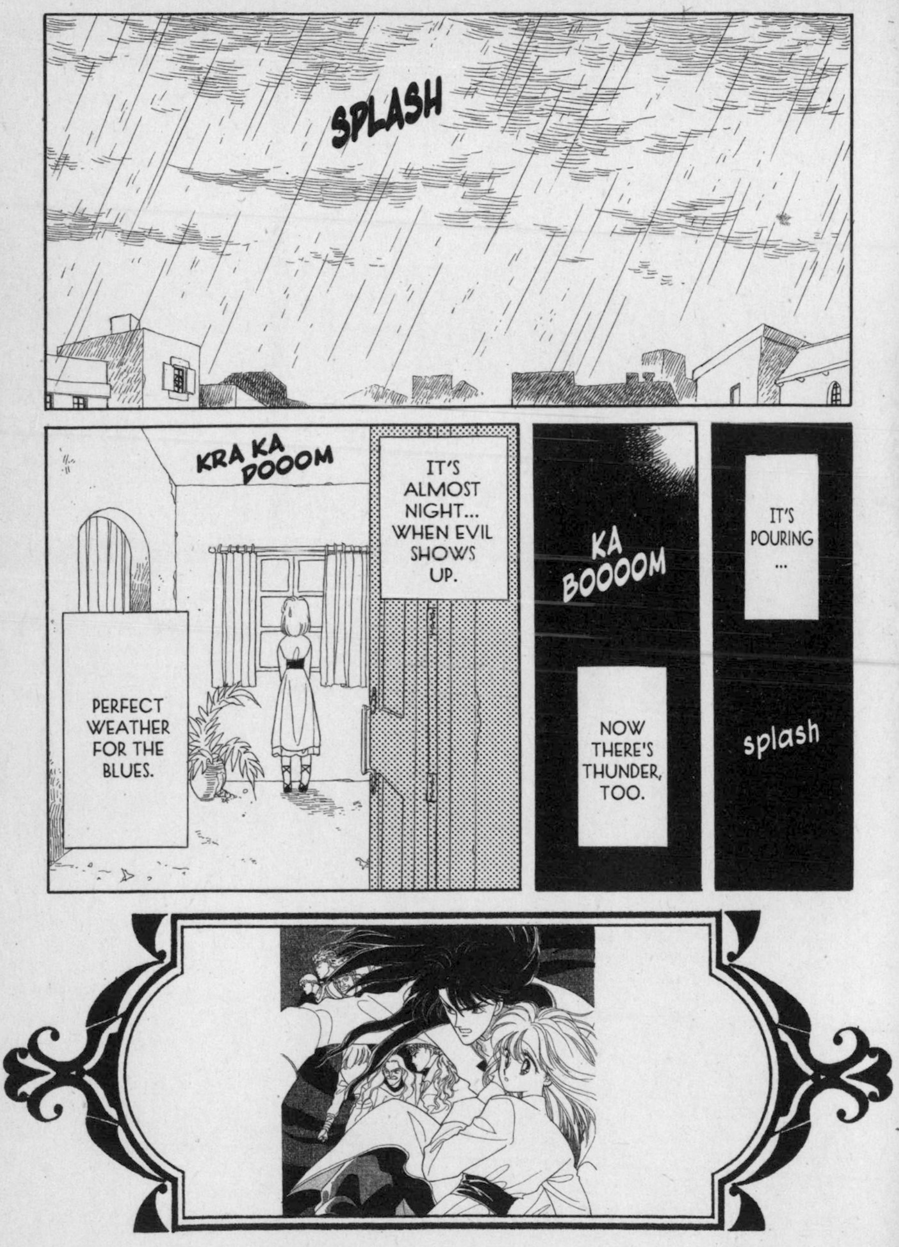
SPLASH
IT'S POURING ...
splash
KA BOOOOM
NOW THERE'S THUNDER, TOO.
IT'S ALMOST NIGHT... WHEN EVIL SHOWS UP.
KRA KA DOOOM
PERFECT WEATHER FOR THE BLUES.

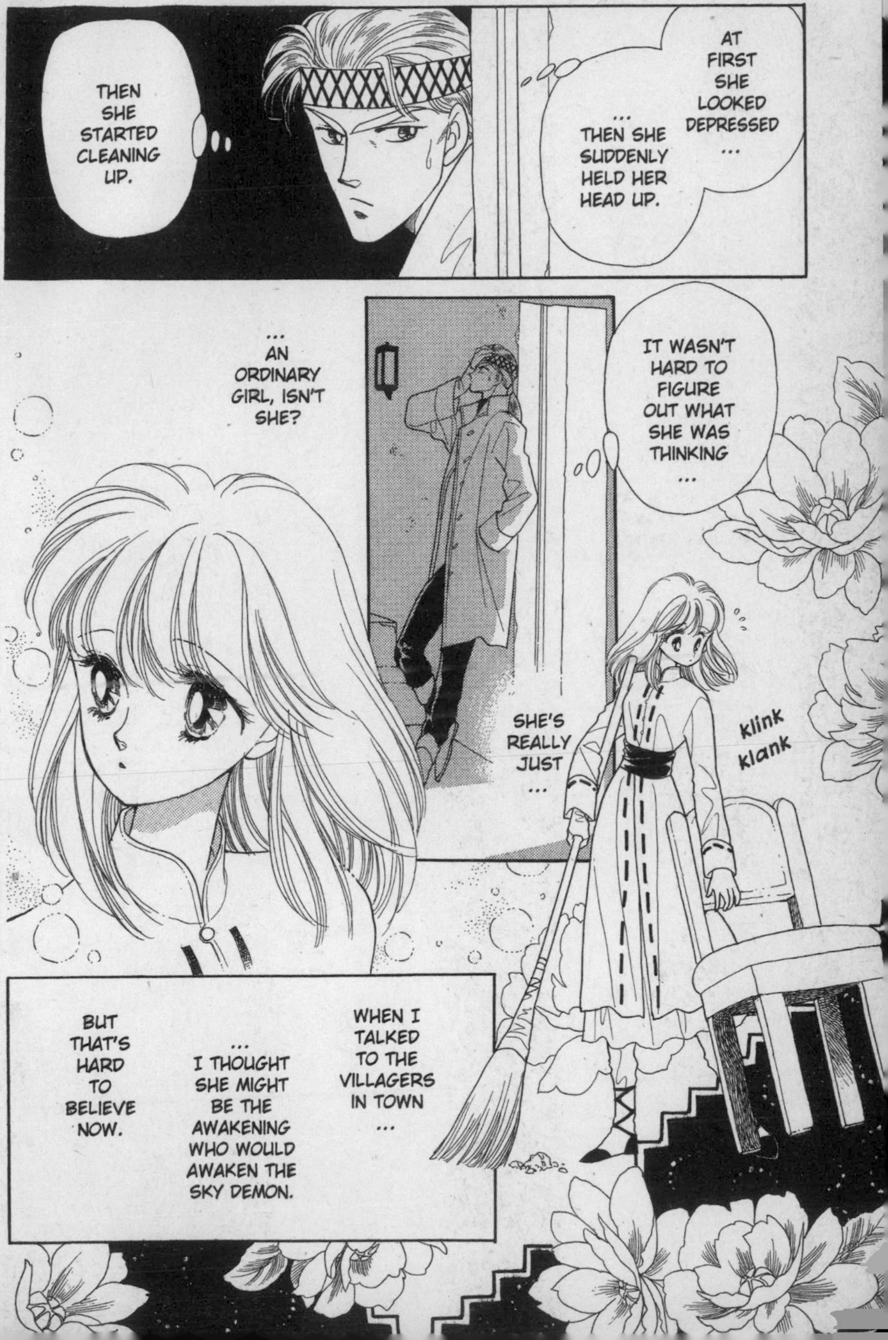
AT FIRST SHE LOOKED DEPRESSED ...
... THEN SHE SUDDENLY HELD HER HEAD UP.
THEN SHE STARTED CLEANING UP.
IT WASN'T HARD TO FIGURE OUT WHAT SHE WAS THINKING ...
Klink klank
SHE'S REALLY JUST ...
... AN ORDINARY GIRL, ISN'T SHE?
WHEN I TALKED TO THE VILLAGERS IN TOWN ...
... I THOUGHT SHE MIGHT BE THE AWAKENING WHO WOULD AWAKEN THE SKY DEMON.
BUT THAT'S HARD TO BELIEVE NOW.

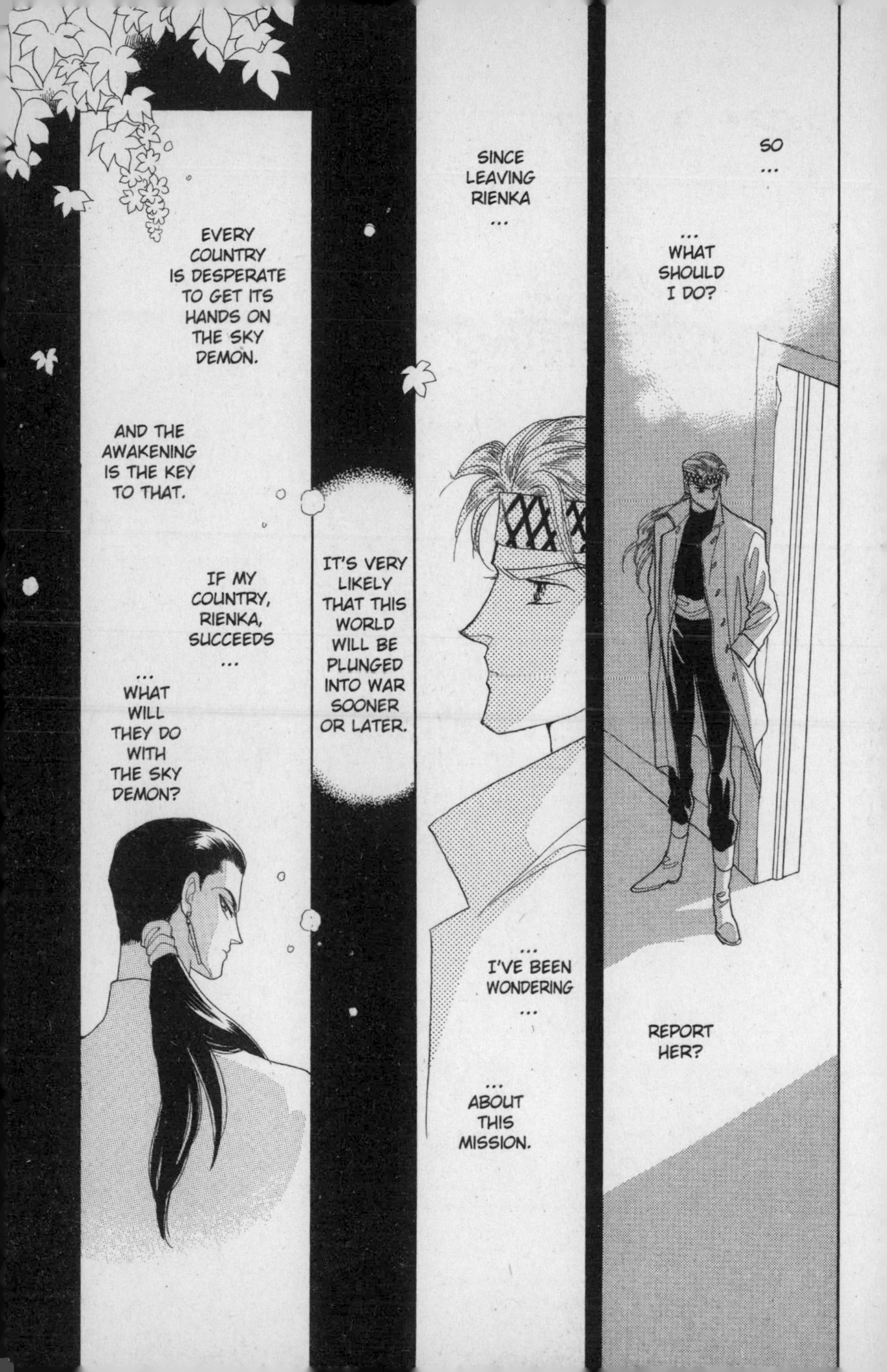
SO ...
... WHAT SHOULD I DO?
REPORT HER?
SINCE LEAVING RIENKA ...
... I'VE BEEN WONDERING ...
... ABOUT THIS MISSION.
IT'S VERY LIKELY THAT THIS WORLD WILL BE PLUNGED INTO WAR SOONER OR LATER.
EVERY COUNTRY IS DESPERATE TO GET ITS HANDS ON THE SKY DEMON.
AND THE AWAKENING IS THE KEY TO THAT.
IF MY COUNTRY, RIENKA, SUCCEEDS ...
... WHAT WILL THEY DO WITH THE SKY DEMON?

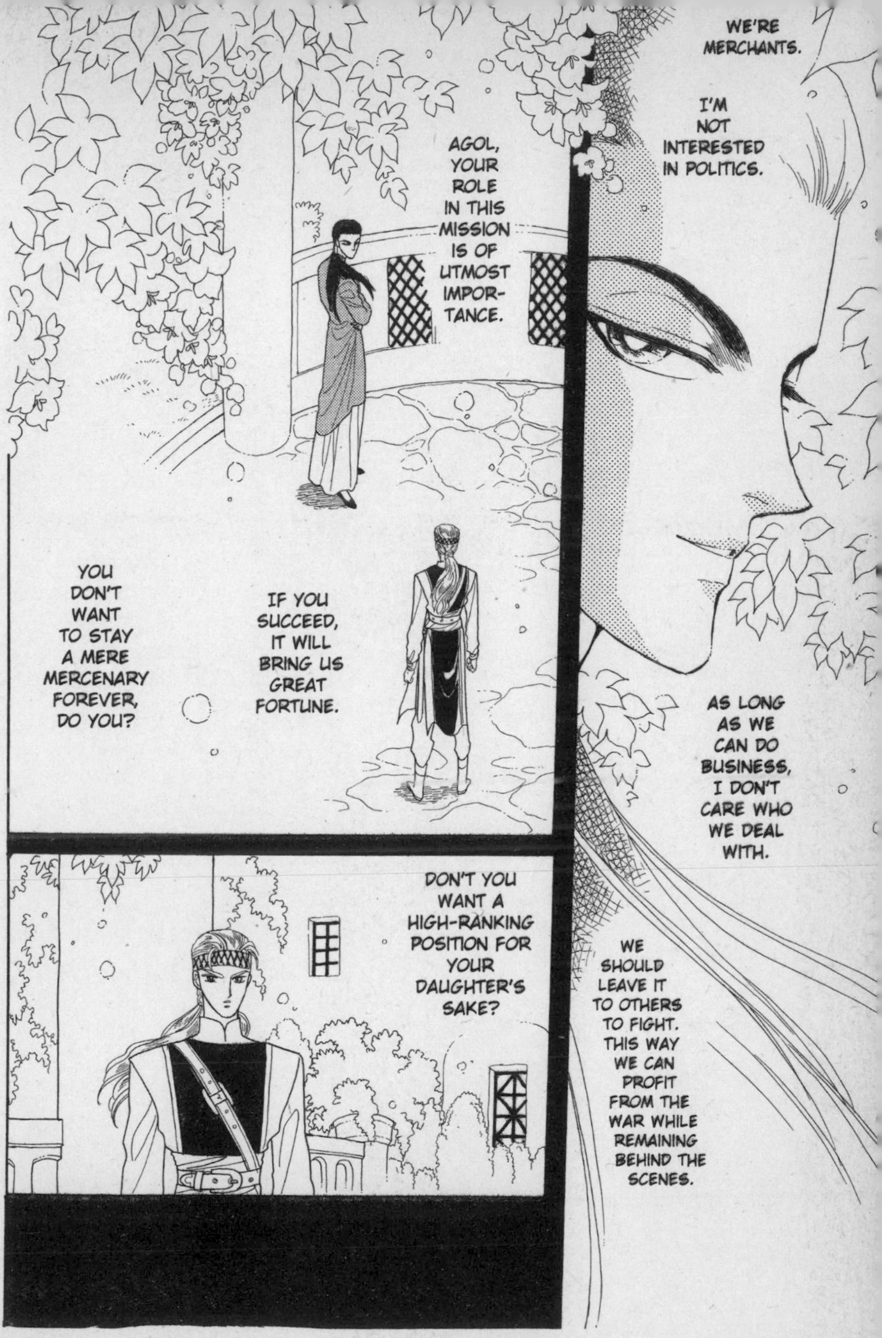
WE'RE MERCHANTS.
I'M NOT INTERESTED IN POLITICS.
AS LONG AS WE CAN DO BUSINESS, I DON'T CARE WHO WE DEAL WITH.
WE SHOULD LEAVE IT TO OTHERS TO FIGHT. THIS WAY WE CAN PROFIT FROM THE WAR WHILE REMAINING BEHIND THE SCENES.
AGOL, YOUR ROLE IN THIS MISSION IS OF UTMOST IMPOR-TANCE.
IF YOU SUCCEED, IT WILL BRING US GREAT FORTUNE.
YOU DON'T WANT TO STAY A MERE MERCENARY FOREVER, DO YOU?
DON'T YOU WANT A HIGH-RANKING POSITION FOR YOUR DAUGHTER'S SAKE?

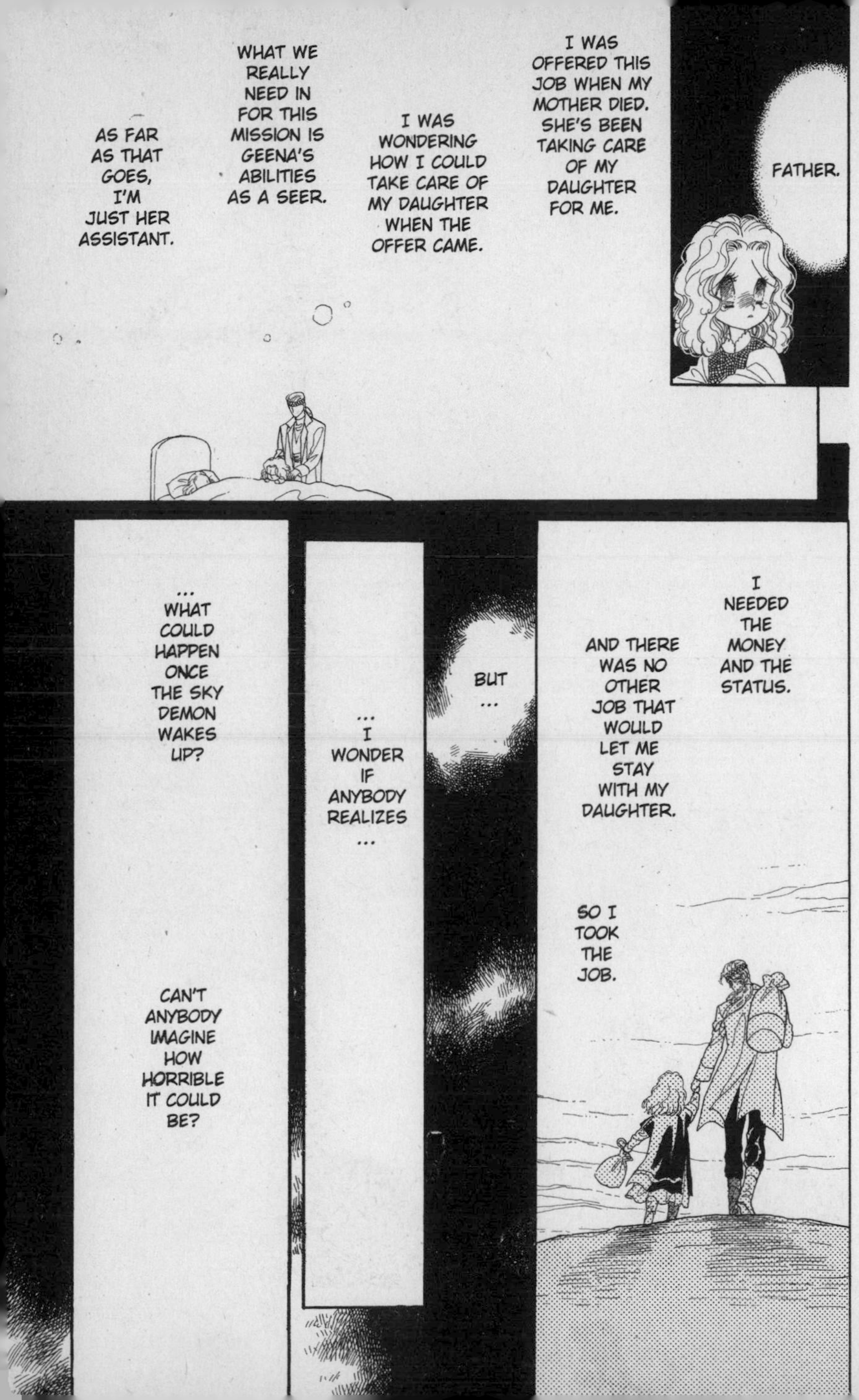
FATHER.
I WAS OFFERED THIS JOB WHEN MY MOTHER DIED. SHE'S BEEN TAKING CARE OF MY DAUGHTER FOR ME.
I WAS WONDERING HOW I COULD TAKE CARE OF MY DAUGHTER WHEN THE OFFER CAME.
WHAT WE REALLY NEED IN FOR THIS MISSION IS GEENA'S ABILITIES AS A SEER.
AS FAR AS THAT GOES, I'M JUST HER ASSISTANT.
I NEEDED THE MONEY AND THE STATUS.
AND THERE WAS NO OTHER JOB THAT WOULD LET ME STAY WITH MY DAUGHTER.
SO I TOOK THE JOB.
BUT ...
... I WONDER IF ANYBODY REALIZES ...
... WHAT COULD HAPPEN ONCE THE SKY DEMON WAKES UP?
CAN'T ANYBODY IMAGINE HOW HORRIBLE IT COULD BE?

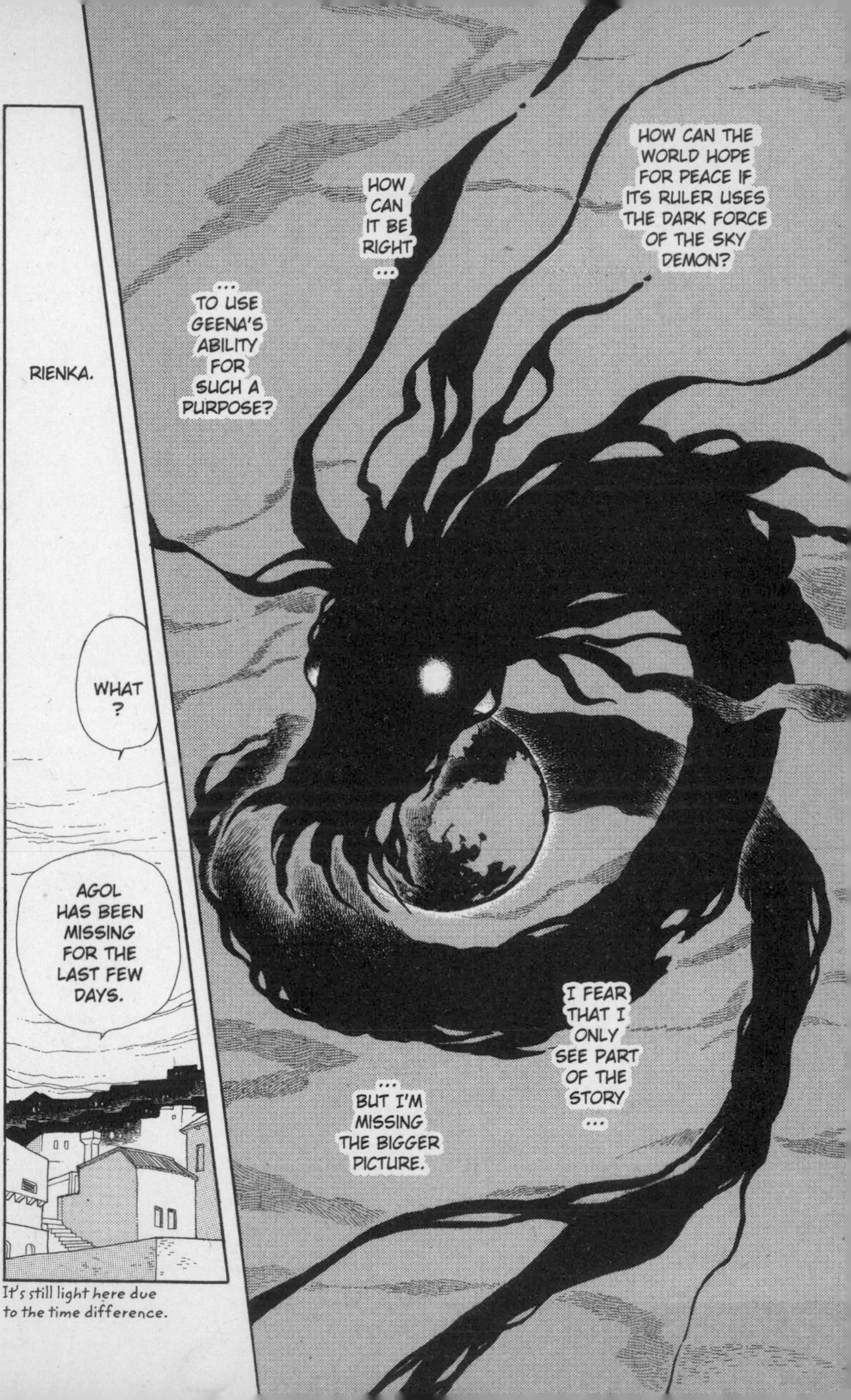
HOW CAN THE WORLD HOPE FOR PEACE IF ITS RULER USES THE DARK FORCE OF THE SKY DEMON?
HOW CAN IT BE RIGHT ...
... TO USE GEENA'S ABILITY FOR SUCH A PURPOSE?
I FEAR THAT I ONLY SEE PART OF THE STORY ...
... BUT I'M MISSING THE BIGGER PICTURE.
RIENKA.
WHAT ?
AGOL HAS BEEN MISSING FOR THE LAST FEW DAYS.

It's still light here due to the time difference.

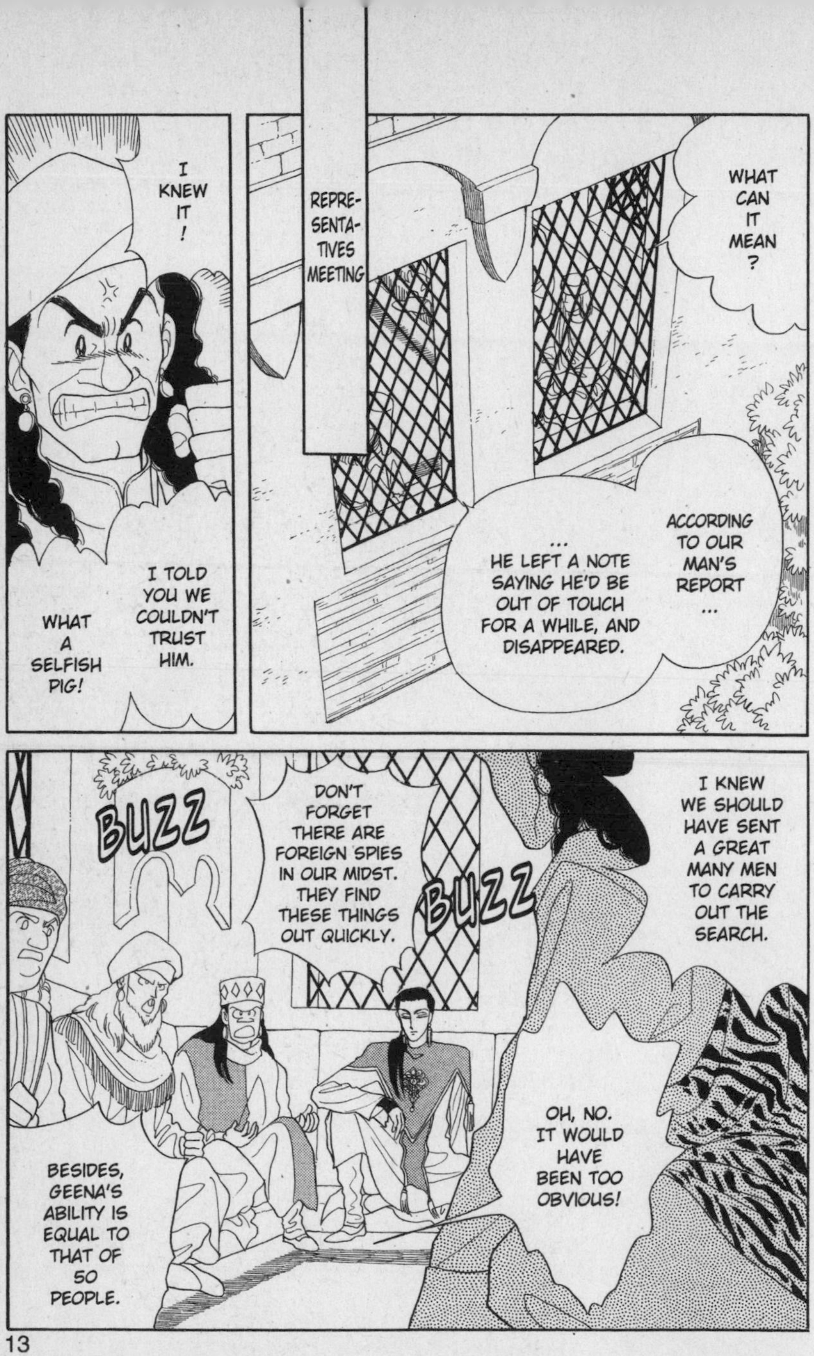
REPRESENTATIVES MEETING
WHAT CAN IT MEAN?
ACCORDING TO OUR MAN'S REPORT...
... HE LEFT A NOTE SAYING HE'D BE OUT OF TOUCH FOR A WHILE, AND DISAPPEARED.
I KNEW IT!
I TOLD YOU WE COULDN'T TRUST HIM.
WHAT A SELFISH PIG!
I KNEW WE SHOULD HAVE SENT A GREAT MANY MEN TO CARRY OUT THE SEARCH.
BUZZ
DON'T FORGET THERE ARE FOREIGN SPIES IN OUR MIDST. THEY FIND THESE THINGS OUT QUICKLY.
BUZZ
OH, NO. IT WOULD HAVE BEEN TOO OBVIOUS!
BESIDES, GEENA'S ABILITY IS EQUAL TO THAT OF 50 PEOPLE.

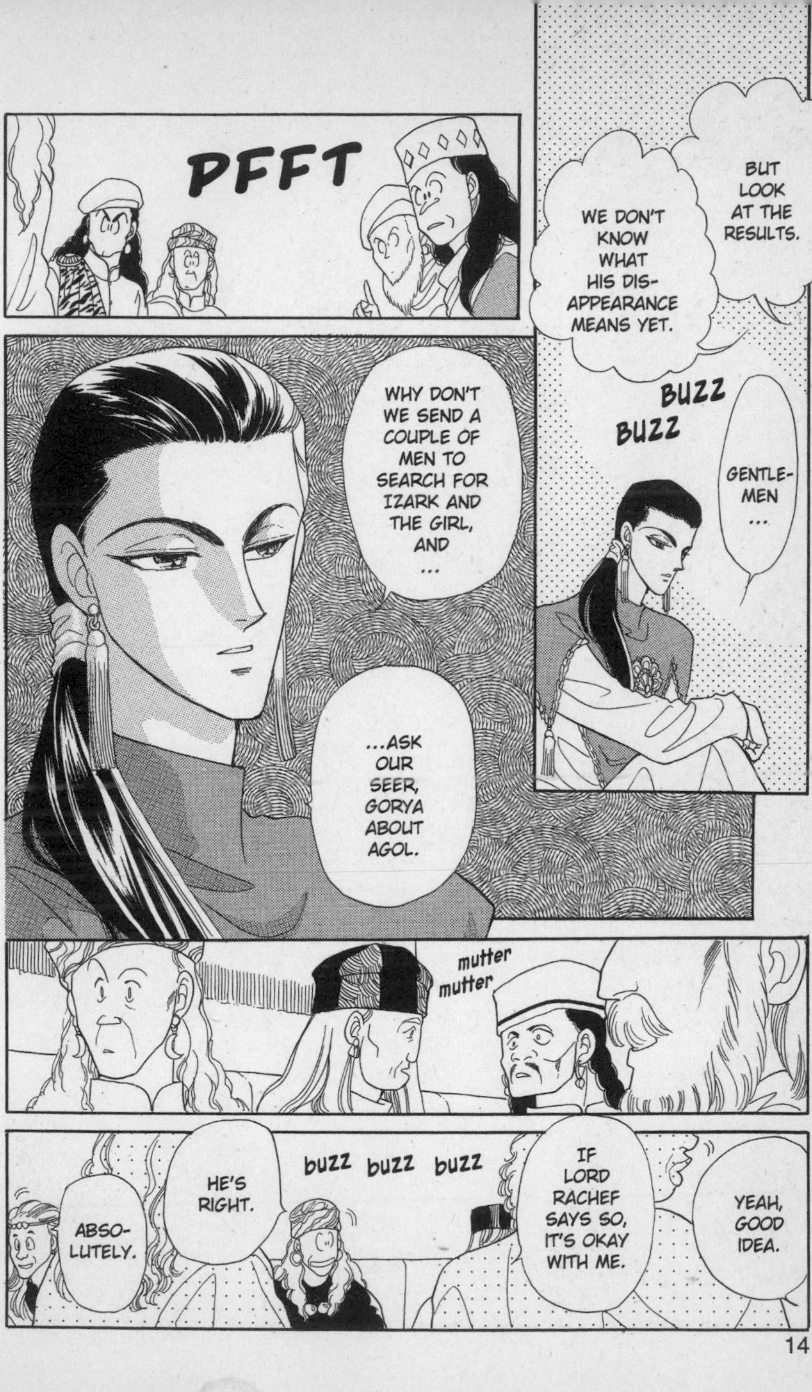

BUT LOOK AT THE RESULTS.
WE DON'T KNOW WHAT HIS DIS-APPEARANCE MEANS YET.
BUZZ BUZZ
GENTLE-MEN ...
PFFT
WHY DON'T WE SEND A COUPLE OF MEN TO SEARCH FOR IZARK AND THE GIRL, AND ...
...ASK OUR SEER, GORYA ABOUT AGOL.
mutter mutter
YEAH, GOOD IDEA.
IF LORD RACHEF SAYS SO, IT'S OKAY WITH ME.
buzz buzz buzz
HE'S RIGHT.
ABSO-LUTELY.

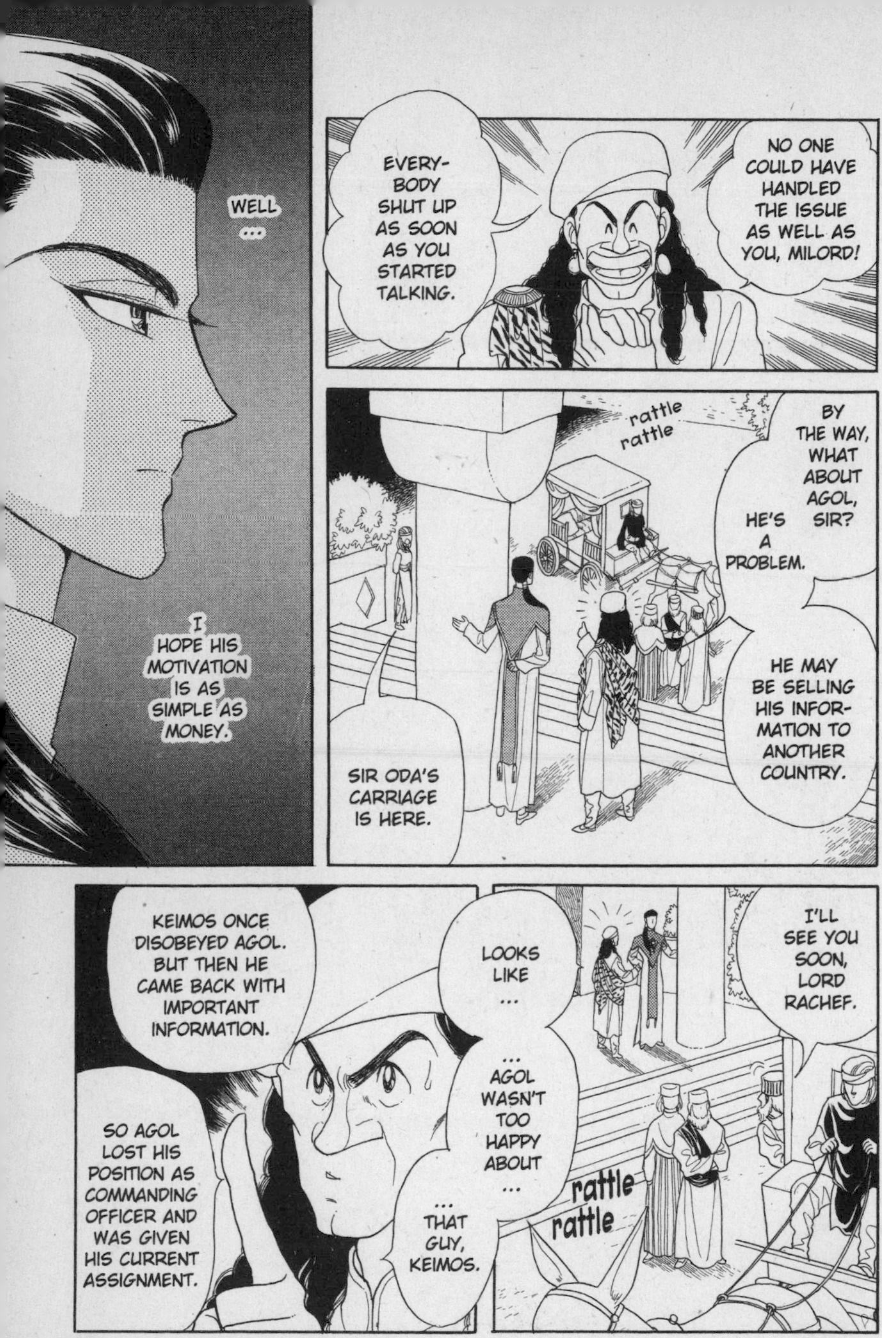
NO ONE COULD HAVE HANDLED THE ISSUE AS WELL AS YOU, MILORD!
EVERY-BODY SHUT UP AS SOON AS YOU STARTED TALKING.
BY THE WAY, WHAT ABOUT AGOL, SIR?
HE'S A PROBLEM.
HE MAY BE SELLING HIS INFOR-MATION TO ANOTHER COUNTRY.
rattle rattle
SIR ODA'S CARRIAGE IS HERE.
WELL ...
I HOPE HIS MOTIVATION IS AS SIMPLE AS MONEY.
I'LL SEE YOU SOON, LORD RACHEF.
rattle rattle
LOOKS LIKE ...
... AGOL WASN'T TOO HAPPY ABOUT ...
... THAT GUY, KEIMOS.
KEIMOS ONCE DISOBEYED AGOL. BUT THEN HE CAME BACK WITH IMPORTANT INFORMATION.
SO AGOL LOST HIS POSITION AS COMMANDING OFFICER AND WAS GIVEN HIS CURRENT ASSIGNMENT.

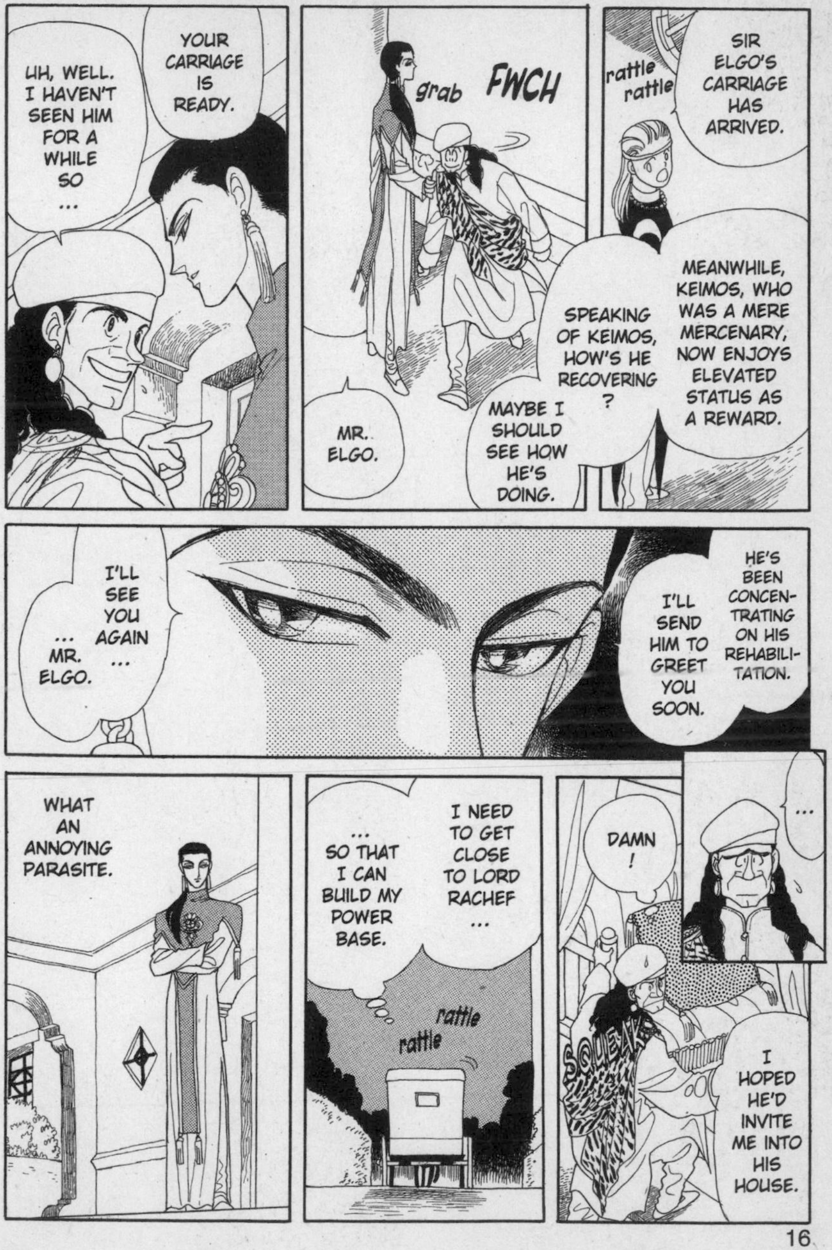
rattle rattle
SIR ELGO'S CARRIAGE HAS ARRIVED.
MEANWHILE, KEIMOS, WHO WAS A MERE MERCENARY, NOW ENJOYS ELEVATED STATUS AS A REWARD.
SPEAKING OF KEIMOS, HOW'S HE RECOVERING ?
MAYBE I SHOULD SEE HOW HE'S DOING.
FWCH
grab
MR. ELGO.
YOUR CARRIAGE IS READY.
UH, WELL. I HAVEN'T SEEN HIM FOR A WHILE SO ...
HE'S BEEN CONCEN-TRATING ON HIS REHABILI-TATION.
I'LL SEND HIM TO GREET YOU SOON.
I'LL SEE YOU AGAIN ... ... MR. ELGO.
...
DAMN !
SQUEAK
I HOPED HE'D INVITE ME INTO HIS HOUSE.
I NEED TO GET CLOSE TO LORD RACHEF ...
... SO THAT I CAN BUILD MY POWER BASE.
rattle
rattle
WHAT AN ANNOYING PARASITE.

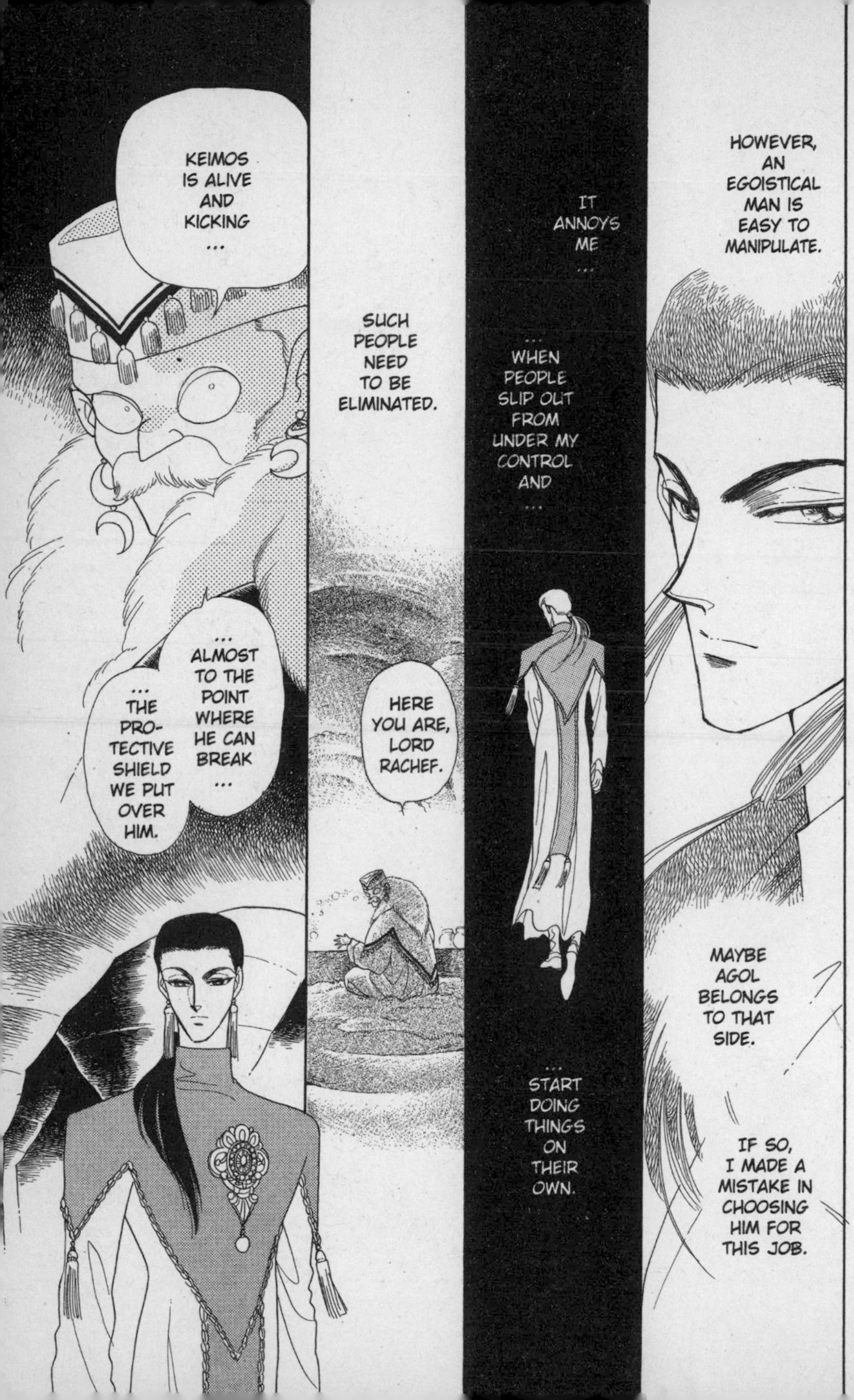
HOWEVER, AN EGOISTICAL MAN IS EASY TO MANIPULATE.
MAYBE AGOL BELONGS TO THAT SIDE.
IF SO, I MADE A MISTAKE IN CHOOSING HIM FOR THIS JOB.
IT ANNOYS ME ...
... WHEN PEOPLE SLIP OUT FROM UNDER MY CONTROL AND ...
... START DOING THINGS ON THEIR OWN.
SUCH PEOPLE NEED TO BE ELIMINATED.
HERE YOU ARE, LORD RACHEF.
KEIMOS IS ALIVE AND KICKING ...
... ALMOST TO THE POINT WHERE HE CAN BREAK ...
... THE PRO-TECTIVE SHIELD WE PUT OVER HIM.

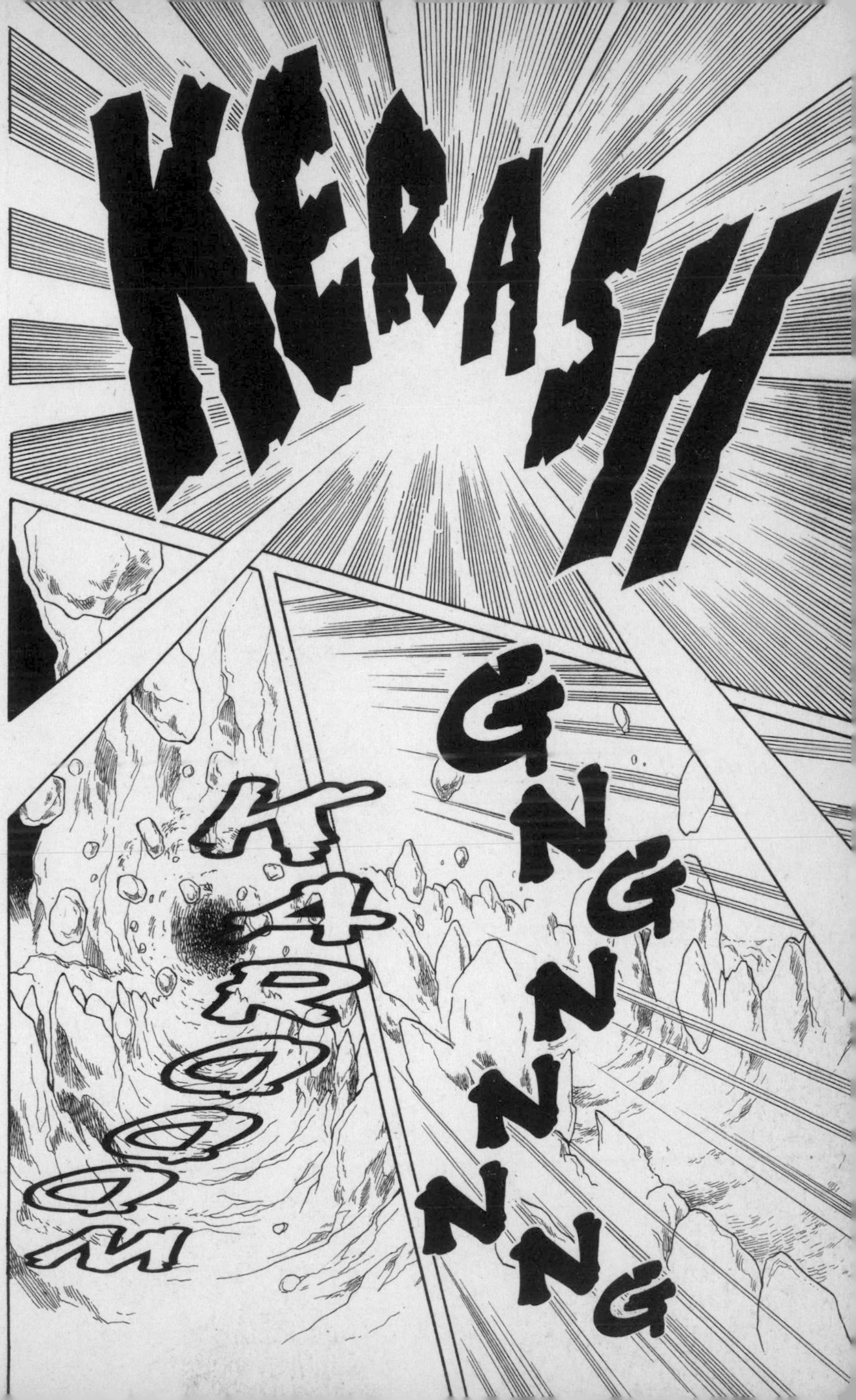
KERASH
GNGNNNNG
KAROOOM

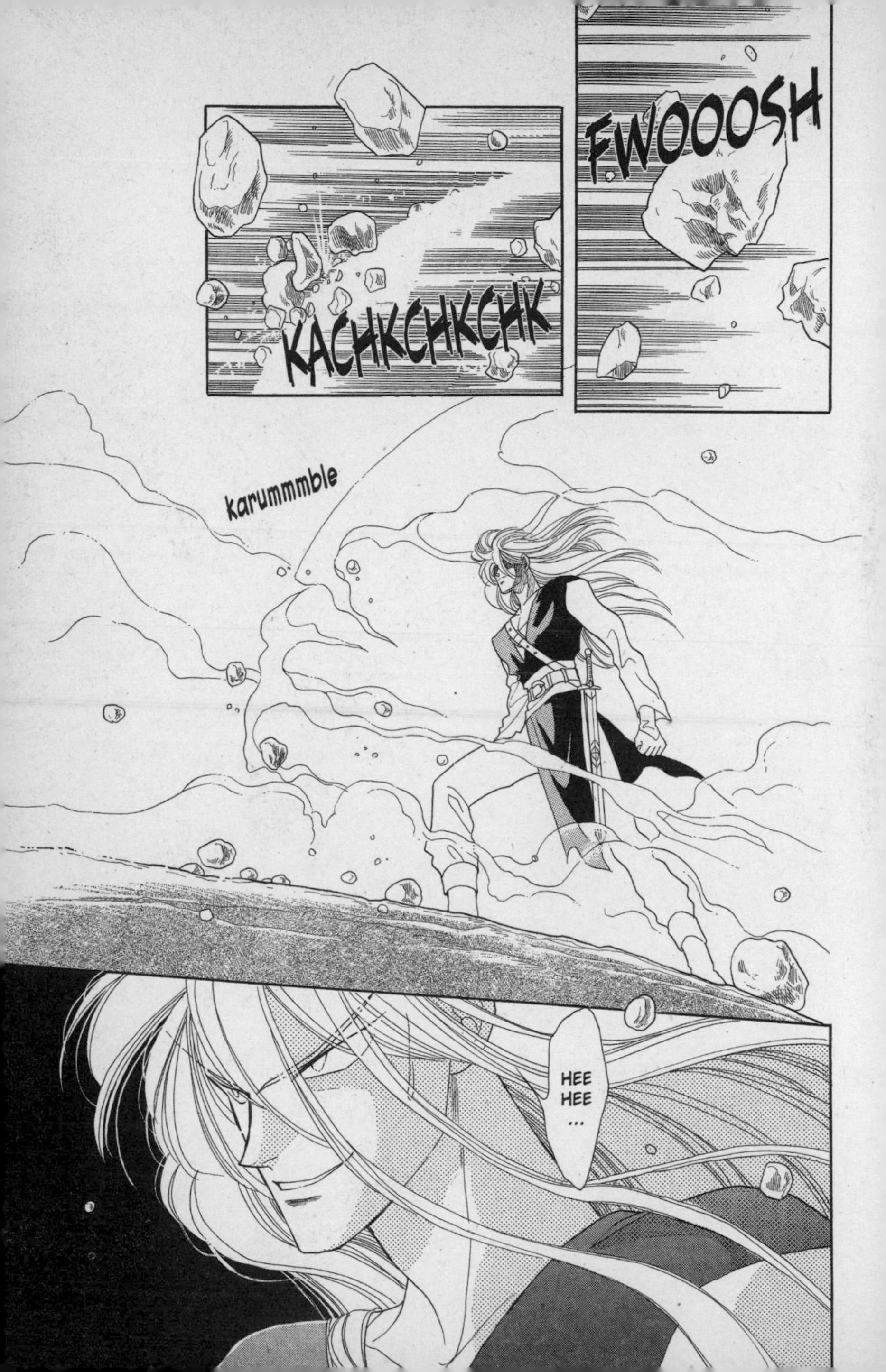
FWOOOSH
KACHKCHKCHK
karummmble
HEE HEE ...

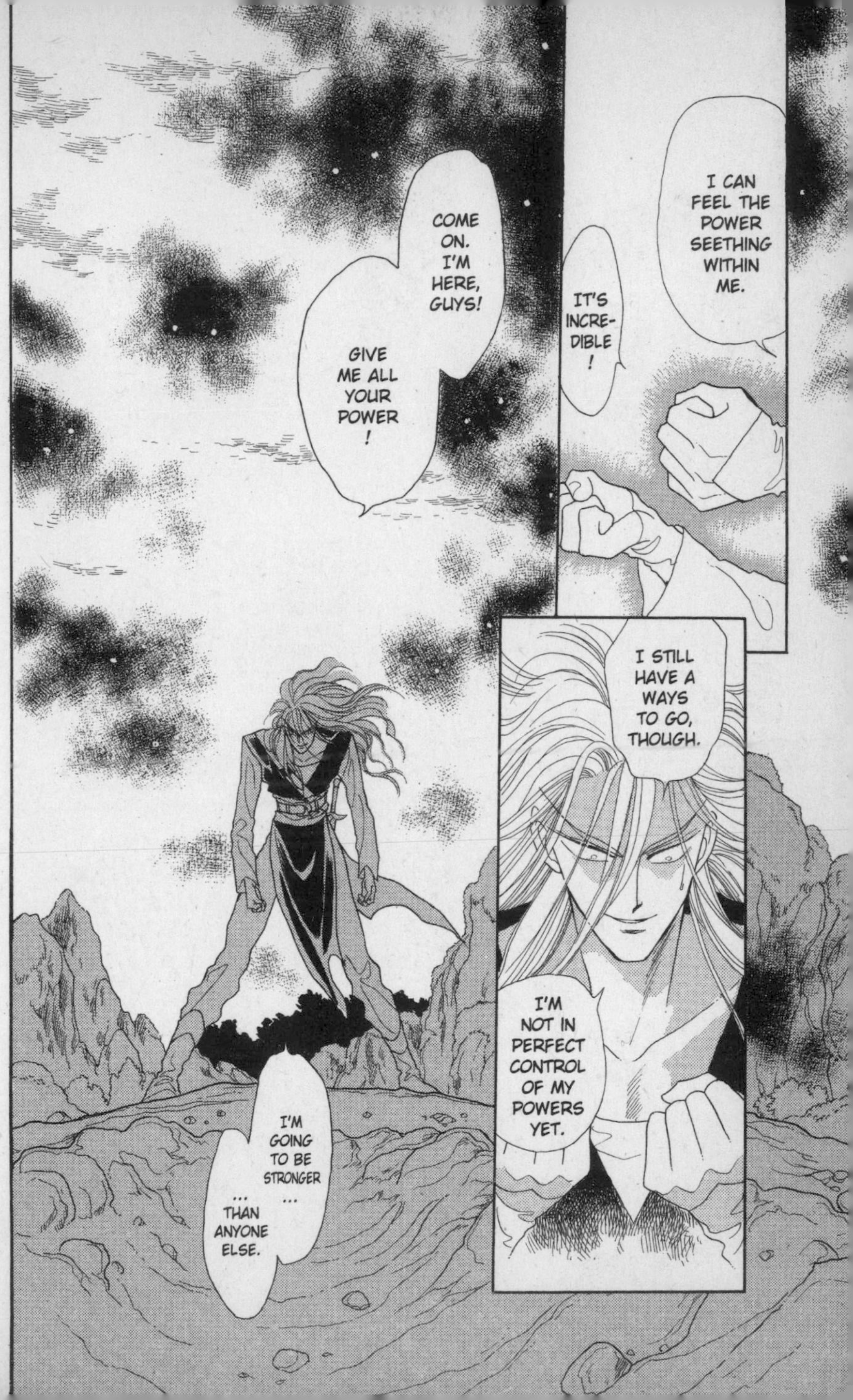
I CAN FEEL THE POWER SEETHING WITHIN ME.
IT'S INCREDIBLE!
I STILL HAVE A WAYS TO GO, THOUGH.
I'M NOT IN PERFECT CONTROL OF MY POWERS YET.
COME ON. I'M HERE, GUYS!
GIVE ME ALL YOUR POWER!
I'M GOING TO BE STRONGER ...
... THAN ANYONE ELSE.

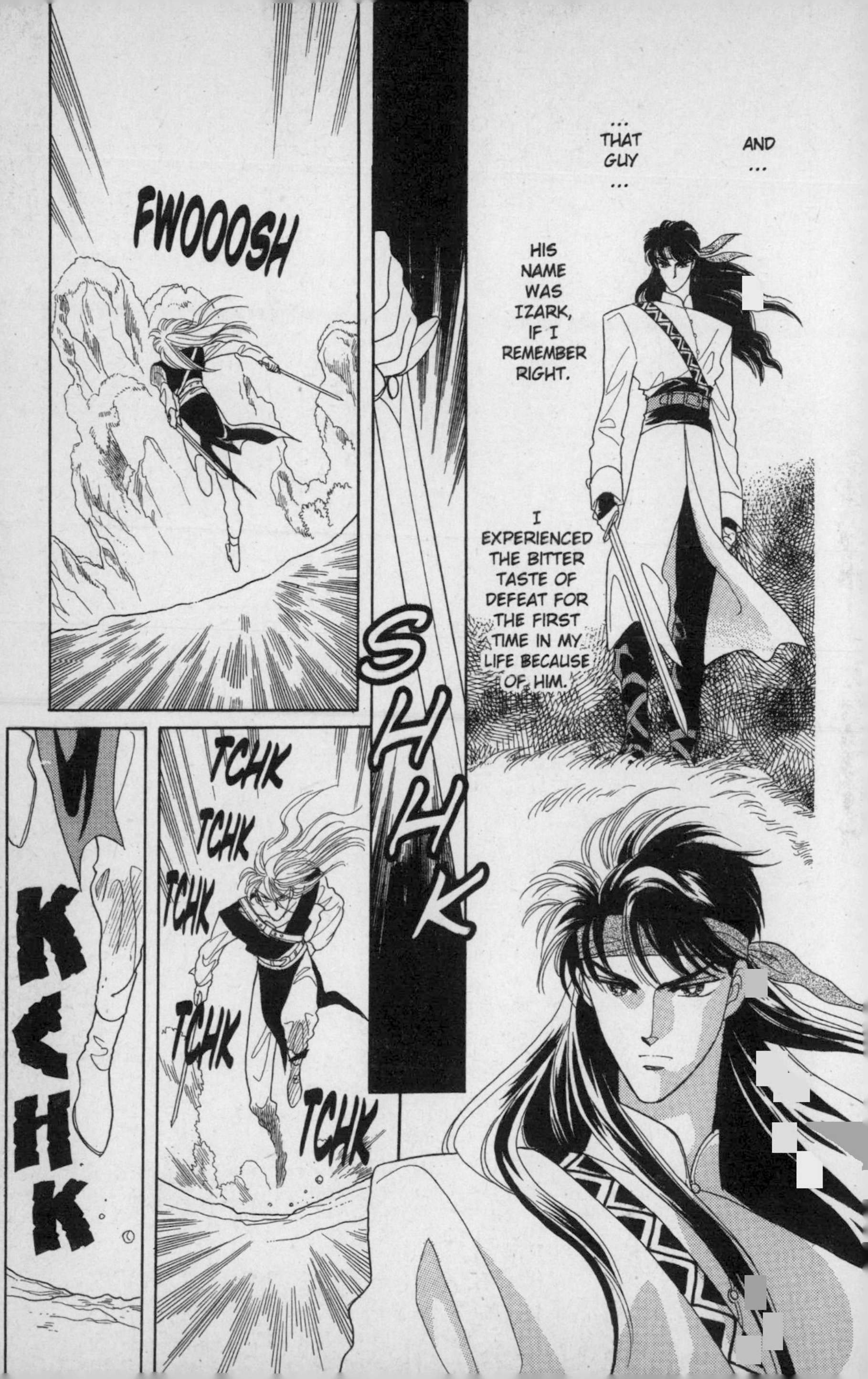
AND ...
... THAT GUY ...
HIS NAME WAS IZARK, IF I REMEMBER RIGHT.
I EXPERIENCED THE BITTER TASTE OF DEFEAT FOR THE FIRST TIME IN MY LIFE BECAUSE OF HIM.
SHHK
FWOOOSH
TCHK
TCHK
TCHK
TCHK
TCHK
KCHK

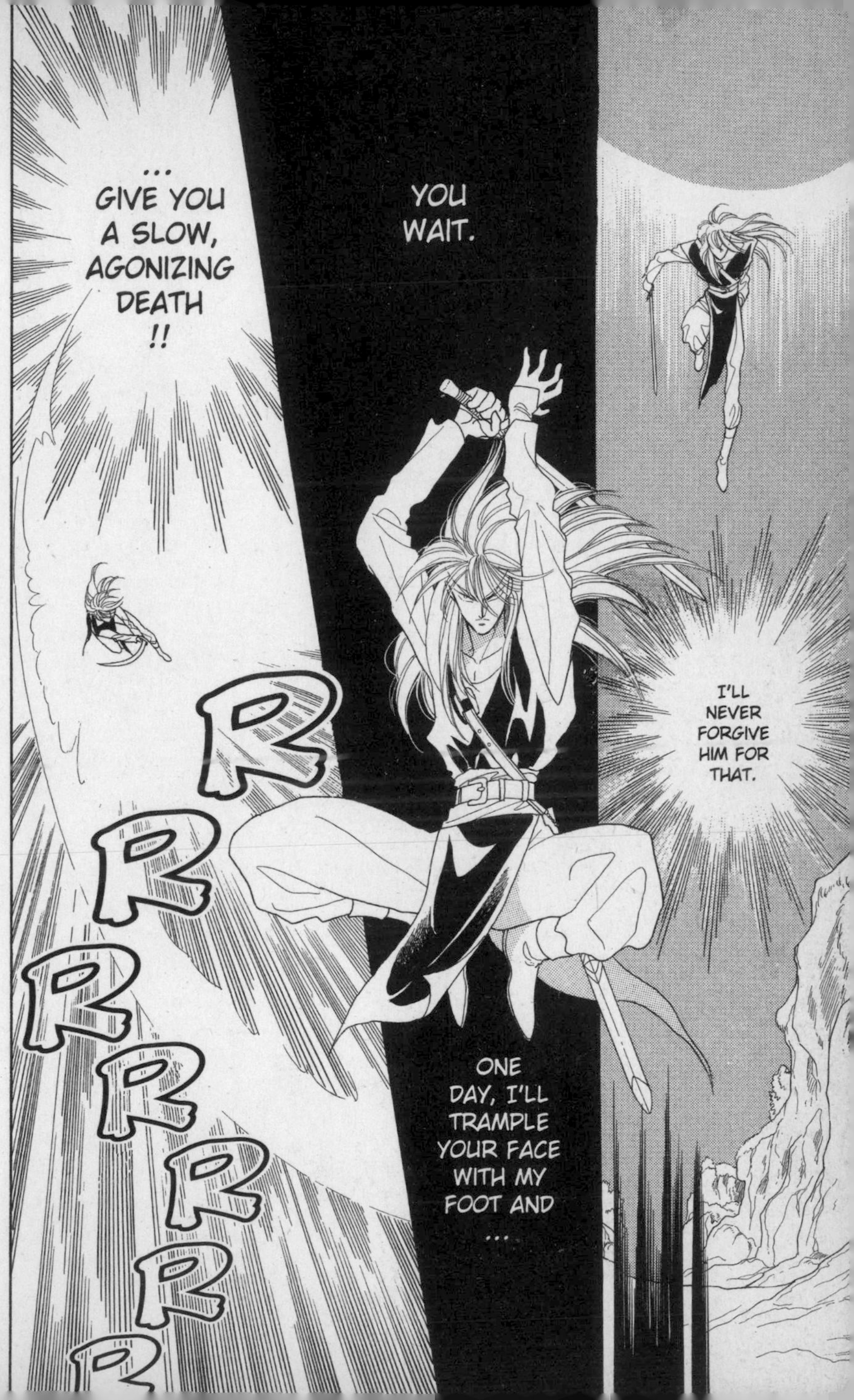
I'LL NEVER FORGIVE HIM FOR THAT.
YOU WAIT.
ONE DAY, I'LL TRAMPLE YOUR FACE WITH MY FOOT AND ...
... GIVE YOU A SLOW, AGONIZING DEATH !!
RRRRRRR

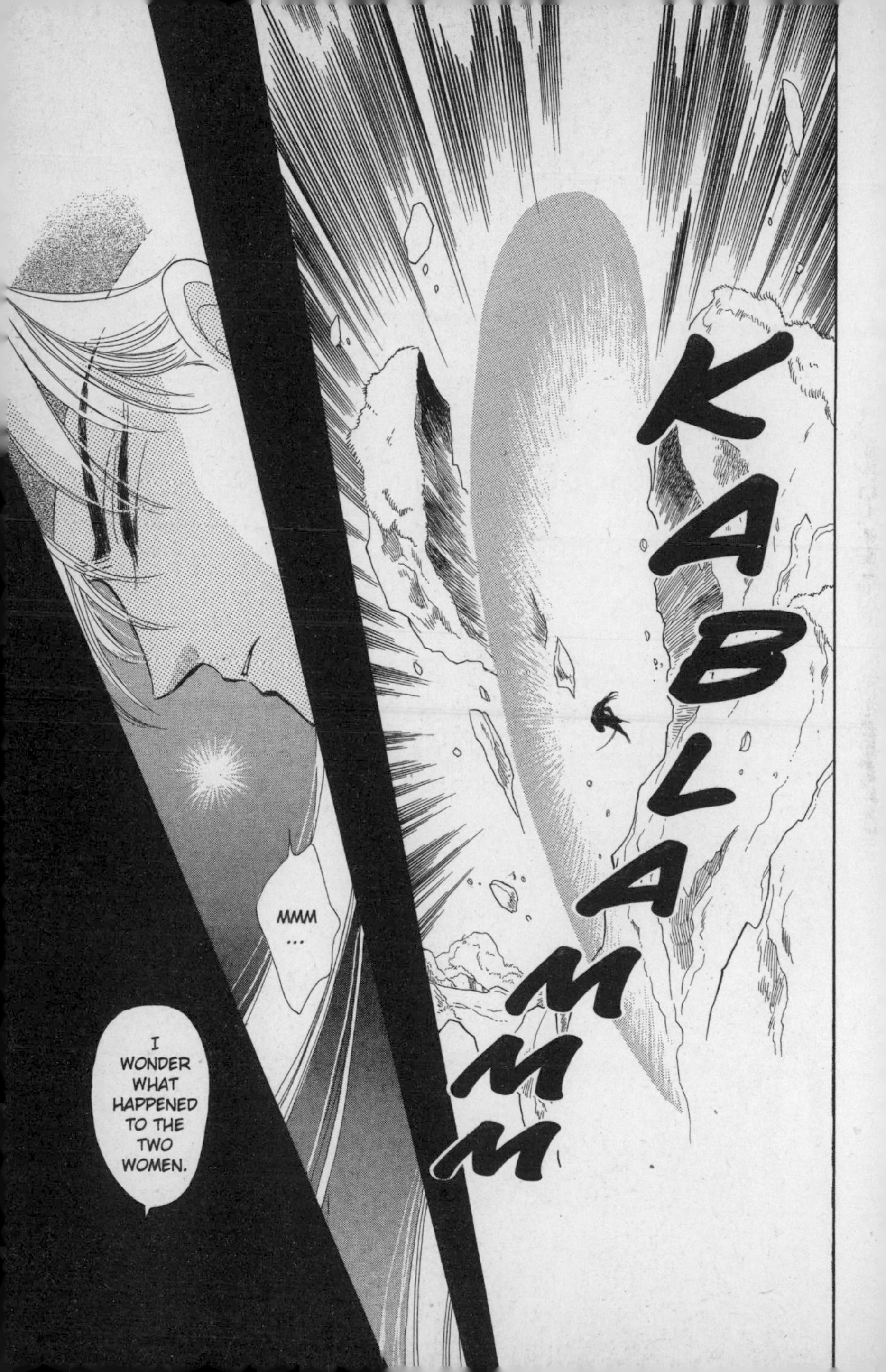
KABLAMMM
MMM ...
I WONDER WHAT HAPPENED TO THE TWO WOMEN.

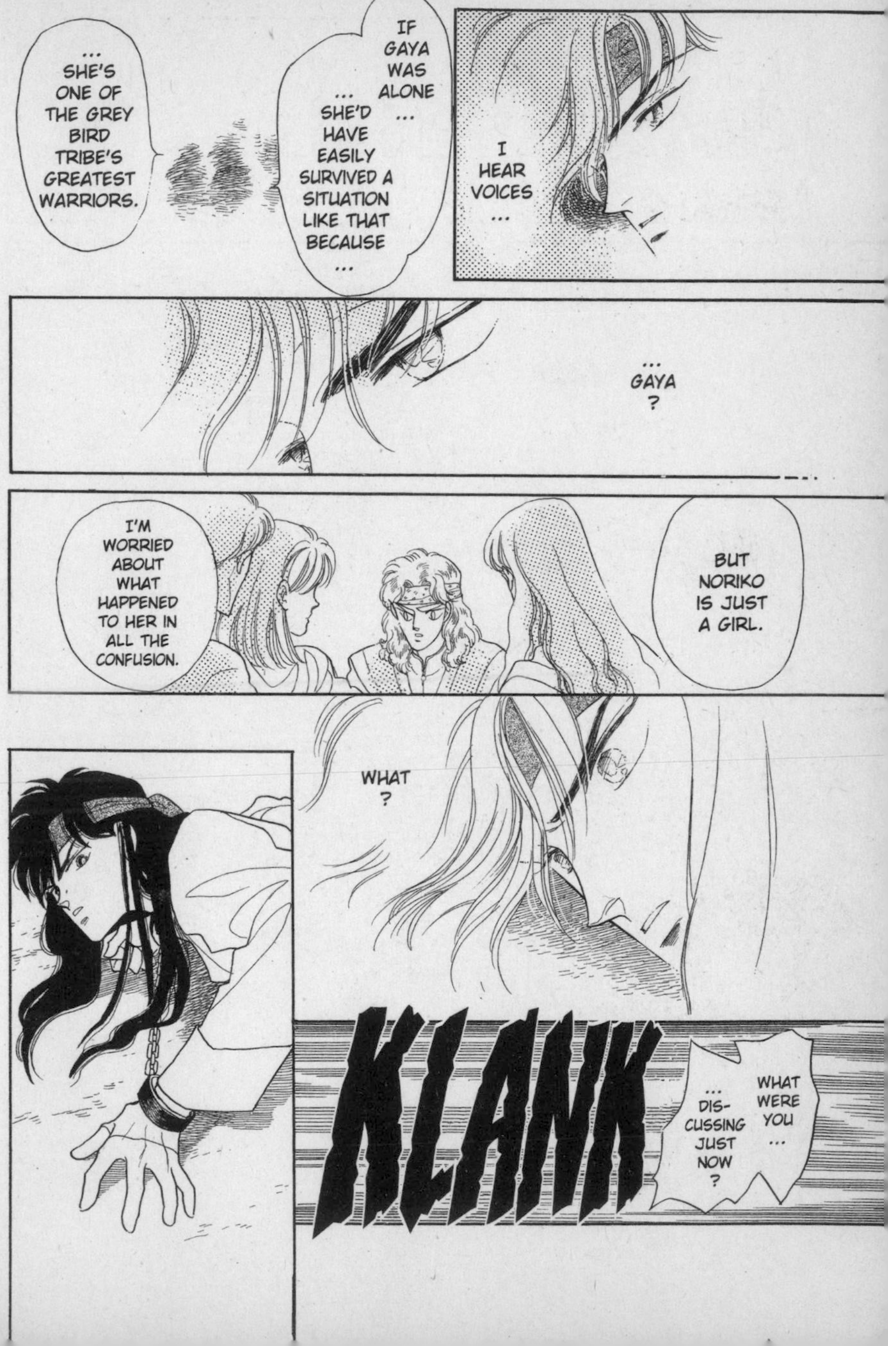
I HEAR VOICES ...
IF GAYA WAS ALONE ...
... SHE'D HAVE EASILY SURVIVED A SITUATION LIKE THAT BECAUSE ...
... SHE'S ONE OF THE GREY BIRD TRIBE'S GREATEST WARRIORS.
... GAYA ?
BUT NORIKO IS JUST A GIRL.
I'M WORRIED ABOUT WHAT HAPPENED TO HER IN ALL THE CONFUSION.
WHAT ?
KLANK
WHAT WERE YOU ...
... DIS-CUSSING JUST NOW ?

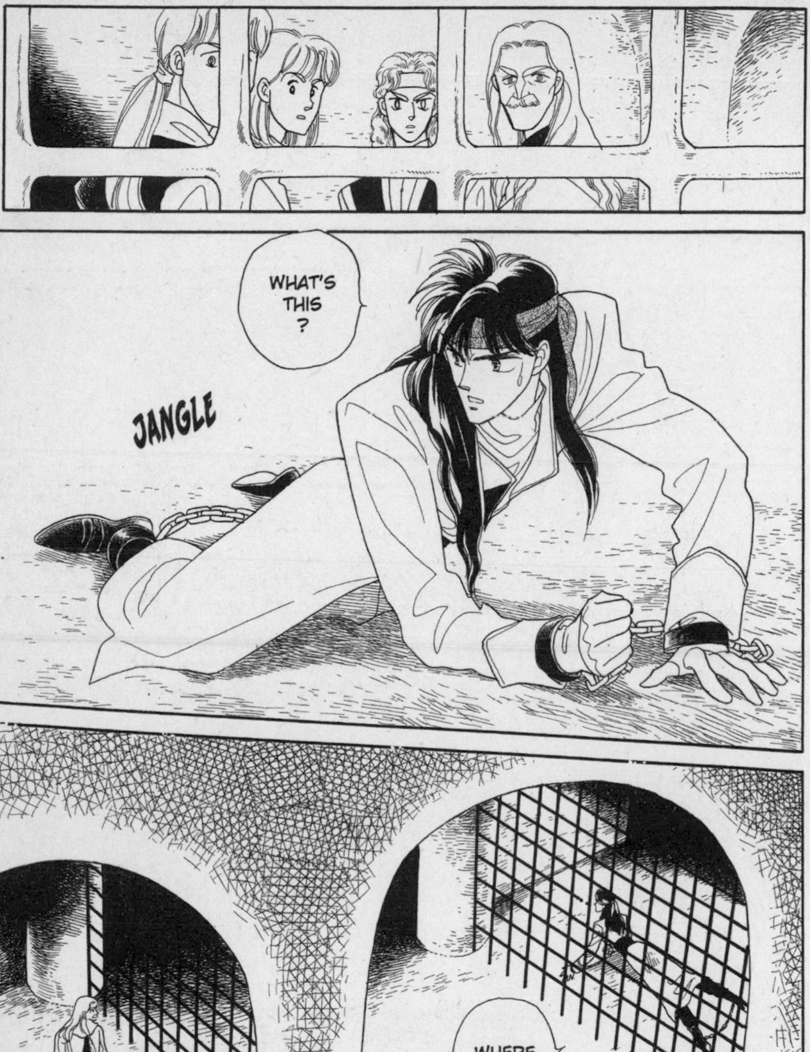
WHAT'S THIS ?
JANGLE
WHERE AM I ?

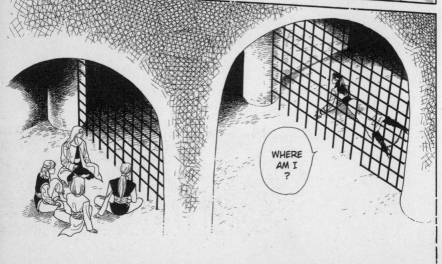

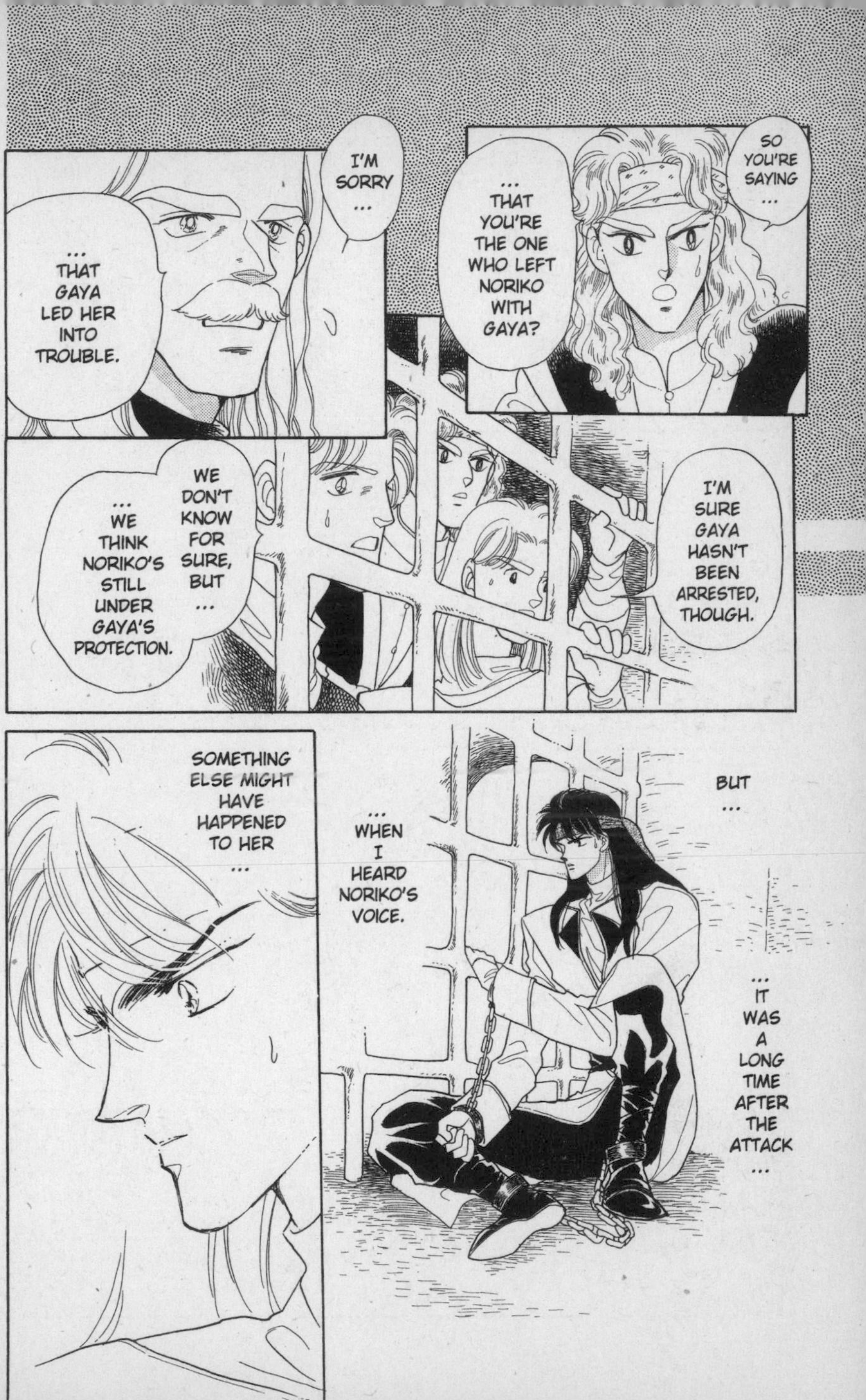
SO YOU'RE SAYING ...
... THAT YOU'RE THE ONE WHO LEFT NORIKO WITH GAYA?
I'M SORRY ...
... THAT GAYA LED HER INTO TROUBLE.
I'M SURE GAYA HASN'T BEEN ARRESTED, THOUGH.
WE DON'T KNOW FOR SURE, BUT ...
... WE THINK NORIKO'S STILL UNDER GAYA'S PROTECTION.
BUT ...
... IT WAS A LONG TIME AFTER THE ATTACK ...
... WHEN I HEARD NORIKO'S VOICE.
SOMETHING ELSE MIGHT HAVE HAPPENED TO HER ...

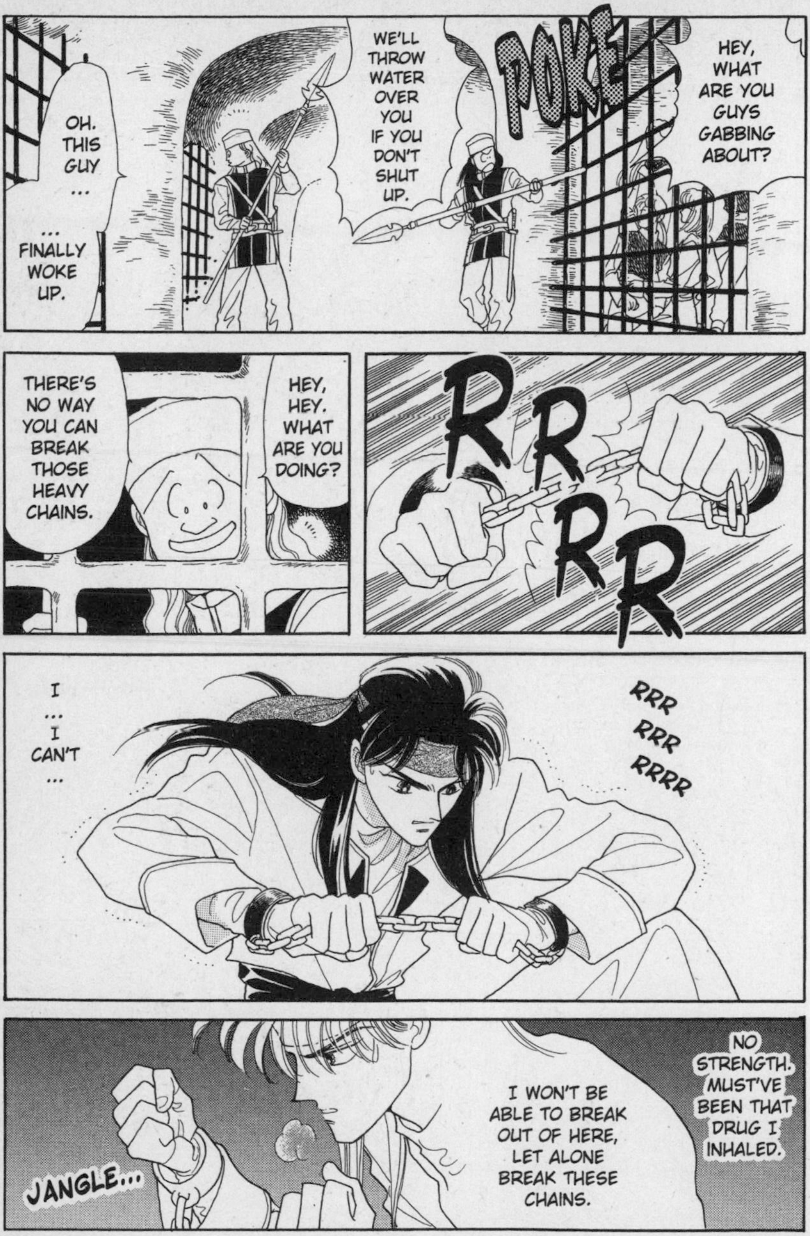
HEY, WHAT ARE YOU GUYS GABBING ABOUT?
POKE
WE'LL THROW WATER OVER YOU IF YOU DON'T SHUT UP.
OH. THIS GUY ...
... FINALLY WOKE UP.
RRRR
HEY, HEY. WHAT ARE YOU DOING?
THERE'S NO WAY YOU CAN BREAK THOSE HEAVY CHAINS.
RRR RRR RRRR
I ... I CAN'T ...
NO STRENGTH. MUST'VE BEEN THAT DRUG I INHALED.
I WON'T BE ABLE TO BREAK OUT OF HERE, LET ALONE BREAK THESE CHAINS.
JANGLE...

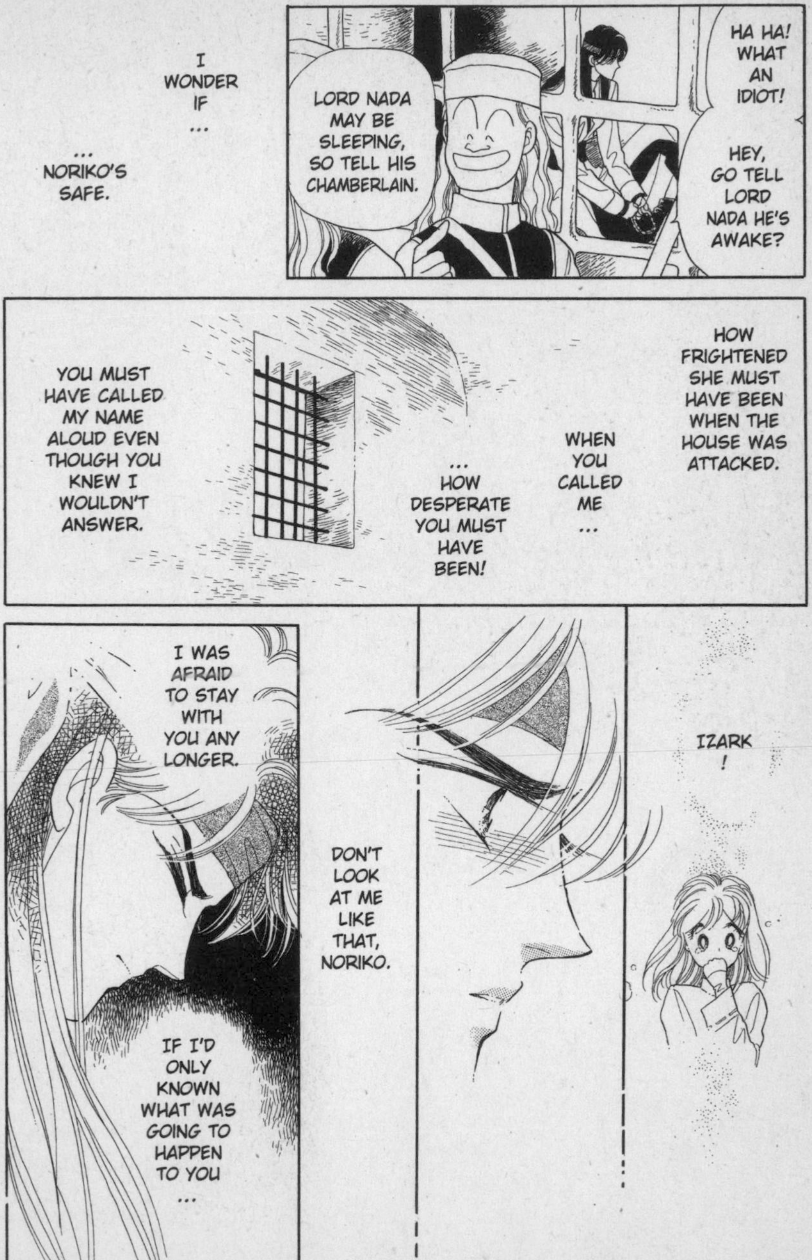
HA HA! WHAT AN IDIOT!
HEY, GO TELL LORD NADA HE'S AWAKE?
LORD NADA MAY BE SLEEPING, SO TELL HIS CHAMBERLAIN.
I WONDER IF ...
... NORIKO'S SAFE.
HOW FRIGHTENED SHE MUST HAVE BEEN WHEN THE HOUSE WAS ATTACKED.
WHEN YOU CALLED ME ...
... HOW DESPERATE YOU MUST HAVE BEEN!
YOU MUST HAVE CALLED MY NAME ALOUD EVEN THOUGH YOU KNEW I WOULDN'T ANSWER.
IZARK!
DON'T LOOK AT ME LIKE THAT, NORIKO.
I WAS AFRAID TO STAY WITH YOU ANY LONGER.
IF I'D ONLY KNOWN WHAT WAS GOING TO HAPPEN TO YOU ...

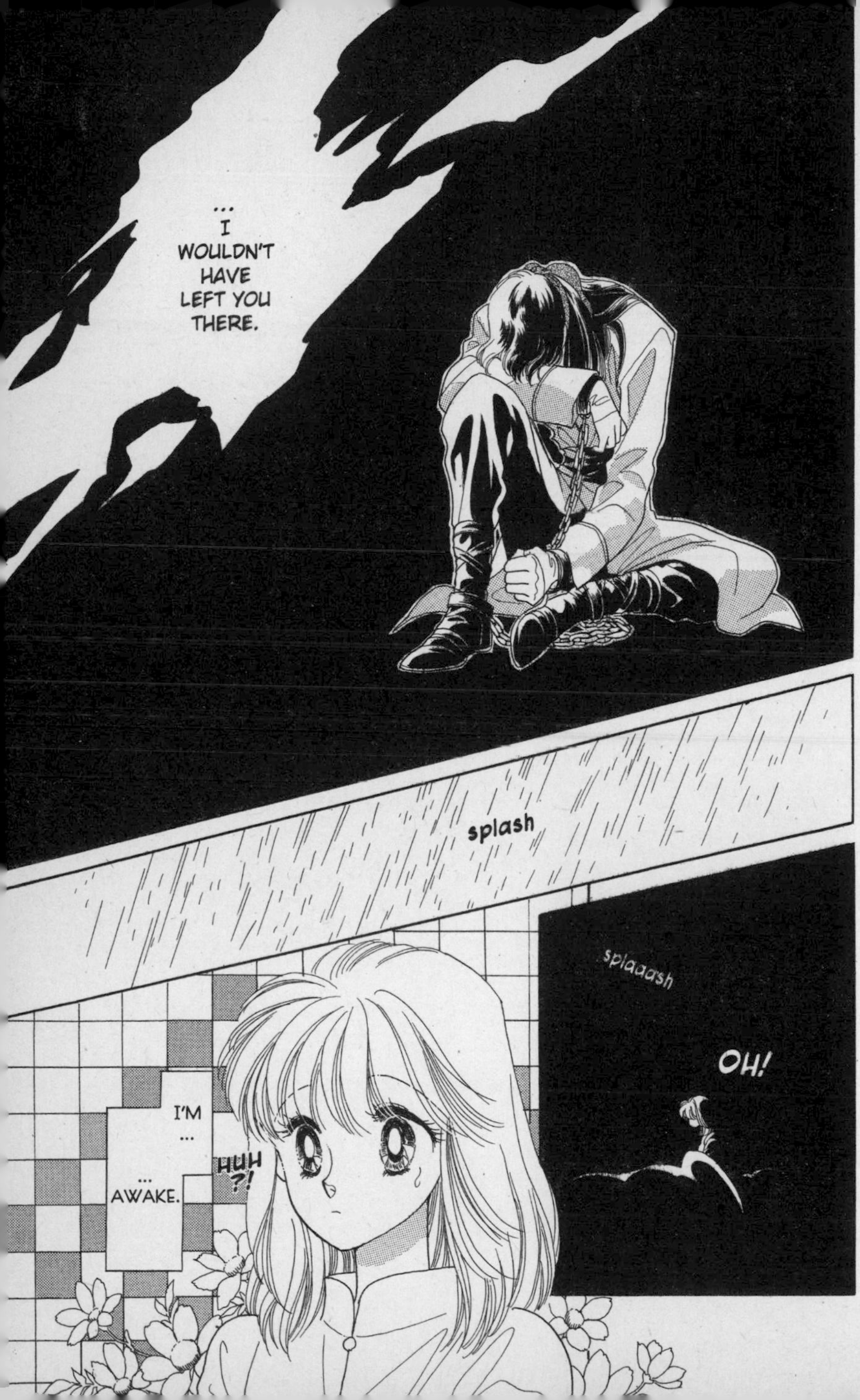
... I WOULDN'T HAVE LEFT YOU THERE.
splash
splaaash
OH!
HUH?!
I'M ... ... AWAKE.

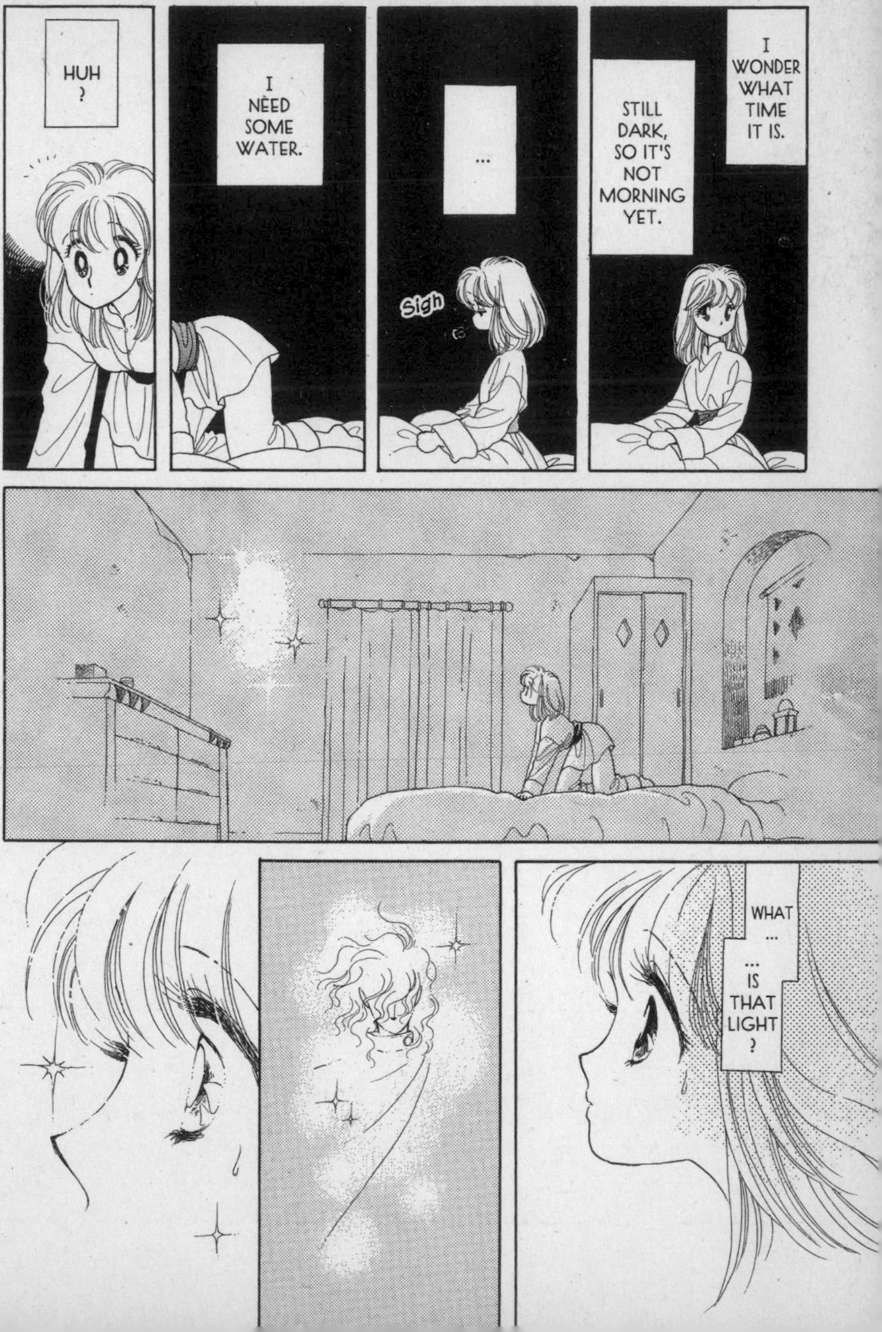
I WONDER WHAT TIME IT IS.
STILL DARK, SO IT'S NOT MORNING YET.
...
Sigh
I NEED SOME WATER.
HUH ?
WHAT ...
... IS THAT LIGHT ?

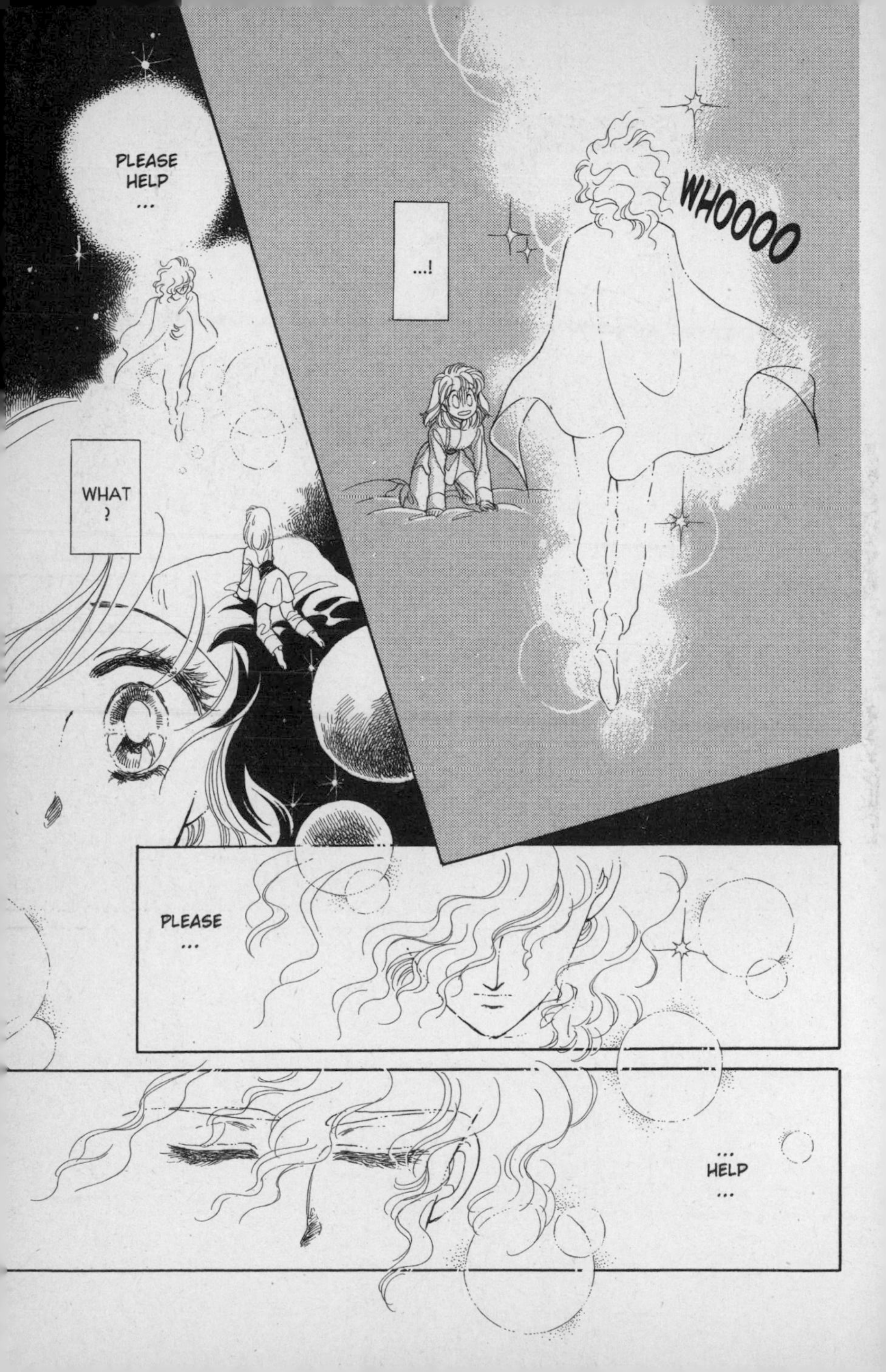
WHOOOO
...!
PLEASE HELP ...
WHAT ?
PLEASE ...
... HELP ...

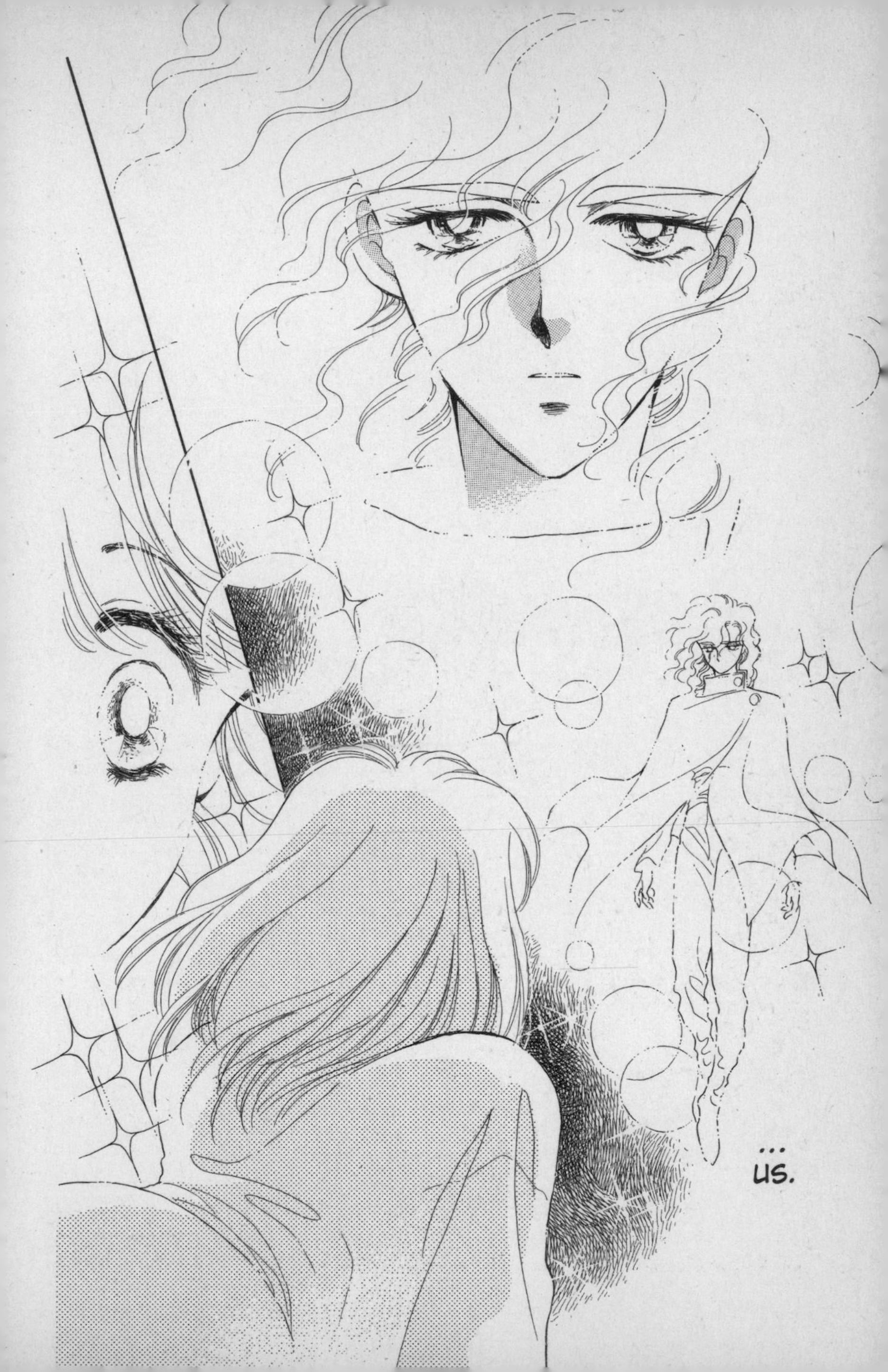

...
US.

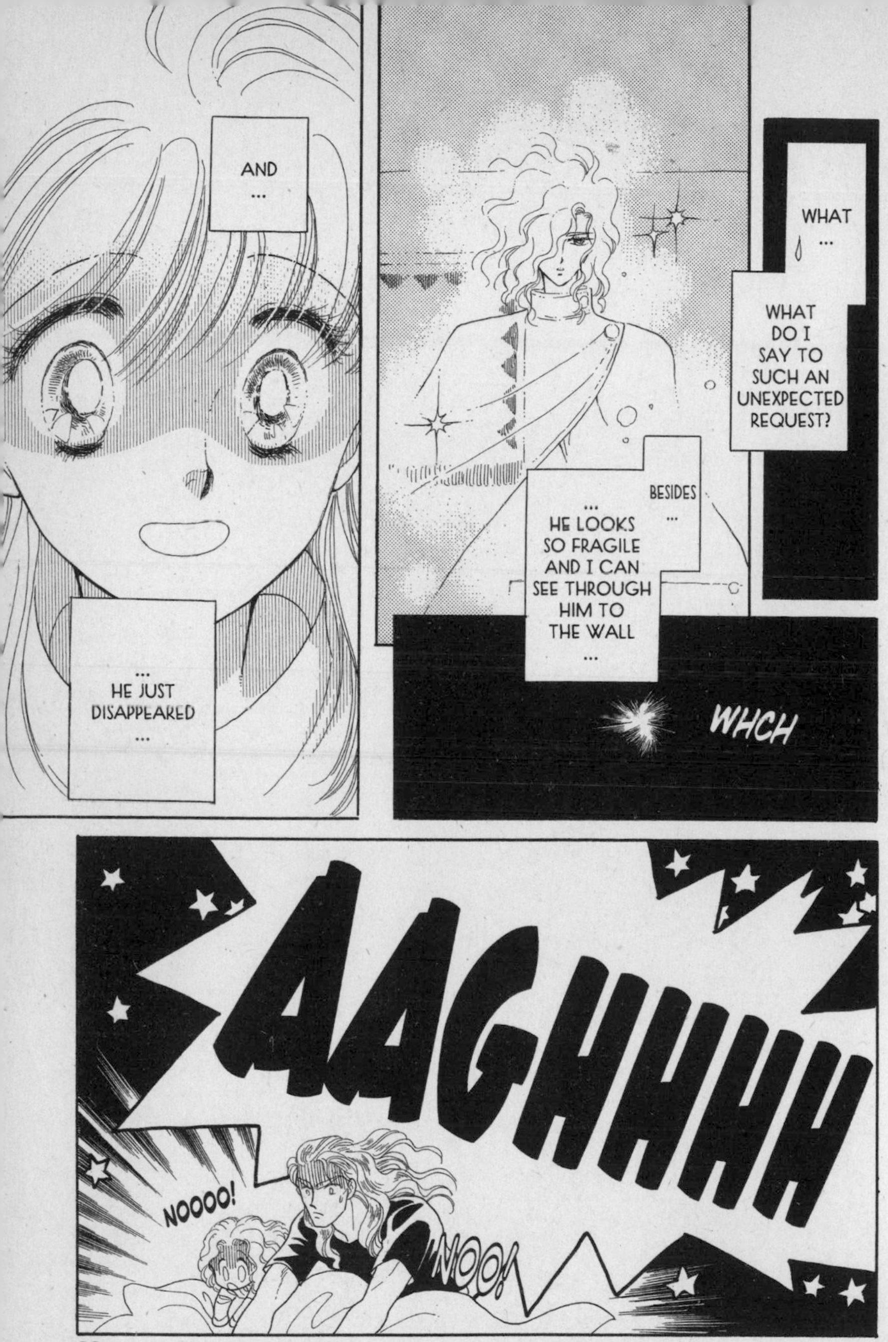
WHAT ...
WHAT DO I SAY TO SUCH AN UNEXPECTED REQUEST?
BESIDES ...
... HE LOOKS SO FRAGILE AND I CAN SEE THROUGH HIM TO THE WALL ...
WHCH
AND ...
... HE JUST DISAPPEARED ...
AAGHHHHH
NOO!
NOOOO!

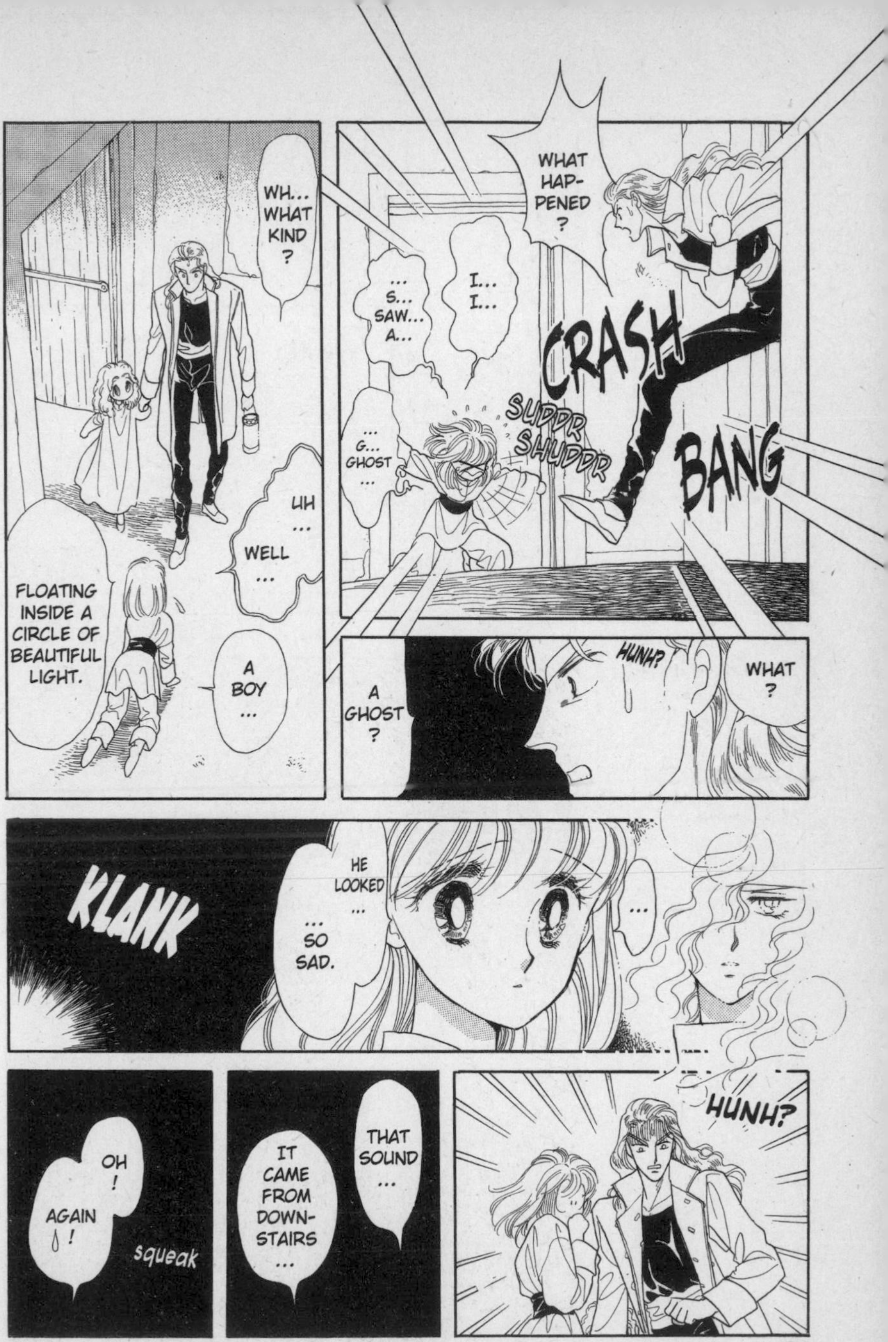
WHAT HAP-PENED?
CRASH
BANG
SUDDR SHUDDR
I... I...
... S... SAW... A...
... G... GHOST ...
WHAT?
HUNH?
A GHOST?
WH... WHAT KIND?
UH ... WELL ...
A BOY ...
FLOATING INSIDE A CIRCLE OF BEAUTIFUL LIGHT.
...
HE LOOKED ...
... SO SAD.
KLANK
HUNH?
THAT SOUND ...
IT CAME FROM DOWN-STAIRS ...
OH!
AGAIN!
squeak

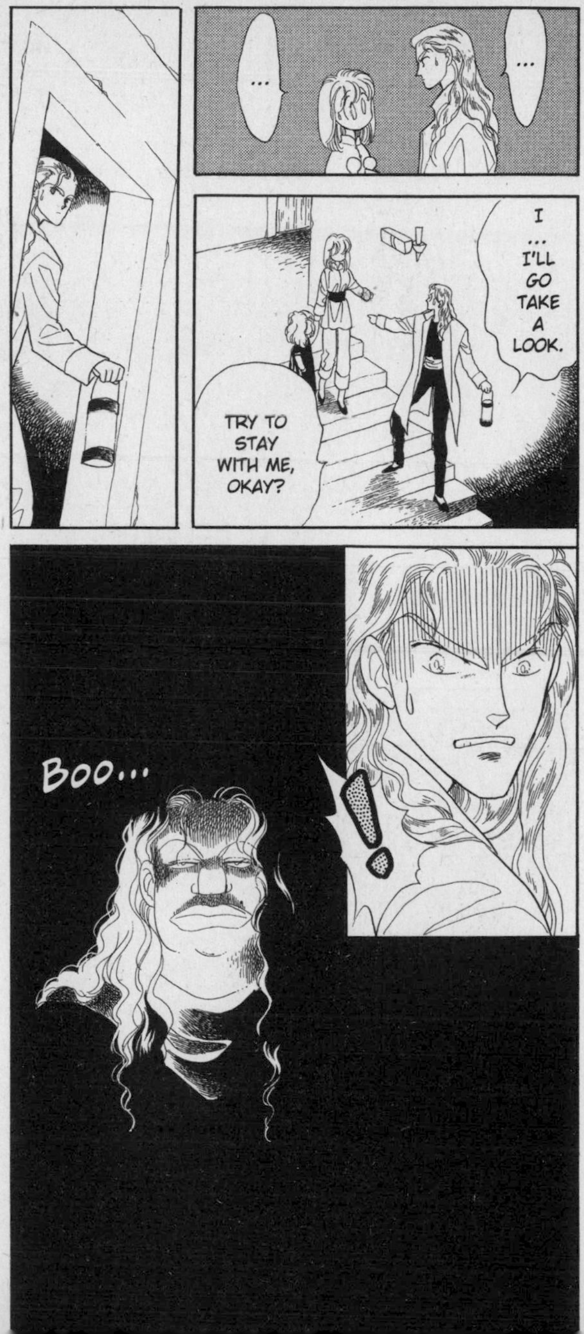
...
...
I ... I'LL GO TAKE A LOOK.
TRY TO STAY WITH ME, OKAY?
!
Boo...

Remember when I wrote about hearing a buzzing sound at night in spring and summer? For some reason, I didn't hear it this year. Why?

I wonder if the mole cricket population has decreased.

Or, could it be a poltergeist?

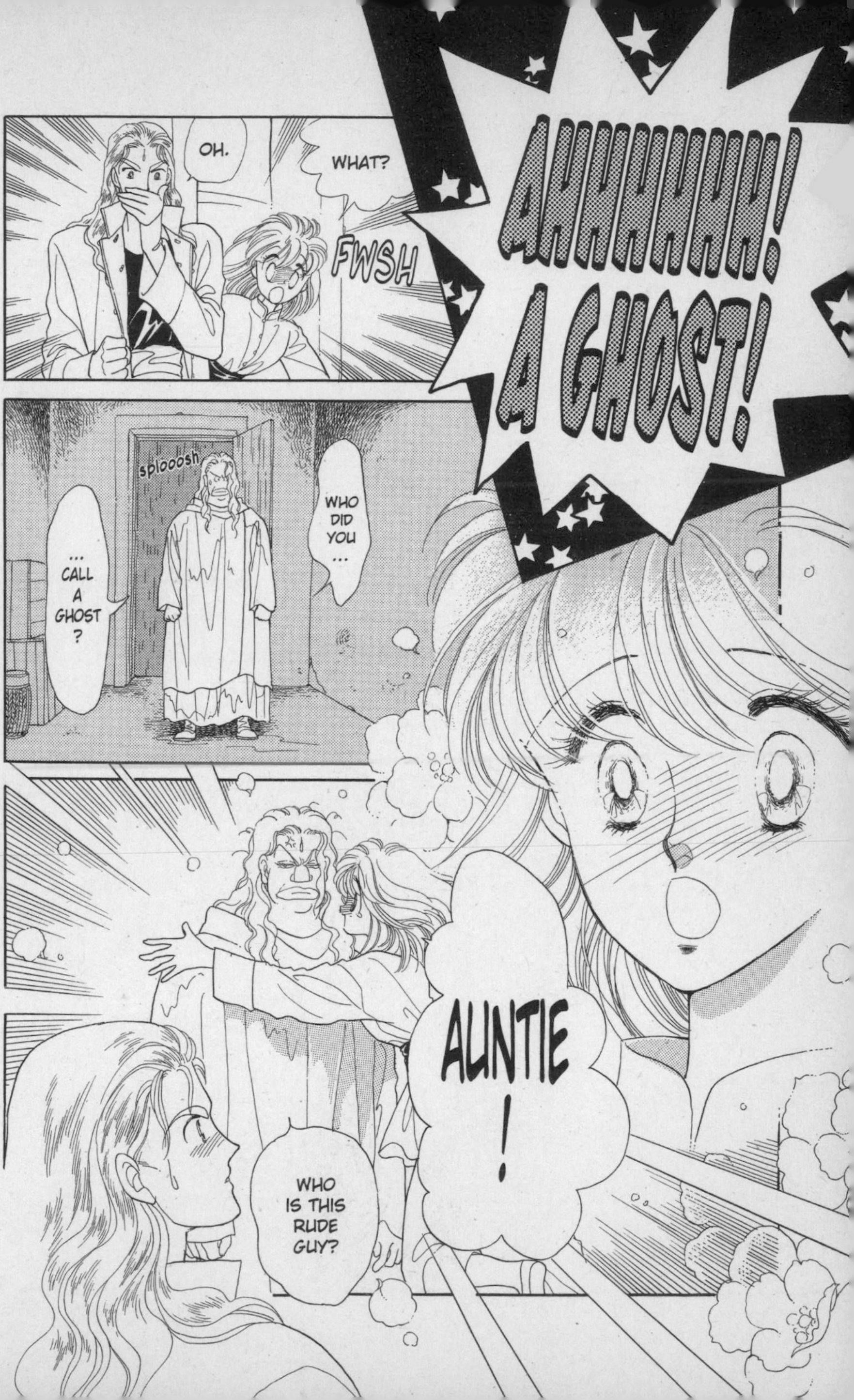
AHHHHHHH! A GHOST!
AUNTIE!
OH.
WHAT?
FWSH
WHO DID YOU ...
... CALL A GHOST?
splooosh
WHO IS THIS RUDE GUY?

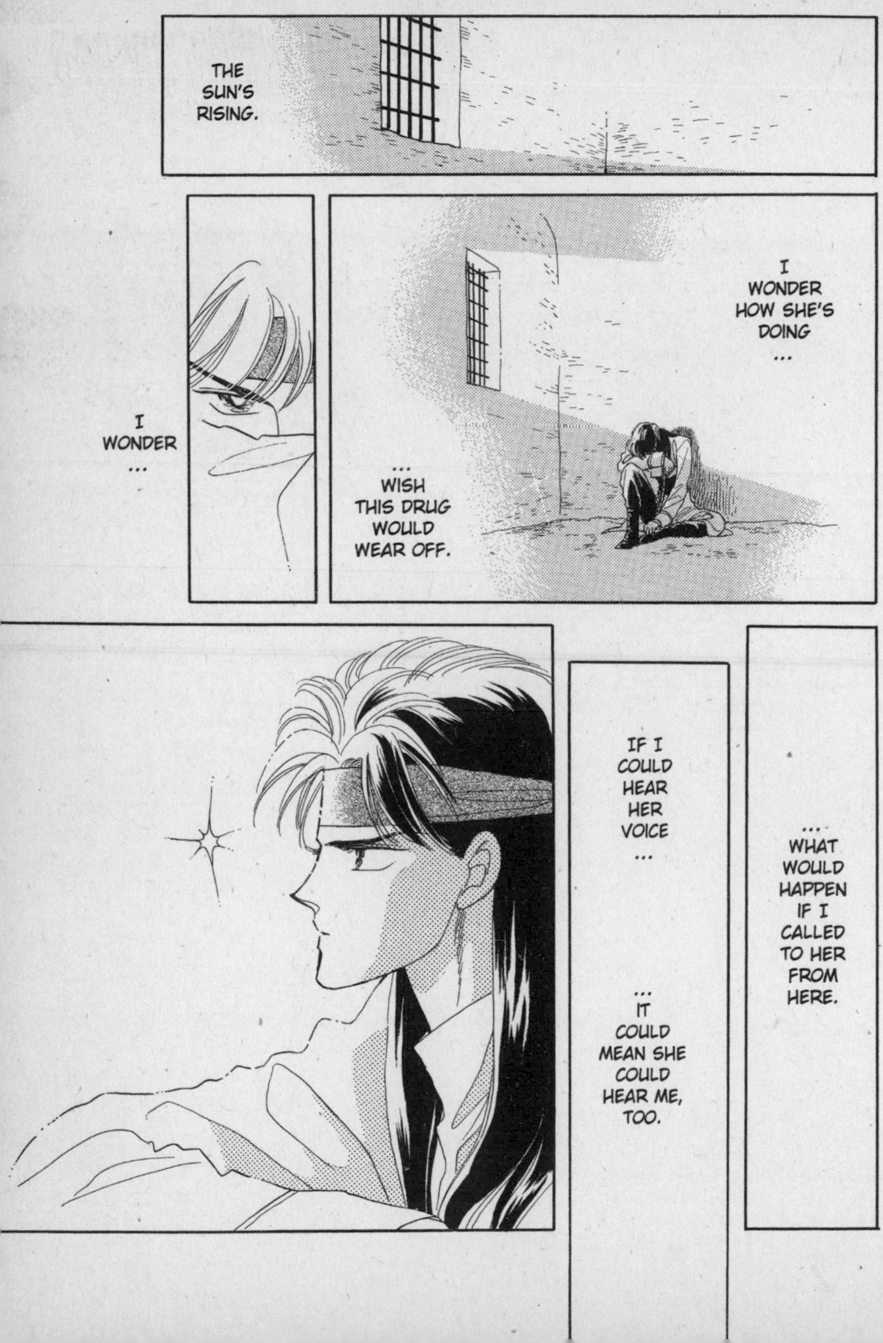
THE SUN'S RISING.
I WONDER HOW SHE'S DOING ...
... WISH THIS DRUG WOULD WEAR OFF.
I WONDER ...
... WHAT WOULD HAPPEN IF I CALLED TO HER FROM HERE.
IF I COULD HEAR HER VOICE ...
... IT COULD MEAN SHE COULD HEAR ME, TOO.

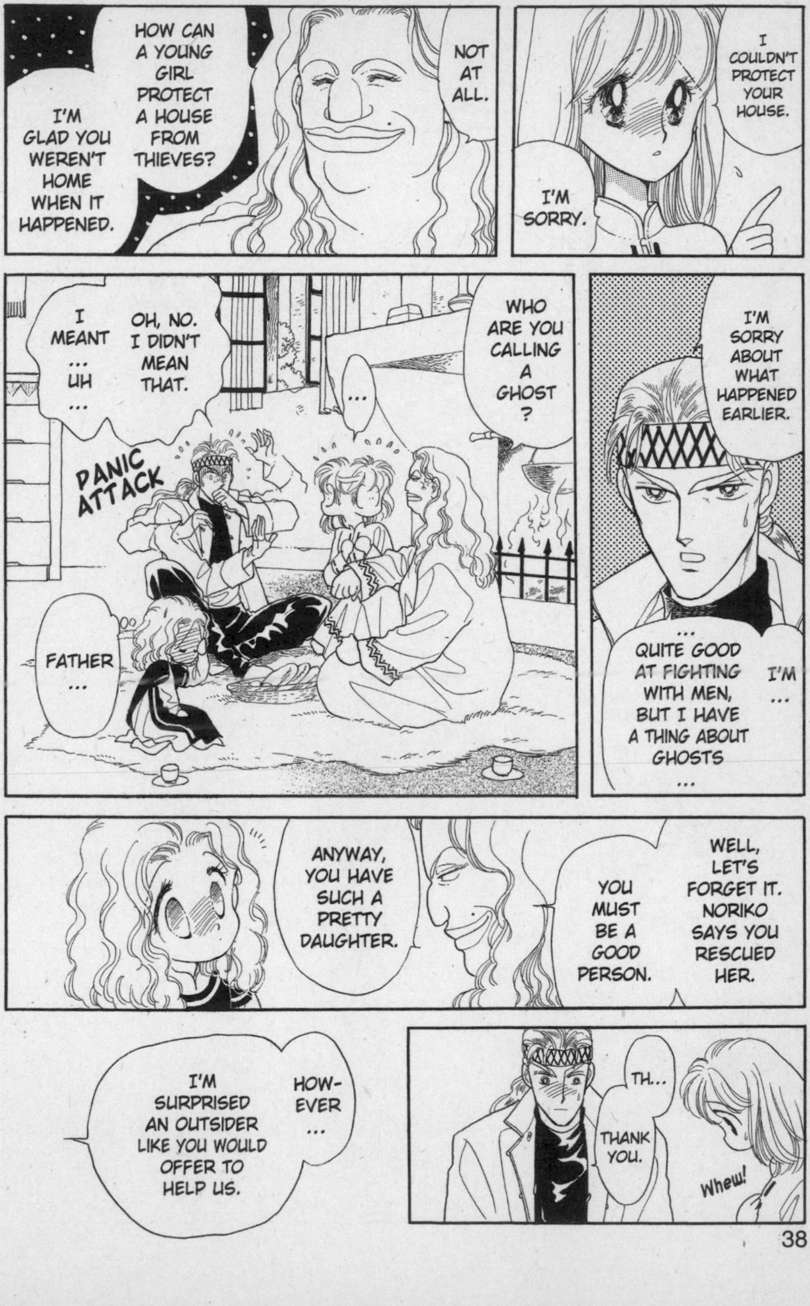
I COULDN'T PROTECT YOUR HOUSE.
I'M SORRY.
NOT AT ALL.
HOW CAN A YOUNG GIRL PROTECT A HOUSE FROM THIEVES?
I'M GLAD YOU WEREN'T HOME WHEN IT HAPPENED.
I'M SORRY ABOUT WHAT HAPPENED EARLIER.
I'M ...
... QUITE GOOD AT FIGHTING WITH MEN, BUT I HAVE A THING ABOUT GHOSTS ...
WHO ARE YOU CALLING A GHOST ?
...
OH, NO. I DIDN'T MEAN THAT.
I MEANT ... UH ...
PANIC ATTACK
FATHER ...
WELL, LET'S FORGET IT. NORIKO SAYS YOU RESCUED HER.
YOU MUST BE A GOOD PERSON.
ANYWAY, YOU HAVE SUCH A PRETTY DAUGHTER.
TH...
THANK YOU.
Whew!
HOW-EVER ...
I'M SURPRISED AN OUTSIDER LIKE YOU WOULD OFFER TO HELP US.

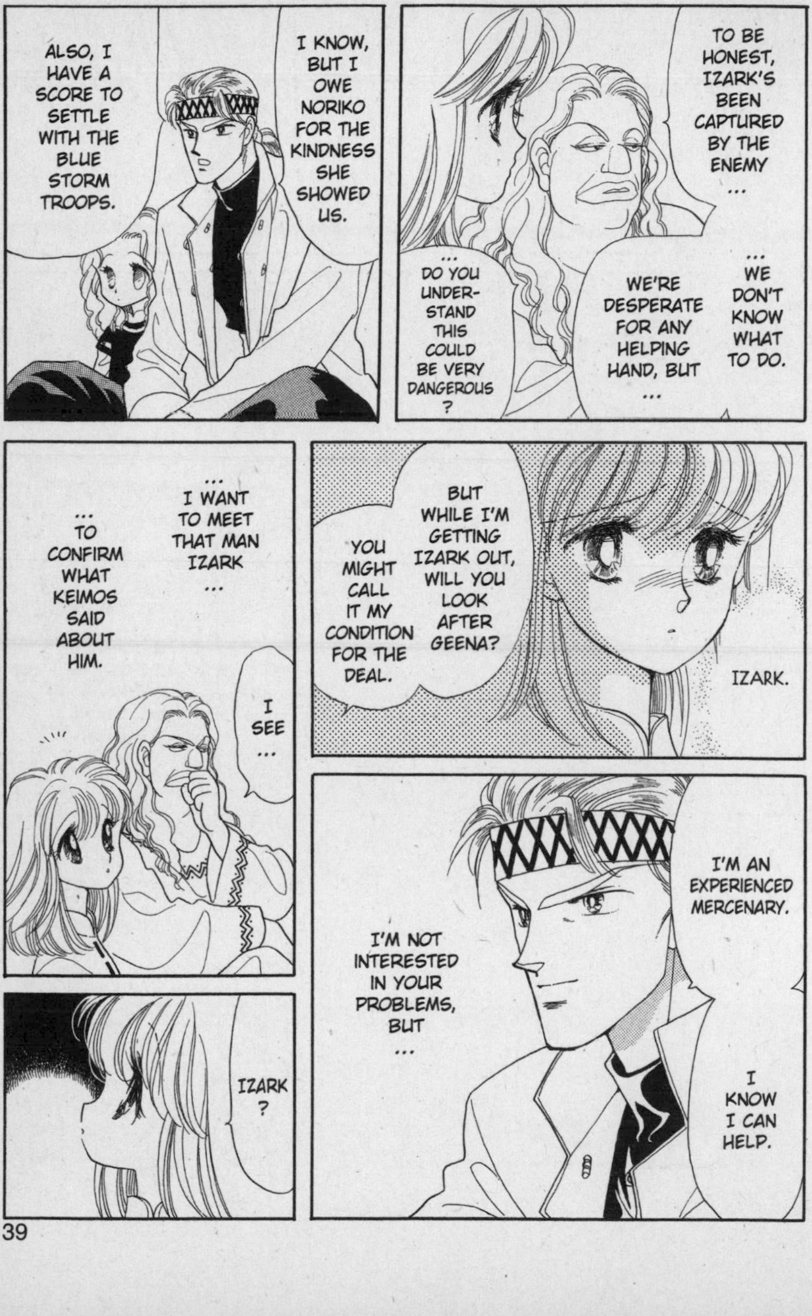
TO BE HONEST, IZARK'S BEEN CAPTURED BY THE ENEMY ...
... WE DON'T KNOW WHAT TO DO.
WE'RE DESPERATE FOR ANY HELPING HAND, BUT ...
... DO YOU UNDER-STAND THIS COULD BE VERY DANGEROUS ?
I KNOW, BUT I OWE NORIKO FOR THE KINDNESS SHE SHOWED US.
ALSO, I HAVE A SCORE TO SETTLE WITH THE BLUE STORM TROOPS.
IZARK.
BUT WHILE I'M GETTING IZARK OUT, WILL YOU LOOK AFTER GEENA?
YOU MIGHT CALL IT MY CONDITION FOR THE DEAL.
... I WANT TO MEET THAT MAN IZARK ...
... TO CONFIRM WHAT KEIMOS SAID ABOUT HIM.
I SEE ...
I'M AN EXPERIENCED MERCENARY.
I KNOW I CAN HELP.
I'M NOT INTERESTED IN YOUR PROBLEMS, BUT ...
IZARK ?

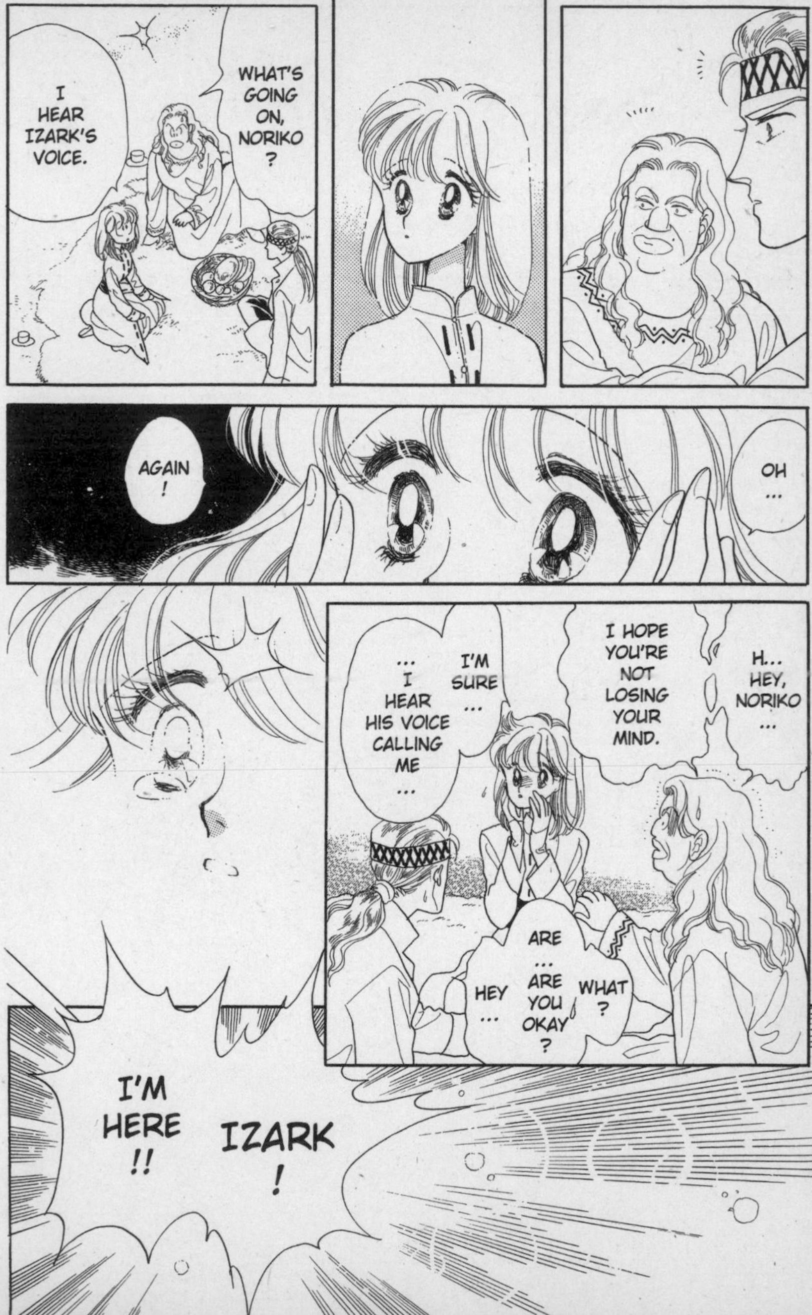
WHAT'S GOING ON, NORIKO?
I HEAR IZARK'S VOICE.
OH...
AGAIN!
H... HEY, NORIKO...
I HOPE YOU'RE NOT LOSING YOUR MIND.
I'M SURE...
... I HEAR HIS VOICE CALLING ME...
WHAT?
ARE... ARE YOU OKAY?
HEY...
IZARK!
I'M HERE!!

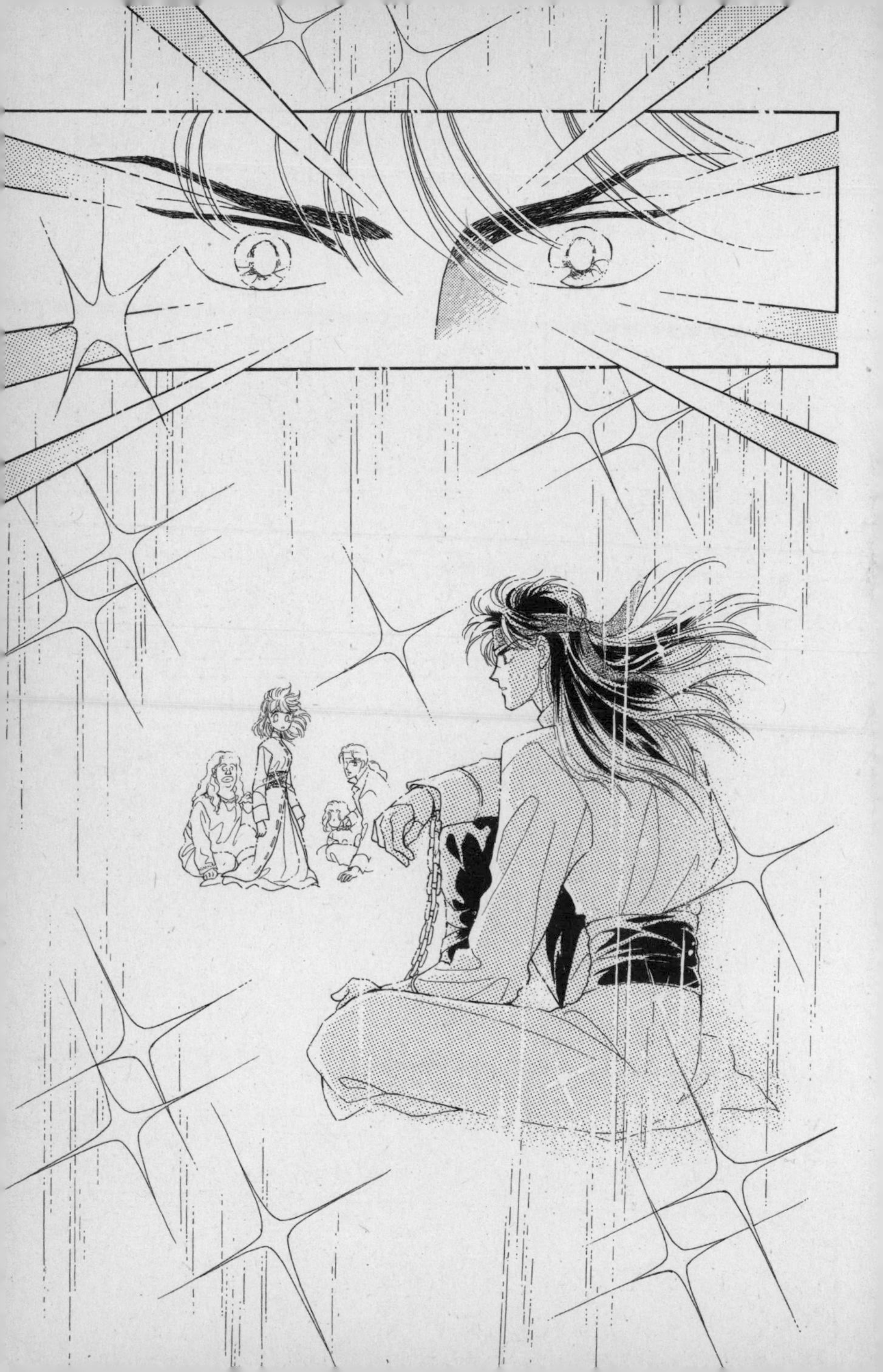

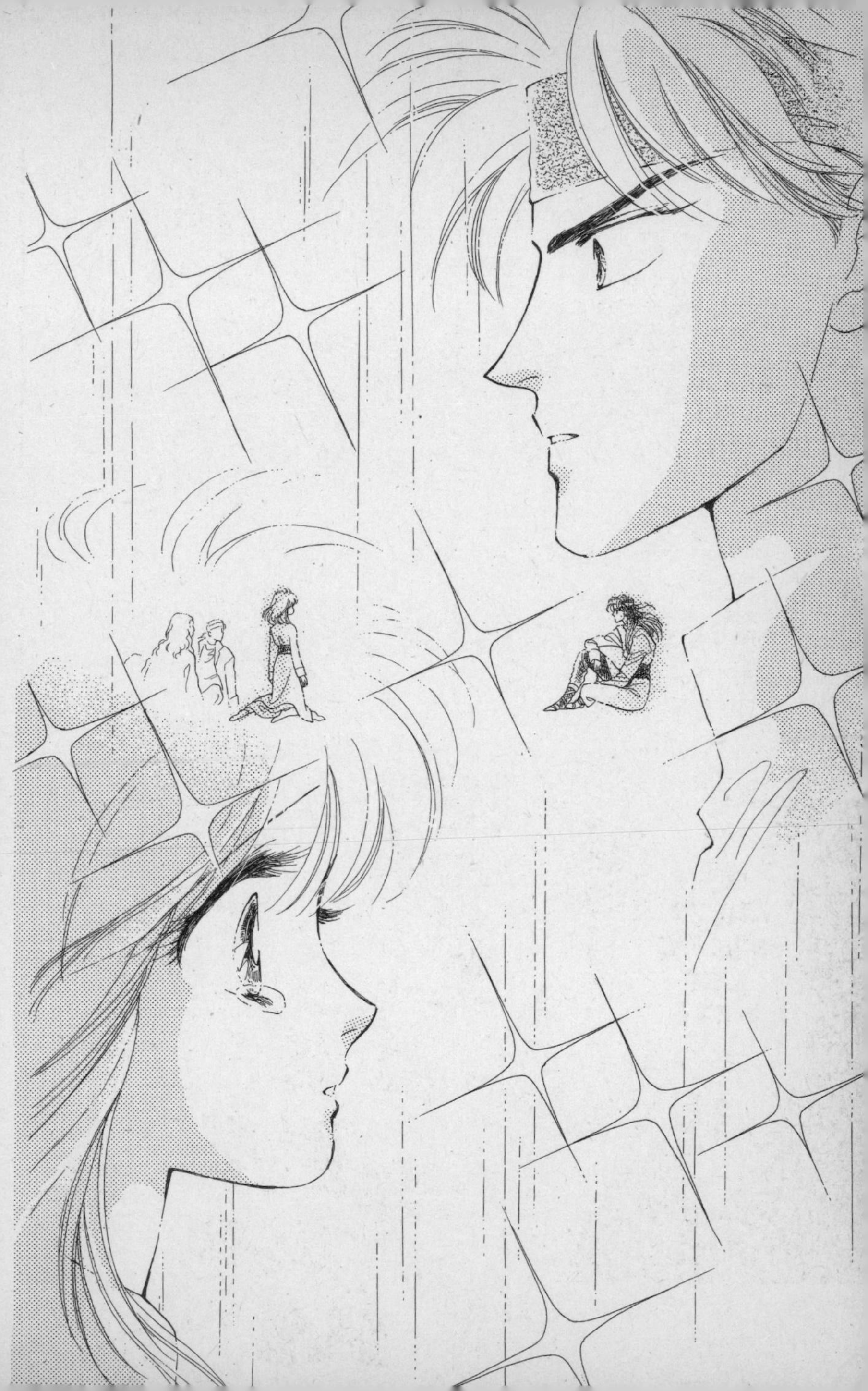

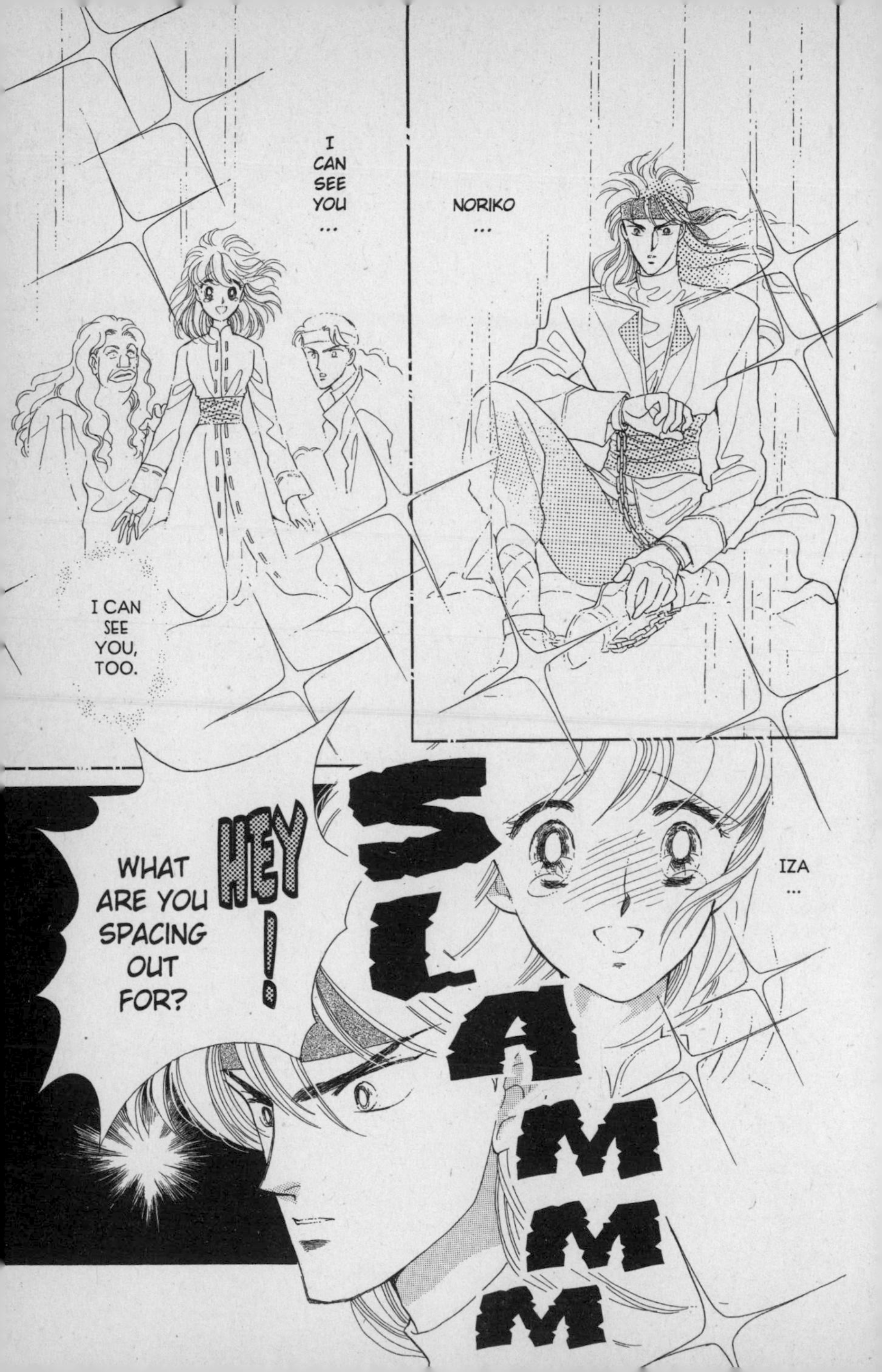
NORIKO ...
I CAN SEE YOU ...
I CAN SEE YOU, TOO.
IZA ...
SLAMMM
HEY!
WHAT ARE YOU SPACING OUT FOR?

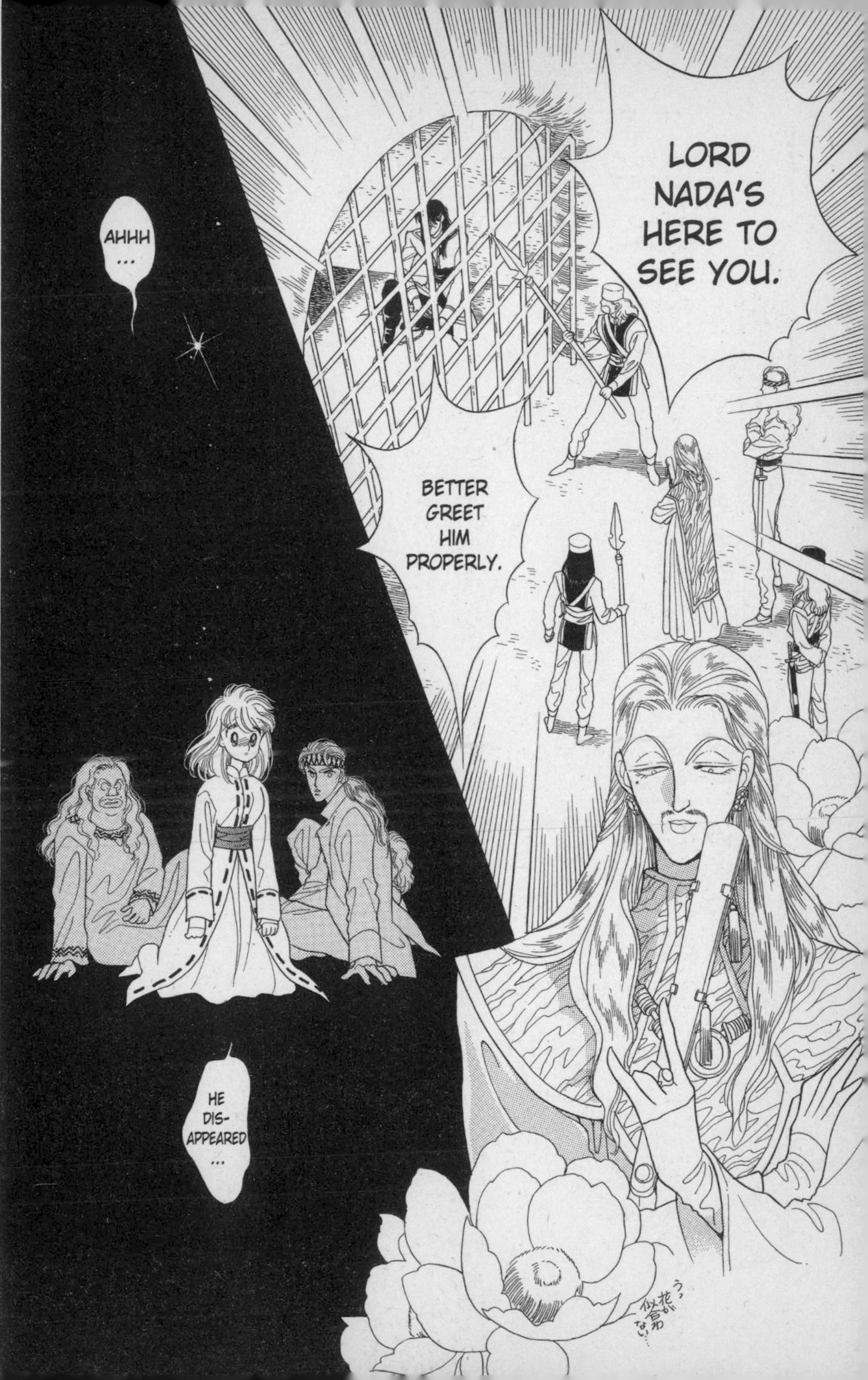
LORD NADA'S HERE TO SEE YOU.
BETTER GREET HIM PROPERLY.
う、花が似合わない…
AHHH ...
HE DIS-APPEARED ...

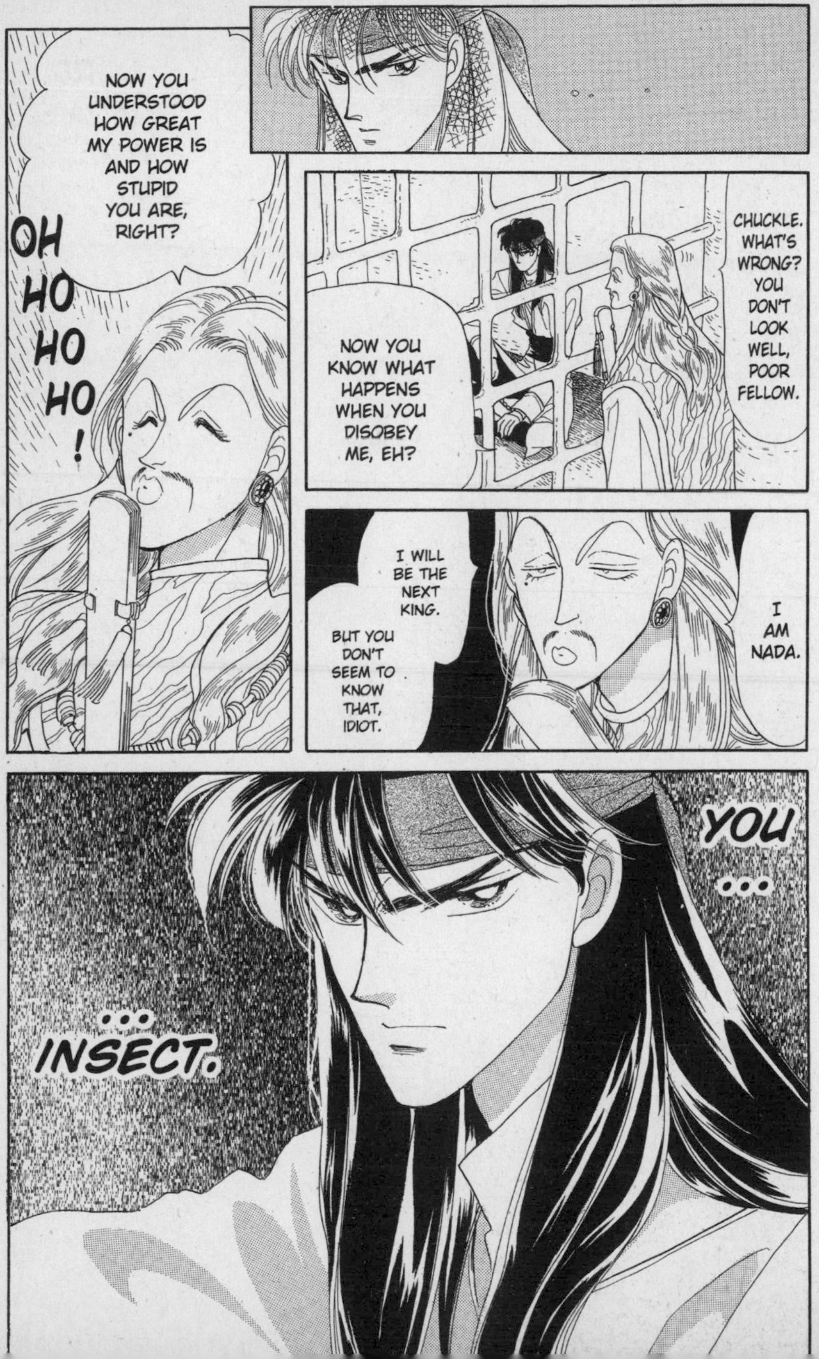
CHUCKLE. WHAT'S WRONG? YOU DON'T LOOK WELL, POOR FELLOW.
NOW YOU KNOW WHAT HAPPENS WHEN YOU DISOBEY ME, EH?
I AM NADA.
I WILL BE THE NEXT KING.
BUT YOU DON'T SEEM TO KNOW THAT, IDIOT.
NOW YOU UNDERSTOOD HOW GREAT MY POWER IS AND HOW STUPID YOU ARE, RIGHT?
OH HO HO HO!
YOU...
...INSECT.

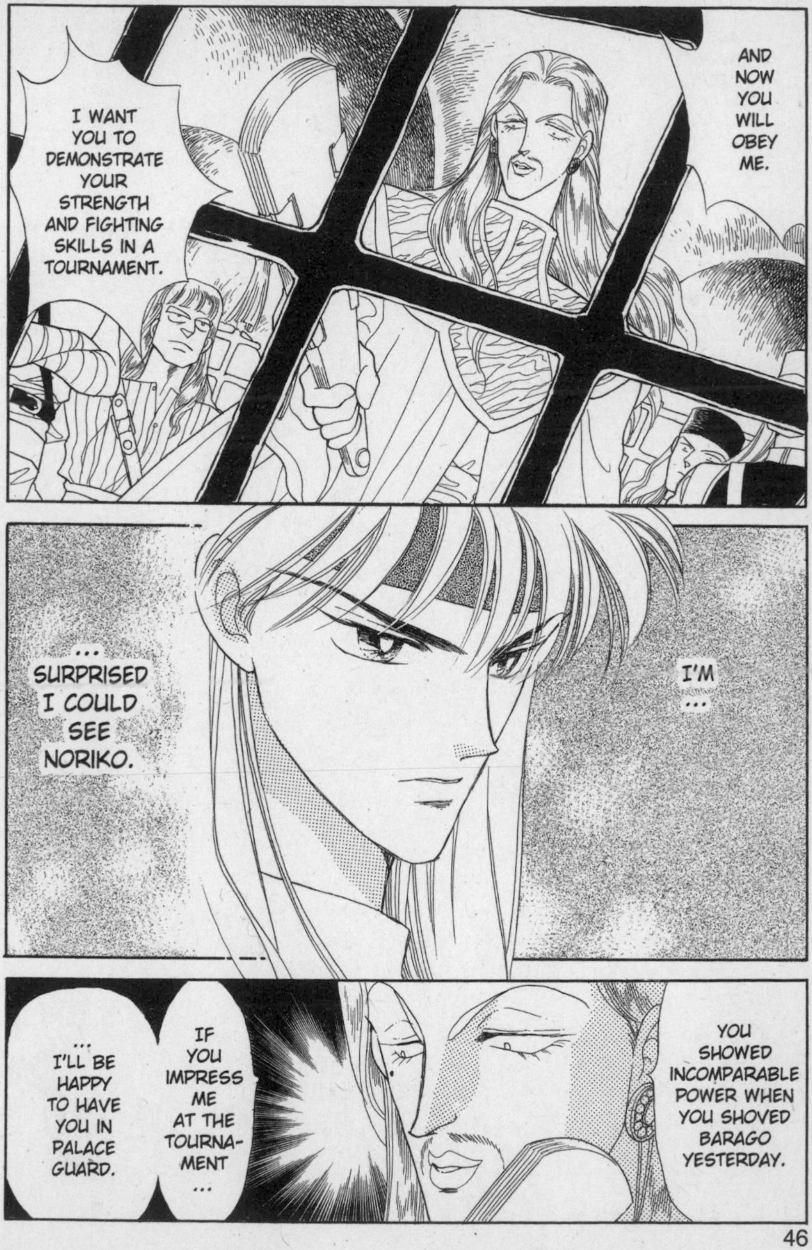
AND NOW YOU WILL OBEY ME.
I WANT YOU TO DEMONSTRATE YOUR STRENGTH AND FIGHTING SKILLS IN A TOURNAMENT.
I'M ...
... SURPRISED I COULD SEE NORIKO.
YOU SHOWED INCOMPARABLE POWER WHEN YOU SHOVED BARAGO YESTERDAY.
IF YOU IMPRESS ME AT THE TOURNA-MENT ...
... I'LL BE HAPPY TO HAVE YOU IN PALACE GUARD.

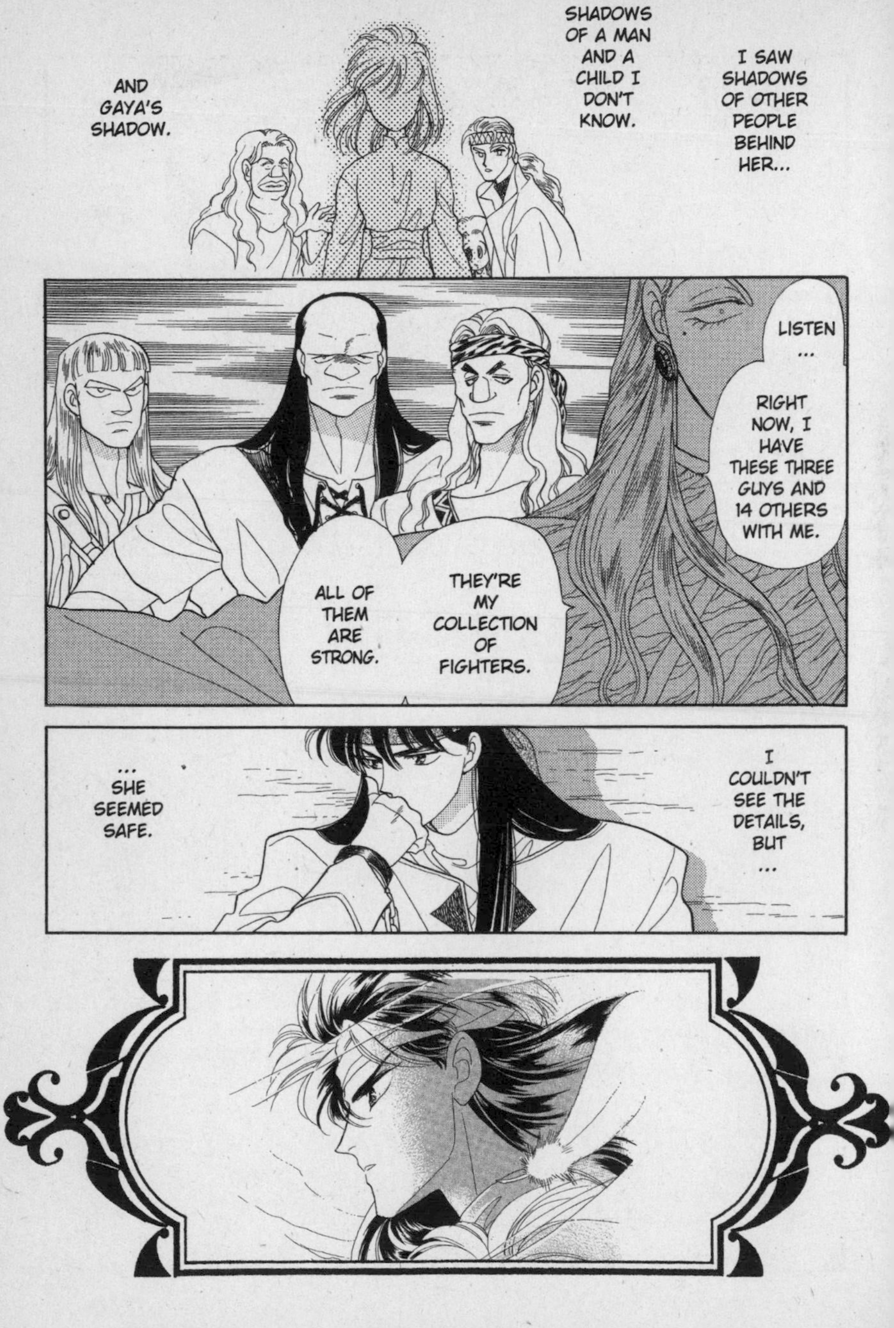
I SAW SHADOWS OF OTHER PEOPLE BEHIND HER...
SHADOWS OF A MAN AND A CHILD I DON'T KNOW.
AND GAYA'S SHADOW.
LISTEN ...
RIGHT NOW, I HAVE THESE THREE GUYS AND 14 OTHERS WITH ME.
THEY'RE MY COLLECTION OF FIGHTERS.
ALL OF THEM ARE STRONG.
I COULDN'T SEE THE DETAILS, BUT ...
... SHE SEEMED SAFE.

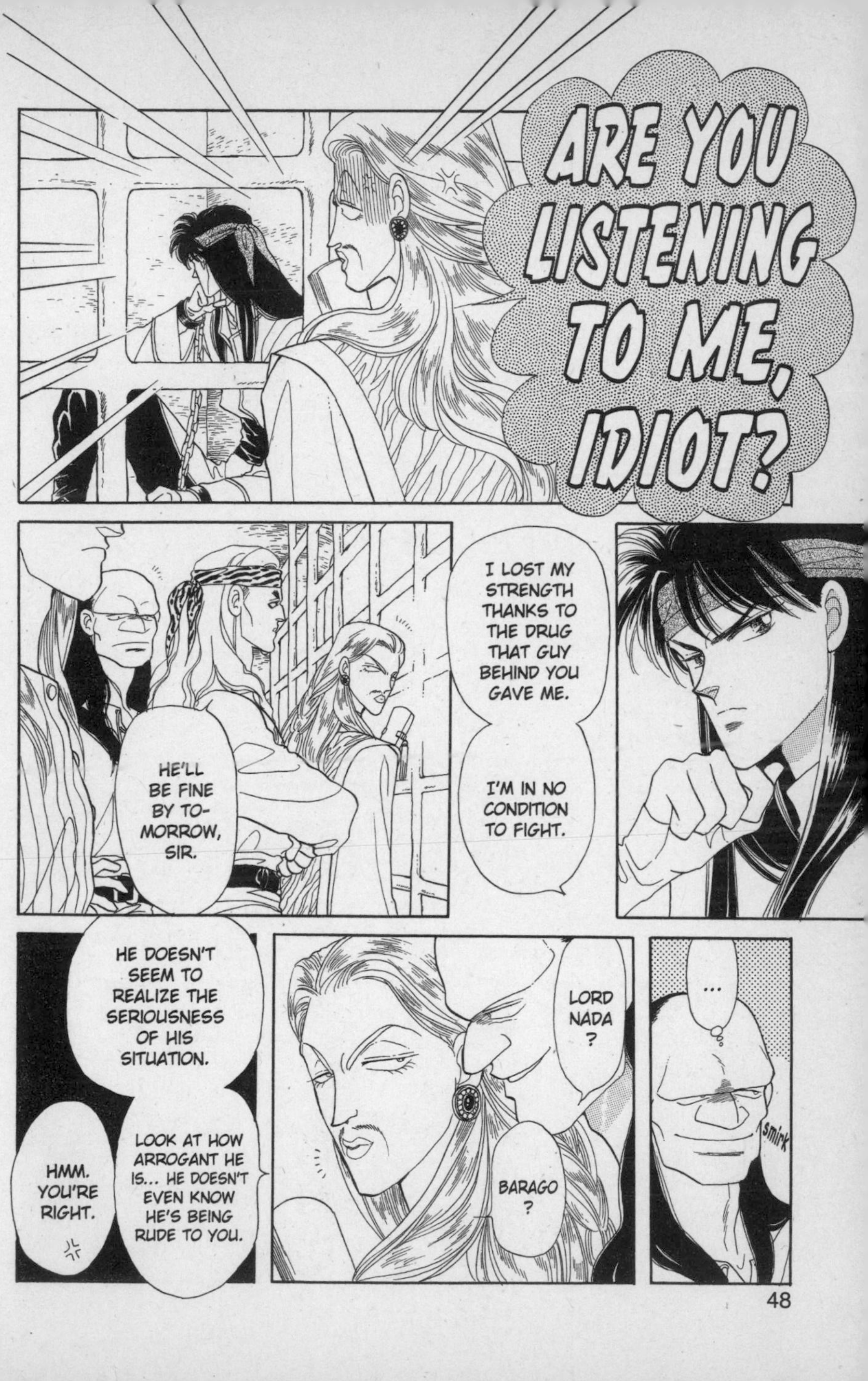
ARE YOU LISTENING TO ME, IDIOT?
I LOST MY STRENGTH THANKS TO THE DRUG THAT GUY BEHIND YOU GAVE ME.
I'M IN NO CONDITION TO FIGHT.
HE'LL BE FINE BY TO-MORROW, SIR.
...
smirk
LORD NADA ?
BARAGO ?
HE DOESN'T SEEM TO REALIZE THE SERIOUSNESS OF HIS SITUATION.
LOOK AT HOW ARROGANT HE IS... HE DOESN'T EVEN KNOW HE'S BEING RUDE TO YOU.
HMM. YOU'RE RIGHT.

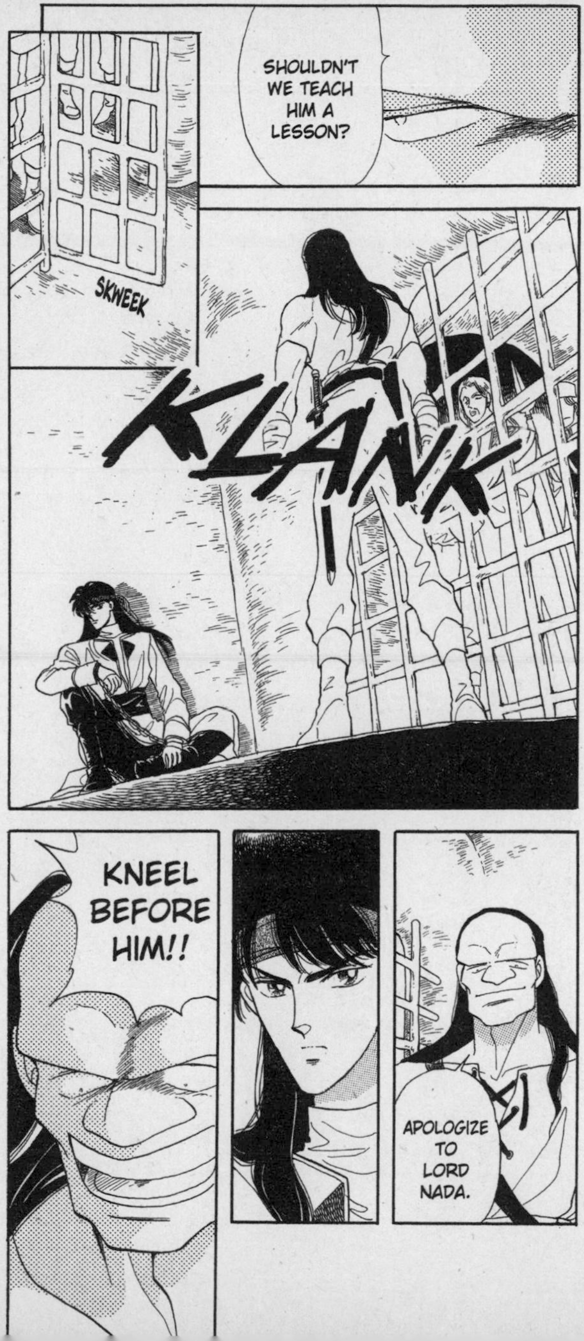
SHOULDN'T WE TEACH HIM A LESSON?
SKWEEK
KLANK
APOLOGIZE TO LORD NADA.
KNEEL BEFORE HIM!!

My strange childhood memories:

Part 1:

There was a house without fences along the road. On the rock in the garden of the house, I saw an old lady with long, loose hair in a white kimono waving at me.

Was it real or a dream?

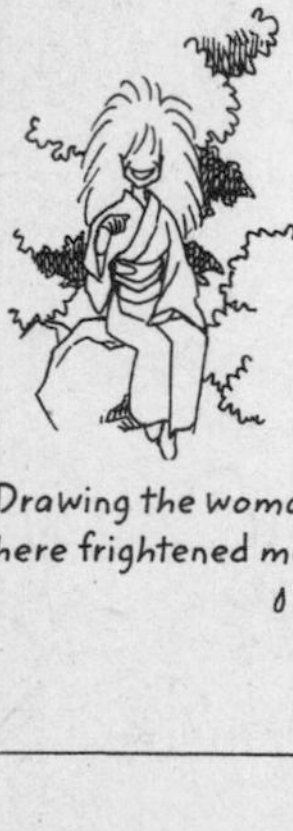

Drawing the woman here frightened me!

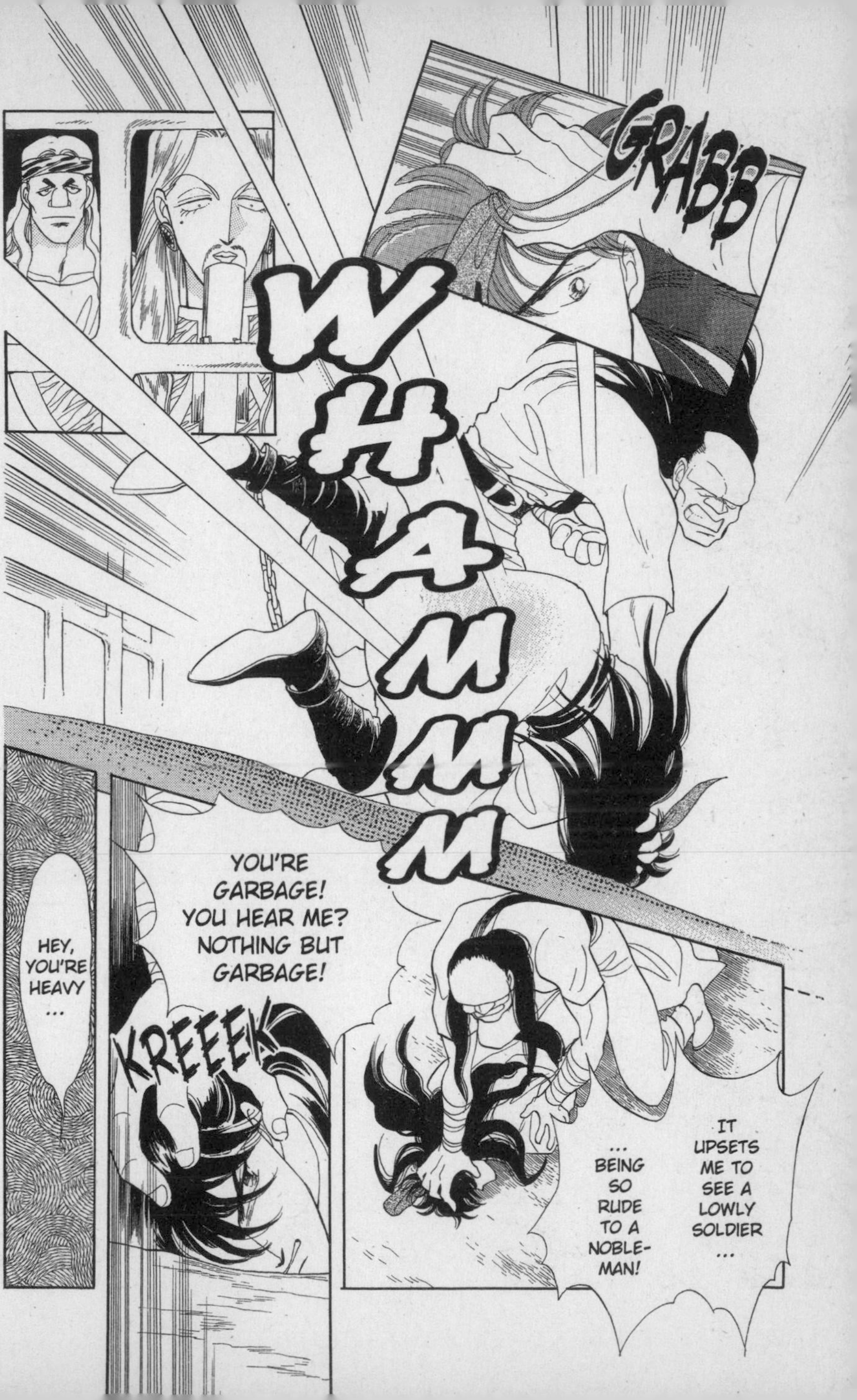
GRABB
WHAMMM
IT UPSETS ME TO SEE A LOWLY SOLDIER ...
... BEING SO RUDE TO A NOBLE-MAN!
YOU'RE GARBAGE! YOU HEAR ME? NOTHING BUT GARBAGE!
KREEEK
HEY, YOU'RE HEAVY ...

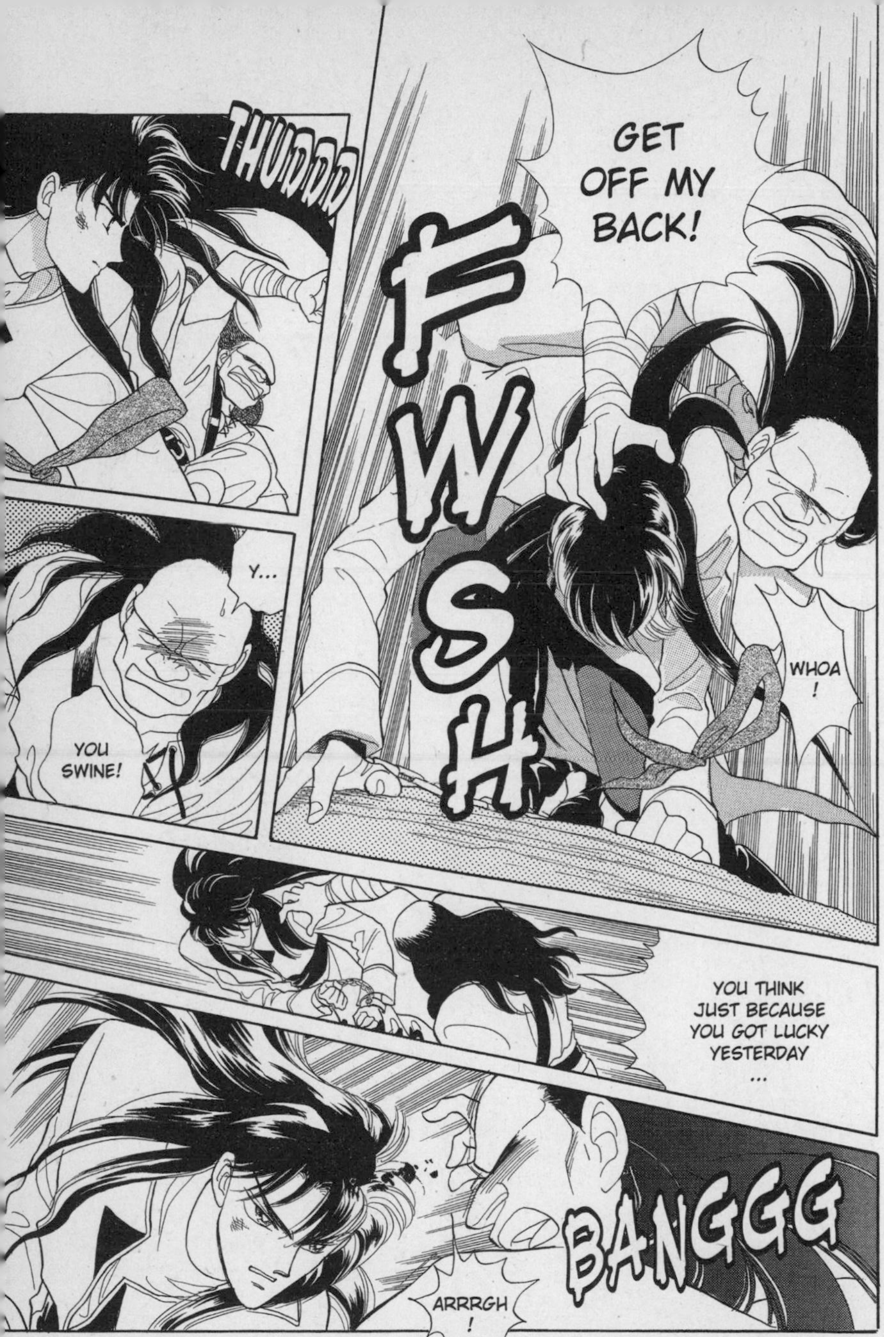
GET OFF MY BACK!
FWSH
WHOA!
THUDDDD
Y...
YOU SWINE!
YOU THINK JUST BECAUSE YOU GOT LUCKY YESTERDAY ...
BANGGG
ARRRGH!

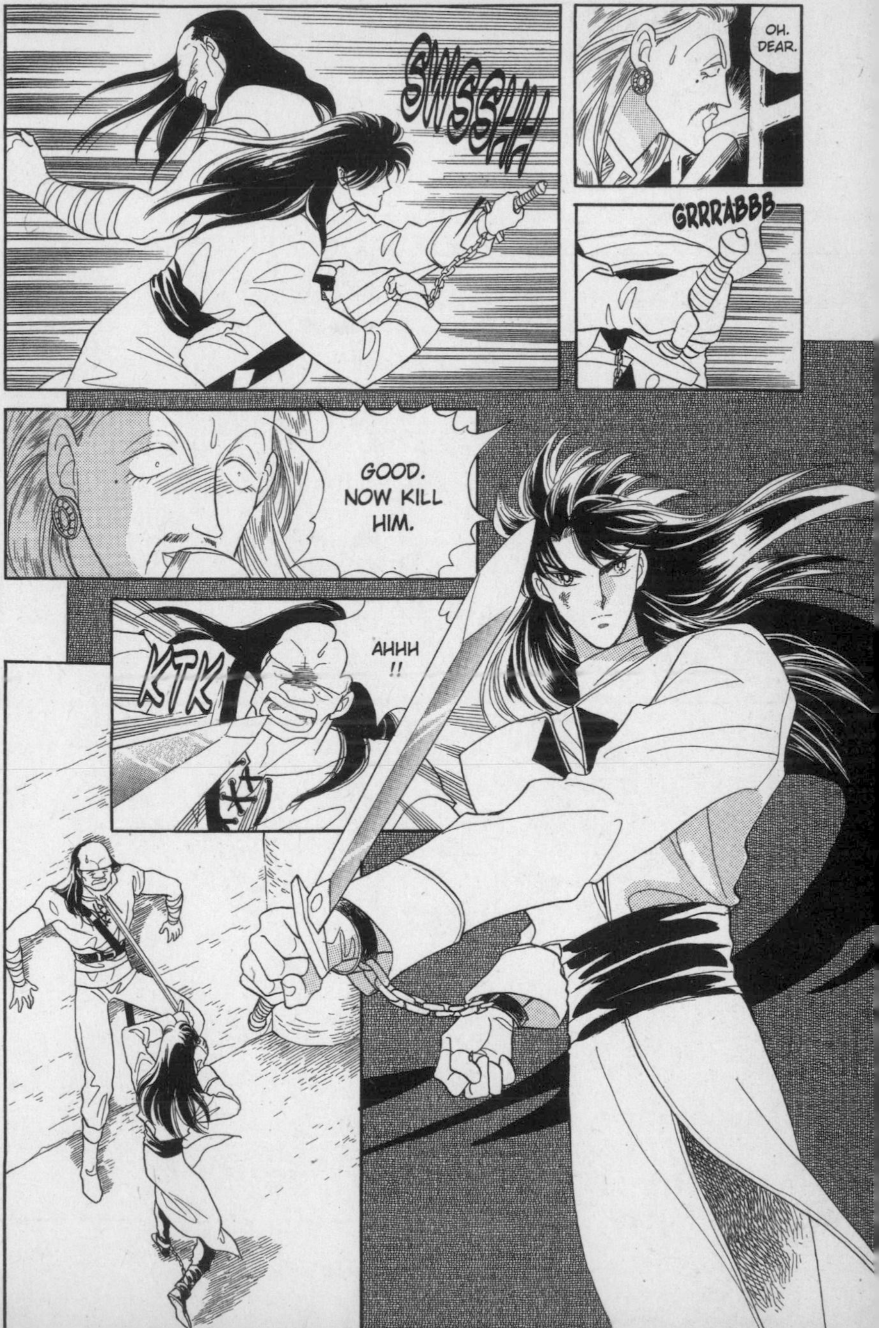
OH. DEAR.
GRRRABBB
SWSSHH
GOOD. NOW KILL HIM.
KTK
AHHH !!

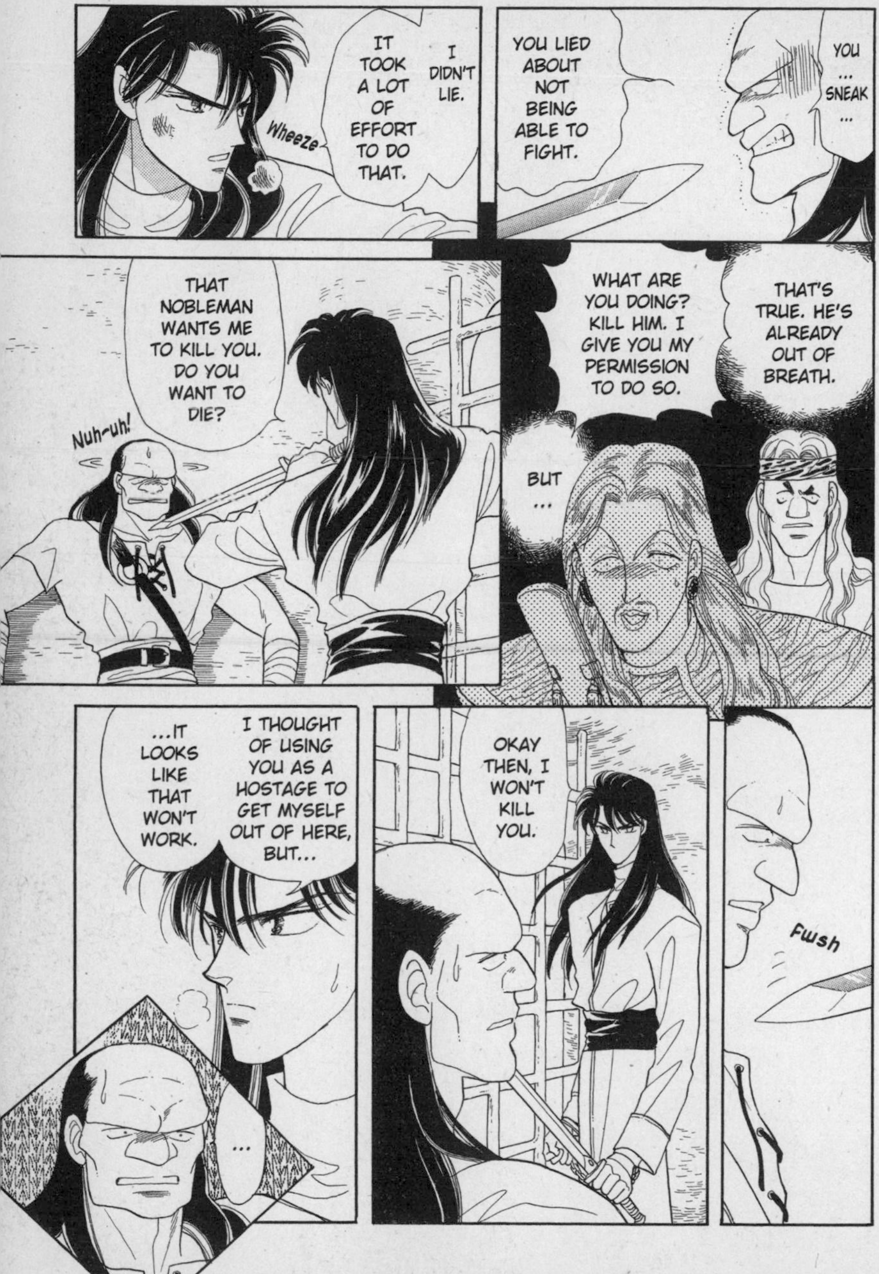
YOU ... SNEAK ...
YOU LIED ABOUT NOT BEING ABLE TO FIGHT.
I DIDN'T LIE.
IT TOOK A LOT OF EFFORT TO DO THAT.
Wheeze
THAT'S TRUE. HE'S ALREADY OUT OF BREATH.
WHAT ARE YOU DOING? KILL HIM. I GIVE YOU MY PERMISSION TO DO SO.
BUT ...
THAT NOBLEMAN WANTS ME TO KILL YOU. DO YOU WANT TO DIE?
Nuh-uh!
Fwsh
OKAY THEN, I WON'T KILL YOU.
I THOUGHT OF USING YOU AS A HOSTAGE TO GET MYSELF OUT OF HERE, BUT...
...IT LOOKS LIKE THAT WON'T WORK.
...

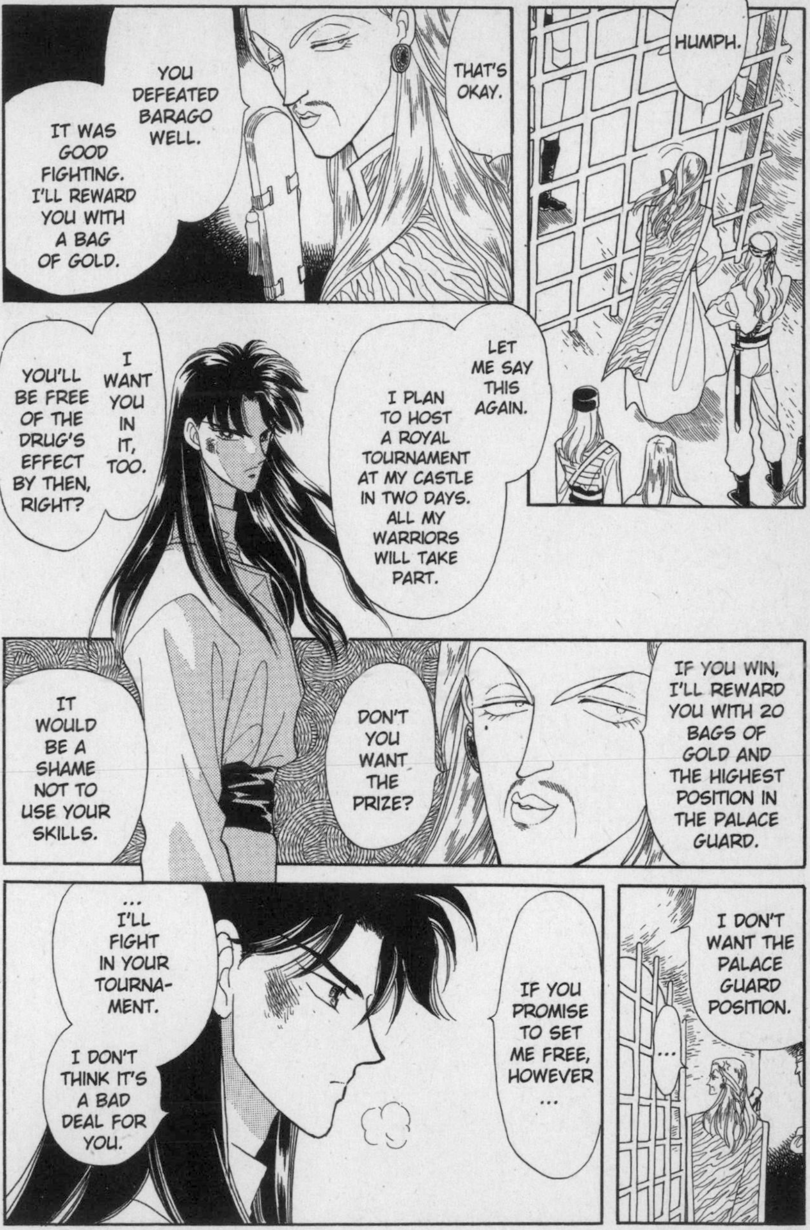
HUMPH.
THAT'S OKAY.
YOU DEFEATED BARAGO WELL.
IT WAS GOOD FIGHTING. I'LL REWARD YOU WITH A BAG OF GOLD.
LET ME SAY THIS AGAIN.
I PLAN TO HOST A ROYAL TOURNAMENT AT MY CASTLE IN TWO DAYS. ALL MY WARRIORS WILL TAKE PART.
I WANT YOU IN IT, TOO.
YOU'LL BE FREE OF THE DRUG'S EFFECT BY THEN, RIGHT?
IF YOU WIN, I'LL REWARD YOU WITH 20 BAGS OF GOLD AND THE HIGHEST POSITION IN THE PALACE GUARD.
DON'T YOU WANT THE PRIZE?
IT WOULD BE A SHAME NOT TO USE YOUR SKILLS.
I DON'T WANT THE PALACE GUARD POSITION.
...
IF YOU PROMISE TO SET ME FREE, HOWEVER ...
... I'LL FIGHT IN YOUR TOURNA-MENT.
I DON'T THINK IT'S A BAD DEAL FOR YOU.

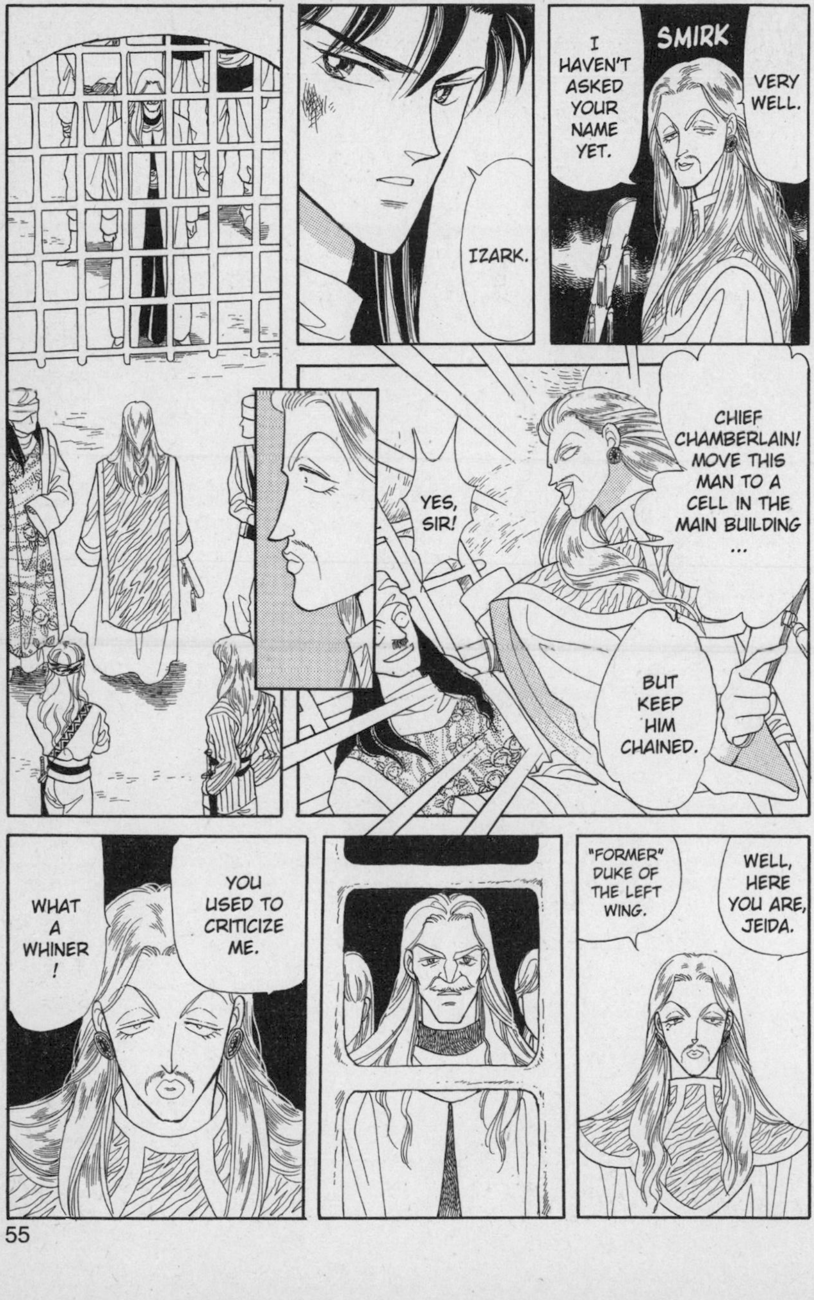
SMIRK
VERY WELL.
I HAVEN'T ASKED YOUR NAME YET.
IZARK.
CHIEF CHAMBERLAIN! MOVE THIS MAN TO A CELL IN THE MAIN BUILDING ...
YES, SIR!
BUT KEEP HIM CHAINED.
WELL, HERE YOU ARE, JEIDA.
"FORMER" DUKE OF THE LEFT WING.
YOU USED TO CRITICIZE ME.
WHAT A WHINER!

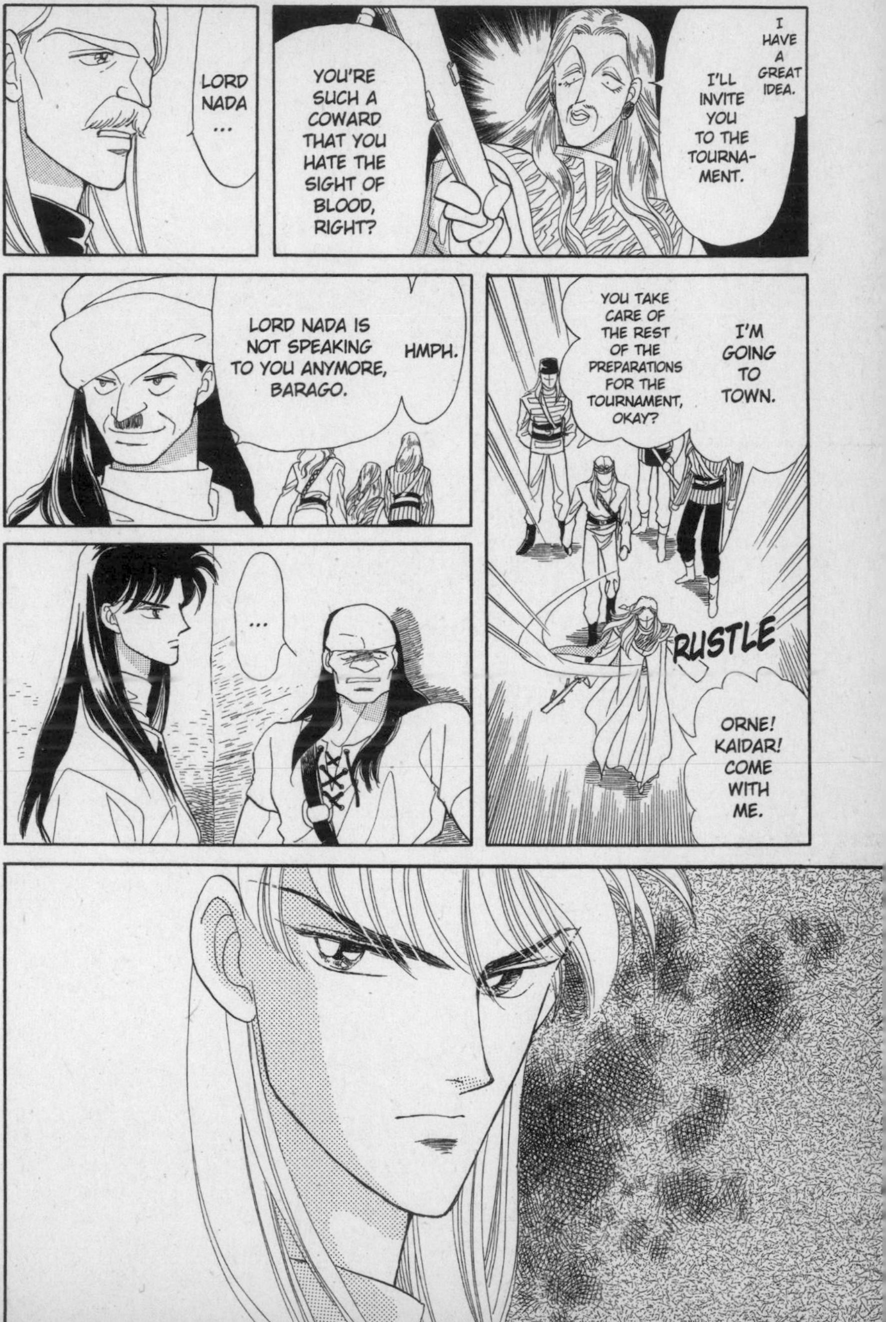
I HAVE A GREAT IDEA.
I'LL INVITE YOU TO THE TOURNAMENT.
YOU'RE SUCH A COWARD THAT YOU HATE THE SIGHT OF BLOOD, RIGHT?
LORD NADA ...
I'M GOING TO TOWN.
YOU TAKE CARE OF THE REST OF THE PREPARATIONS FOR THE TOURNAMENT, OKAY?
RUSTLE
ORNE! KAIDAR! COME WITH ME.
HMPH.
LORD NADA IS NOT SPEAKING TO YOU ANYMORE, BARAGO.
...

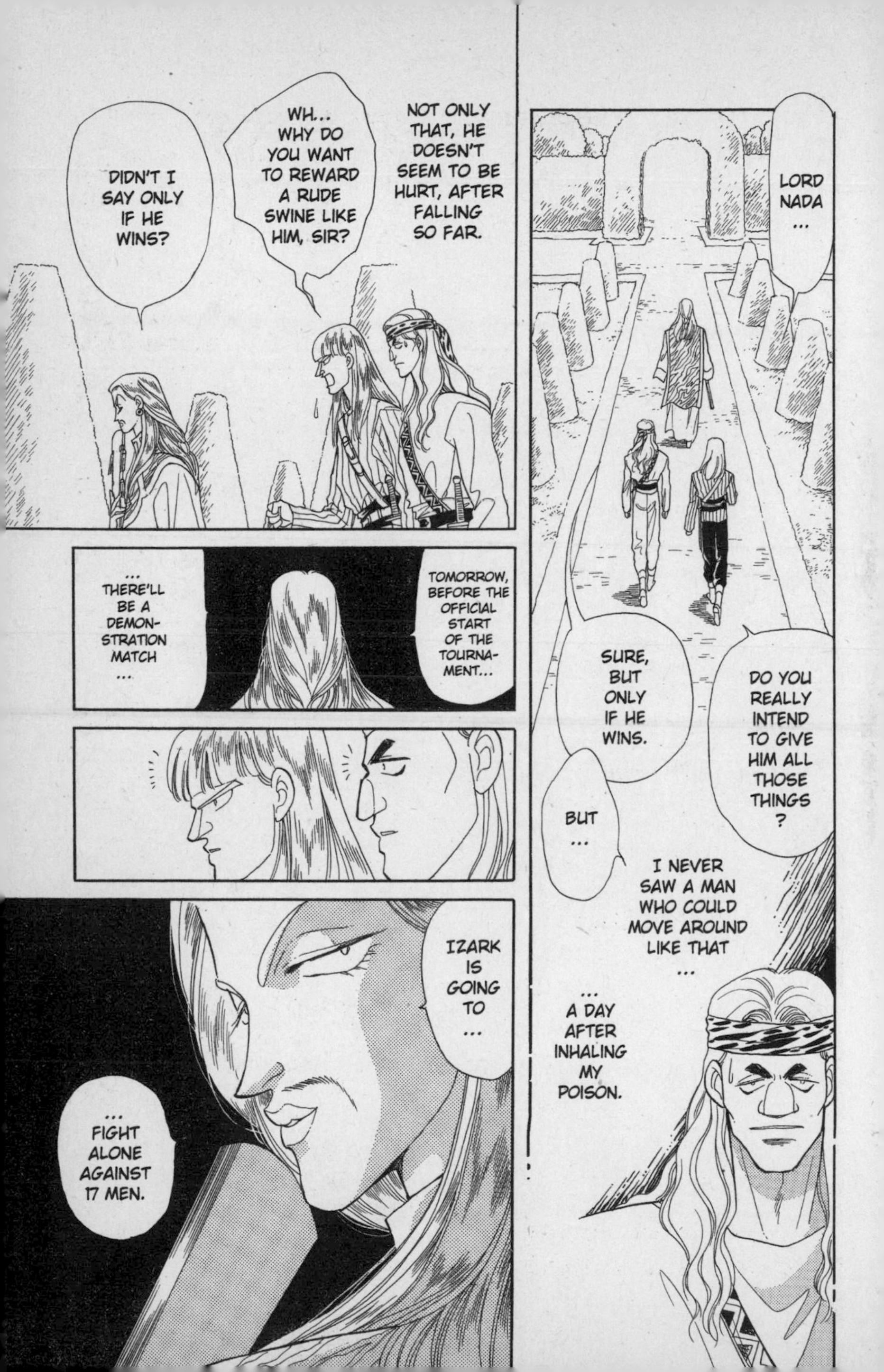
LORD NADA ...
DO YOU REALLY INTEND TO GIVE HIM ALL THOSE THINGS ?
SURE, BUT ONLY IF HE WINS.
BUT ...
I NEVER SAW A MAN WHO COULD MOVE AROUND LIKE THAT ...
... A DAY AFTER INHALING MY POISON.
NOT ONLY THAT, HE DOESN'T SEEM TO BE HURT, AFTER FALLING SO FAR.
WH... WHY DO YOU WANT TO REWARD A RUDE SWINE LIKE HIM, SIR?
DIDN'T I SAY ONLY IF HE WINS?
TOMORROW, BEFORE THE OFFICIAL START OF THE TOURNA-MENT...
... THERE'LL BE A DEMON-STRATION MATCH ...
IZARK IS GOING TO ...
... FIGHT ALONE AGAINST 17 MEN.

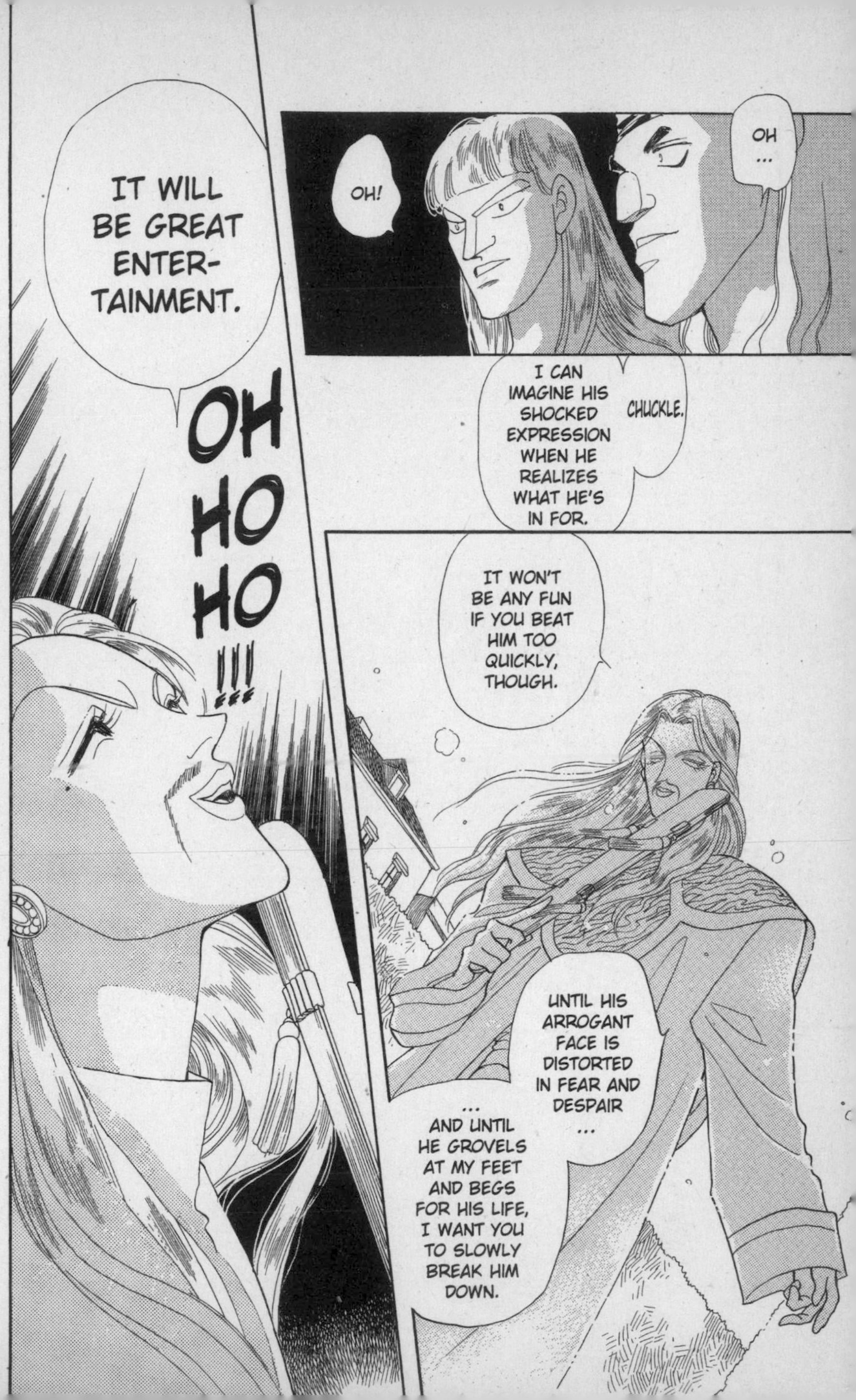
OH ...
OH!
I CAN IMAGINE HIS SHOCKED EXPRESSION WHEN HE REALIZES WHAT HE'S IN FOR.
CHUCKLE.
IT WON'T BE ANY FUN IF YOU BEAT HIM TOO QUICKLY, THOUGH.
UNTIL HIS ARROGANT FACE IS DISTORTED IN FEAR AND DESPAIR ...
... AND UNTIL HE GROVELS AT MY FEET AND BEGS FOR HIS LIFE, I WANT YOU TO SLOWLY BREAK HIM DOWN.
IT WILL BE GREAT ENTER-TAINMENT.
OH HO HO !!!

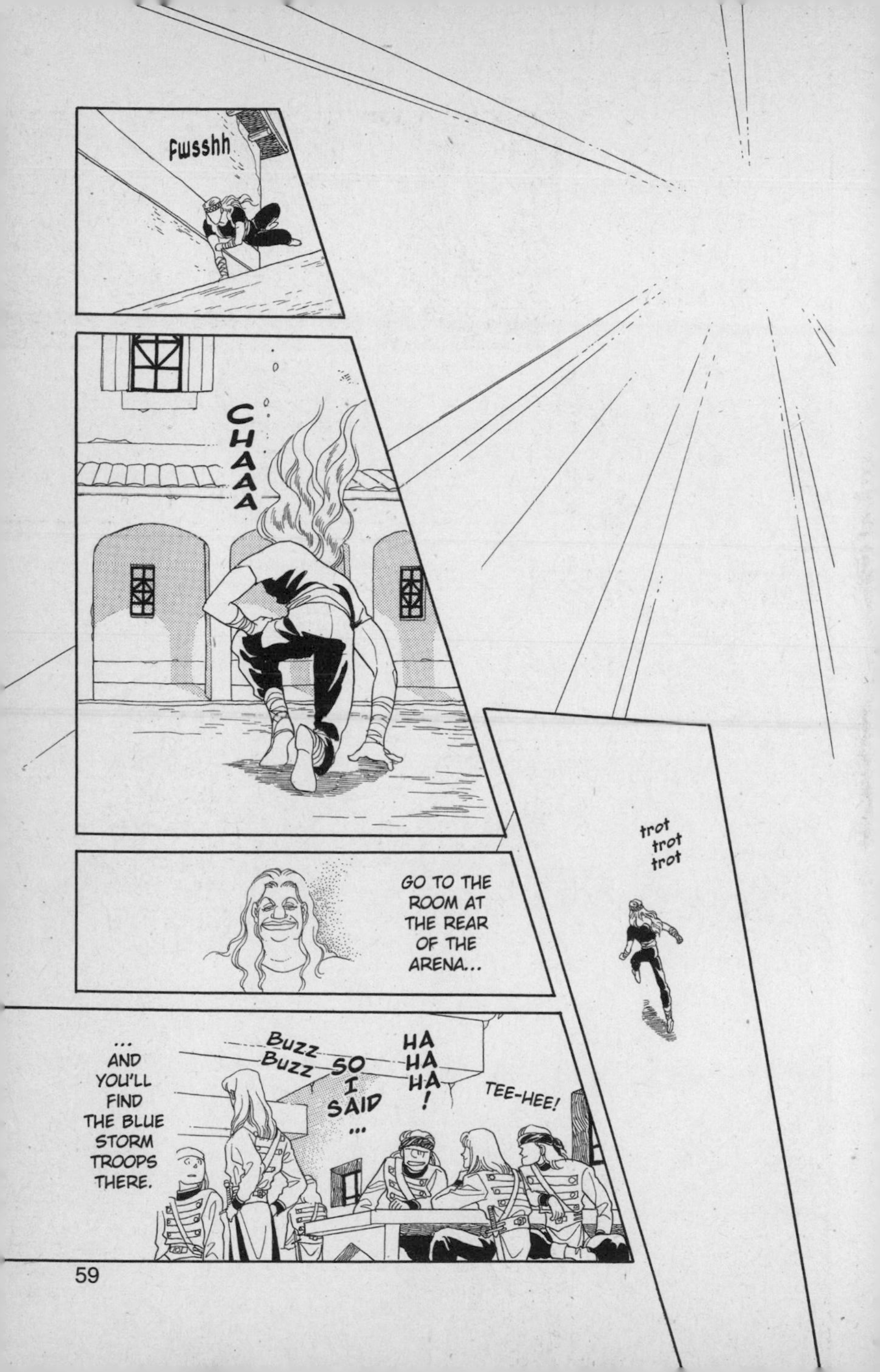
Fwsshh
CHAAA
GO TO THE ROOM AT THE REAR OF THE ARENA...
... AND YOU'LL FIND THE BLUE STORM TROOPS THERE.
Buzz Buzz
SO I SAID ...
HA HA HA!
TEE-HEE!
trot trot trot

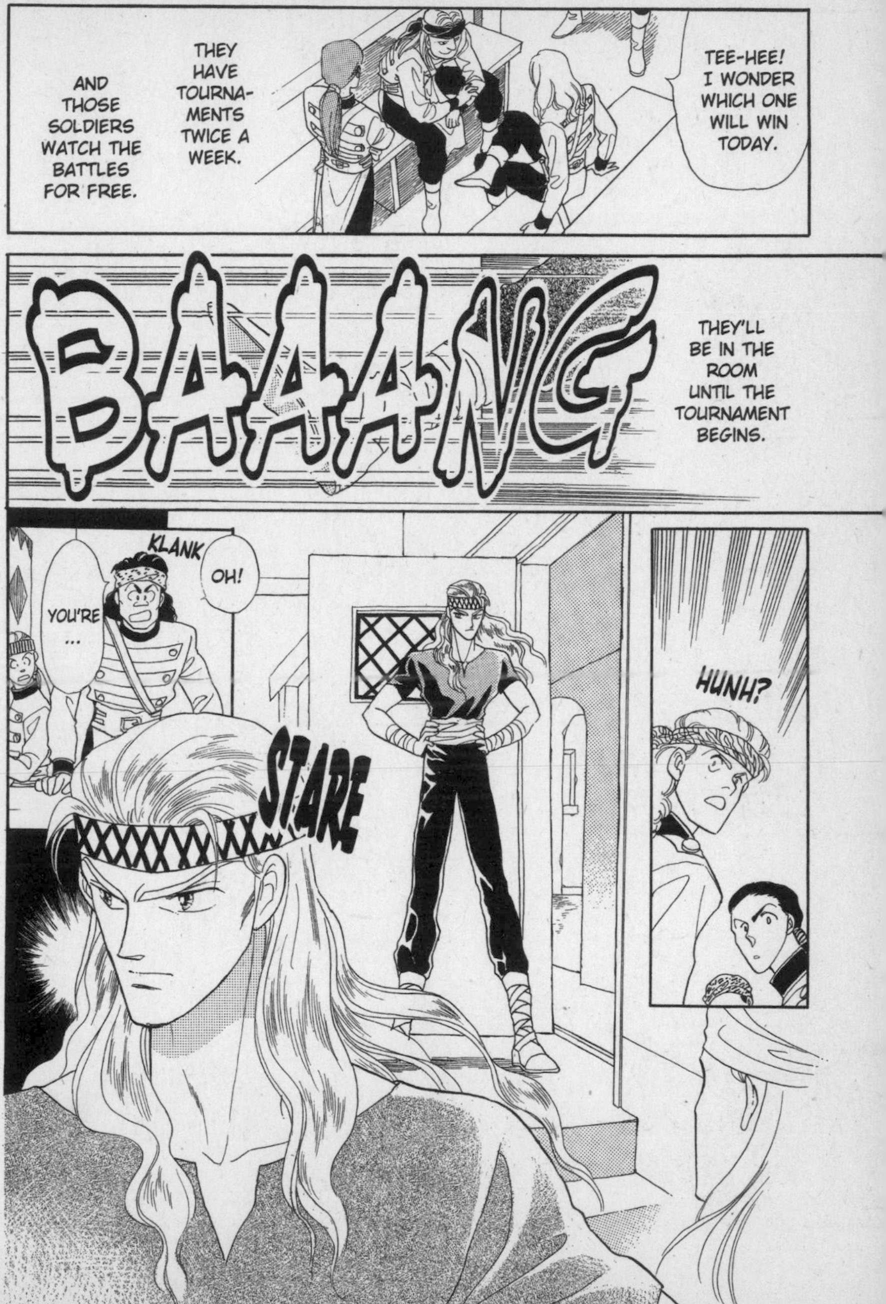
TEE-HEE! I WONDER WHICH ONE WILL WIN TODAY.
THEY HAVE TOURNA- MENTS TWICE A WEEK.
AND THOSE SOLDIERS WATCH THE BATTLES FOR FREE.
THEY'LL BE IN THE ROOM UNTIL THE TOURNAMENT BEGINS.
BAAANG
HUNH?
OH!
KLANK
YOU'RE ...
STARE

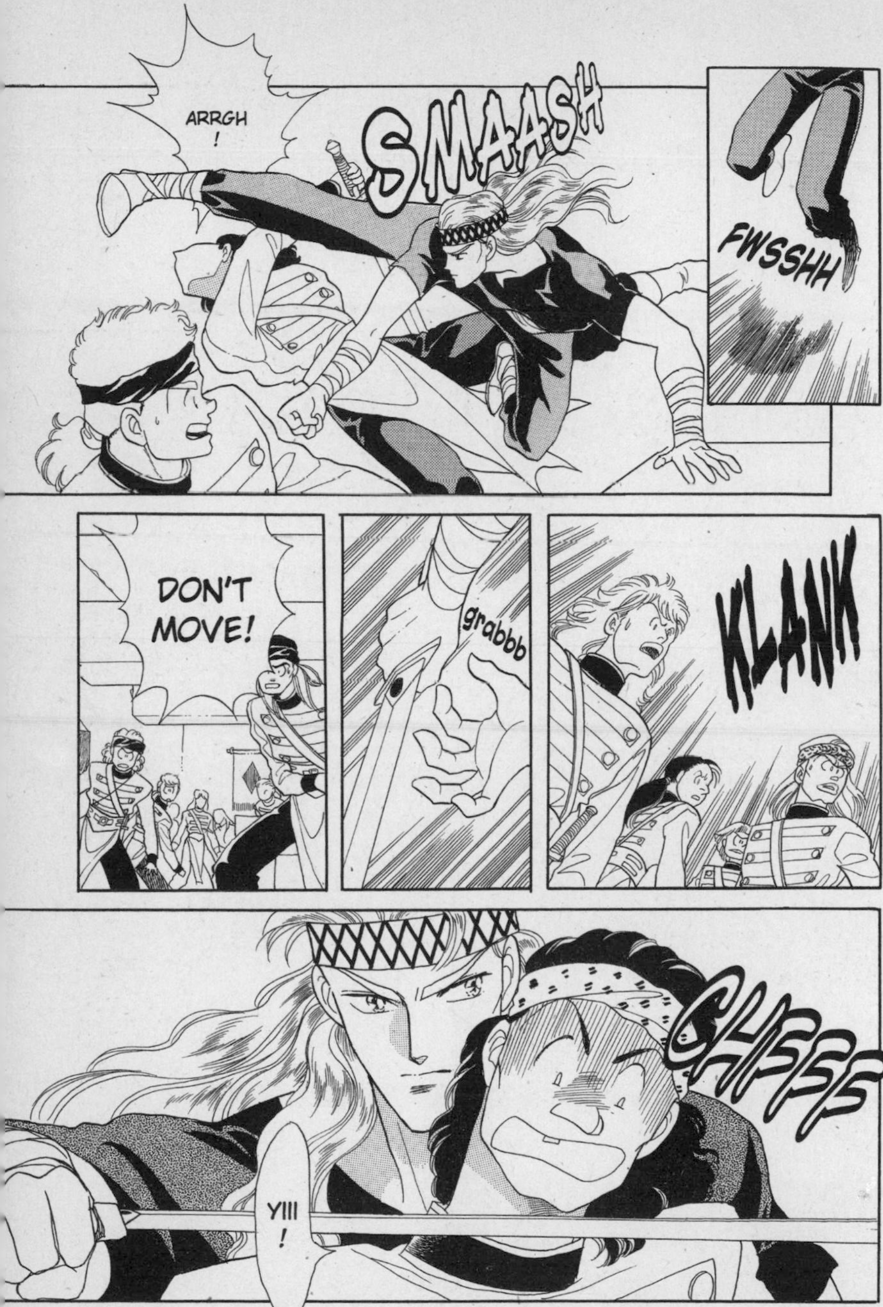
FWSSHH
SMAASH
ARRGH!
KLANK
grabbb
DON'T MOVE!
CHSSSS
YIII!

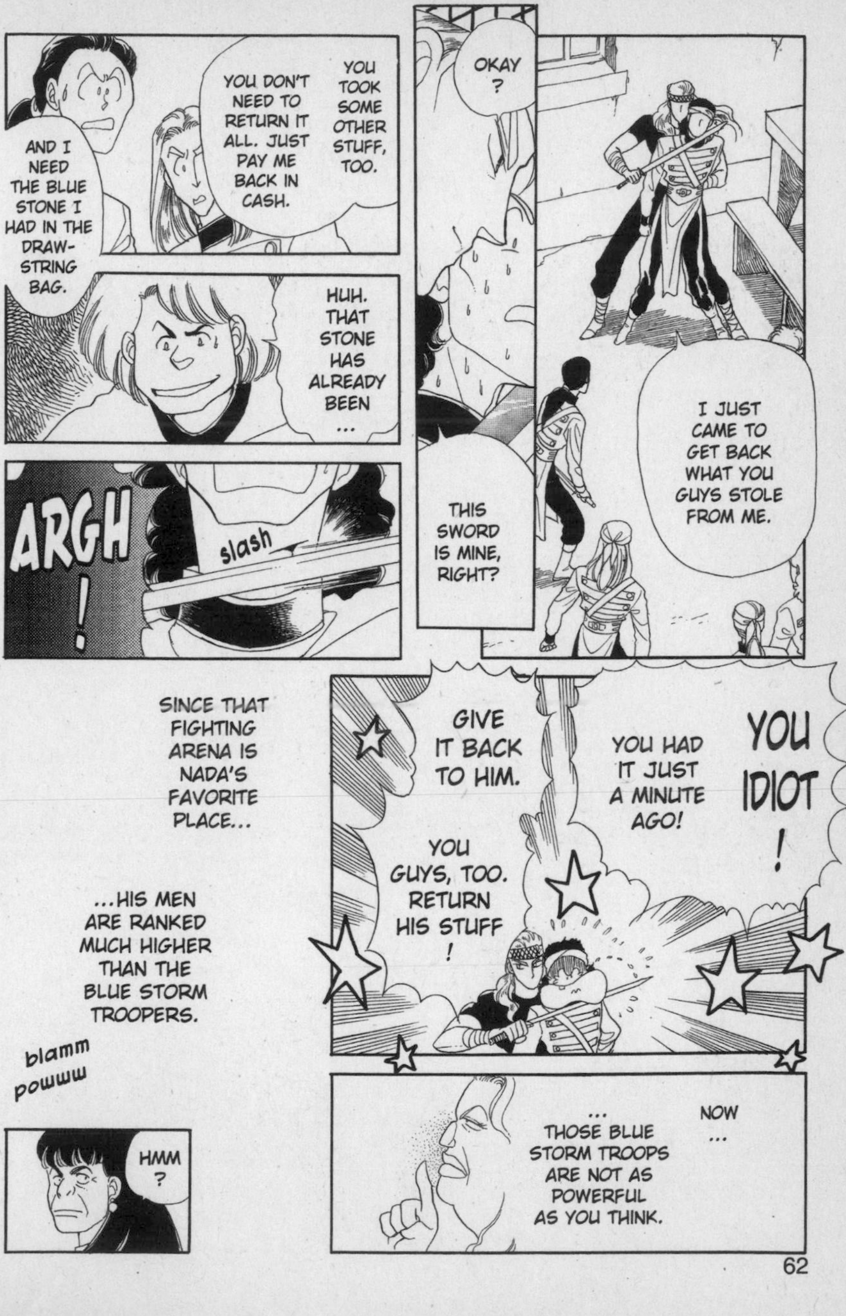
I JUST CAME TO GET BACK WHAT YOU GUYS STOLE FROM ME.
OKAY?
THIS SWORD IS MINE, RIGHT?
YOU TOOK SOME OTHER STUFF, TOO.
YOU DON'T NEED TO RETURN IT ALL. JUST PAY ME BACK IN CASH.
AND I NEED THE BLUE STONE I HAD IN THE DRAW-STRING BAG.
HUH. THAT STONE HAS ALREADY BEEN...
ARGH!
slash
YOU IDIOT!
YOU HAD IT JUST A MINUTE AGO!
GIVE IT BACK TO HIM.
YOU GUYS, TOO. RETURN HIS STUFF!
SINCE THAT FIGHTING ARENA IS NADA'S FAVORITE PLACE...
...HIS MEN ARE RANKED MUCH HIGHER THAN THE BLUE STORM TROOPERS.
blamm
powww
NOW...
...THOSE BLUE STORM TROOPS ARE NOT AS POWERFUL AS YOU THINK.
HMM?

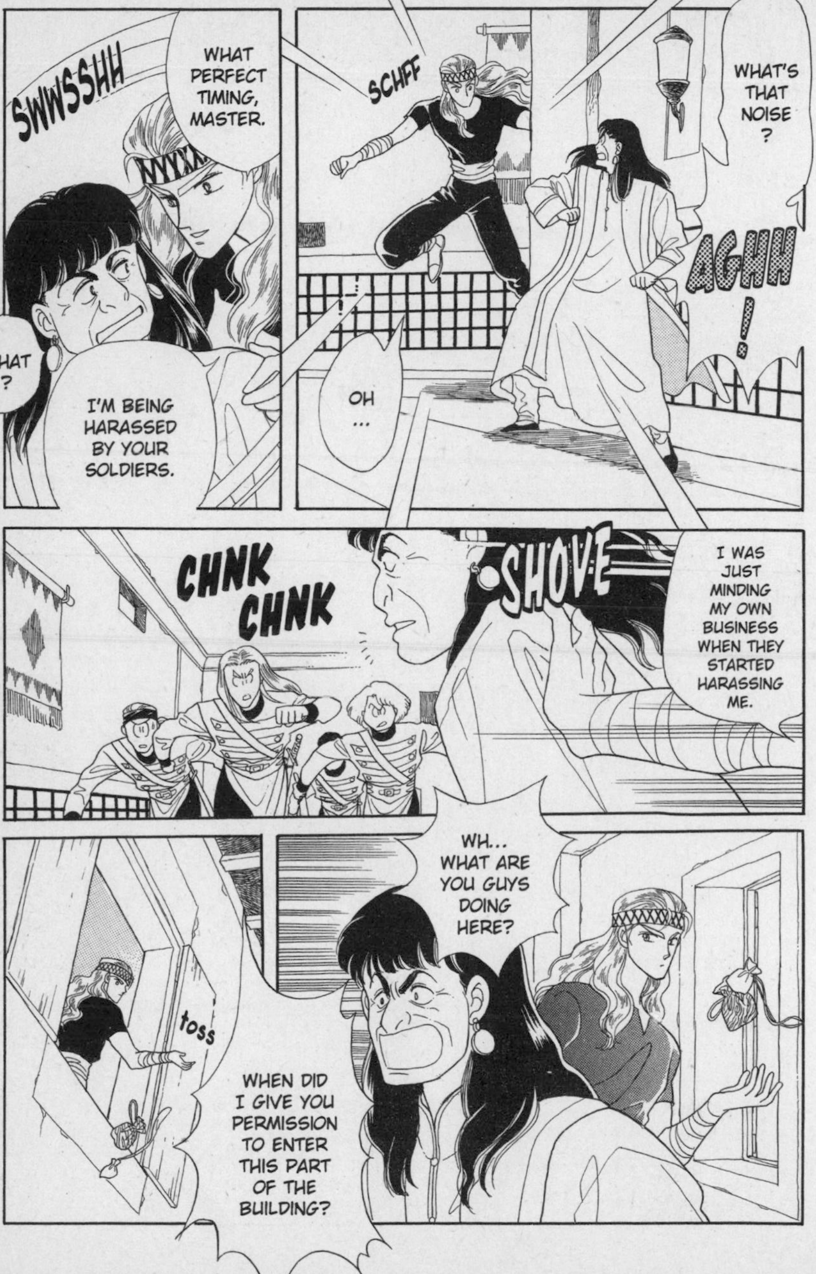
WHAT'S THAT NOISE ?
SCHFF
AGHH !
OH ...
WHAT PERFECT TIMING, MASTER.
SWWSSHH
WHAT ?
I'M BEING HARASSED BY YOUR SOLDIERS.
I WAS JUST MINDING MY OWN BUSINESS WHEN THEY STARTED HARASSING ME.
SHOVE
CHNK CHNK
WH... WHAT ARE YOU GUYS DOING HERE?
WHEN DID I GIVE YOU PERMISSION TO ENTER THIS PART OF THE BUILDING?
toss

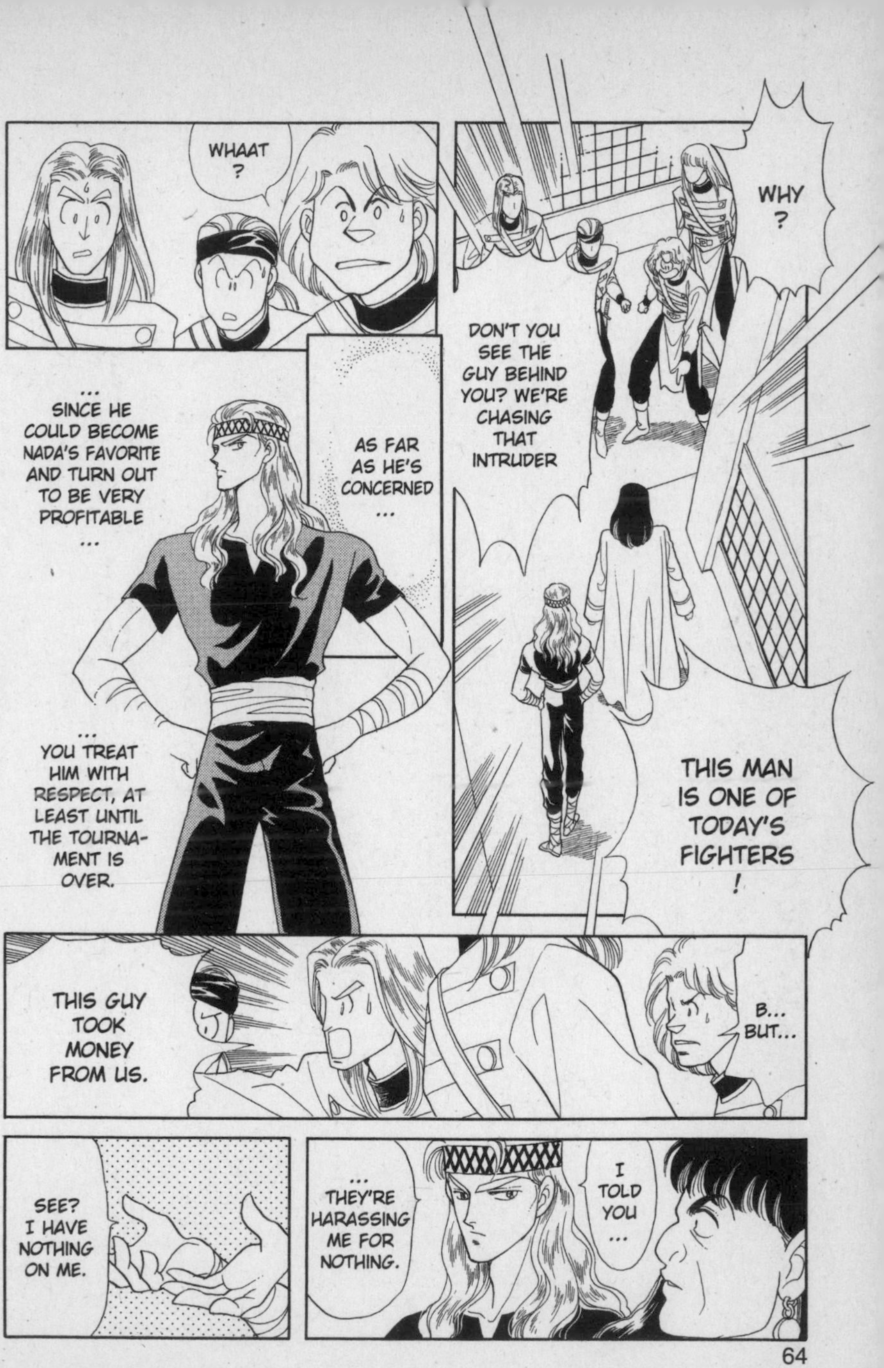
WHY?
DON'T YOU SEE THE GUY BEHIND YOU? WE'RE CHASING THAT INTRUDER
THIS MAN IS ONE OF TODAY'S FIGHTERS!
WHAAT?
AS FAR AS HE'S CONCERNED ...
... SINCE HE COULD BECOME NADA'S FAVORITE AND TURN OUT TO BE VERY PROFITABLE ...
... YOU TREAT HIM WITH RESPECT, AT LEAST UNTIL THE TOURNAMENT IS OVER.
B... BUT...
THIS GUY TOOK MONEY FROM US.
I TOLD YOU ...
... THEY'RE HARASSING ME FOR NOTHING.
SEE? I HAVE NOTHING ON ME.

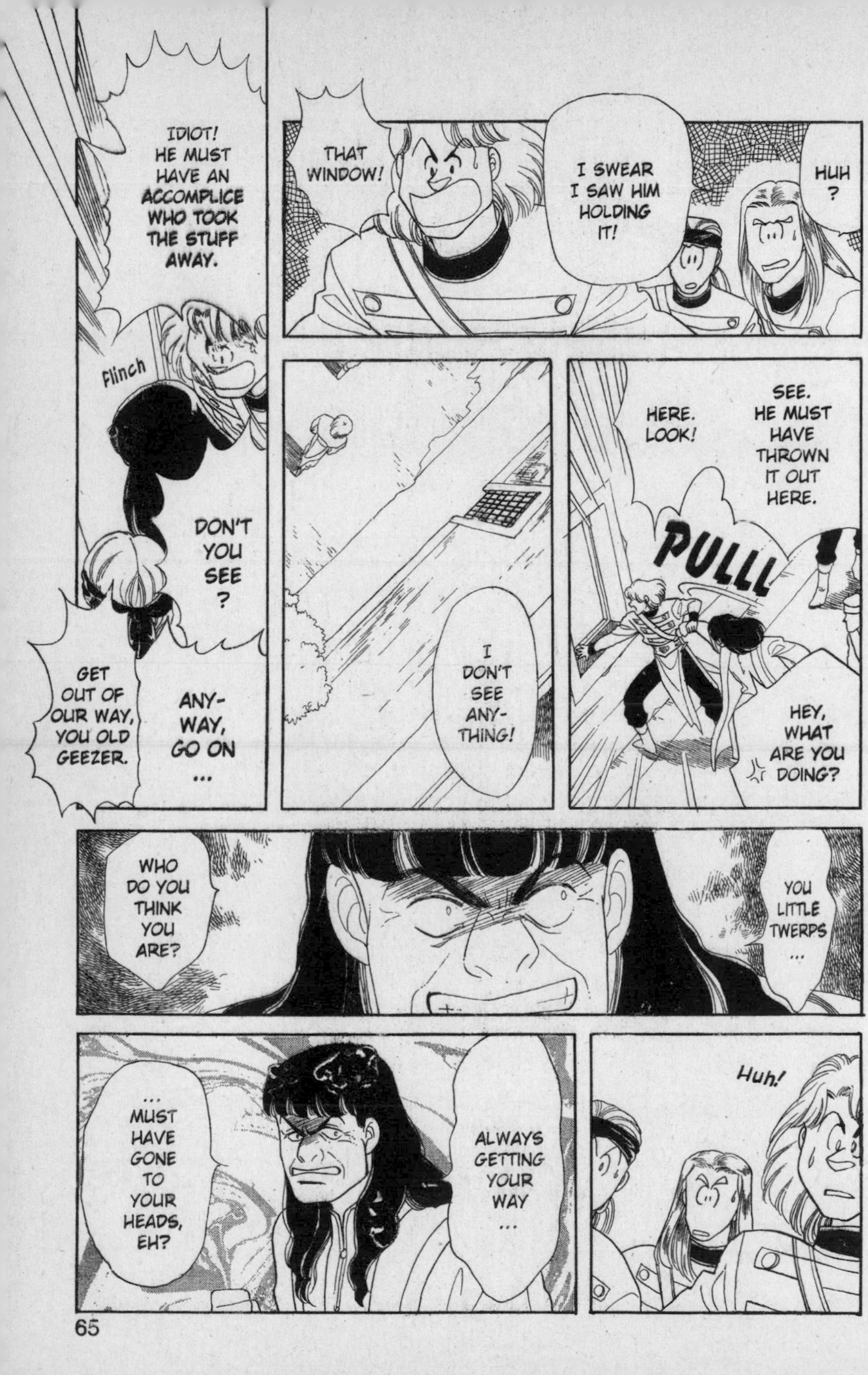
HUH?
I SWEAR I SAW HIM HOLDING IT!
THAT WINDOW!
SEE. HE MUST HAVE THROWN IT OUT HERE.
HERE. LOOK!
PULLL
HEY, WHAT ARE YOU DOING?
I DON'T SEE ANY-THING!
IDIOT! HE MUST HAVE AN ACCOMPLICE WHO TOOK THE STUFF AWAY.
Flinch
DON'T YOU SEE?
ANY-WAY, GO ON ...
GET OUT OF OUR WAY, YOU OLD GEEZER.
YOU LITTLE TWERPS ...
WHO DO YOU THINK YOU ARE?
Huh!
ALWAYS GETTING YOUR WAY ...
... MUST HAVE GONE TO YOUR HEADS, EH?

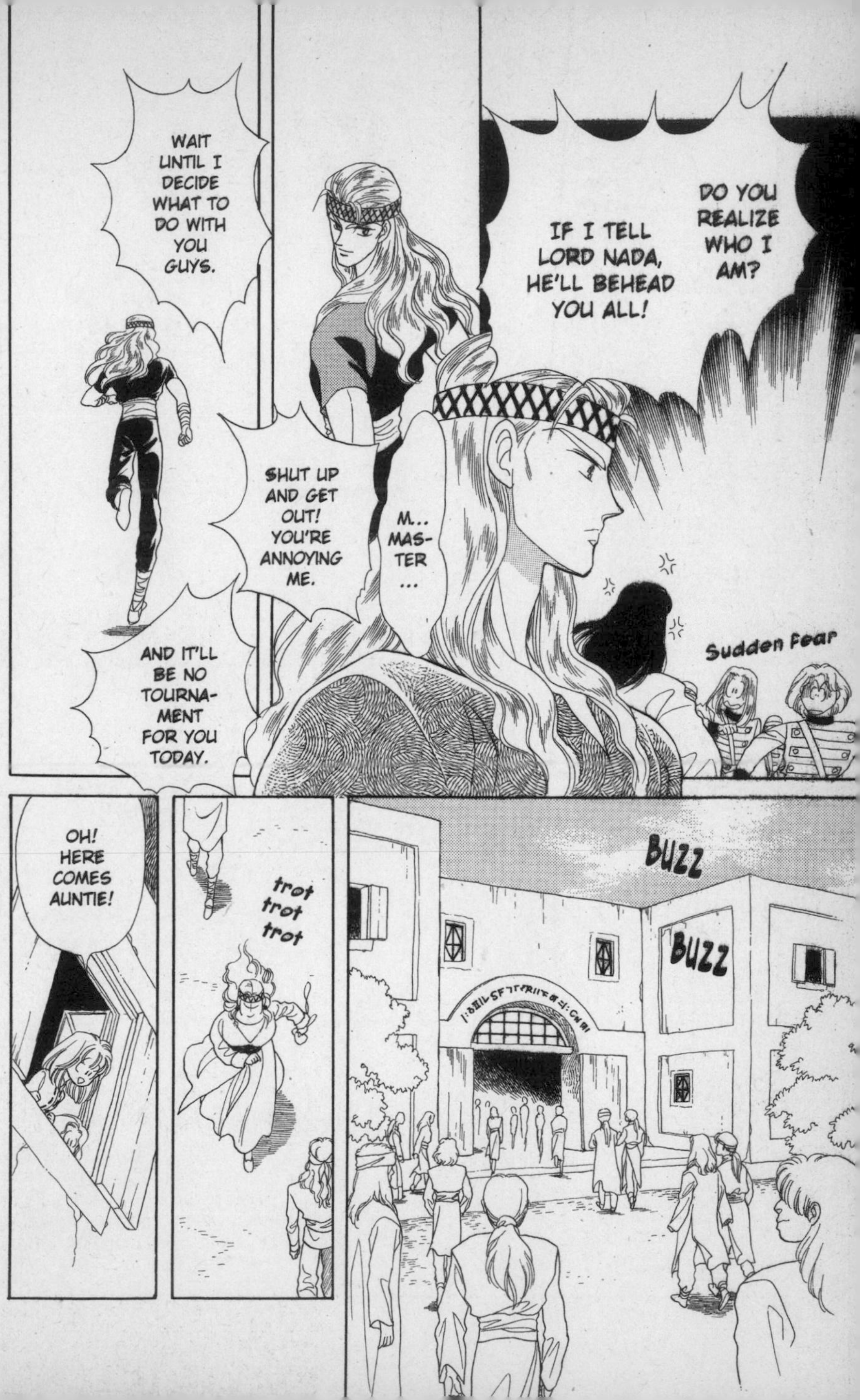
DO YOU REALIZE WHO I AM?
IF I TELL LORD NADA, HE'LL BEHEAD YOU ALL!
Sudden Fear
M... MAS-TER ...
SHUT UP AND GET OUT! YOU'RE ANNOYING ME.
WAIT UNTIL I DECIDE WHAT TO DO WITH YOU GUYS.
AND IT'LL BE NO TOURNA-MENT FOR YOU TODAY.
BUZZ
BUZZ
trot trot trot
OH! HERE COMES AUNTIE!

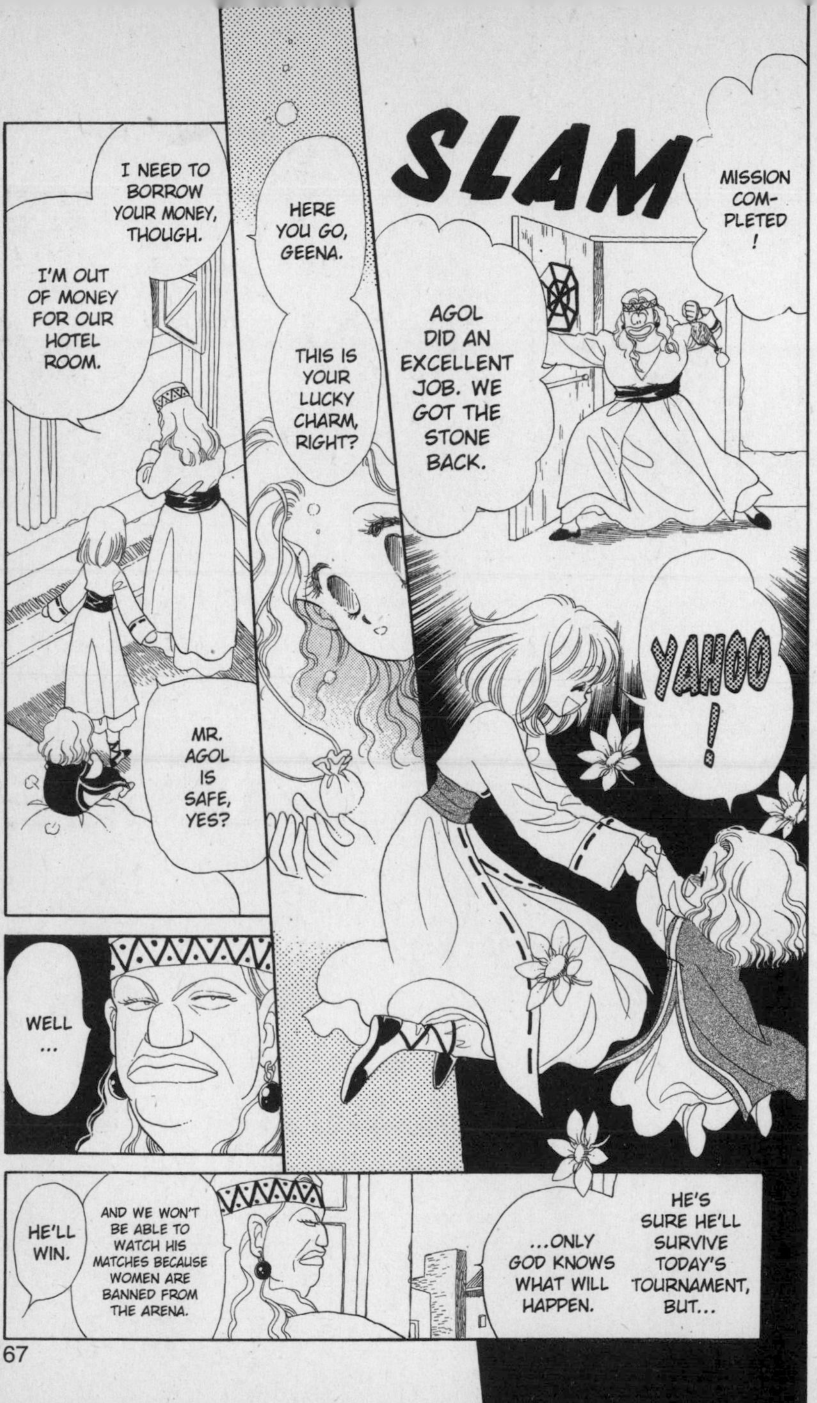
SLAM
MISSION COM-PLETED !
AGOL DID AN EXCELLENT JOB. WE GOT THE STONE BACK.
YAHOO !
HERE YOU GO, GEENA.
THIS IS YOUR LUCKY CHARM, RIGHT?
I NEED TO BORROW YOUR MONEY, THOUGH.
I'M OUT OF MONEY FOR OUR HOTEL ROOM.
MR. AGOL IS SAFE, YES?
WELL ...
HE'S SURE HE'LL SURVIVE TODAY'S TOURNAMENT, BUT...
...ONLY GOD KNOWS WHAT WILL HAPPEN.
AND WE WON'T BE ABLE TO WATCH HIS MATCHES BECAUSE WOMEN ARE BANNED FROM THE ARENA.
HE'LL WIN.

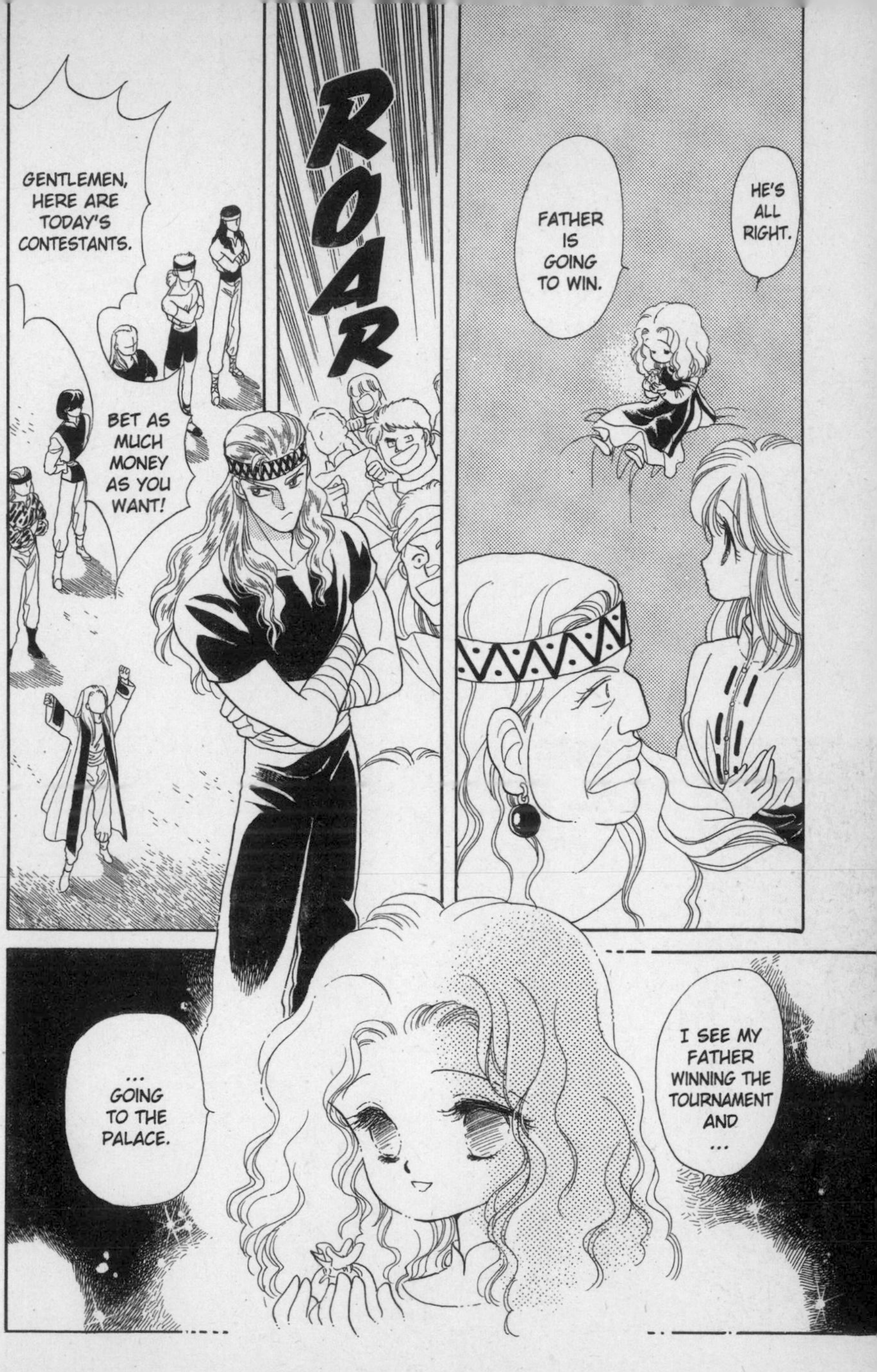
HE'S ALL RIGHT.
FATHER IS GOING TO WIN.
ROAR
GENTLEMEN, HERE ARE TODAY'S CONTESTANTS.
BET AS MUCH MONEY AS YOU WANT!
I SEE MY FATHER WINNING THE TOURNAMENT AND ...
... GOING TO THE PALACE.

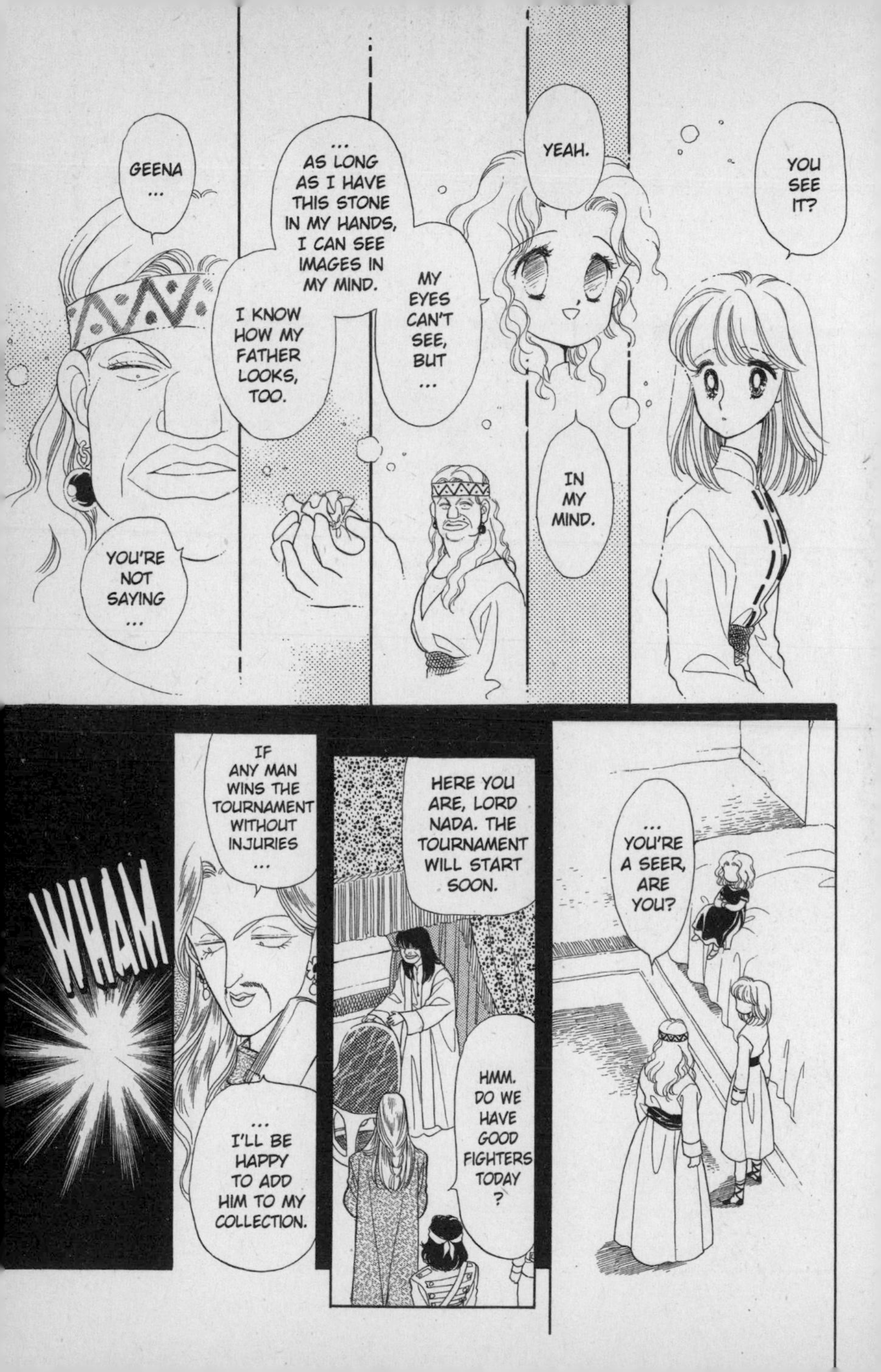
YOU SEE IT?
YEAH.
IN MY MIND.
MY EYES CAN'T SEE, BUT ...
... AS LONG AS I HAVE THIS STONE IN MY HANDS, I CAN SEE IMAGES IN MY MIND.
I KNOW HOW MY FATHER LOOKS, TOO.
GEENA ...
YOU'RE NOT SAYING ...
... YOU'RE A SEER, ARE YOU?
HERE YOU ARE, LORD NADA. THE TOURNAMENT WILL START SOON.
HMM. DO WE HAVE GOOD FIGHTERS TODAY ?
IF ANY MAN WINS THE TOURNAMENT WITHOUT INJURIES ...
... I'LL BE HAPPY TO ADD HIM TO MY COLLECTION.
WHAM

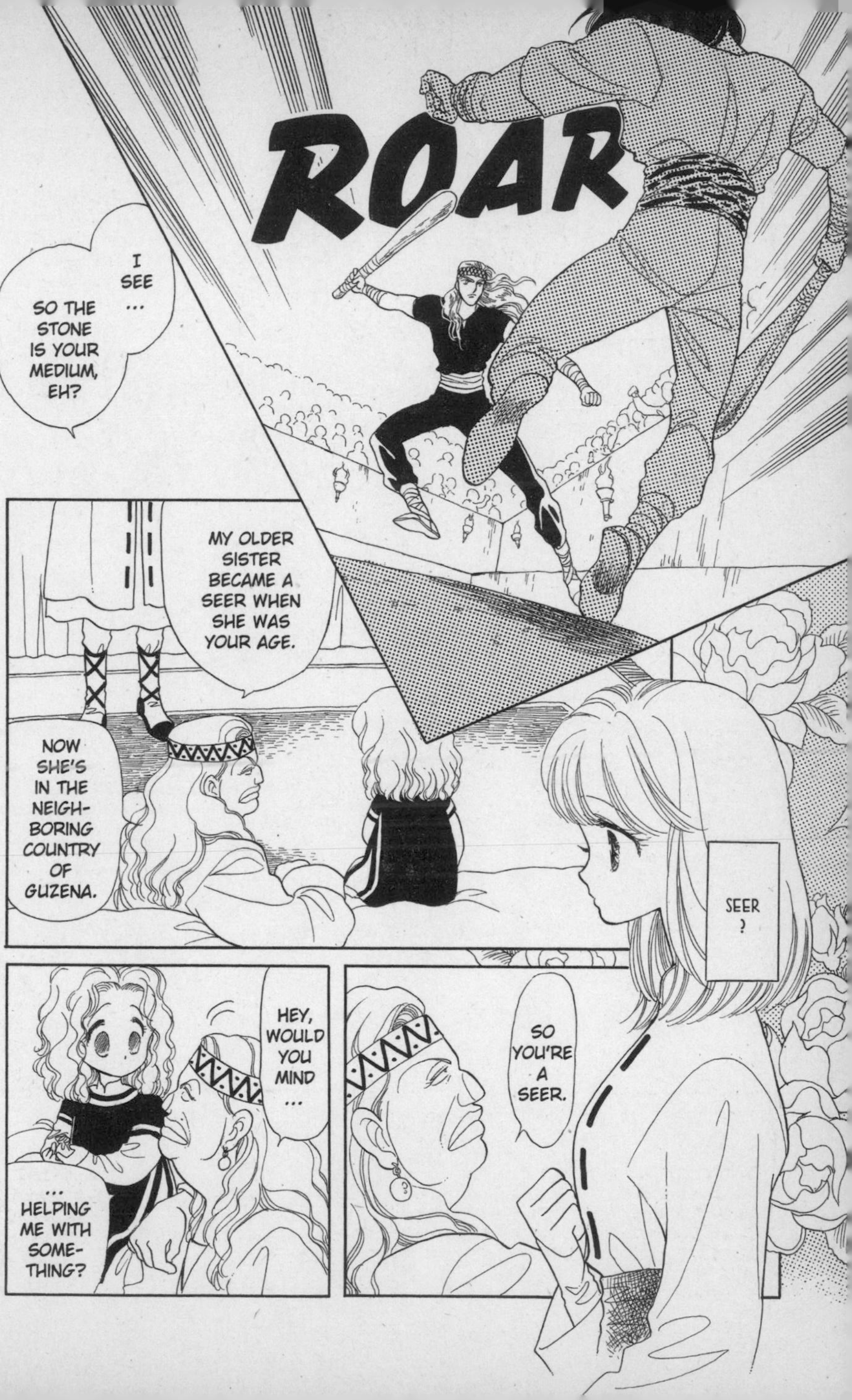
ROAR
I SEE ... SO THE STONE IS YOUR MEDIUM, EH?
SEER ?
MY OLDER SISTER BECAME A SEER WHEN SHE WAS YOUR AGE.
NOW SHE'S IN THE NEIGH-BORING COUNTRY OF GUZENA.
SO YOU'RE A SEER.
HEY, WOULD YOU MIND ...
... HELPING ME WITH SOME-THING?

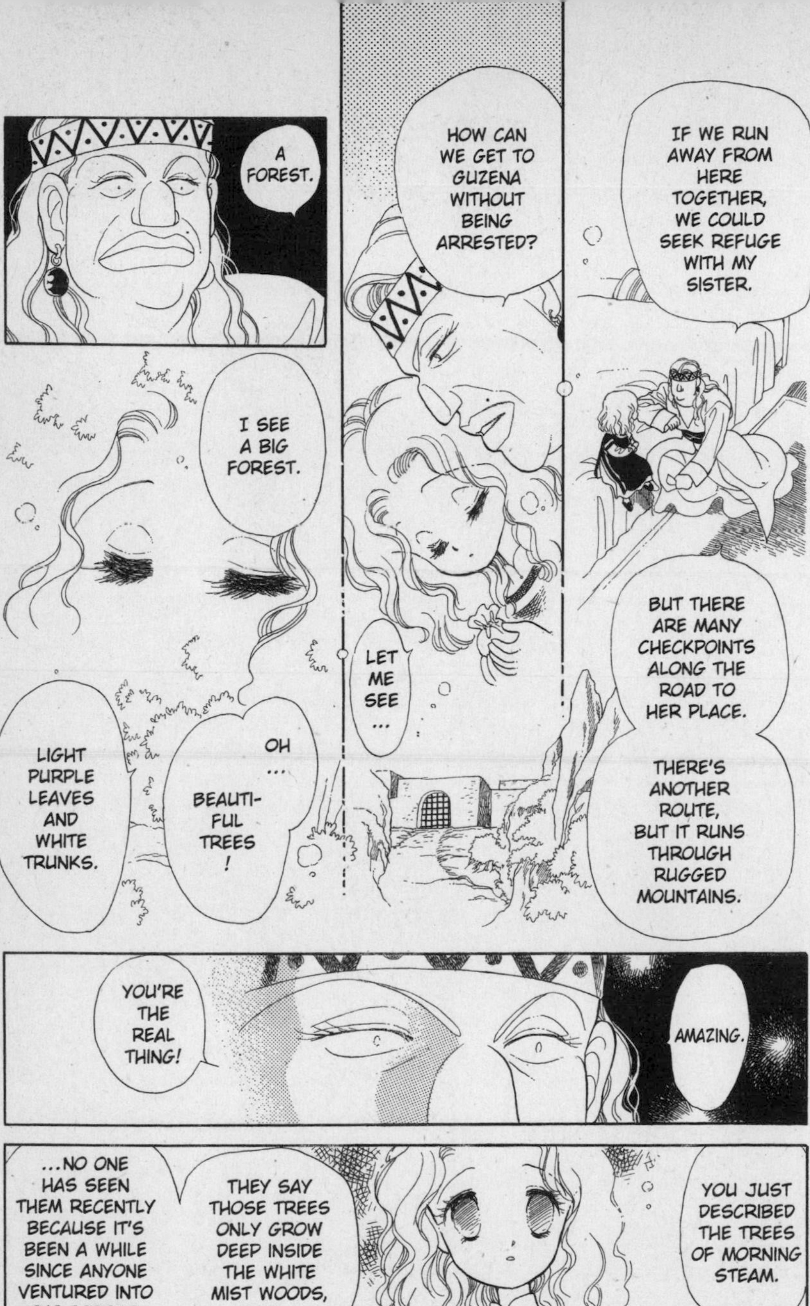
IF WE RUN AWAY FROM HERE TOGETHER, WE COULD SEEK REFUGE WITH MY SISTER.
BUT THERE ARE MANY CHECKPOINTS ALONG THE ROAD TO HER PLACE.
THERE'S ANOTHER ROUTE, BUT IT RUNS THROUGH RUGGED MOUNTAINS.
HOW CAN WE GET TO GUZENA WITHOUT BEING ARRESTED?
LET ME SEE...
A FOREST.
I SEE A BIG FOREST.
OH... BEAUTIFUL TREES!
LIGHT PURPLE LEAVES AND WHITE TRUNKS.
AMAZING.
YOU'RE THE REAL THING!
YOU JUST DESCRIBED THE TREES OF MORNING STEAM.
THEY SAY THOSE TREES ONLY GROW DEEP INSIDE THE WHITE MIST WOODS, BUT...
...NO ONE HAS SEEN THEM RECENTLY BECAUSE IT'S BEEN A WHILE SINCE ANYONE VENTURED INTO THE FOREST.

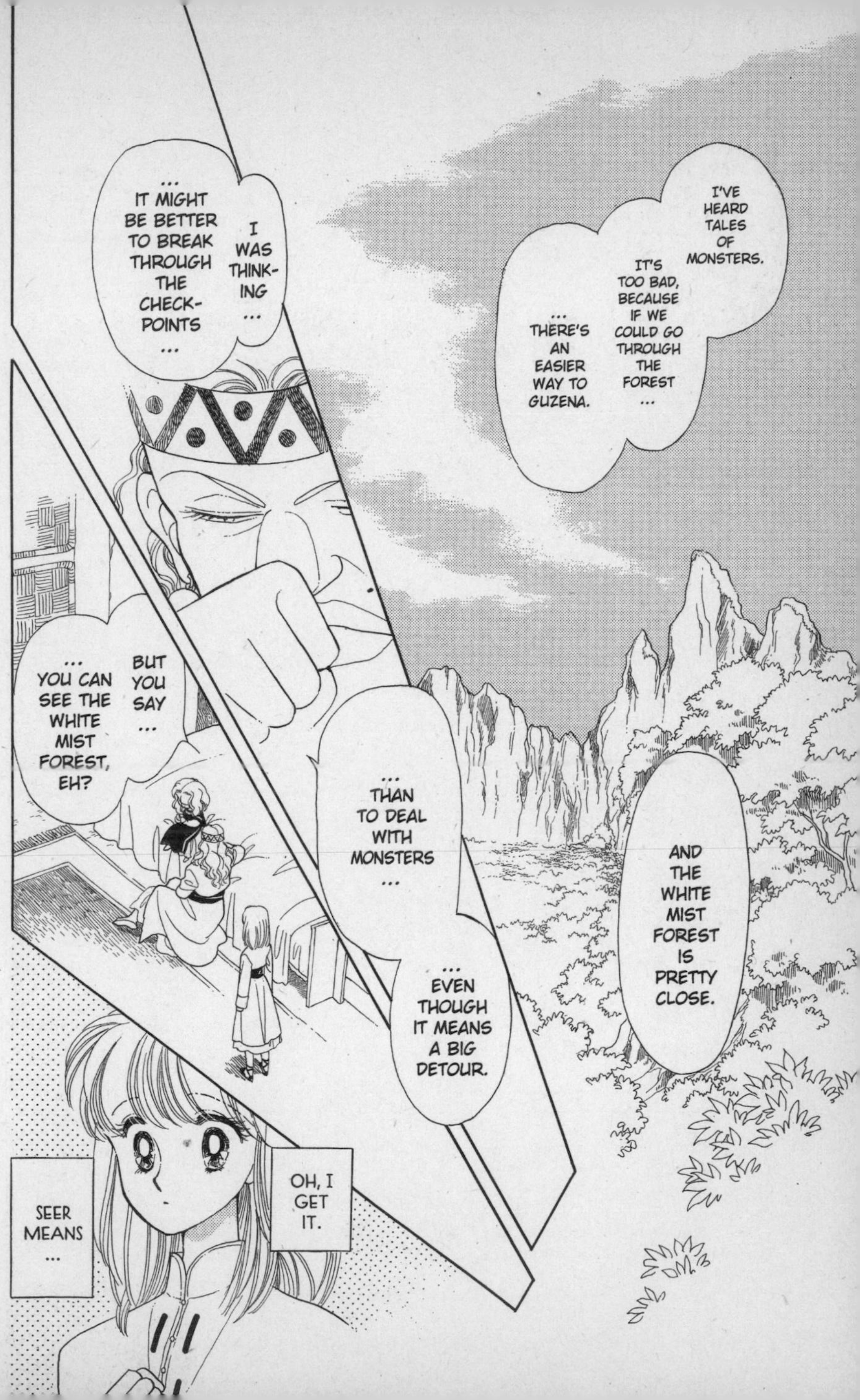
I'VE HEARD TALES OF MONSTERS.
IT'S TOO BAD, BECAUSE IF WE COULD GO THROUGH THE FOREST...
...THERE'S AN EASIER WAY TO GUZENA.
AND THE WHITE MIST FOREST IS PRETTY CLOSE.
I WAS THINKING...
...IT MIGHT BE BETTER TO BREAK THROUGH THE CHECK-POINTS...
...THAN TO DEAL WITH MONSTERS...
...EVEN THOUGH IT MEANS A BIG DETOUR.
BUT YOU SAY...
...YOU CAN SEE THE WHITE MIST FOREST, EH?
OH, I GET IT.
SEER MEANS...

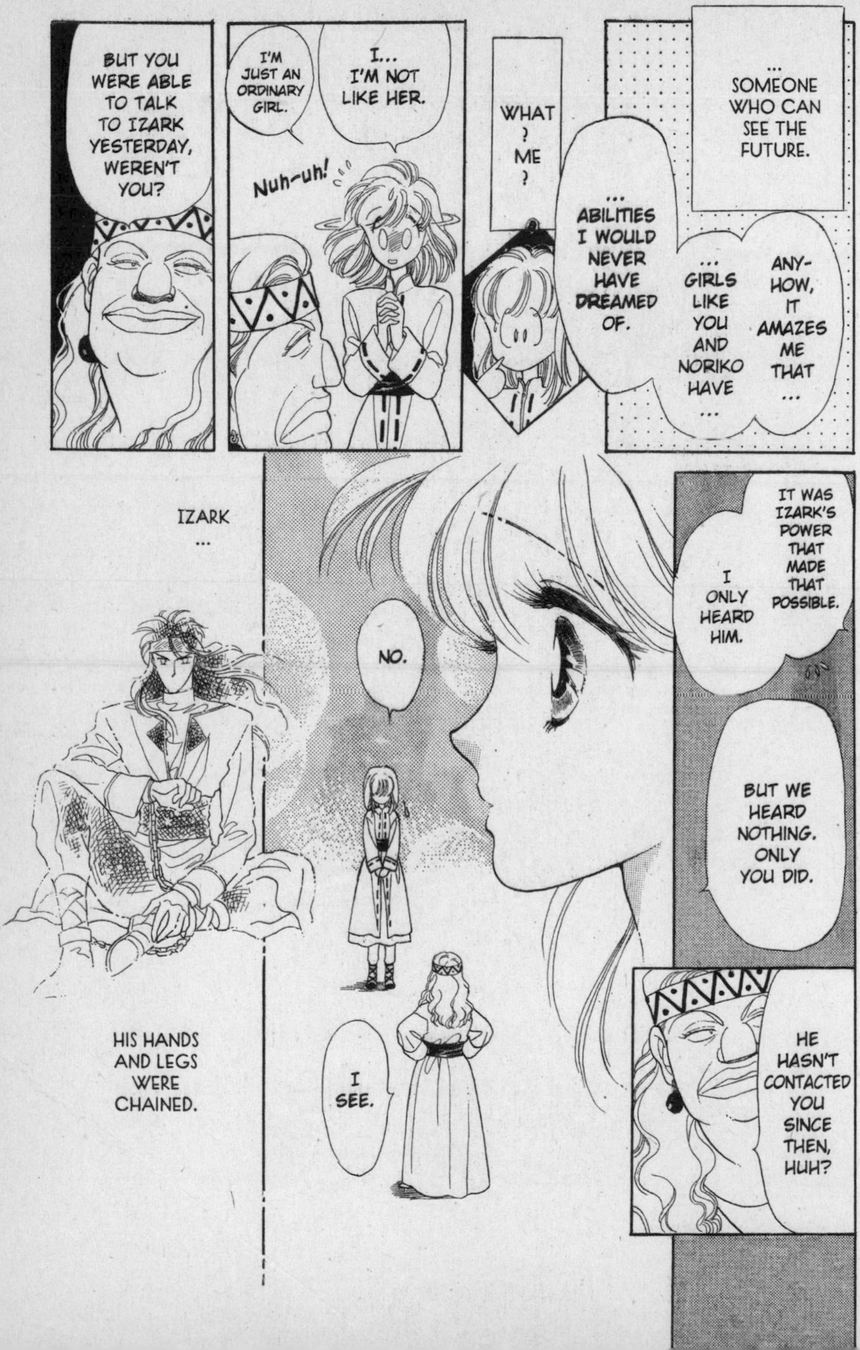
... SOMEONE WHO CAN SEE THE FUTURE.
ANY-HOW, IT AMAZES ME THAT ...
... GIRLS LIKE YOU AND NORIKO HAVE ...
... ABILITIES I WOULD NEVER HAVE DREAMED OF.
WHAT? ME?
I... I'M NOT LIKE HER.
I'M JUST AN ORDINARY GIRL.
Nuh-uh!
BUT YOU WERE ABLE TO TALK TO IZARK YESTERDAY, WEREN'T YOU?
IT WAS IZARK'S POWER THAT MADE THAT POSSIBLE.
I ONLY HEARD HIM.
BUT WE HEARD NOTHING. ONLY YOU DID.
HE HASN'T CONTACTED YOU SINCE THEN, HUH?
NO.
I SEE.
IZARK ...
HIS HANDS AND LEGS WERE CHAINED.

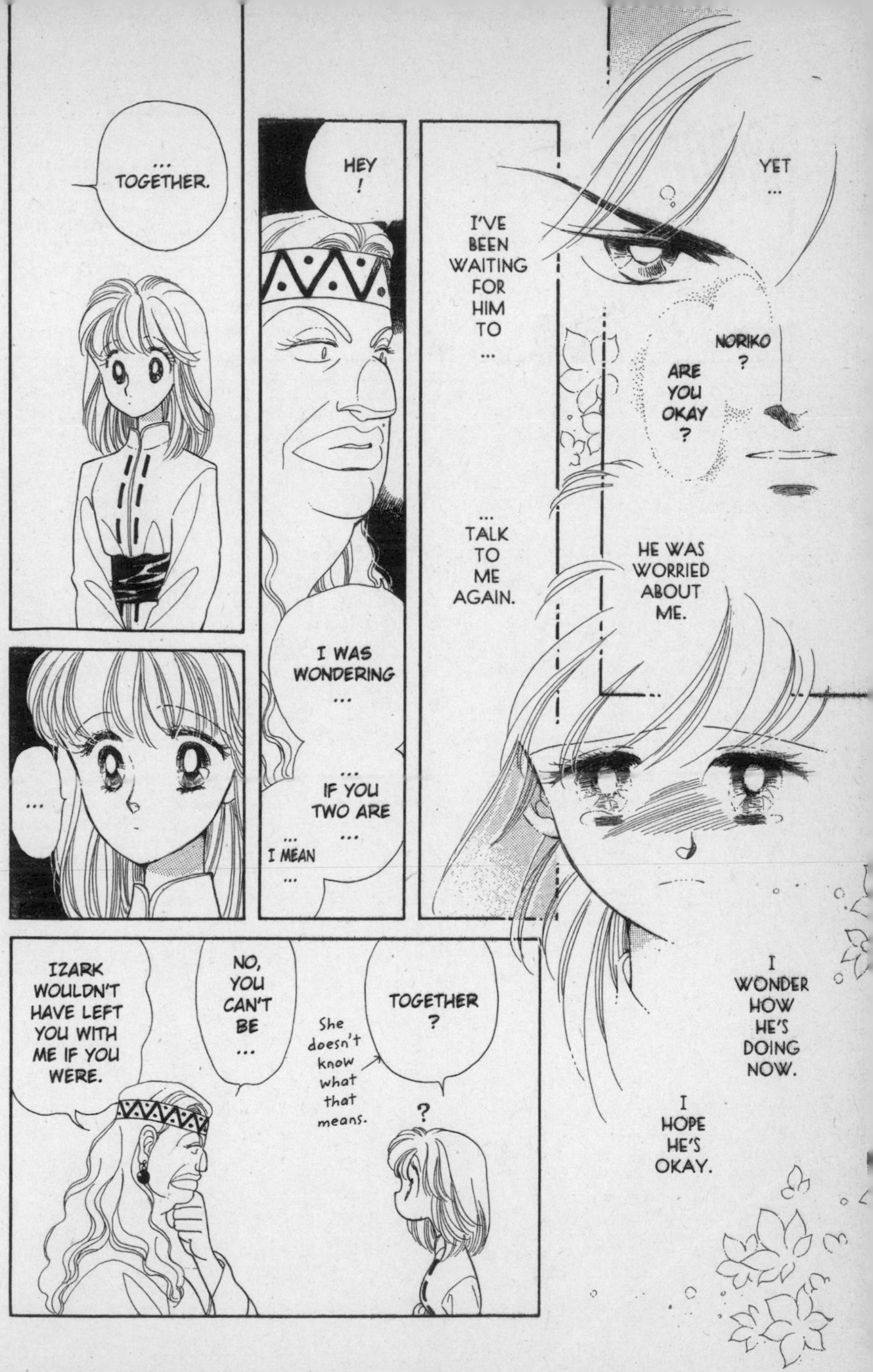
I'VE BEEN WAITING FOR HIM TO ...
... TALK TO ME AGAIN.
YET ...
NORIKO ?
ARE YOU OKAY ?
HE WAS WORRIED ABOUT ME.
I WONDER HOW HE'S DOING NOW.
I HOPE HE'S OKAY.
HEY !
I WAS WONDERING ...
... IF YOU TWO ARE ...
... I MEAN ...
... TOGETHER.
...
TOGETHER ?
She doesn't know what that means.
?
NO, YOU CAN'T BE ...
IZARK WOULDN'T HAVE LEFT YOU WITH ME IF YOU WERE.

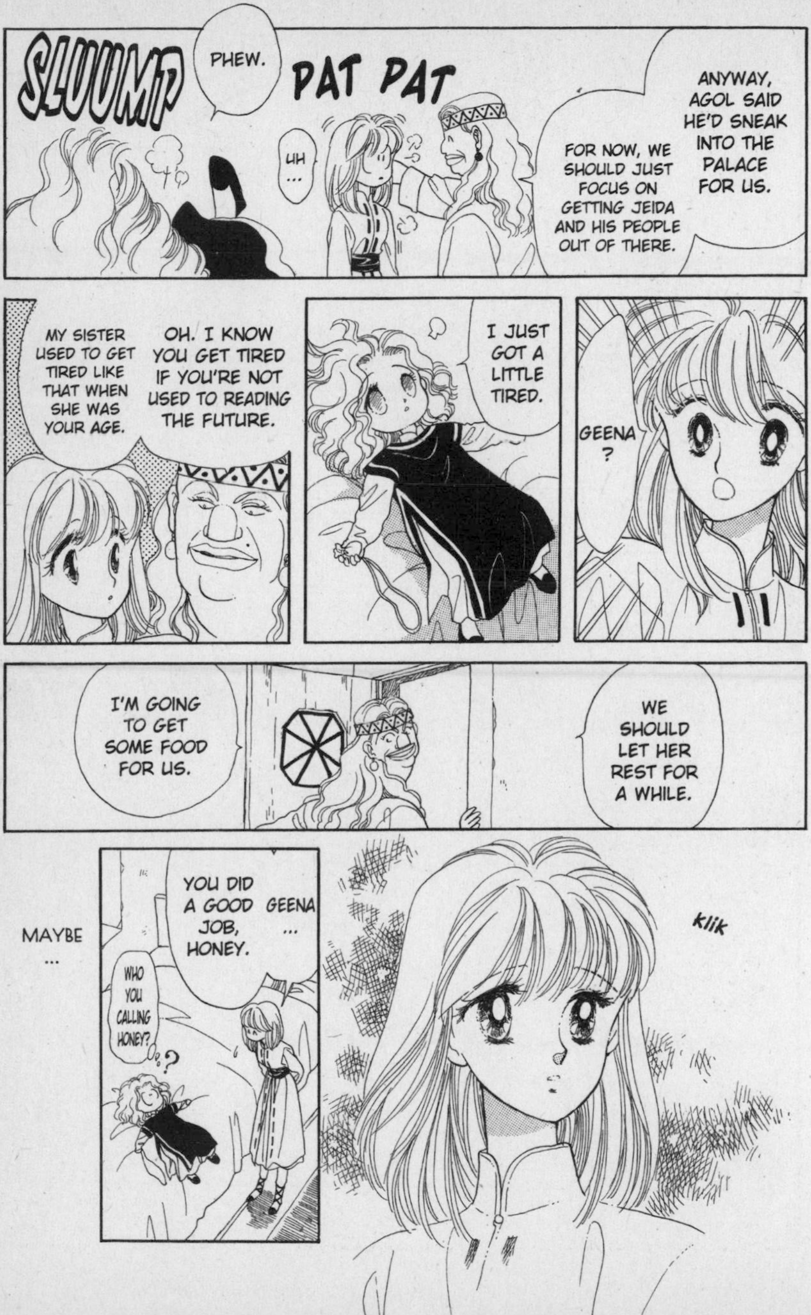
ANYWAY, AGOL SAID HE'D SNEAK INTO THE PALACE FOR US.
FOR NOW, WE SHOULD JUST FOCUS ON GETTING JEIDA AND HIS PEOPLE OUT OF THERE.
PAT PAT
UH ...
PHEW.
SLUUMP
GEENA ?
I JUST GOT A LITTLE TIRED.
OH. I KNOW YOU GET TIRED IF YOU'RE NOT USED TO READING THE FUTURE.
MY SISTER USED TO GET TIRED LIKE THAT WHEN SHE WAS YOUR AGE.
WE SHOULD LET HER REST FOR A WHILE.
I'M GOING TO GET SOME FOOD FOR US.
klik
GEENA ...
YOU DID A GOOD JOB, HONEY.
WHO YOU CALLING HONEY?
MAYBE ...

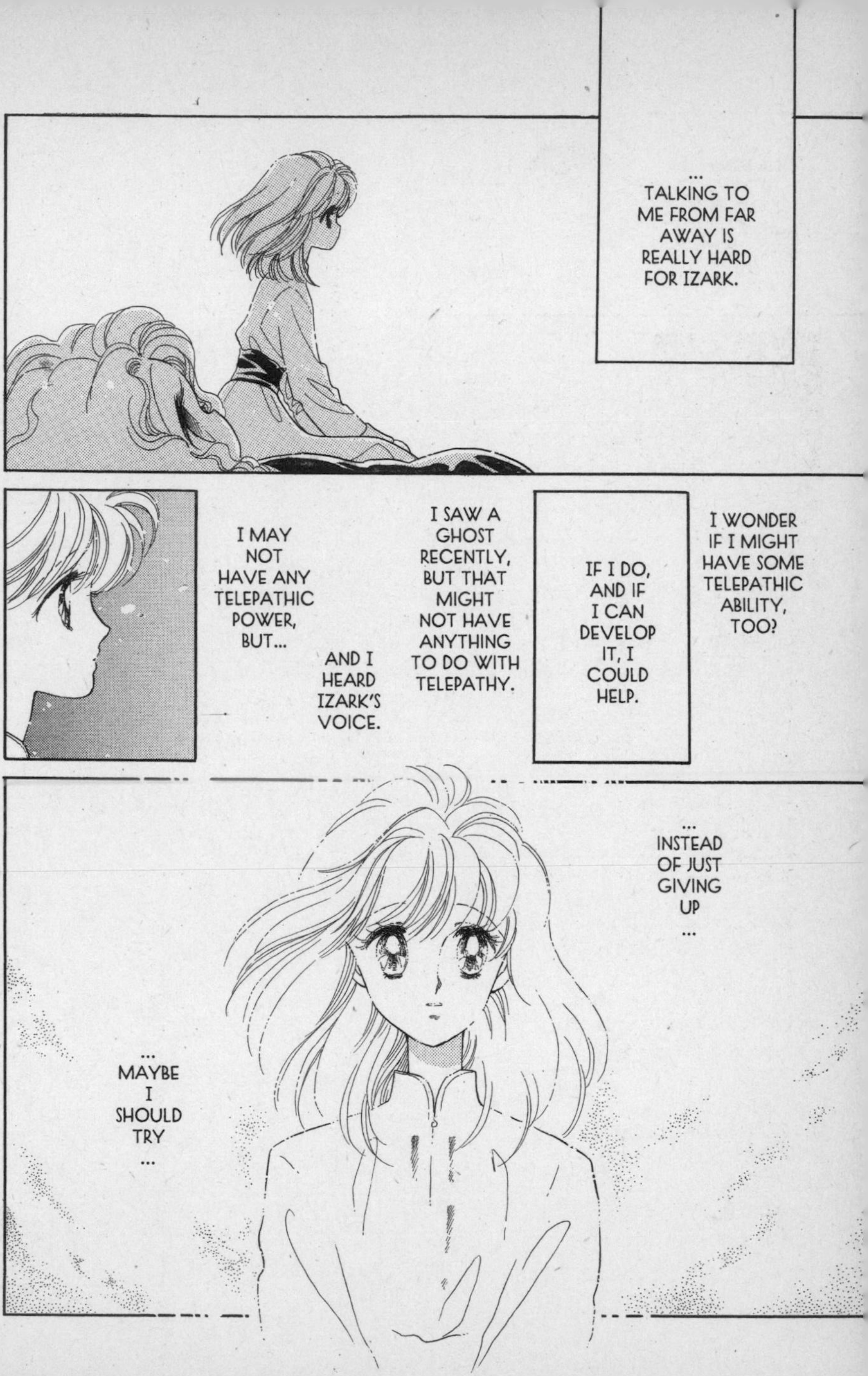
... TALKING TO ME FROM FAR AWAY IS REALLY HARD FOR IZARK.
I WONDER IF I MIGHT HAVE SOME TELEPATHIC ABILITY, TOO?
IF I DO, AND IF I CAN DEVELOP IT, I COULD HELP.
I SAW A GHOST RECENTLY, BUT THAT MIGHT NOT HAVE ANYTHING TO DO WITH TELEPATHY.
AND I HEARD IZARK'S VOICE.
I MAY NOT HAVE ANY TELEPATHIC POWER, BUT...
... INSTEAD OF JUST GIVING UP ...
... MAYBE I SHOULD TRY ...

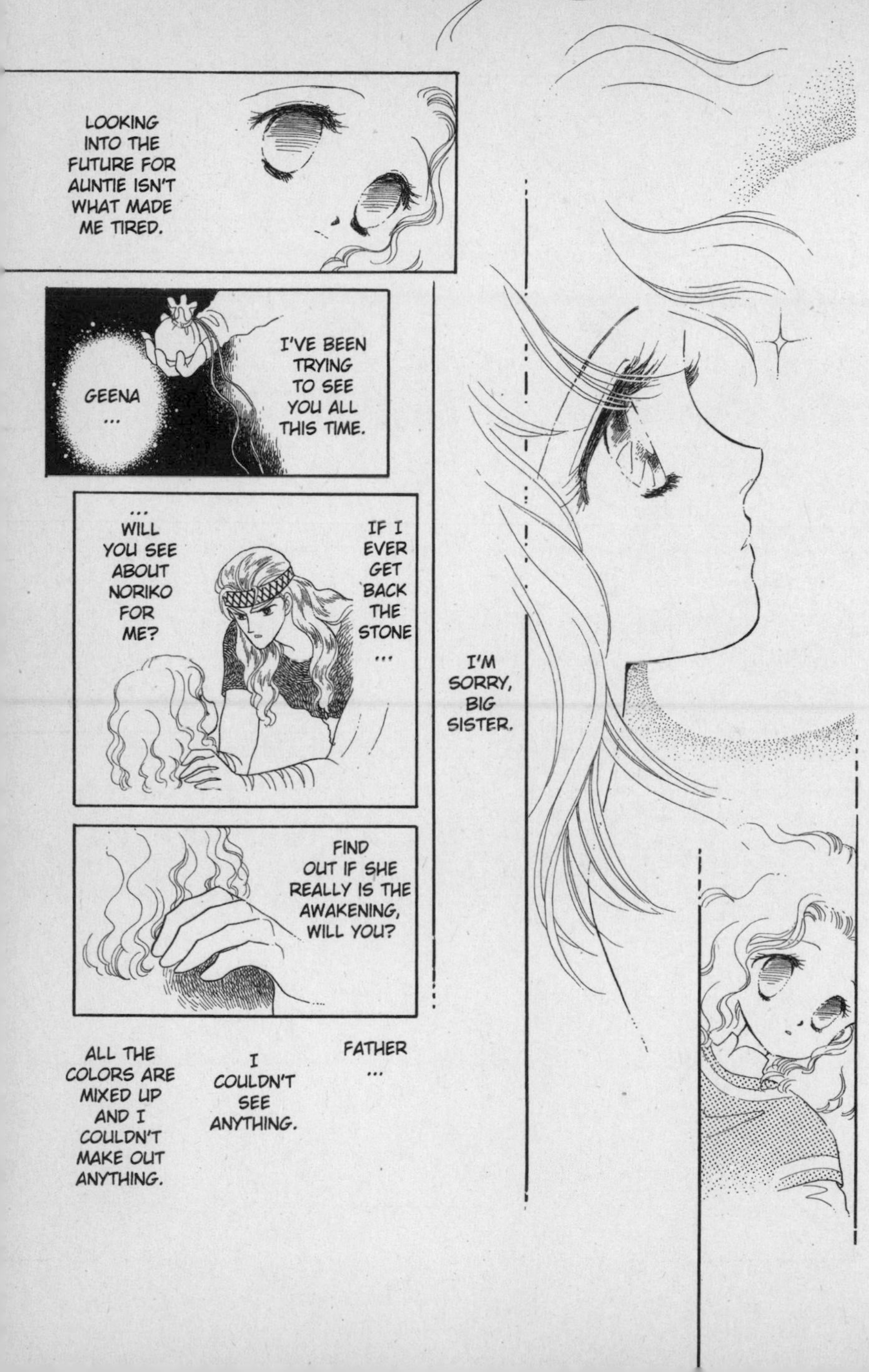
LOOKING INTO THE FUTURE FOR AUNTIE ISN'T WHAT MADE ME TIRED.
I'VE BEEN TRYING TO SEE YOU ALL THIS TIME.
GEENA ...
IF I EVER GET BACK THE STONE ...
... WILL YOU SEE ABOUT NORIKO FOR ME?
FIND OUT IF SHE REALLY IS THE AWAKENING, WILL YOU?
FATHER ...
I COULDN'T SEE ANYTHING.
ALL THE COLORS ARE MIXED UP AND I COULDN'T MAKE OUT ANYTHING.
I'M SORRY, BIG SISTER.

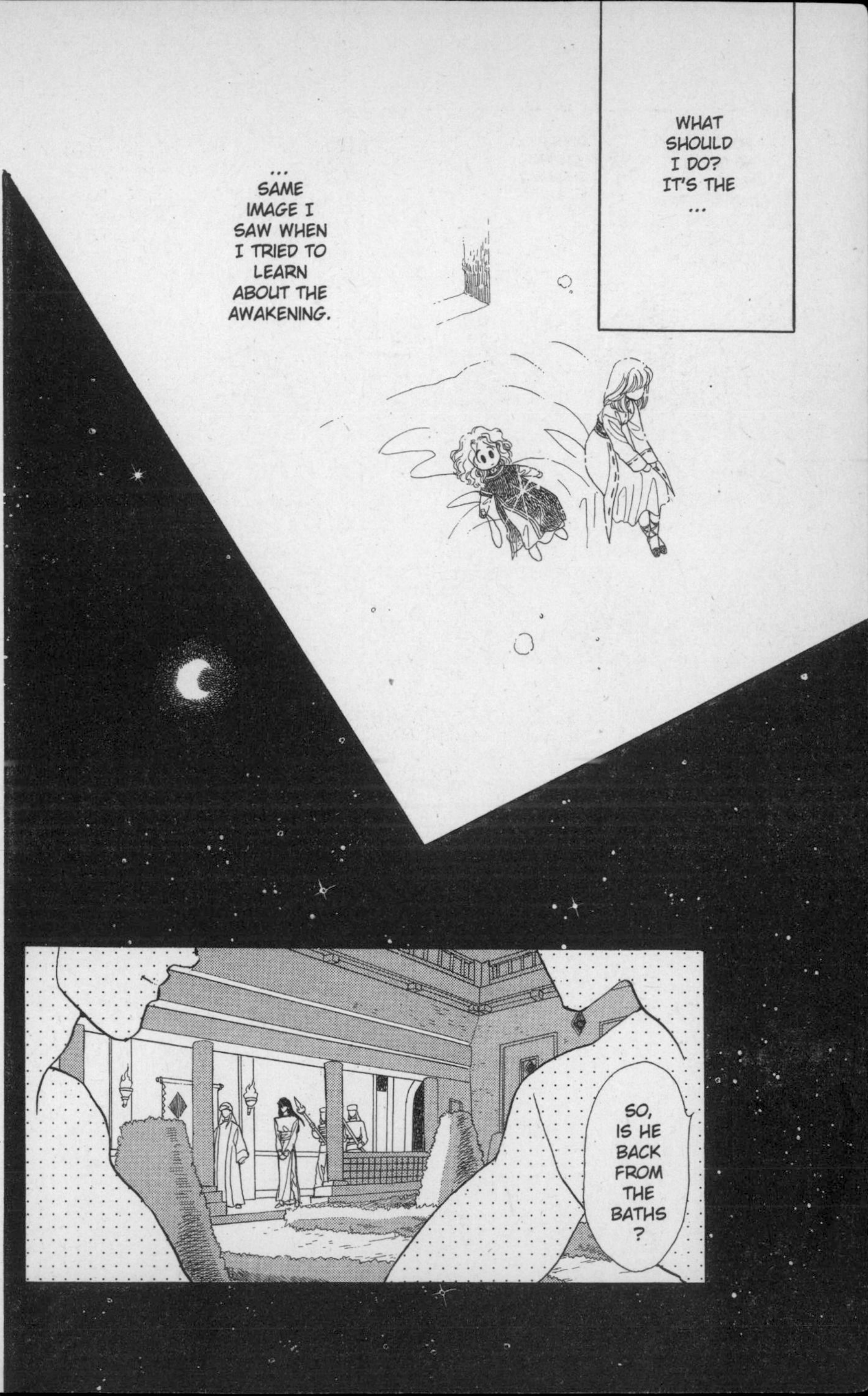
WHAT SHOULD I DO? IT'S THE ...
... SAME IMAGE I SAW WHEN I TRIED TO LEARN ABOUT THE AWAKENING.
SO, IS HE BACK FROM THE BATHS ?

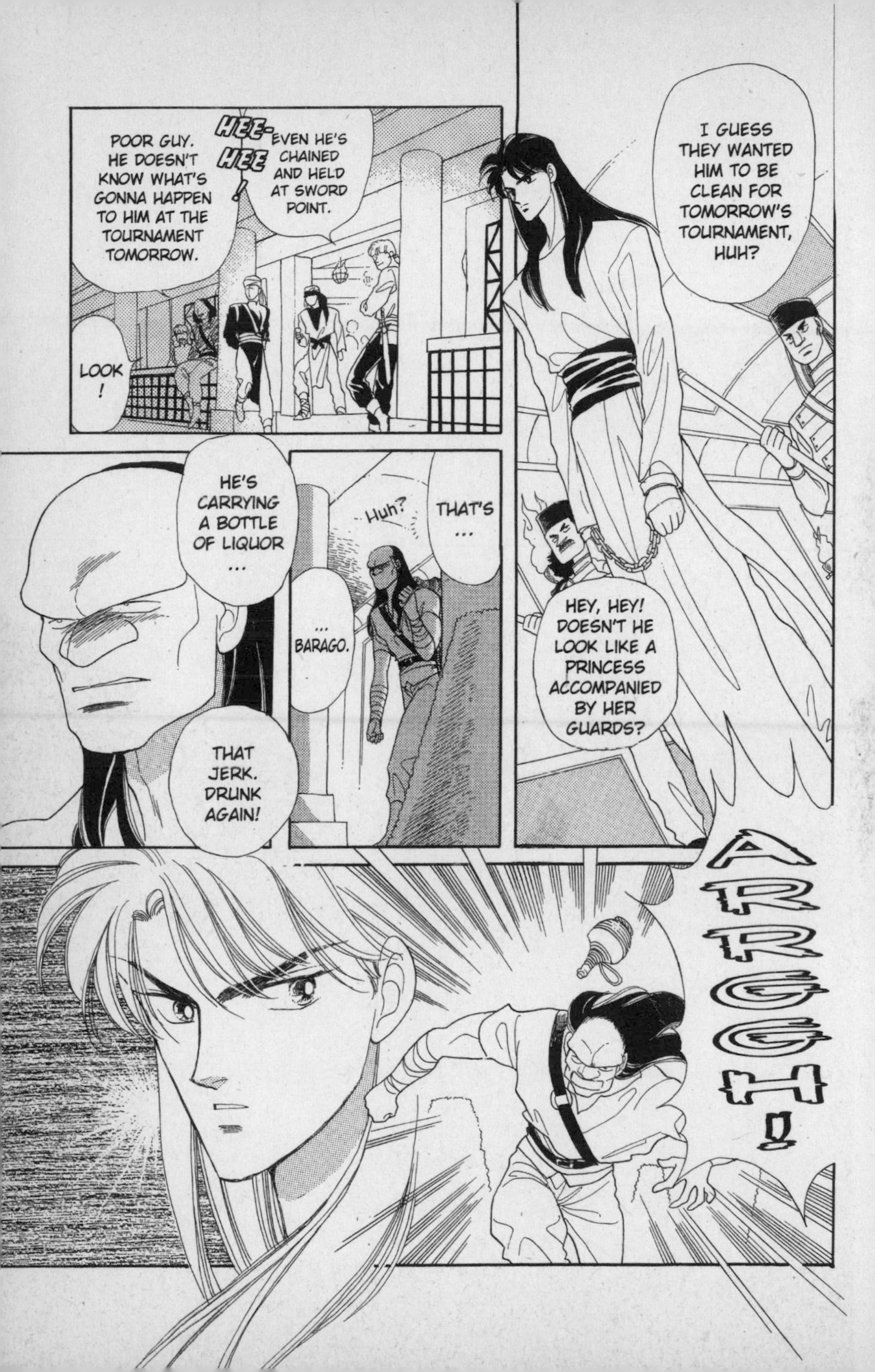
I GUESS THEY WANTED HIM TO BE CLEAN FOR TOMORROW'S TOURNAMENT, HUH?
HEY, HEY! DOESN'T HE LOOK LIKE A PRINCESS ACCOMPANIED BY HER GUARDS?
EVEN HE'S CHAINED AND HELD AT SWORD POINT.
HEE-HEE!
POOR GUY. HE DOESN'T KNOW WHAT'S GONNA HAPPEN TO HIM AT THE TOURNAMENT TOMORROW.
LOOK!
THAT'S ...
Huh?
... BARAGO.
HE'S CARRYING A BOTTLE OF LIQUOR ...
THAT JERK. DRUNK AGAIN!
ARRGGH!

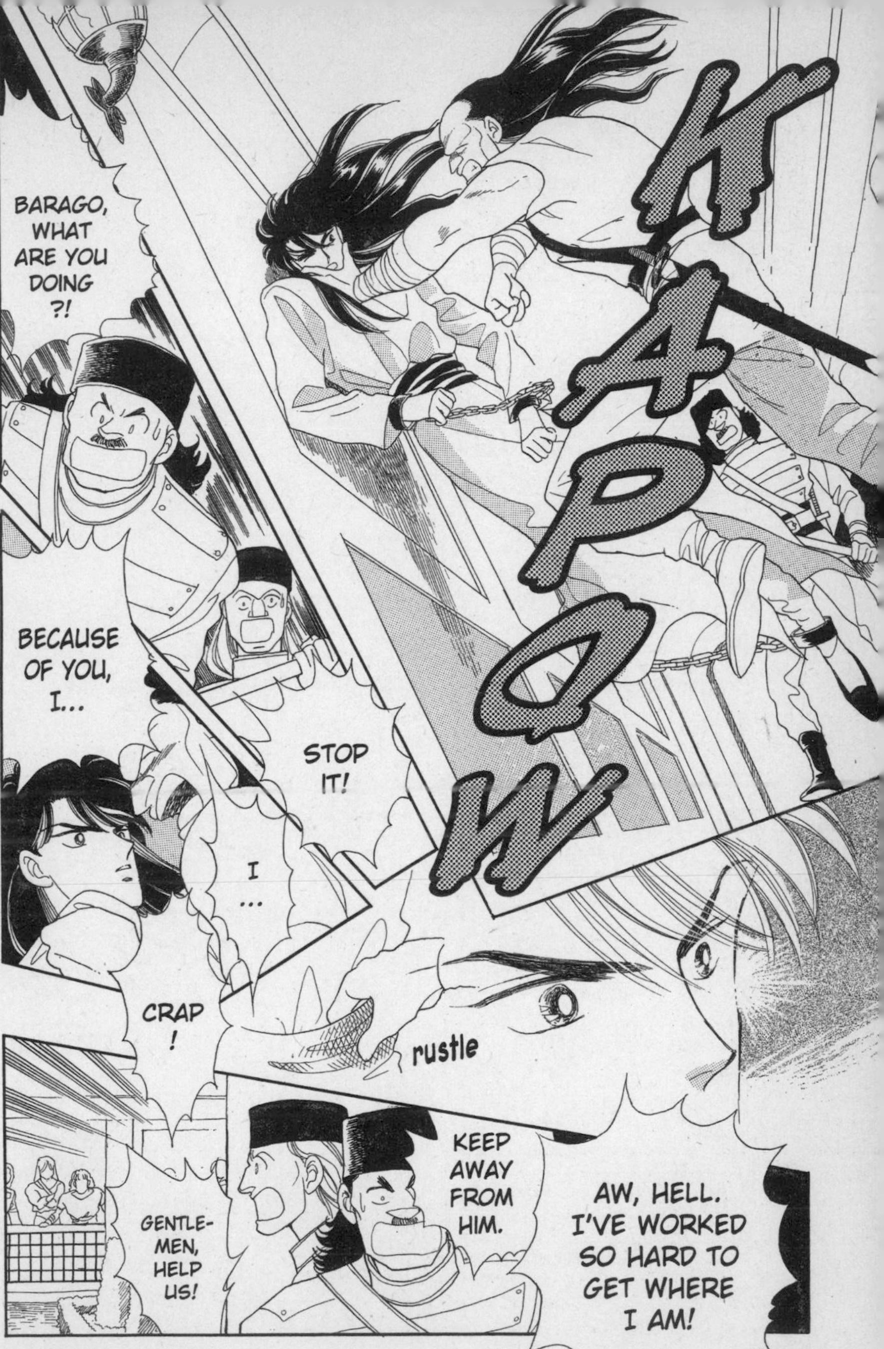
KAPOW
BARAGO, WHAT ARE YOU DOING ?!
BECAUSE OF YOU, I...
STOP IT!
I ...
CRAP !
rustle
AW, HELL. I'VE WORKED SO HARD TO GET WHERE I AM!
KEEP AWAY FROM HIM.
GENTLEMEN, HELP US!

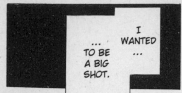

SCHK
HUNH! HE MUST'VE LOST HIS MIND.
WHAT IS THAT FOOL DOING?
THUD
KCHK
HEY.
CALM DOWN, BOSS.
WE'LL TAKE CARE OF HIM. YOU CAN GO NOW.
I WANTED ...
... TO BE A BIG SHOT.
UH-OH. YOU LOOK MISER-ABLE.
WHY DON'T YOU WAIT UNTIL TOMORROW TO GET EVEN WITH HIM?
I COULDA BEEN A CONTENDER!
SO, EVEN IF YOU GET HIM TOMORROW, YOU STILL HAVE NO CHANCE OF PROMOTION, HUH?
SO NOW YOU HAVE NO FUTURE, EH?
I'VE WORKED SO HARD ALL MY LIFE!
HE'S PATHETIC. I DON'T WANT TO BE A LOSER LIKE HIM.
HAW HAW
BUT ...

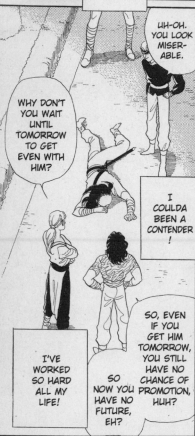

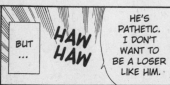

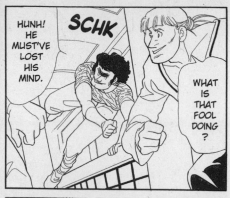

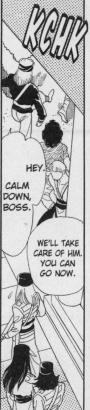

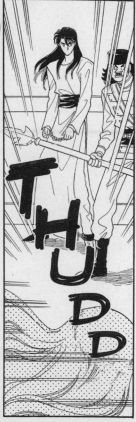

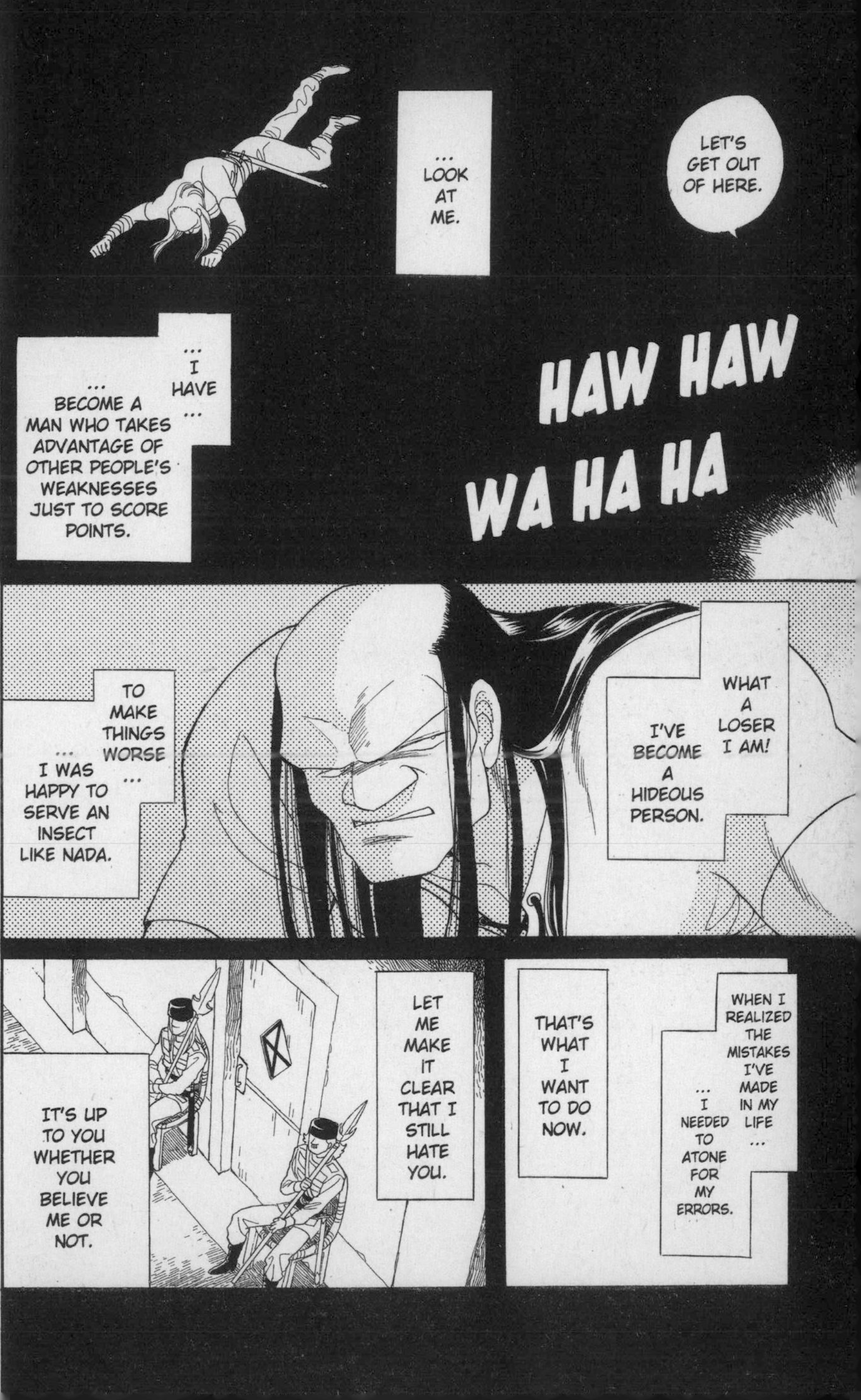
LET'S GET OUT OF HERE.
... LOOK AT ME.
HAW HAW
WA HA HA
... I HAVE ...
... BECOME A MAN WHO TAKES ADVANTAGE OF OTHER PEOPLE'S WEAKNESSES JUST TO SCORE POINTS.
WHAT A LOSER I AM!
I'VE BECOME A HIDEOUS PERSON.
TO MAKE THINGS WORSE ...
... I WAS HAPPY TO SERVE AN INSECT LIKE NADA.
WHEN I REALIZED THE MISTAKES I'VE MADE IN MY LIFE ...
... I NEEDED TO ATONE FOR MY ERRORS.
THAT'S WHAT I WANT TO DO NOW.
LET ME MAKE IT CLEAR THAT I STILL HATE YOU.
IT'S UP TO YOU WHETHER YOU BELIEVE ME OR NOT.

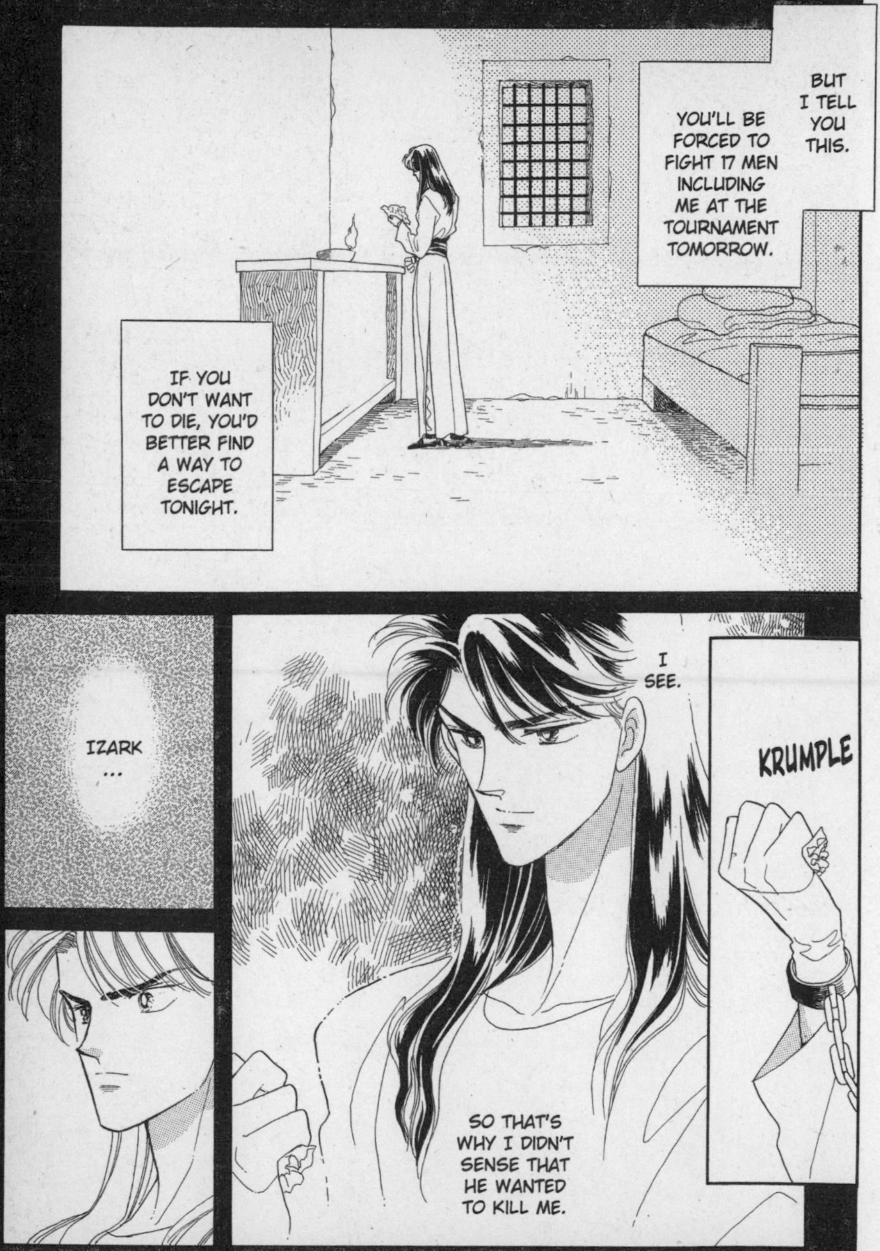
BUT I TELL YOU THIS.
YOU'LL BE FORCED TO FIGHT 17 MEN INCLUDING ME AT THE TOURNAMENT TOMORROW.
IF YOU DON'T WANT TO DIE, YOU'D BETTER FIND A WAY TO ESCAPE TONIGHT.
KRUMPLE
I SEE.
SO THAT'S WHY I DIDN'T SENSE THAT HE WANTED TO KILL ME.
IZARK ...

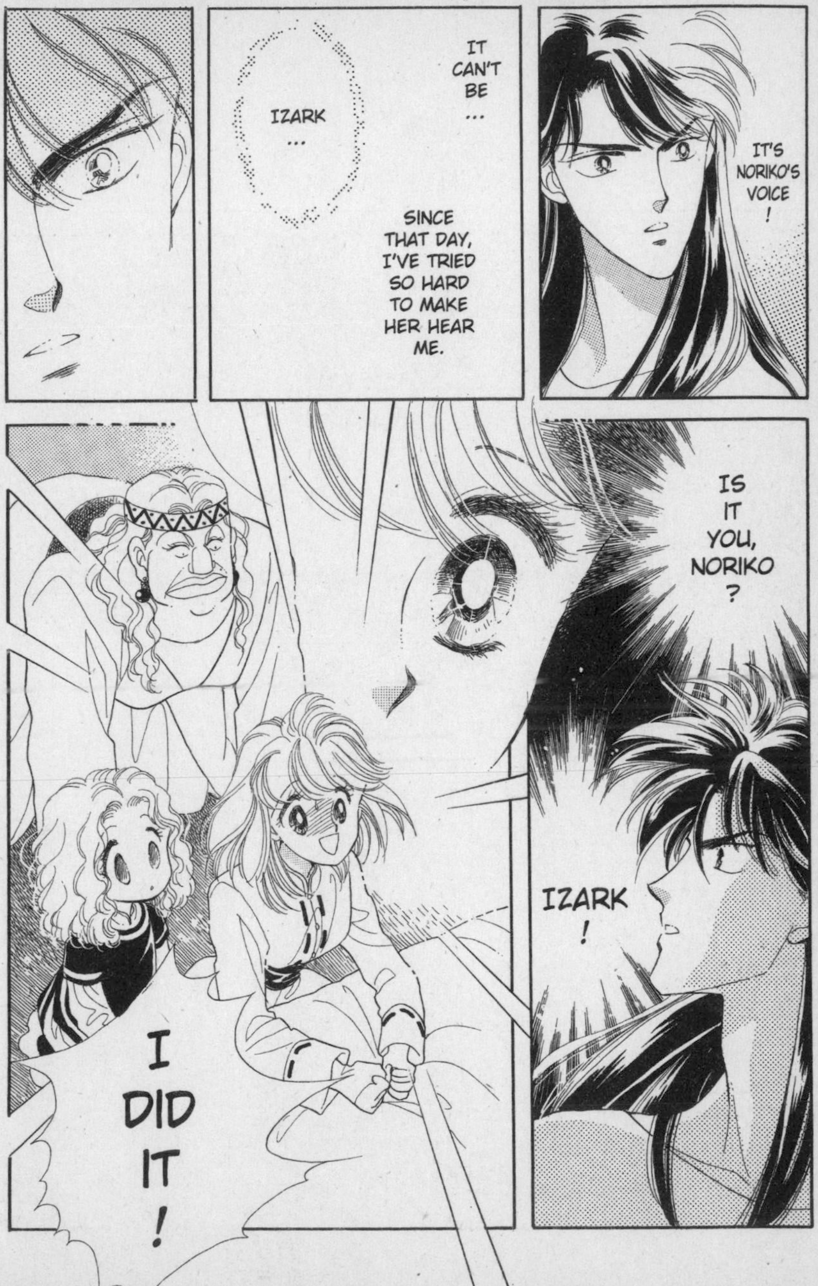
IT'S NORIKO'S VOICE !
IT CAN'T BE ...
IZARK ...
SINCE THAT DAY, I'VE TRIED SO HARD TO MAKE HER HEAR ME.
IS IT YOU, NORIKO ?
IZARK !
I DID IT !

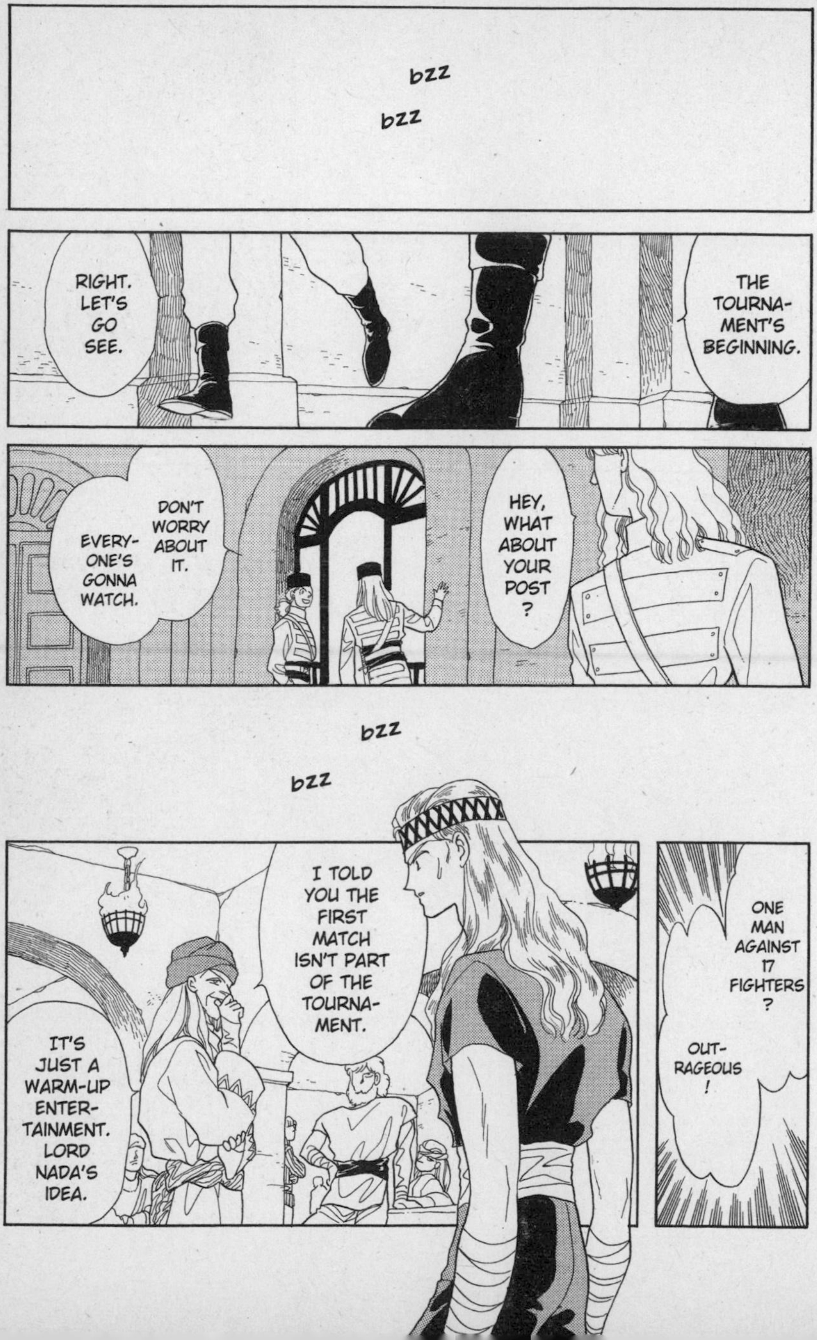
bzz
bzz
THE TOURNAMENT'S BEGINNING.
RIGHT. LET'S GO SEE.
HEY, WHAT ABOUT YOUR POST?
DON'T WORRY ABOUT IT.
EVERYONE'S GONNA WATCH.
bzz
bzz
ONE MAN AGAINST 17 FIGHTERS?
OUTRAGEOUS!
I TOLD YOU THE FIRST MATCH ISN'T PART OF THE TOURNAMENT.
IT'S JUST A WARM-UP ENTERTAINMENT. LORD NADA'S IDEA.

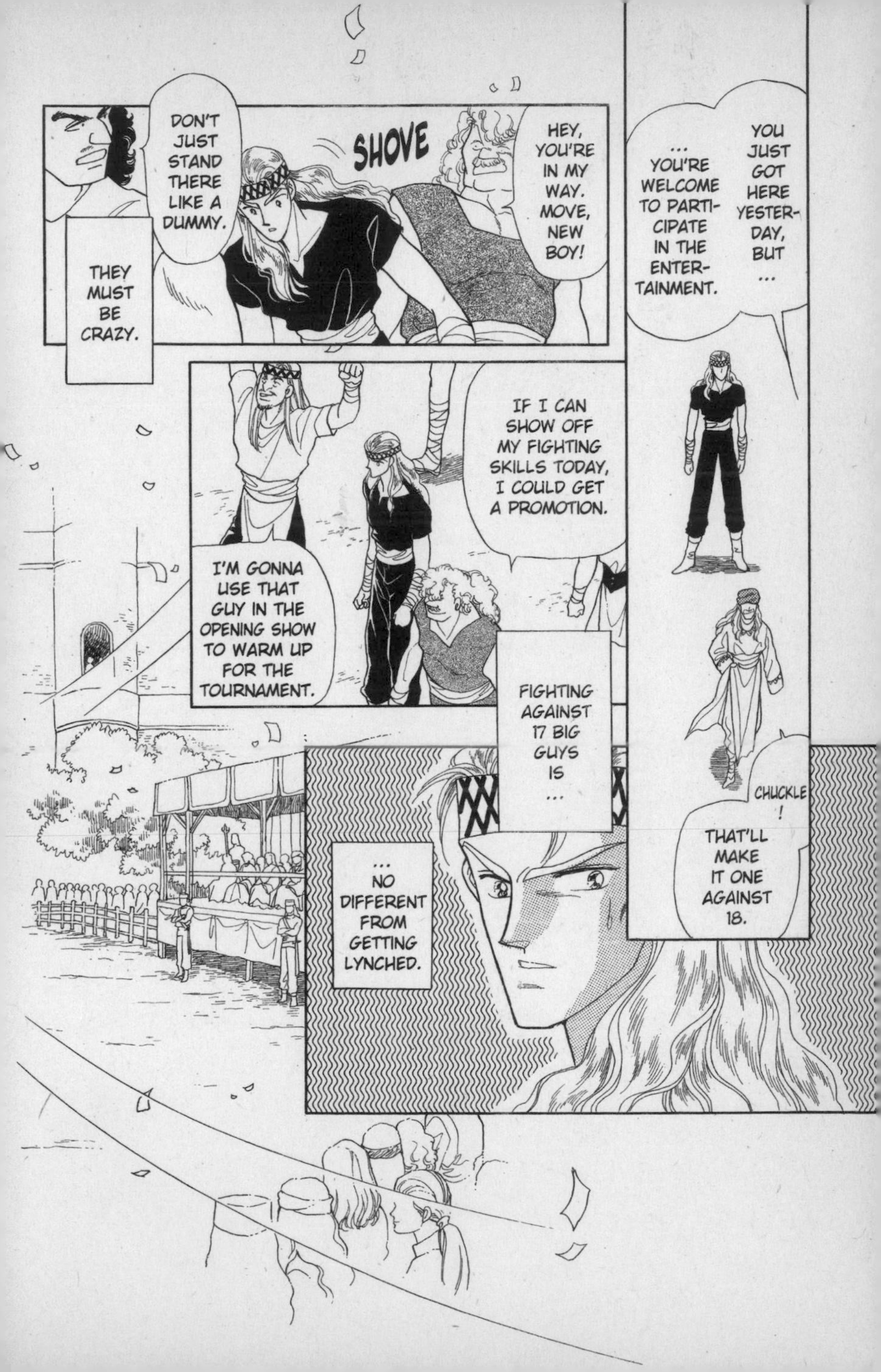

YOU JUST GOT HERE YESTERDAY, BUT ...
... YOU'RE WELCOME TO PARTICIPATE IN THE ENTERTAINMENT.
CHUCKLE!
THAT'LL MAKE IT ONE AGAINST 18.
HEY, YOU'RE IN MY WAY. MOVE, NEW BOY!
SHOVE
DON'T JUST STAND THERE LIKE A DUMMY.
THEY MUST BE CRAZY.
IF I CAN SHOW OFF MY FIGHTING SKILLS TODAY, I COULD GET A PROMOTION.
I'M GONNA USE THAT GUY IN THE OPENING SHOW TO WARM UP FOR THE TOURNAMENT.
FIGHTING AGAINST 17 BIG GUYS IS ...
... NO DIFFERENT FROM GETTING LYNCHED.

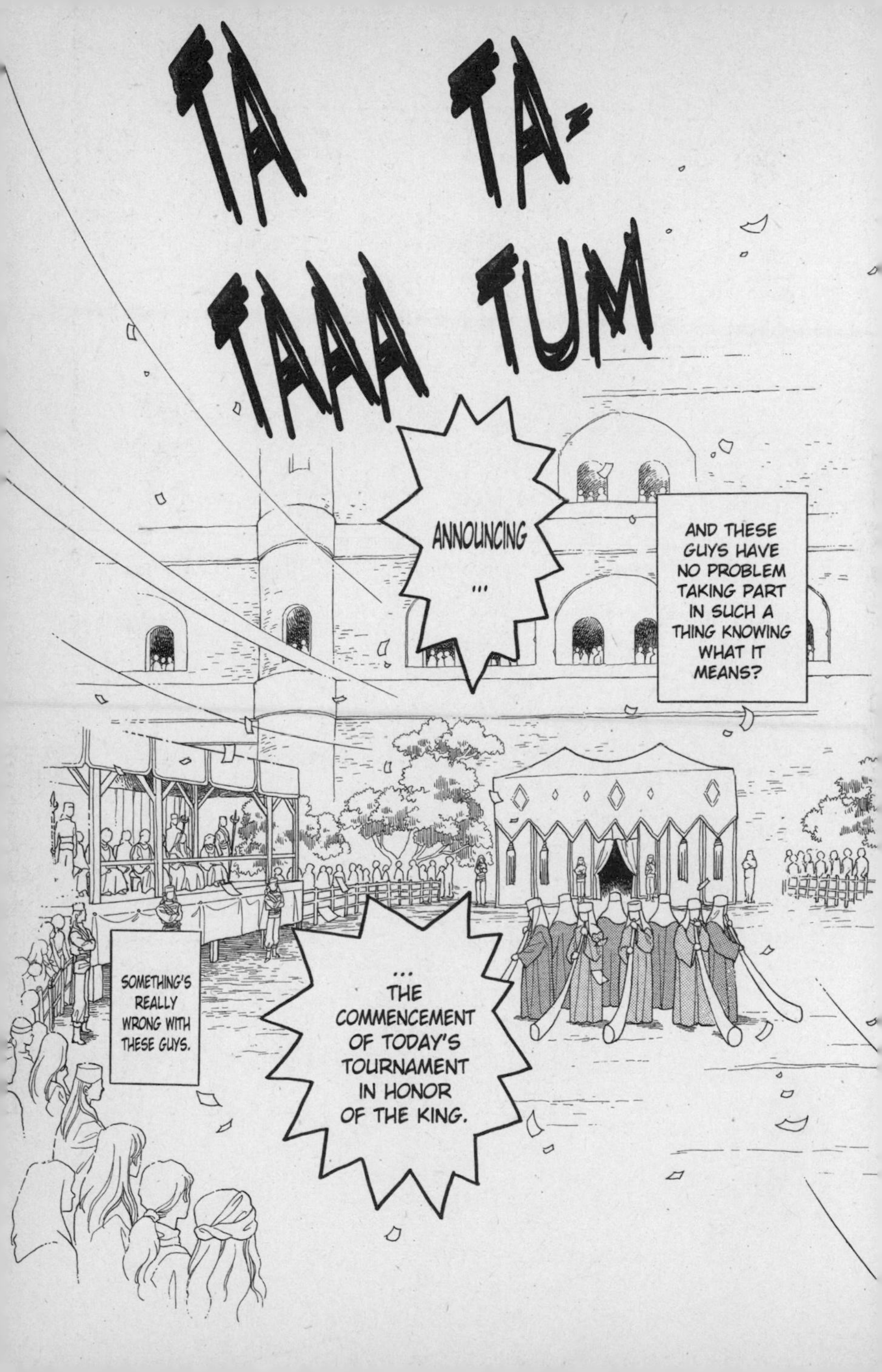
TA TA-
TAAA TUM
ANNOUNCING ...
AND THESE GUYS HAVE NO PROBLEM TAKING PART IN SUCH A THING KNOWING WHAT IT MEANS?
... THE COMMENCEMENT OF TODAY'S TOURNAMENT IN HONOR OF THE KING.
SOMETHING'S REALLY WRONG WITH THESE GUYS.

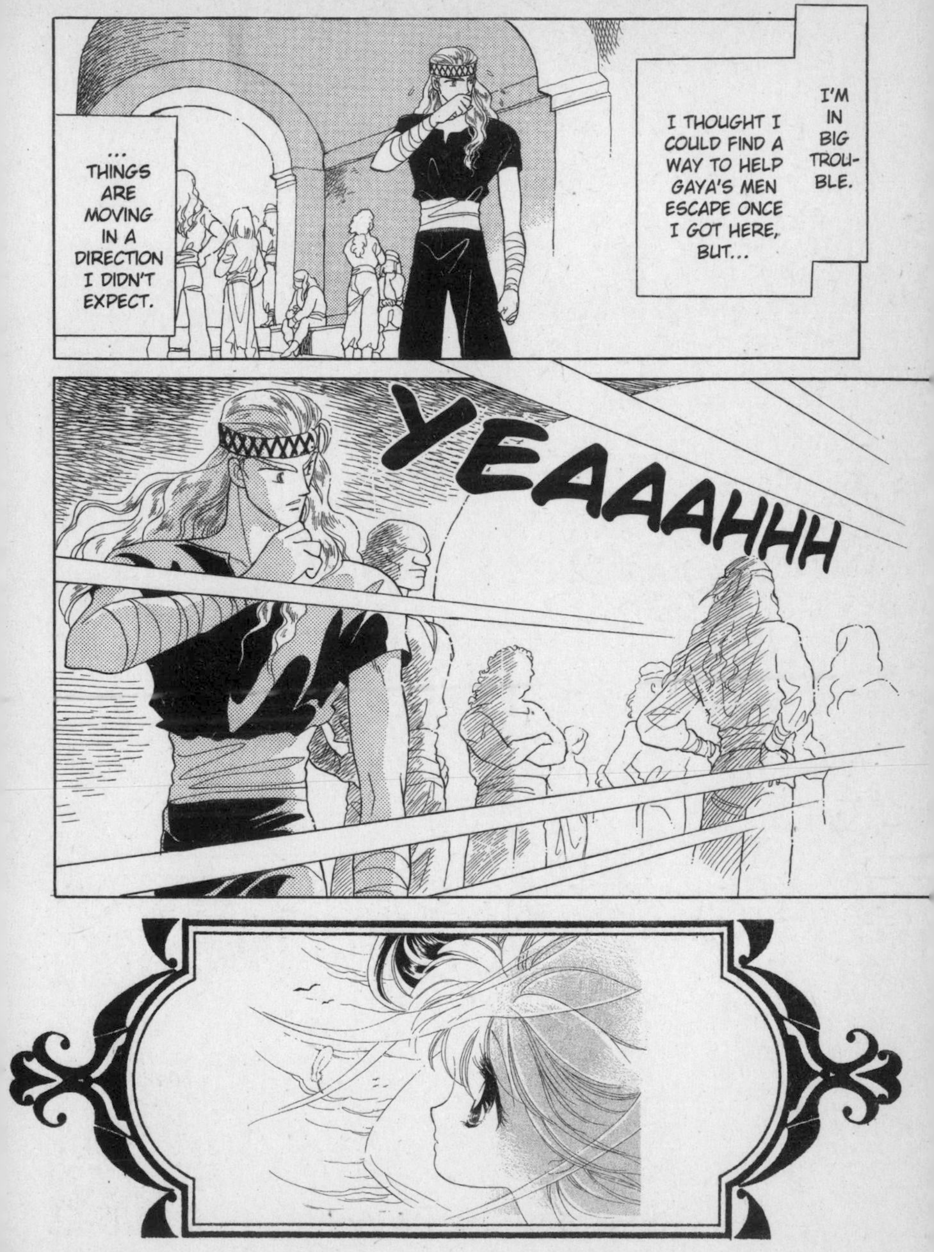
I'M IN BIG TROU-BLE.
I THOUGHT I COULD FIND A WAY TO HELP GAYA'S MEN ESCAPE ONCE I GOT HERE, BUT...
...THINGS ARE MOVING IN A DIRECTION I DIDN'T EXPECT.
YEAAAAHHH

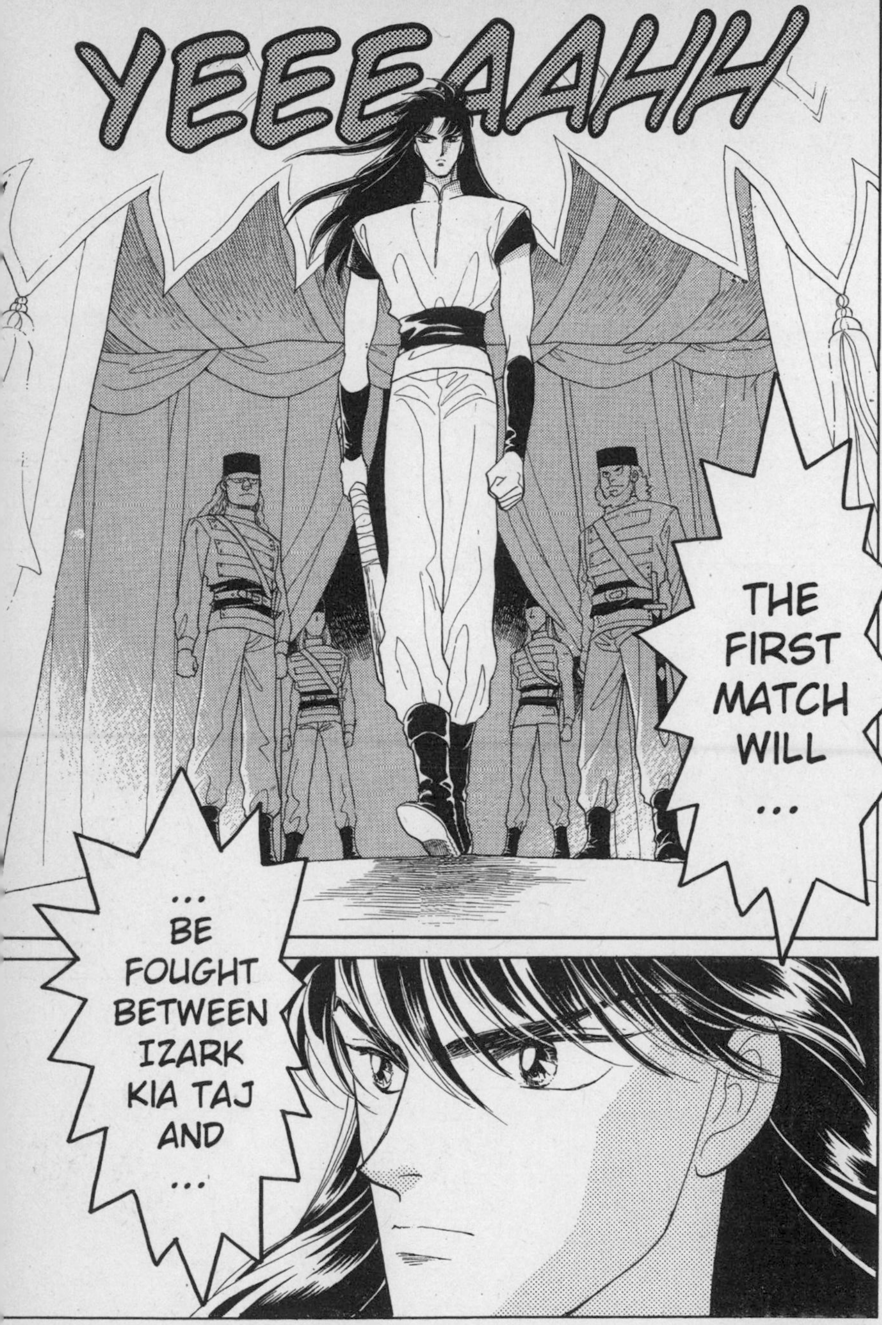
YEEEAAHH
THE FIRST MATCH WILL ...
... BE FOUGHT BETWEEN IZARK KIA TAJ AND ...

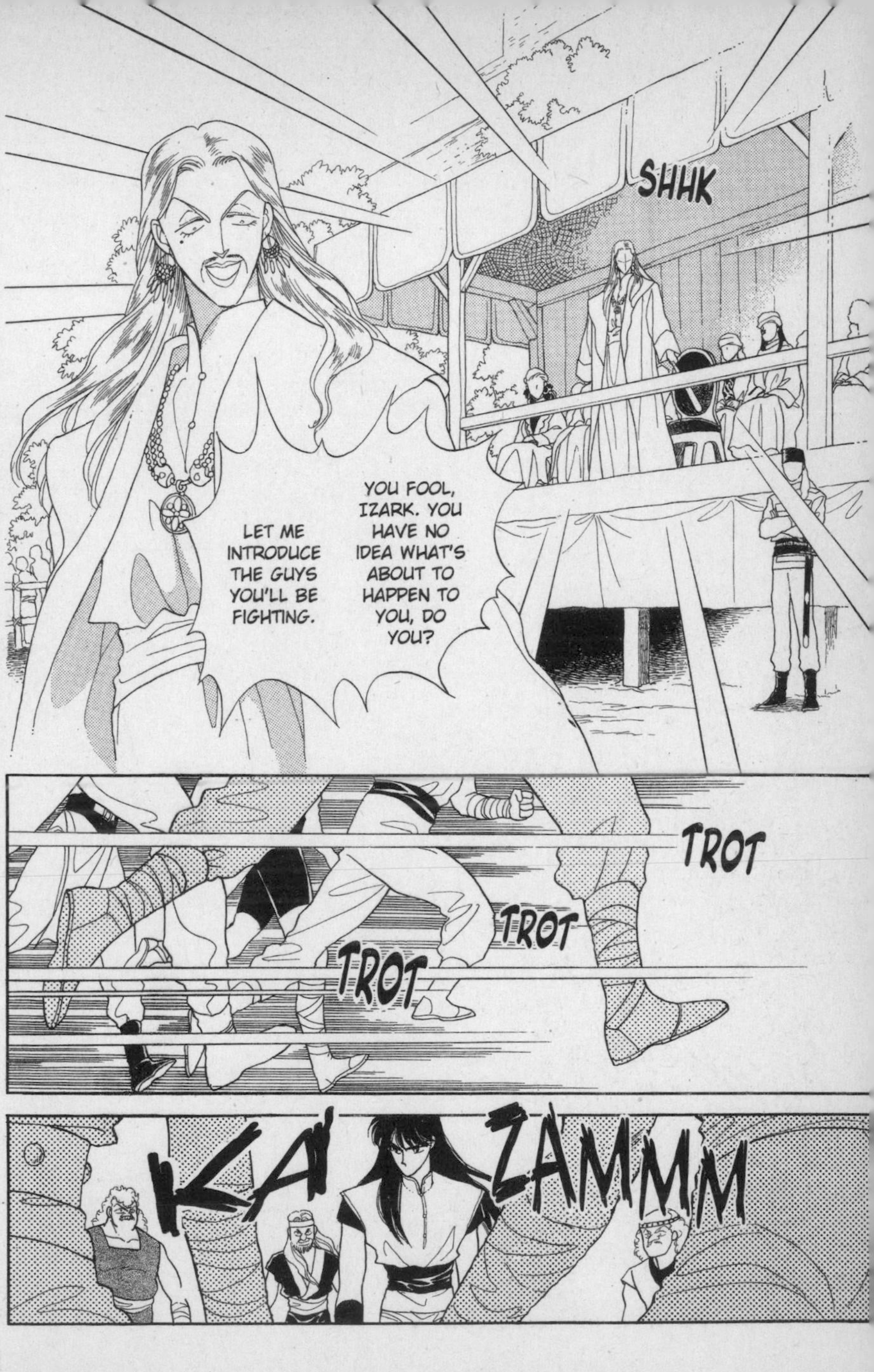
SHHK
YOU FOOL, IZARK. YOU HAVE NO IDEA WHAT'S ABOUT TO HAPPEN TO YOU, DO YOU?
LET ME INTRODUCE THE GUYS YOU'LL BE FIGHTING.
TROT
TROT
TROT
KA-ZAMMM

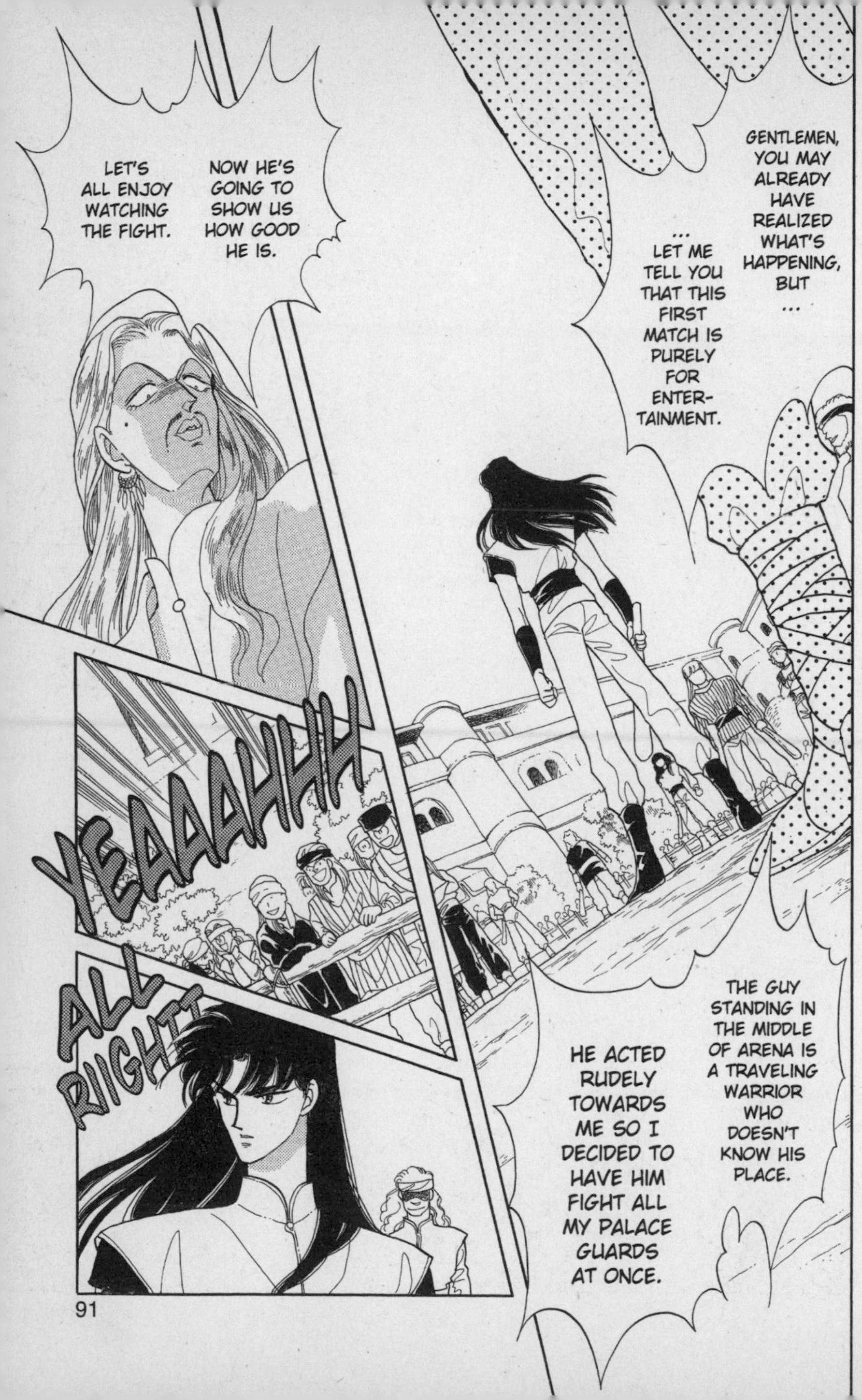
GENTLEMEN, YOU MAY ALREADY HAVE REALIZED WHAT'S HAPPENING, BUT ...
... LET ME TELL YOU THAT THIS FIRST MATCH IS PURELY FOR ENTERTAINMENT.
THE GUY STANDING IN THE MIDDLE OF ARENA IS A TRAVELING WARRIOR WHO DOESN'T KNOW HIS PLACE.
HE ACTED RUDELY TOWARDS ME SO I DECIDED TO HAVE HIM FIGHT ALL MY PALACE GUARDS AT ONCE.
NOW HE'S GOING TO SHOW US HOW GOOD HE IS.
LET'S ALL ENJOY WATCHING THE FIGHT.
YEAAAHHH
ALL RIGHT!!

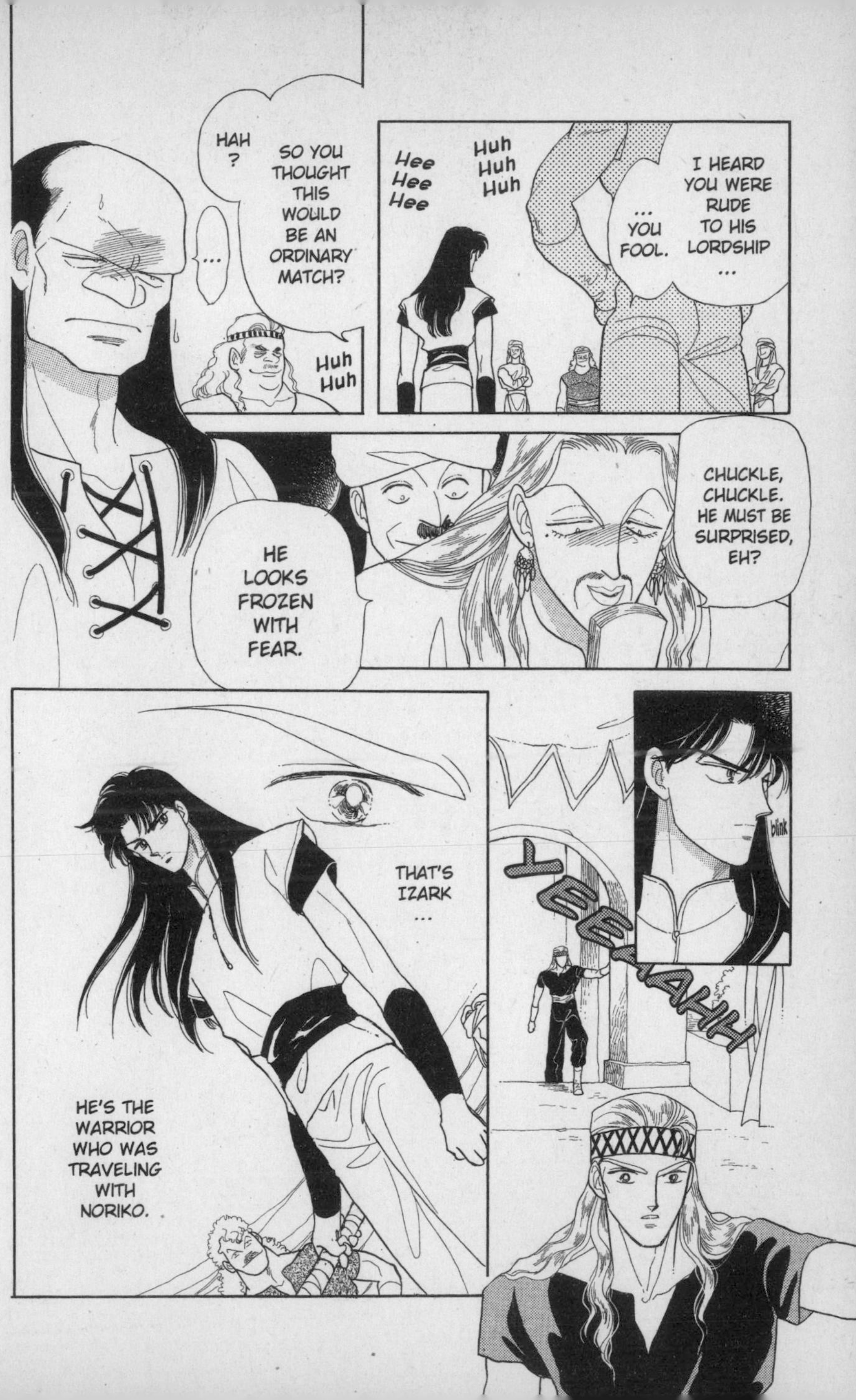
I HEARD YOU WERE RUDE TO HIS LORDSHIP ...
... YOU FOOL.
Huh Huh Huh
Hee Hee Hee
SO YOU THOUGHT THIS WOULD BE AN ORDINARY MATCH?
HAH ?
...
Huh Huh
CHUCKLE, CHUCKLE. HE MUST BE SURPRISED, EH?
HE LOOKS FROZEN WITH FEAR.
blink
YEEAAHH
THAT'S IZARK ...
HE'S THE WARRIOR WHO WAS TRAVELING WITH NORIKO.

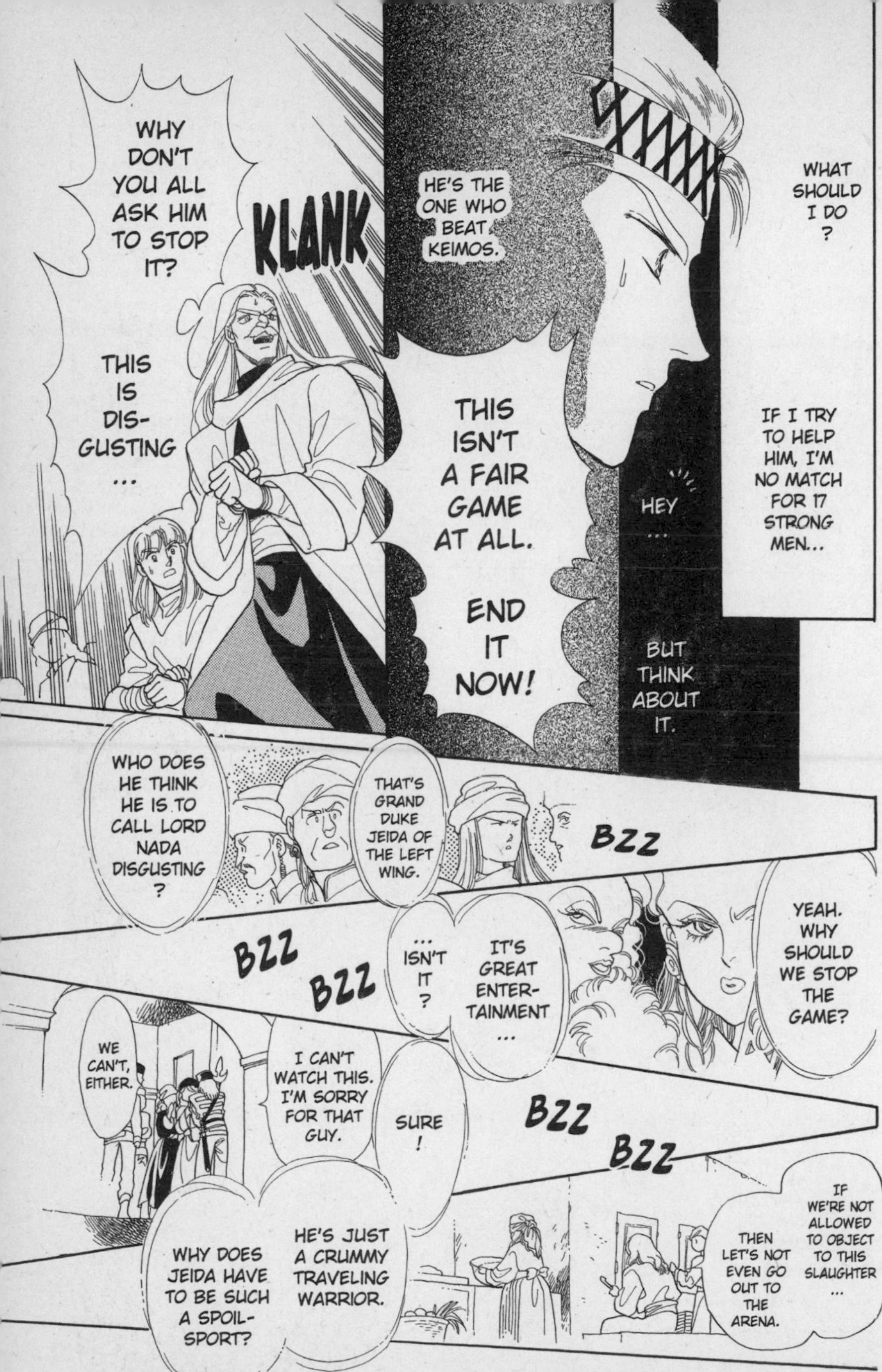
WHAT SHOULD I DO?
IF I TRY TO HELP HIM, I'M NO MATCH FOR 17 STRONG MEN...
HEY...
BUT THINK ABOUT IT.
HE'S THE ONE WHO BEAT KEIMOS.
THIS ISN'T A FAIR GAME AT ALL.
END IT NOW!
WHY DON'T YOU ALL ASK HIM TO STOP IT?
KLANK
THIS IS DIS-GUSTING...
BZZ
THAT'S GRAND DUKE JEIDA OF THE LEFT WING.
WHO DOES HE THINK HE IS TO CALL LORD NADA DISGUSTING?
YEAH. WHY SHOULD WE STOP THE GAME?
IT'S GREAT ENTER-TAINMENT...
...ISN'T IT?
BZZ
BZZ
BZZ
BZZ
SURE!
I CAN'T WATCH THIS. I'M SORRY FOR THAT GUY.
WE CAN'T, EITHER.
IF WE'RE NOT ALLOWED TO OBJECT TO THIS SLAUGHTER...
THEN LET'S NOT EVEN GO OUT TO THE ARENA.
HE'S JUST A CRUMMY TRAVELING WARRIOR.
WHY DOES JEIDA HAVE TO BE SUCH A SPOIL-SPORT?

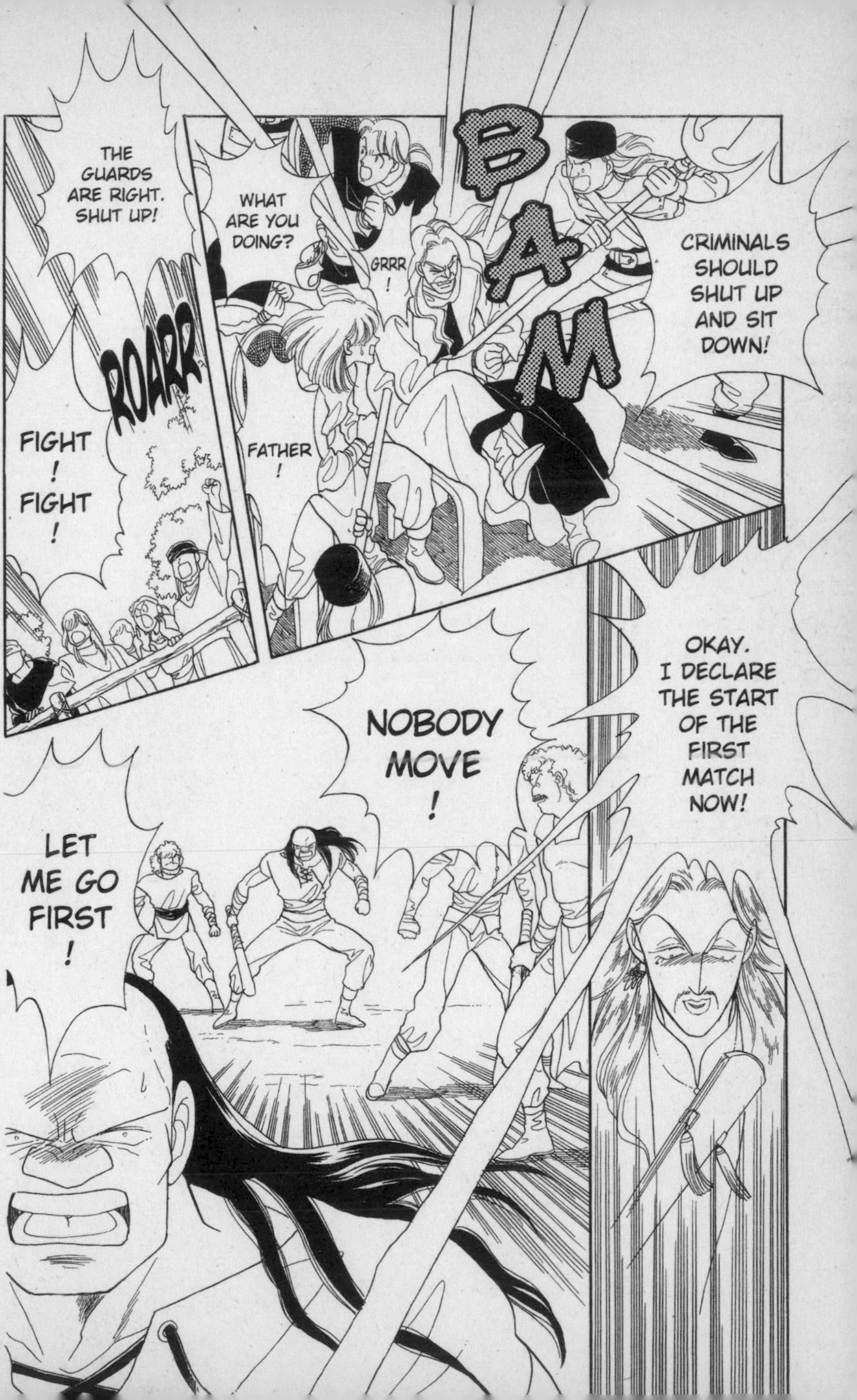
CRIMINALS SHOULD SHUT UP AND SIT DOWN!
BAM
WHAT ARE YOU DOING?
GRRR!
FATHER!
THE GUARDS ARE RIGHT. SHUT UP!
ROARR
FIGHT! FIGHT!
OKAY. I DECLARE THE START OF THE FIRST MATCH NOW!
NOBODY MOVE!
LET ME GO FIRST!

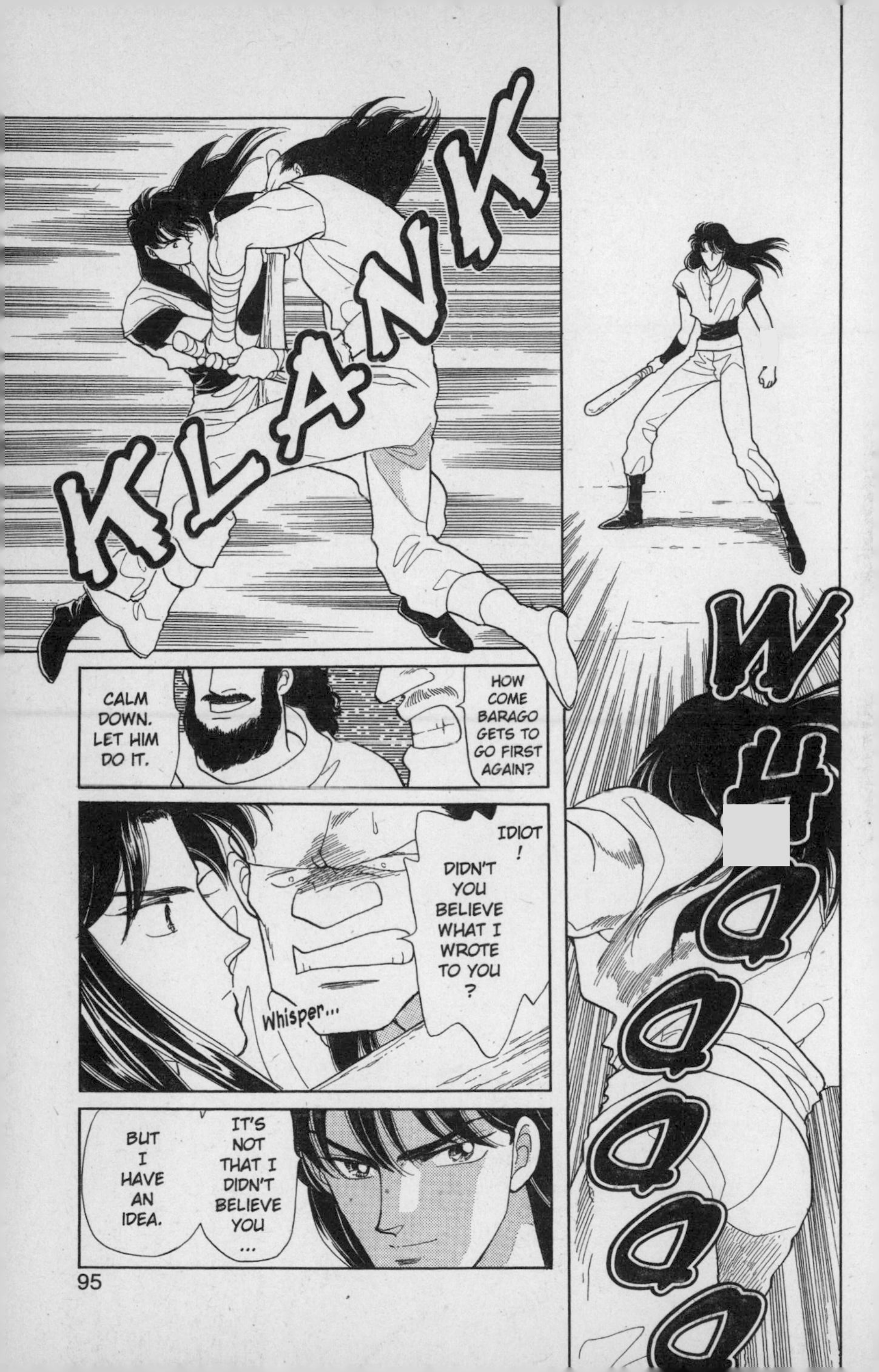
WHOOOOO
KLANK
HOW COME BARAGO GETS TO GO FIRST AGAIN?
CALM DOWN. LET HIM DO IT.
IDIOT! DIDN'T YOU BELIEVE WHAT I WROTE TO YOU?
Whisper...
IT'S NOT THAT I DIDN'T BELIEVE YOU...
BUT I HAVE AN IDEA.

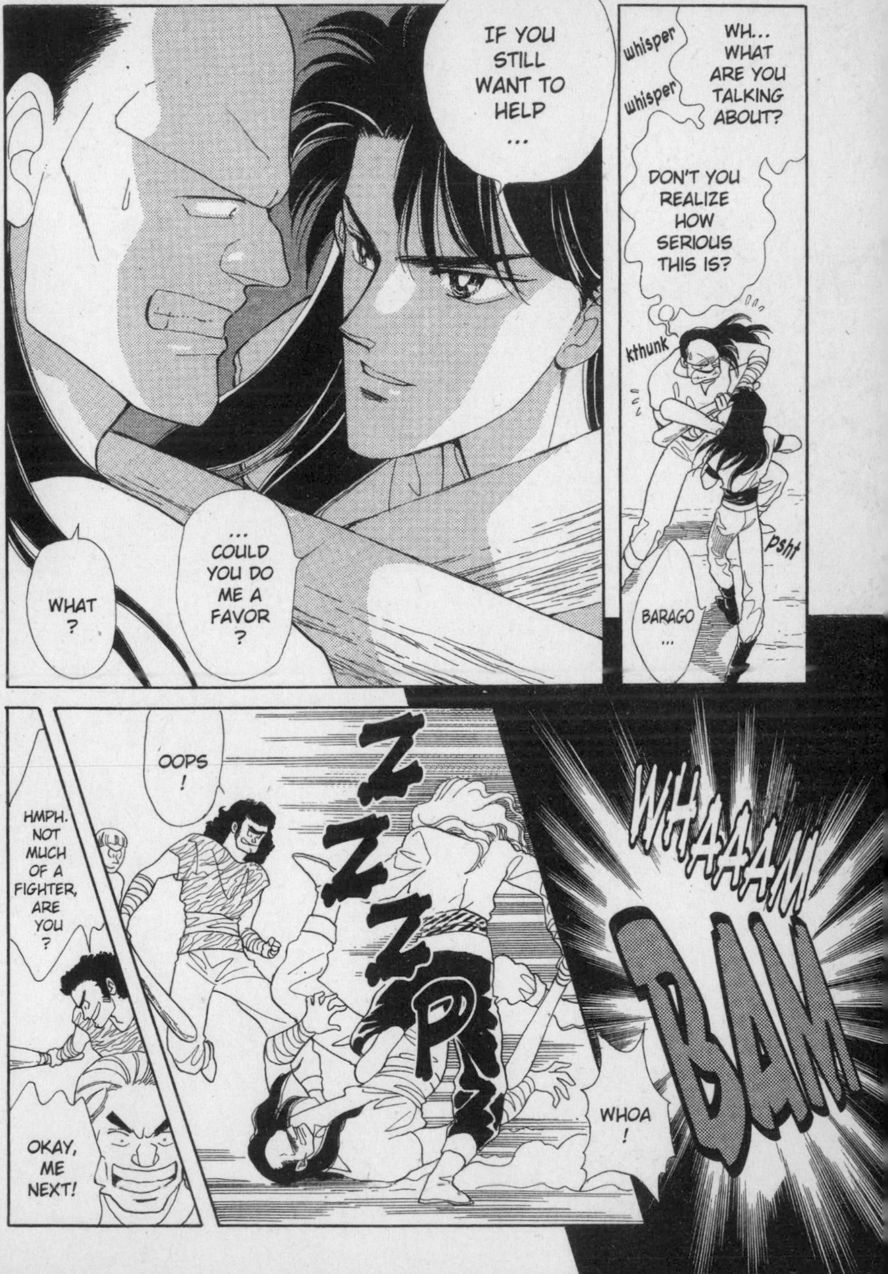
WH... WHAT ARE YOU TALKING ABOUT?
whisper
whisper
DON'T YOU REALIZE HOW SERIOUS THIS IS?
kthunk
psht
BARAGO ...
IF YOU STILL WANT TO HELP ...
... COULD YOU DO ME A FAVOR ?
WHAT ?
WHAAAM
BAM
ZZZP
OOPS !
WHOA !
HMPH. NOT MUCH OF A FIGHTER, ARE YOU ?
OKAY, ME NEXT!

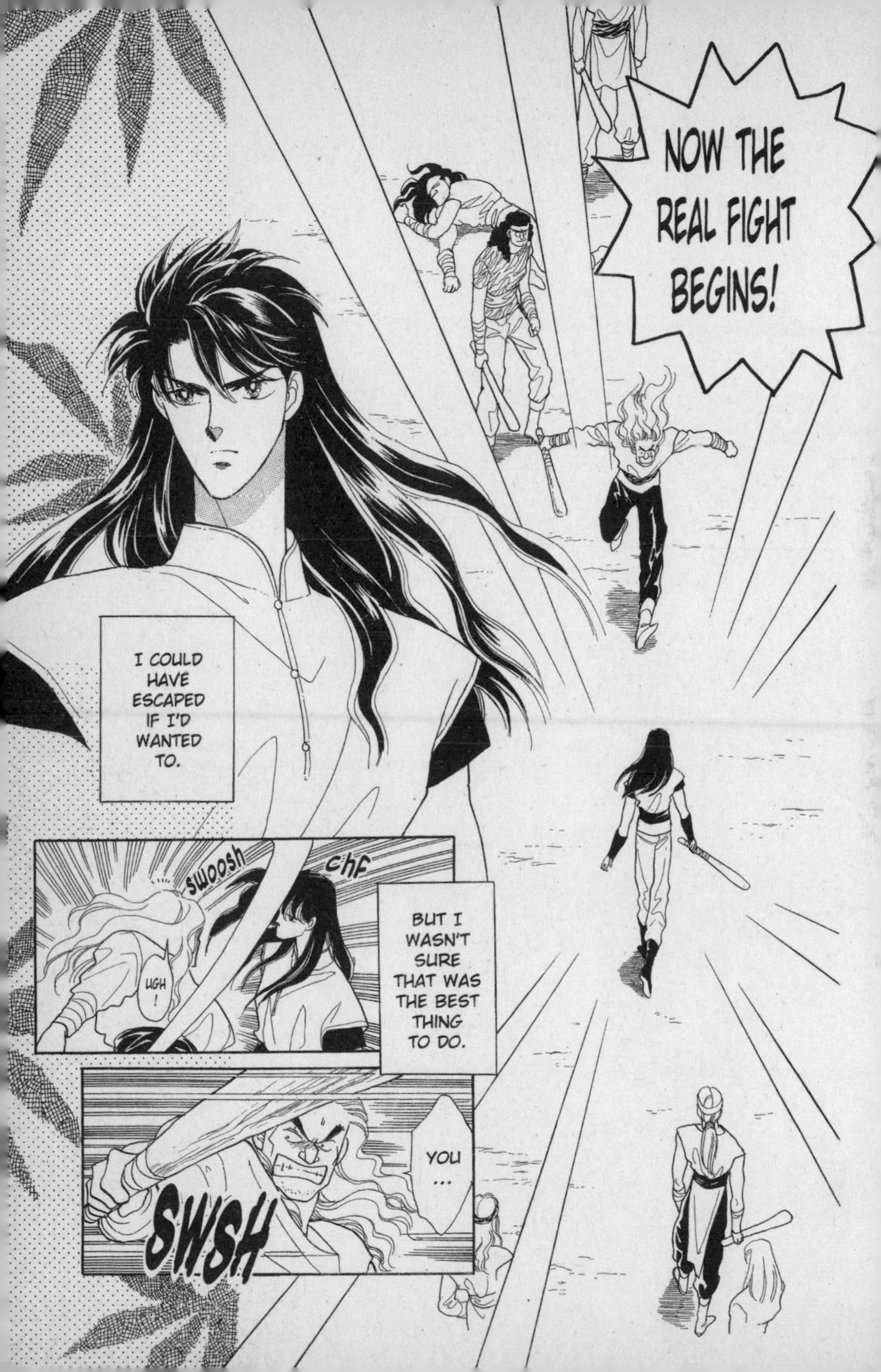
NOW THE REAL FIGHT BEGINS!
I COULD HAVE ESCAPED IF I'D WANTED TO.
BUT I WASN'T SURE THAT WAS THE BEST THING TO DO.
chF
swoosh
UGH!
YOU...
SWSH

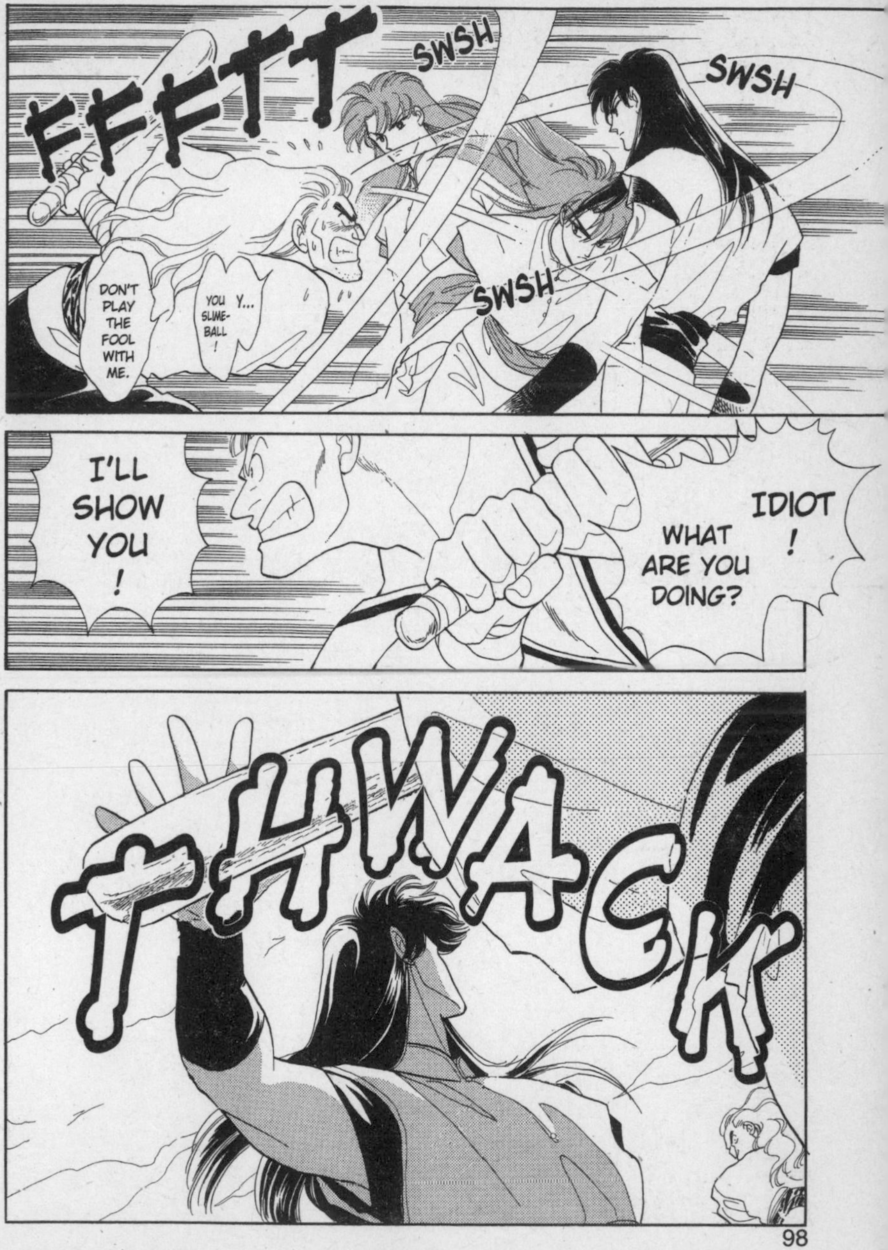
SWSH
SWSH
FFFTT
SWSH
YOU Y... SLIME-BALL!
DON'T PLAY THE FOOL WITH ME.
IDIOT!
WHAT ARE YOU DOING?
I'LL SHOW YOU!
THWACK

GRRR.
UNGH.
grrrippp
SHOVE
WHAMMM
ARGH !
WHOA !
THUDD
UNGH.
Y... YOU RAT ...
FWSH
GRABBB
FWSH
YOU CAN'T MAKE FOOLS OF US!

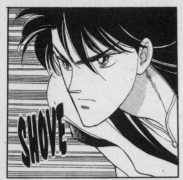

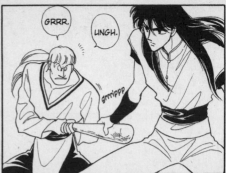

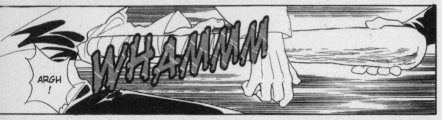

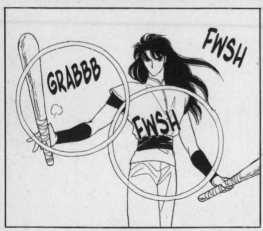

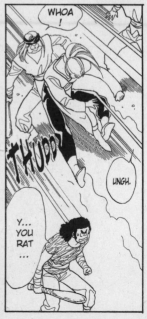

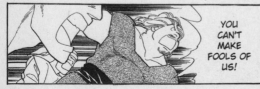

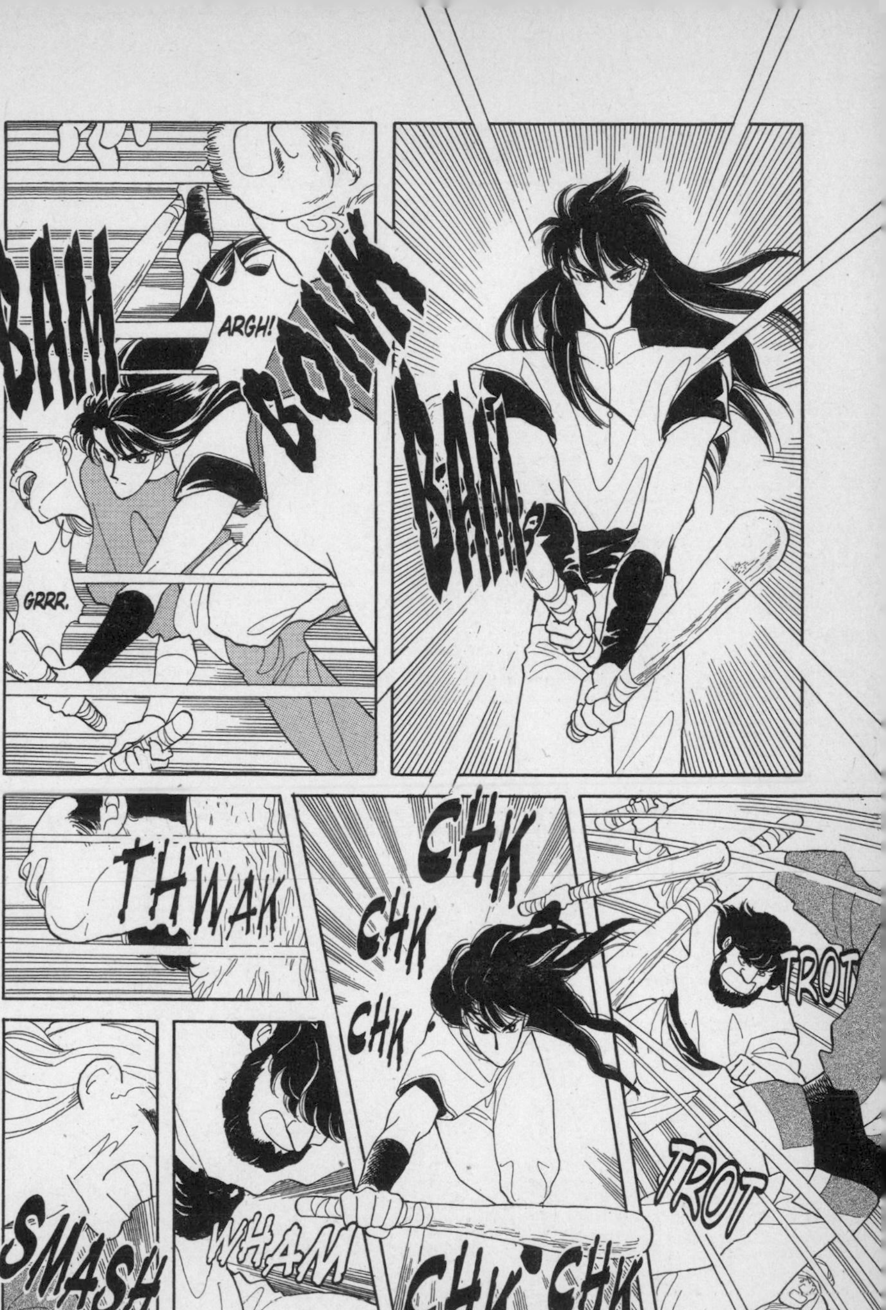
BAM
BONK
ARGH!
BAM
GRRR.
TROT
TROT
CHK
CHK
CHK
CHK
CHK
THWAK
WHAM
SMASH

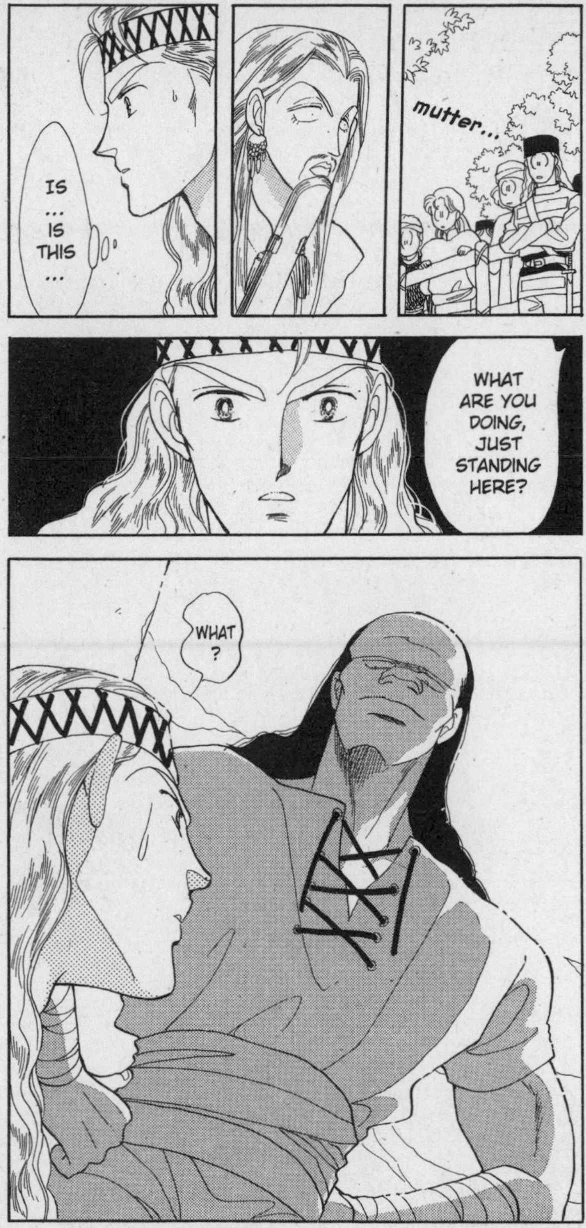
mutter...
IS ... IS THIS ...
WHAT ARE YOU DOING, JUST STANDING HERE?
WHAT?

My strange childhood memories:
Part 2:

There was a huge warehouse next to a train station. It was abandoned and full of rubble. The place had become a playground for the kids in the neighborhood.

The warehouse had a window high up on the wall. When I looked up, I saw a face at the window that looked like okame, a fat-face woman's mask!

I was curious so I went outside and looked up toward the window. There was nothing there.

Was this all just a dream?

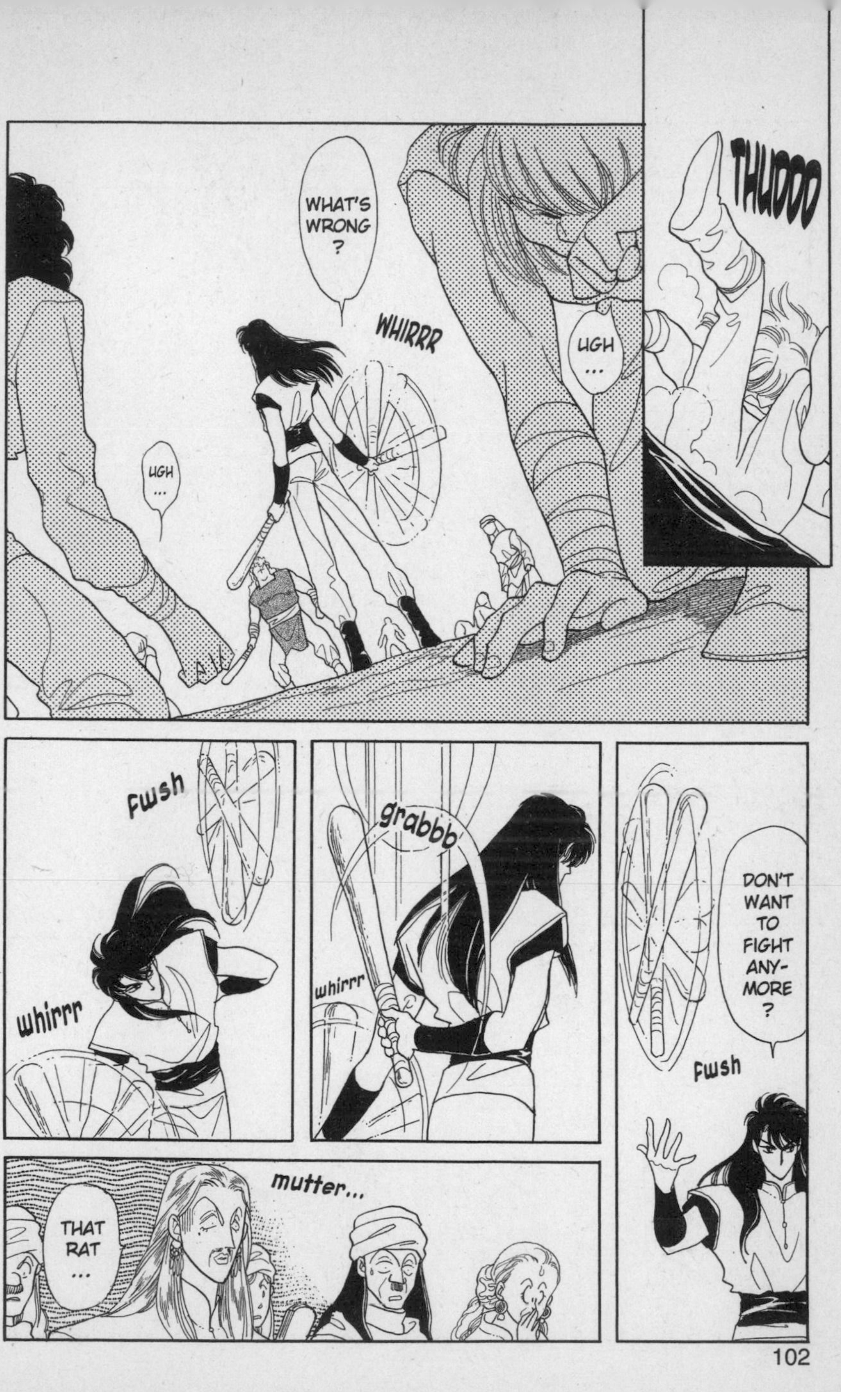
THUDDD
UGH ...
WHAT'S WRONG ?
WHIRRR
UGH ...
DON'T WANT TO FIGHT ANY-MORE ?
Fwsh
grabbb
whirrr
Fwsh
whirrr
mutter...
THAT RAT ...

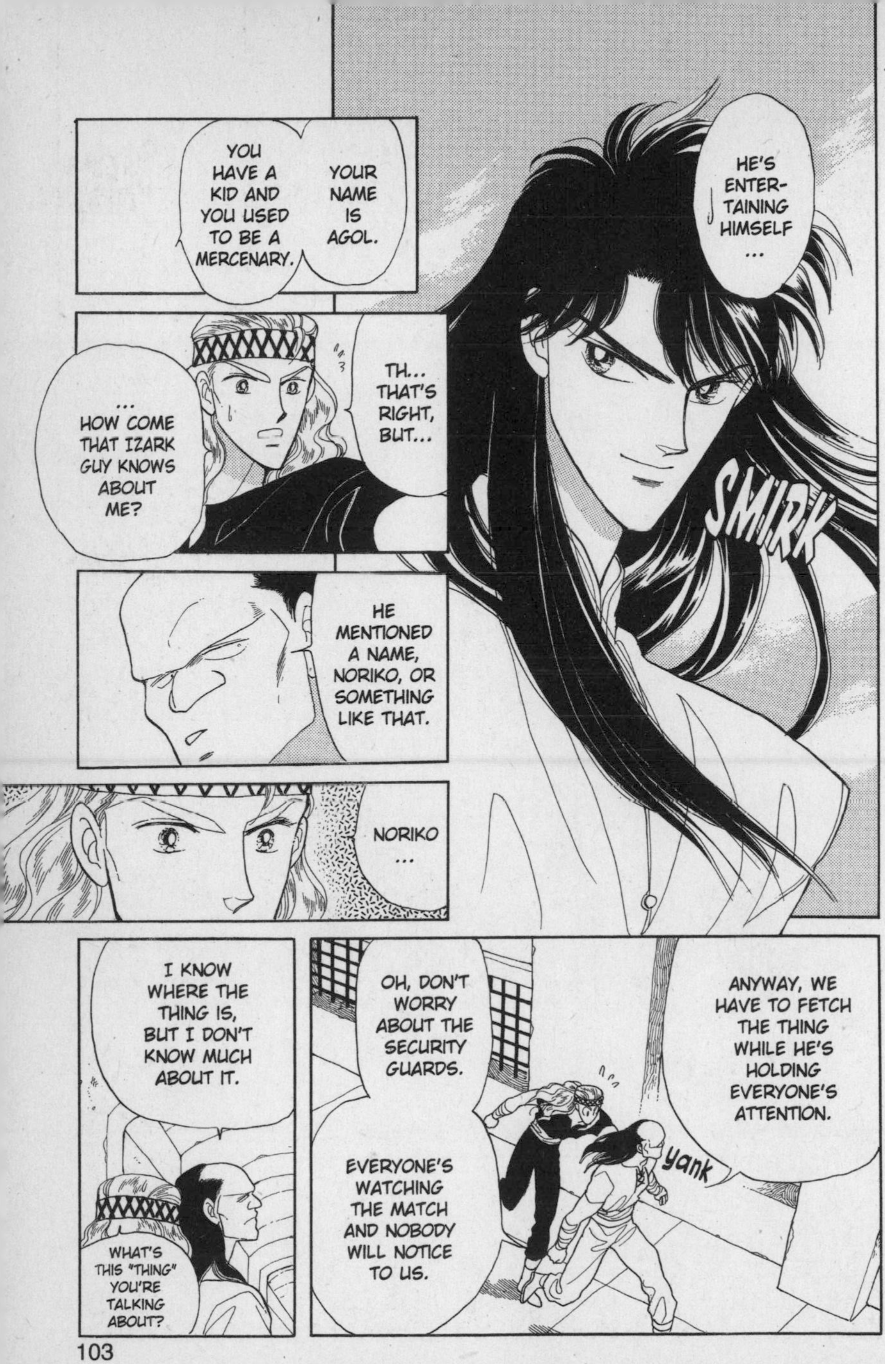
HE'S ENTERTAINING HIMSELF ...
SMIRK
YOUR NAME IS AGOL.
YOU HAVE A KID AND YOU USED TO BE A MERCENARY.
TH... THAT'S RIGHT, BUT...
... HOW COME THAT IZARK GUY KNOWS ABOUT ME?
HE MENTIONED A NAME, NORIKO, OR SOMETHING LIKE THAT.
NORIKO ...
ANYWAY, WE HAVE TO FETCH THE THING WHILE HE'S HOLDING EVERYONE'S ATTENTION.
yank
OH, DON'T WORRY ABOUT THE SECURITY GUARDS.
EVERYONE'S WATCHING THE MATCH AND NOBODY WILL NOTICE TO US.
WHAT'S THIS "THING" YOU'RE TALKING ABOUT?
I KNOW WHERE THE THING IS, BUT I DON'T KNOW MUCH ABOUT IT.

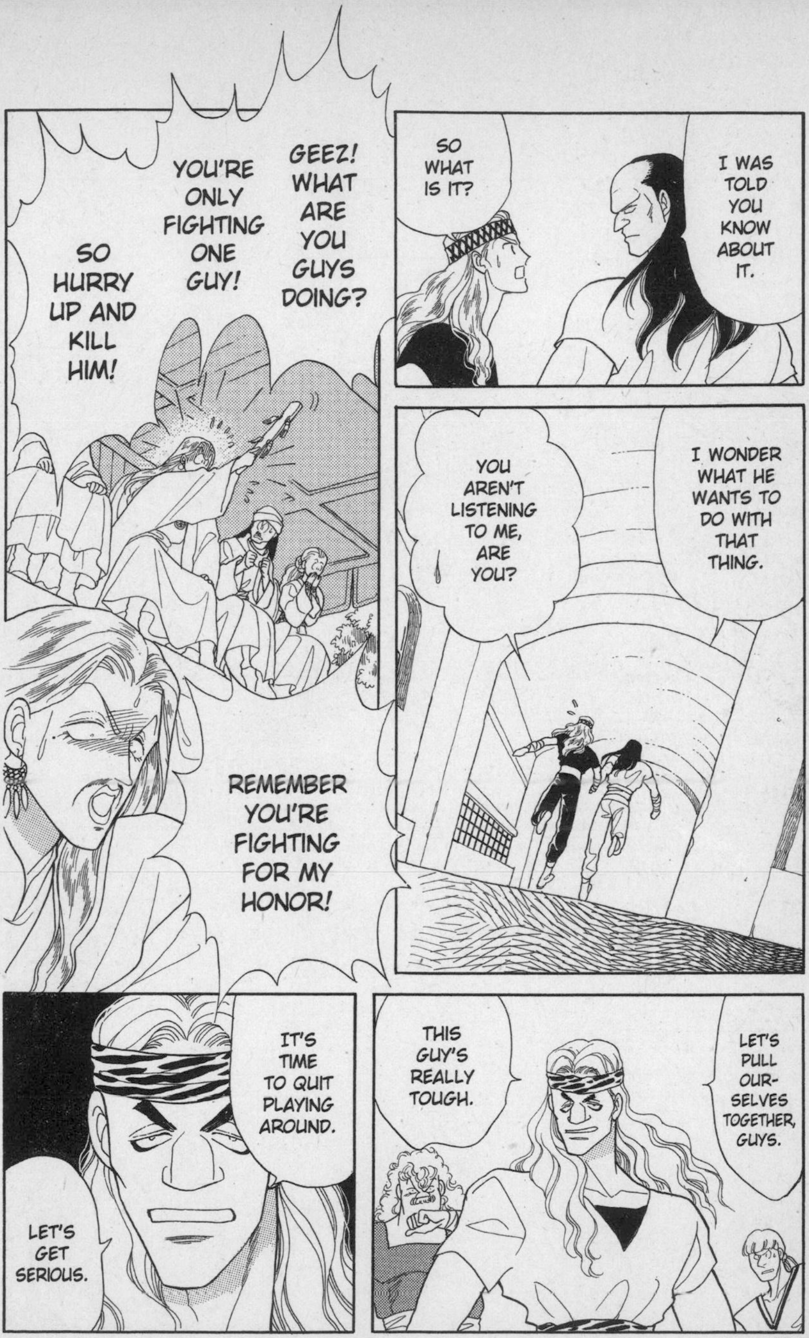
I WAS TOLD YOU KNOW ABOUT IT.
SO WHAT IS IT?
I WONDER WHAT HE WANTS TO DO WITH THAT THING.
YOU AREN'T LISTENING TO ME, ARE YOU?
GEEZ! WHAT ARE YOU GUYS DOING?
YOU'RE ONLY FIGHTING ONE GUY!
SO HURRY UP AND KILL HIM!
REMEMBER YOU'RE FIGHTING FOR MY HONOR!
LET'S PULL OURSELVES TOGETHER, GUYS.
THIS GUY'S REALLY TOUGH.
IT'S TIME TO QUIT PLAYING AROUND.
LET'S GET SERIOUS.

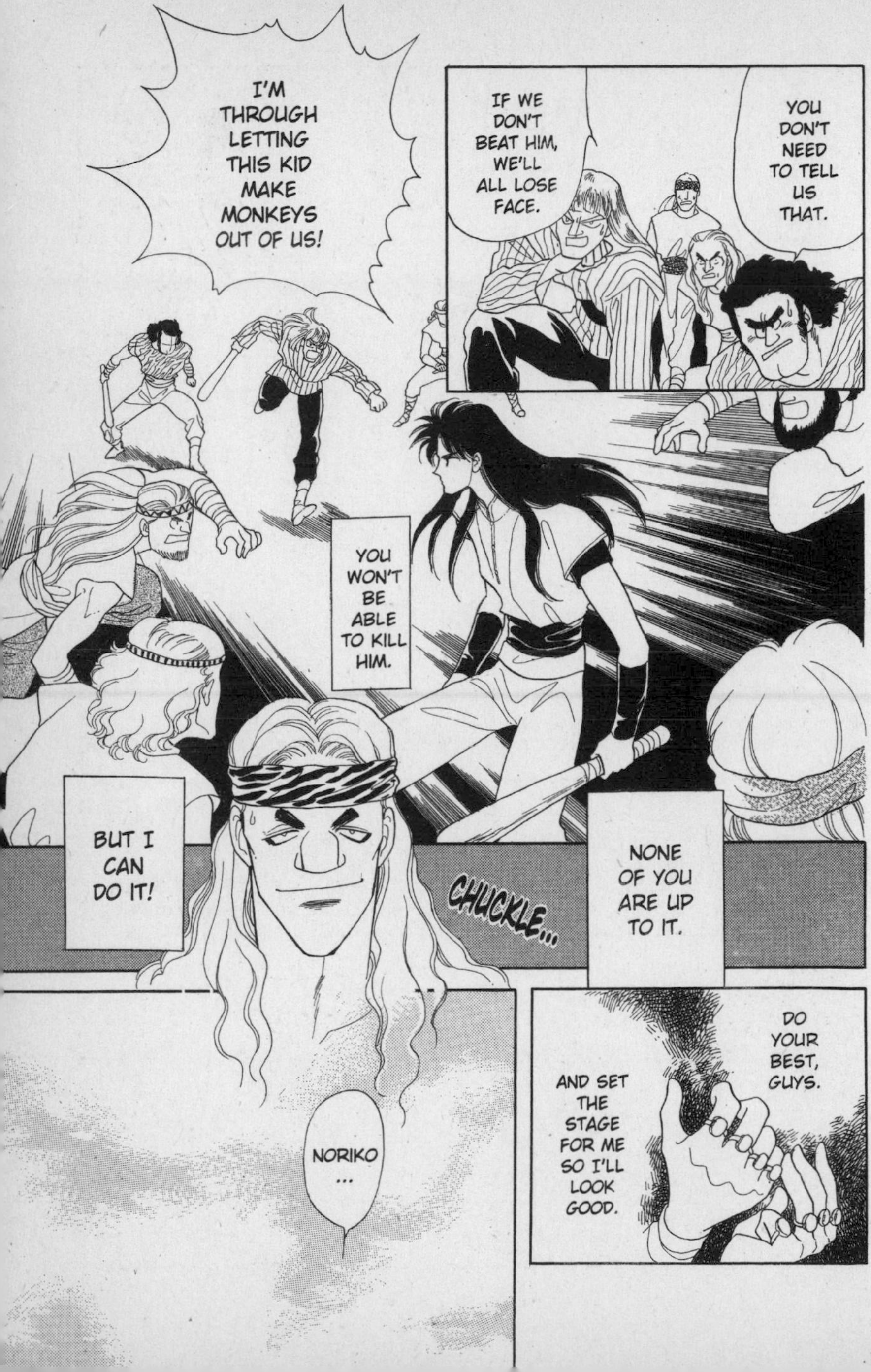
IF WE DON'T BEAT HIM, WE'LL ALL LOSE FACE.
YOU DON'T NEED TO TELL US THAT.
I'M THROUGH LETTING THIS KID MAKE MONKEYS OUT OF US!
YOU WON'T BE ABLE TO KILL HIM.
NONE OF YOU ARE UP TO IT.
CHUCKLE...
BUT I CAN DO IT!
DO YOUR BEST, GUYS.
AND SET THE STAGE FOR ME SO I'LL LOOK GOOD.
NORIKO ...

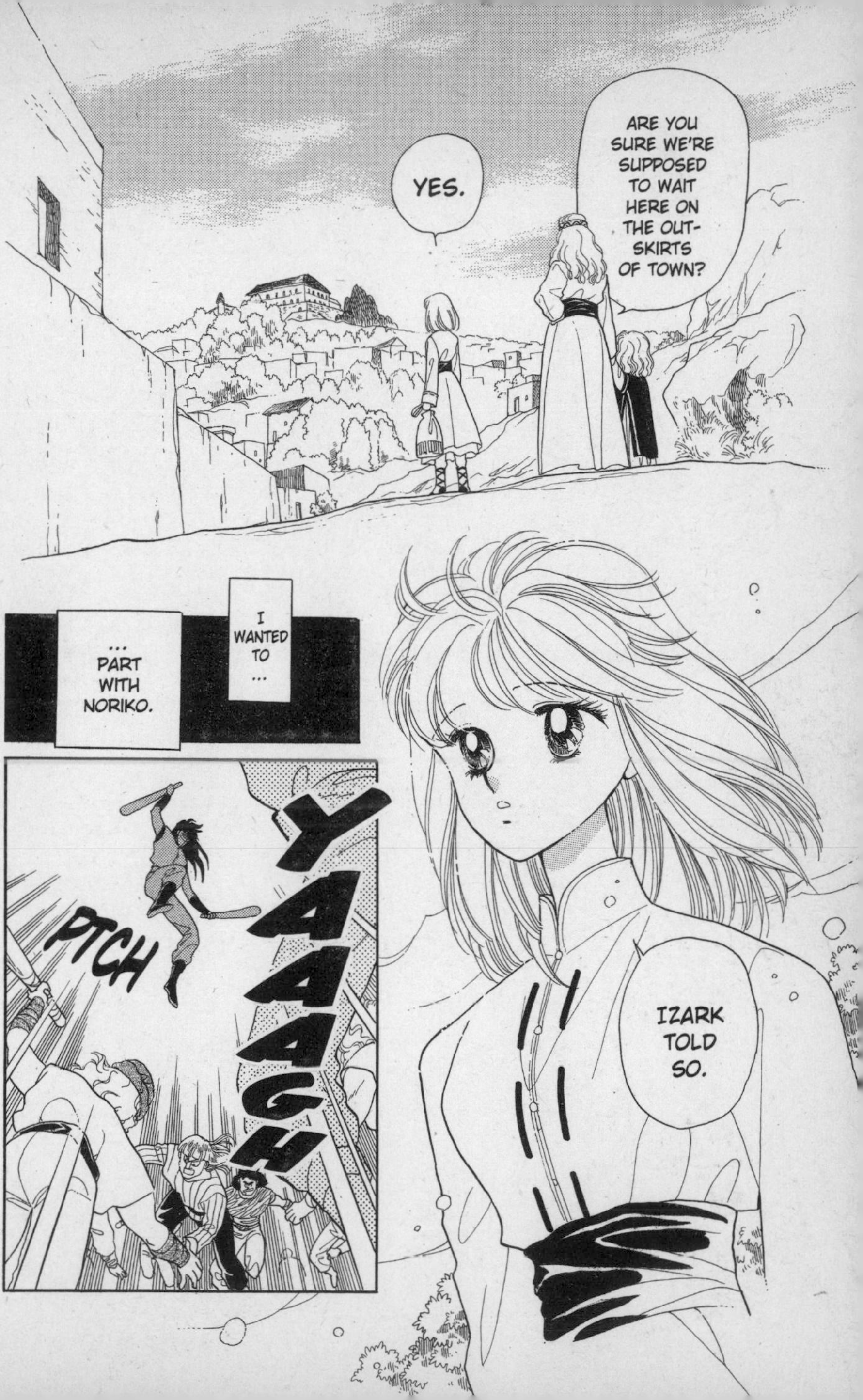
ARE YOU SURE WE'RE SUPPOSED TO WAIT HERE ON THE OUT-SKIRTS OF TOWN?
YES.
IZARK TOLD SO.
I WANTED TO ...
... PART WITH NORIKO.
YAAAAGH
PTCH

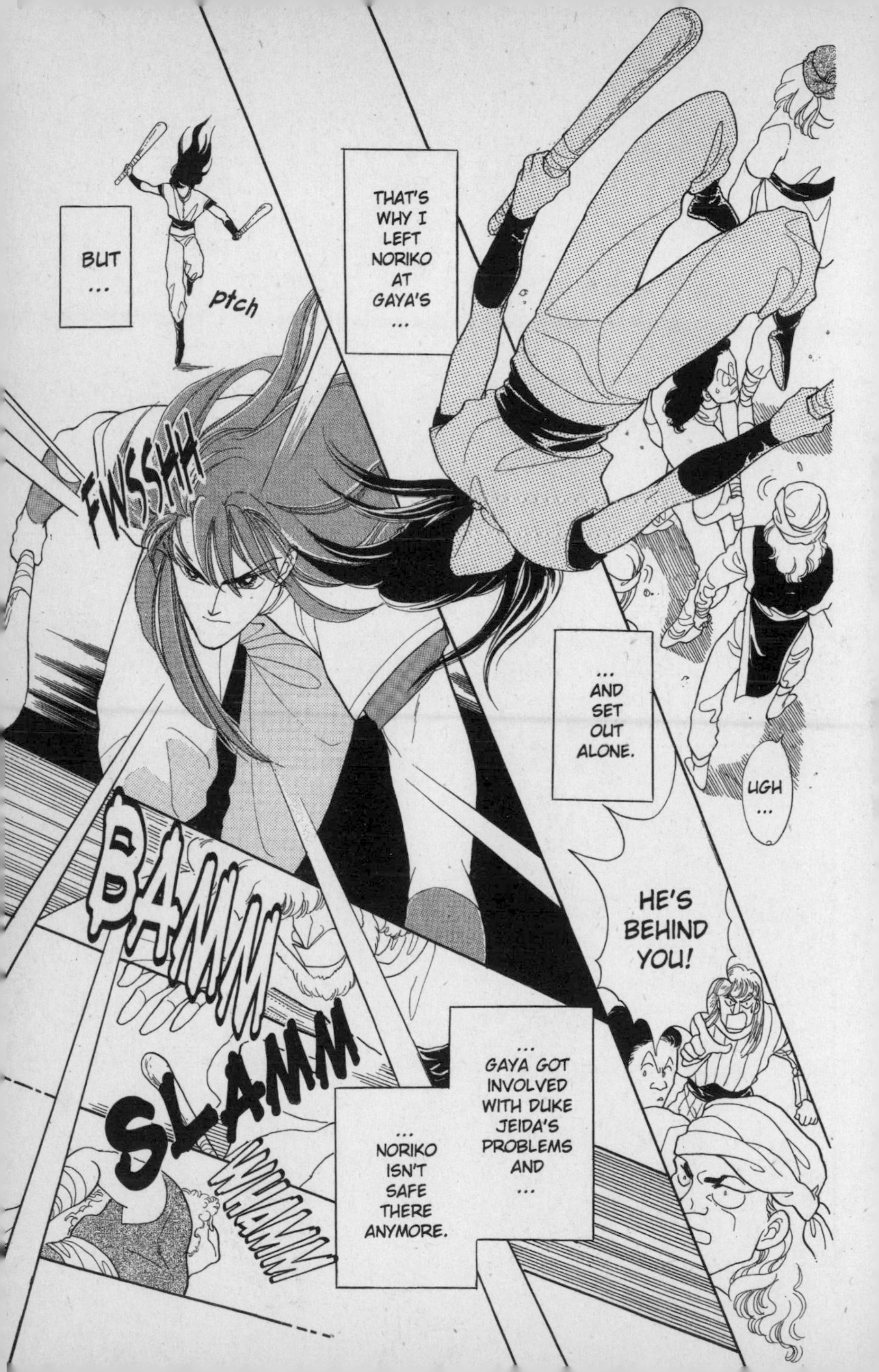
THAT'S WHY I LEFT NORIKO AT GAYA'S ...
... AND SET OUT ALONE.
UGH ...
BUT ...
ptch
FWSSHH
HE'S BEHIND YOU!
... GAYA GOT INVOLVED WITH DUKE JEIDA'S PROBLEMS AND ...
... NORIKO ISN'T SAFE THERE ANYMORE.
BAMM
SLAMM
WHAMM

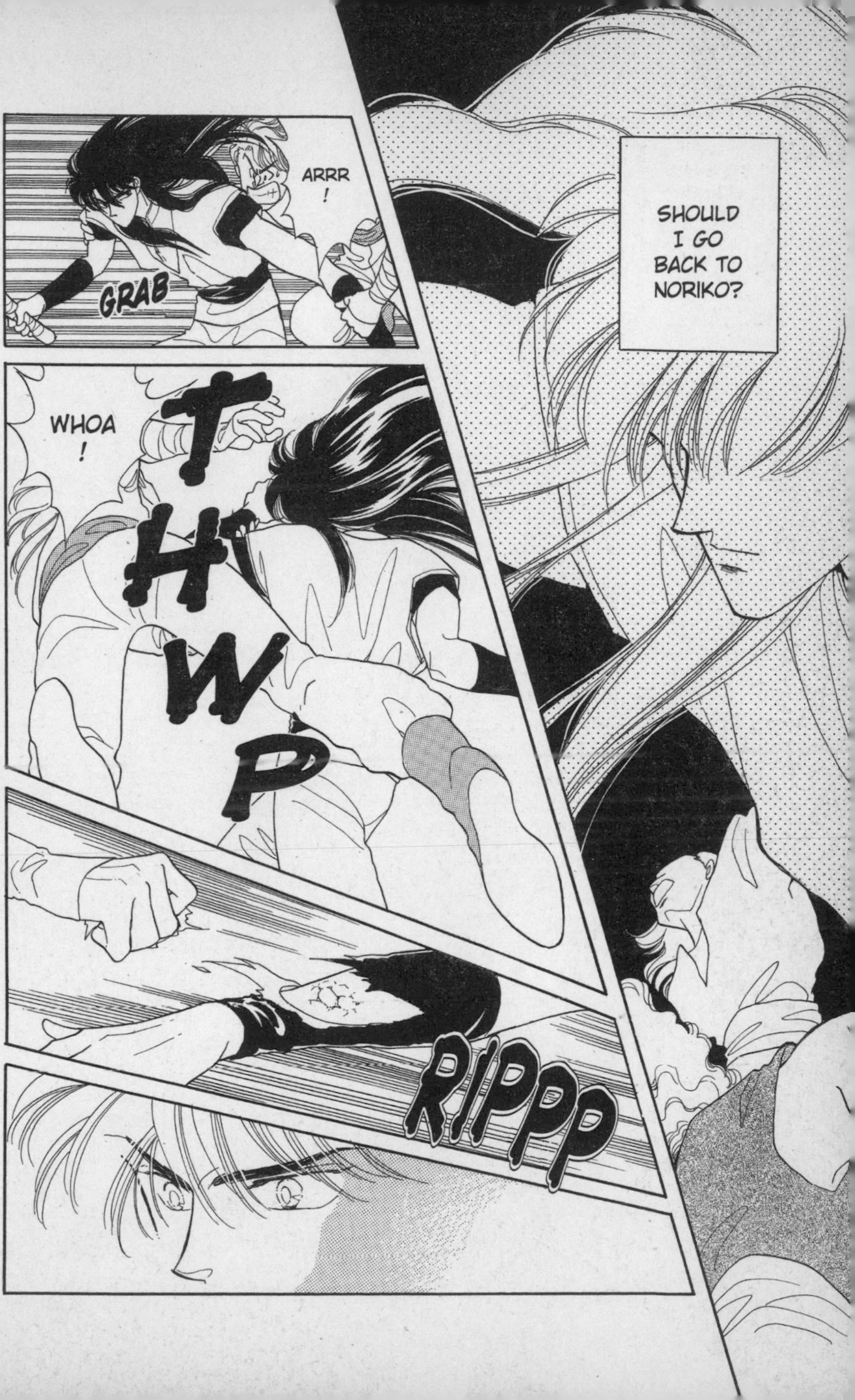
SHOULD I GO BACK TO NORIKO?
ARRR!
GRAB
WHOA!
THWP
RIPPP

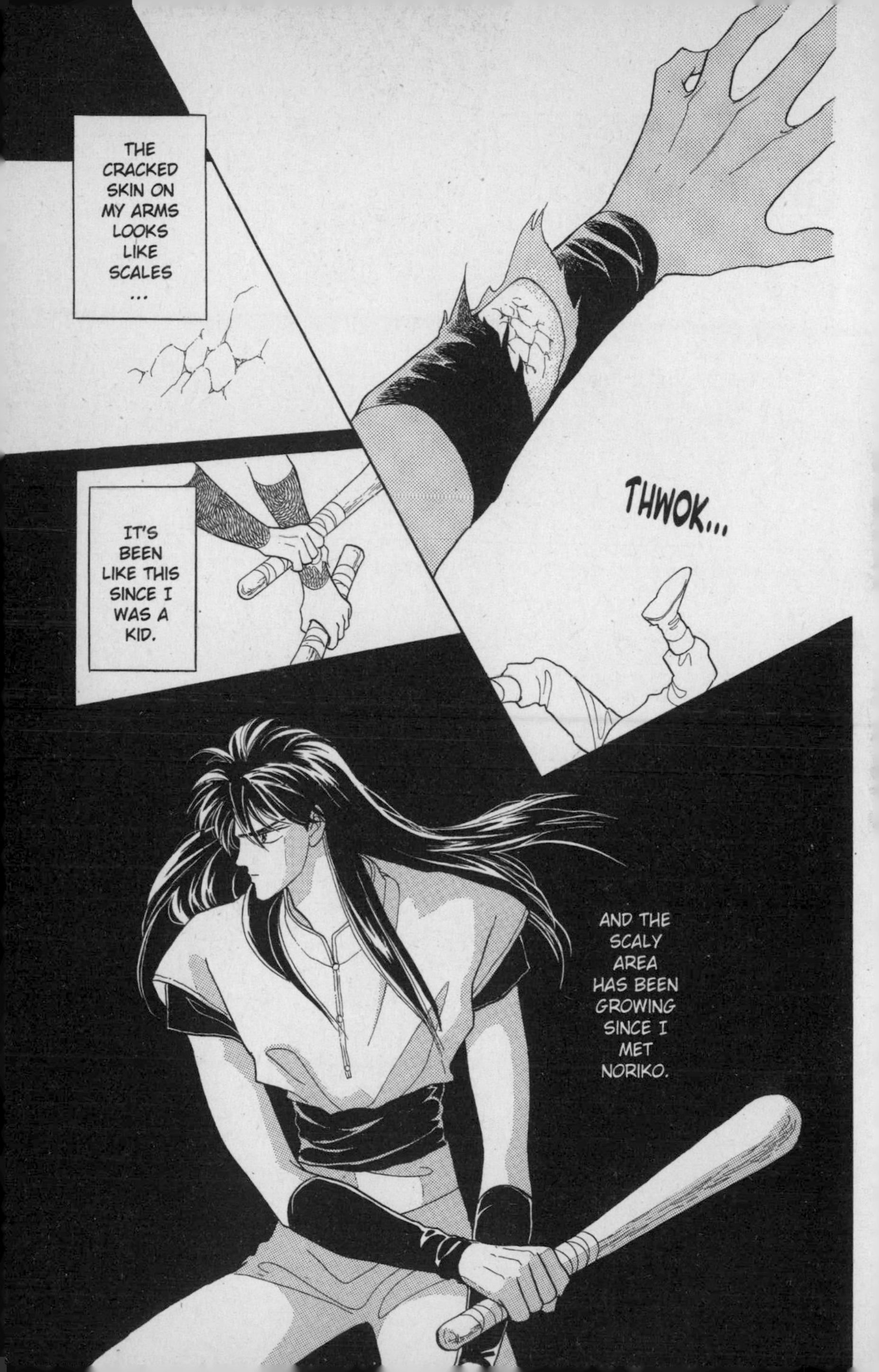
THE CRACKED SKIN ON MY ARMS LOOKS LIKE SCALES ...
THWOK...
IT'S BEEN LIKE THIS SINCE I WAS A KID.
AND THE SCALY AREA HAS BEEN GROWING SINCE I MET NORIKO.

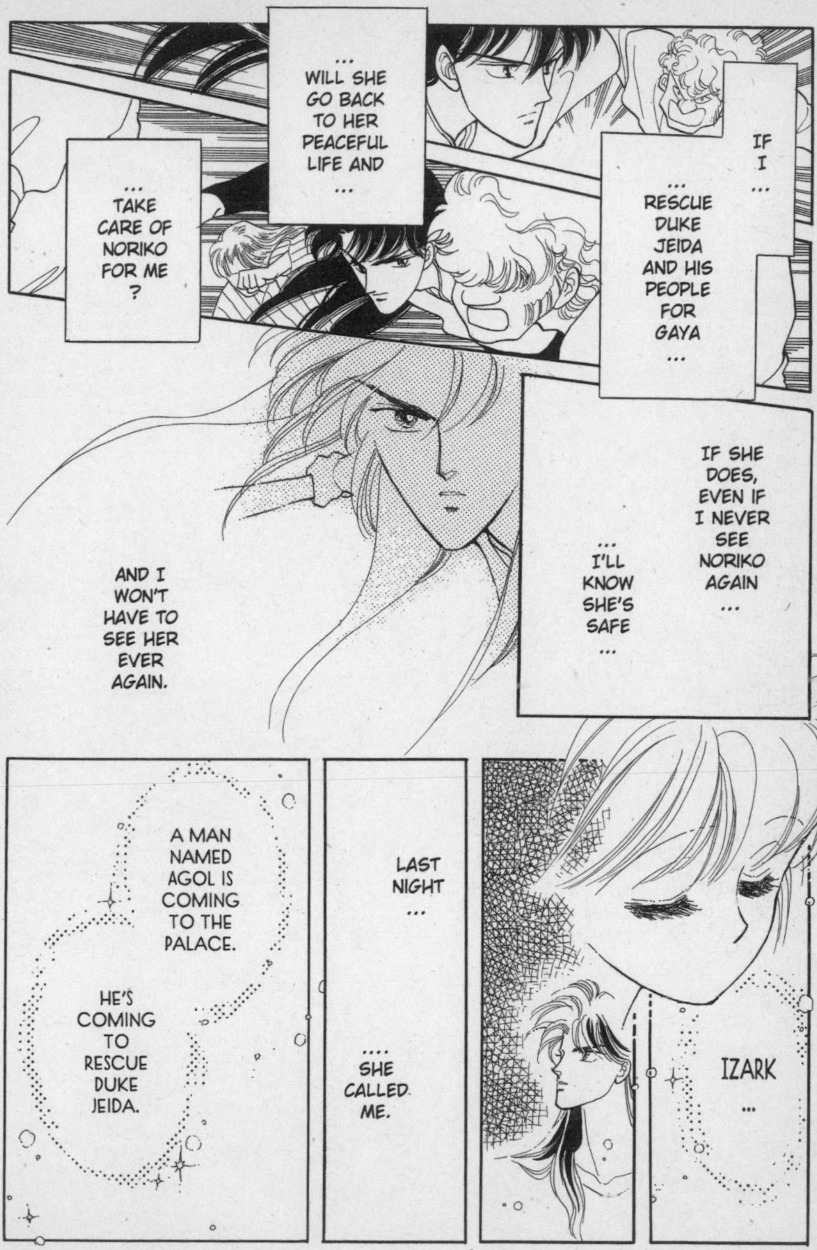
IF I ...
... RESCUE DUKE JEIDA AND HIS PEOPLE FOR GAYA ...
... WILL SHE GO BACK TO HER PEACEFUL LIFE AND ...
... TAKE CARE OF NORIKO FOR ME ?
IF SHE DOES, EVEN IF I NEVER SEE NORIKO AGAIN ...
... I'LL KNOW SHE'S SAFE ...
AND I WON'T HAVE TO SEE HER EVER AGAIN.
IZARK ...
LAST NIGHT ...
.... SHE CALLED ME.
A MAN NAMED AGOL IS COMING TO THE PALACE.
HE'S COMING TO RESCUE DUKE JEIDA.

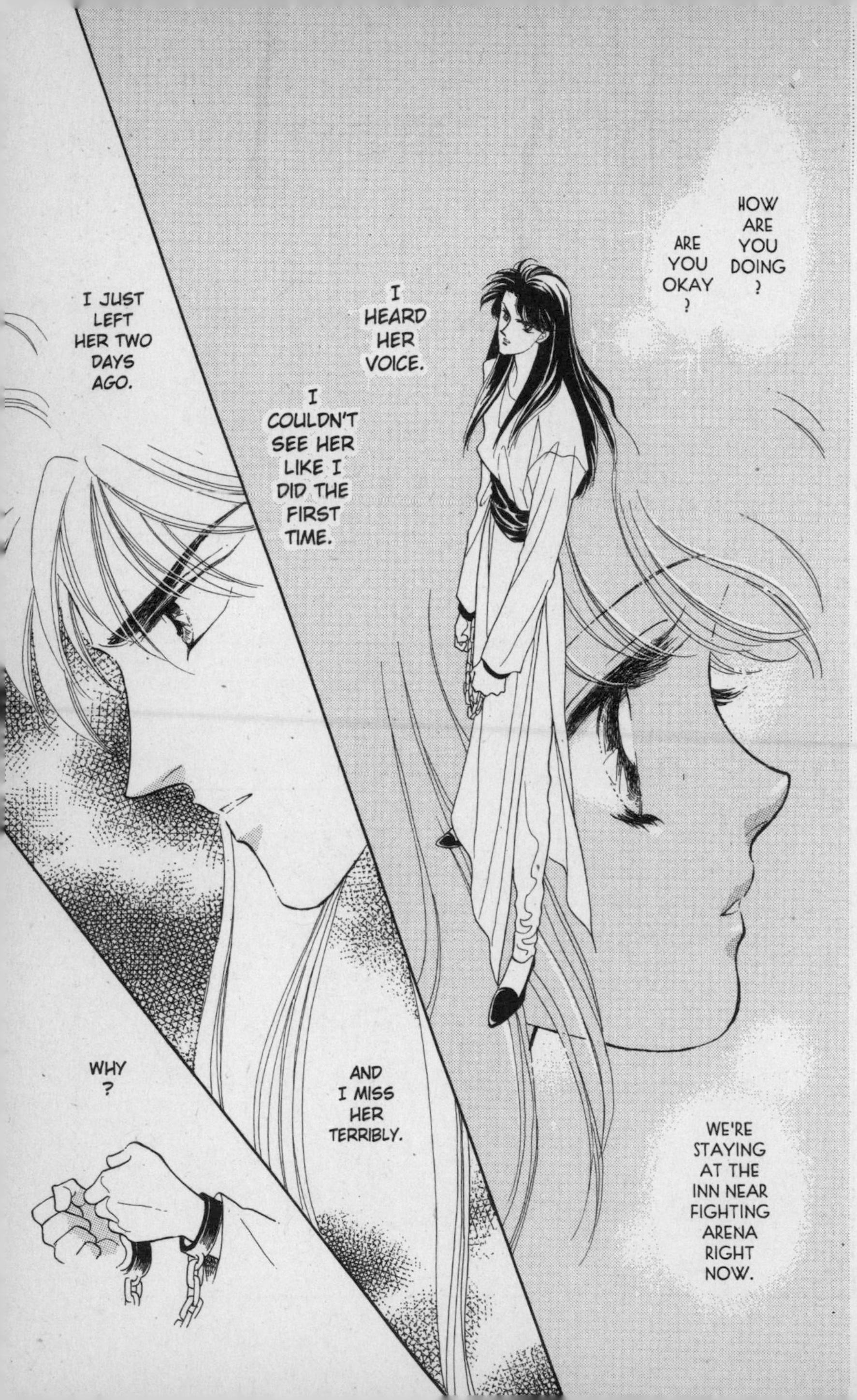
HOW ARE YOU DOING ?
ARE YOU OKAY ?
I HEARD HER VOICE.
I COULDN'T SEE HER LIKE I DID THE FIRST TIME.
WE'RE STAYING AT THE INN NEAR FIGHTING ARENA RIGHT NOW.
AND I MISS HER TERRIBLY.
I JUST LEFT HER TWO DAYS AGO.
WHY ?

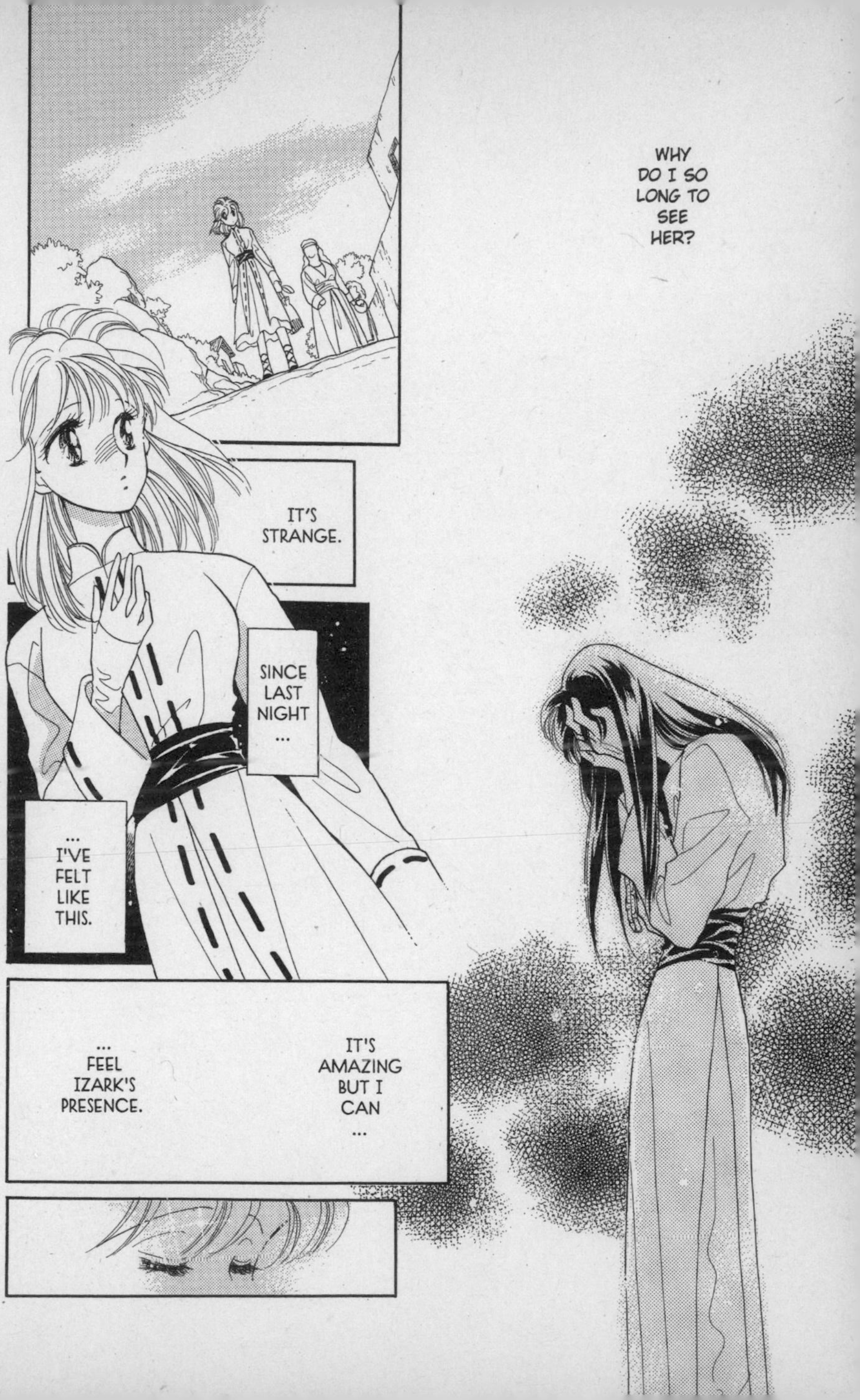
WHY DO I SO LONG TO SEE HER?
IT'S STRANGE.
SINCE LAST NIGHT ...
... I'VE FELT LIKE THIS.
IT'S AMAZING BUT I CAN ...
... FEEL IZARK'S PRESENCE.

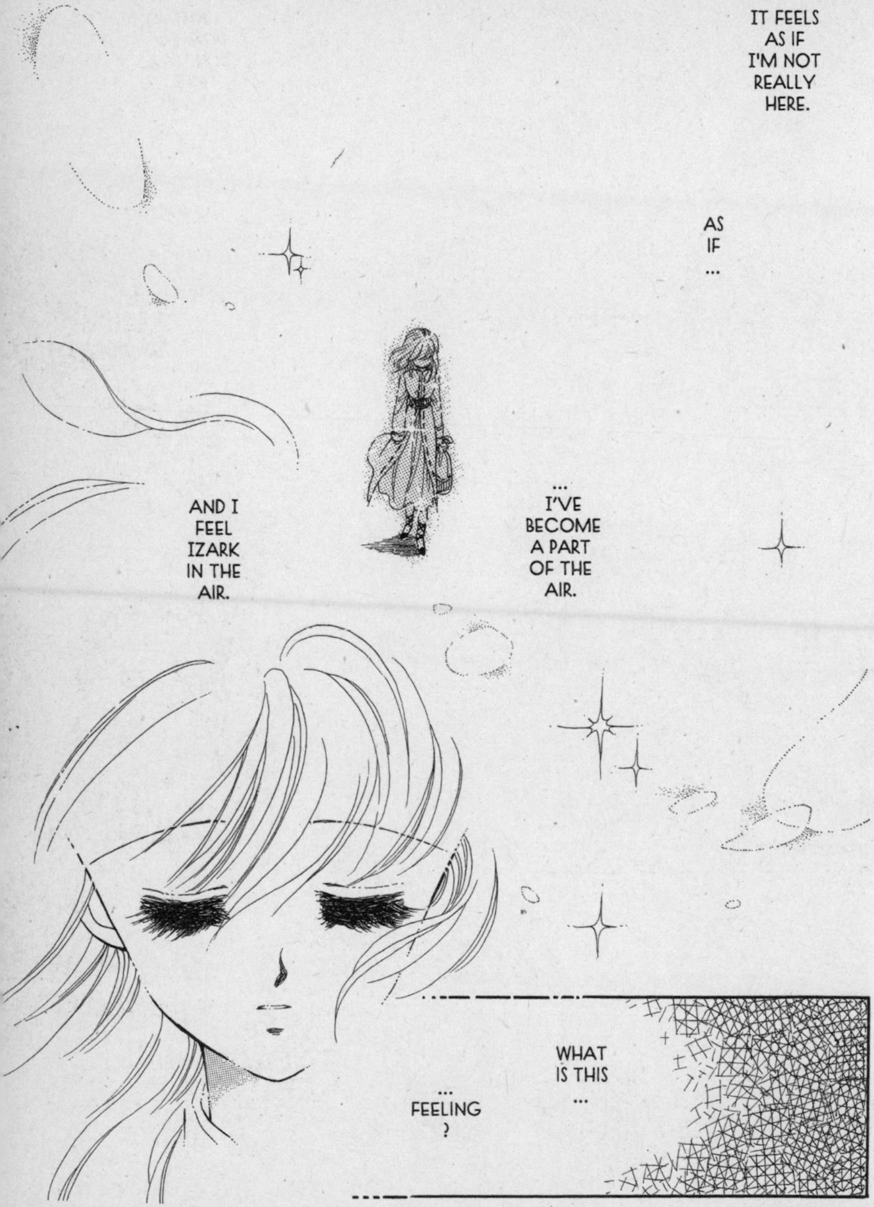
IT FEELS AS IF I'M NOT REALLY HERE.
AS IF ...
... I'VE BECOME A PART OF THE AIR.
AND I FEEL IZARK IN THE AIR.
WHAT IS THIS ...
... FEELING ?

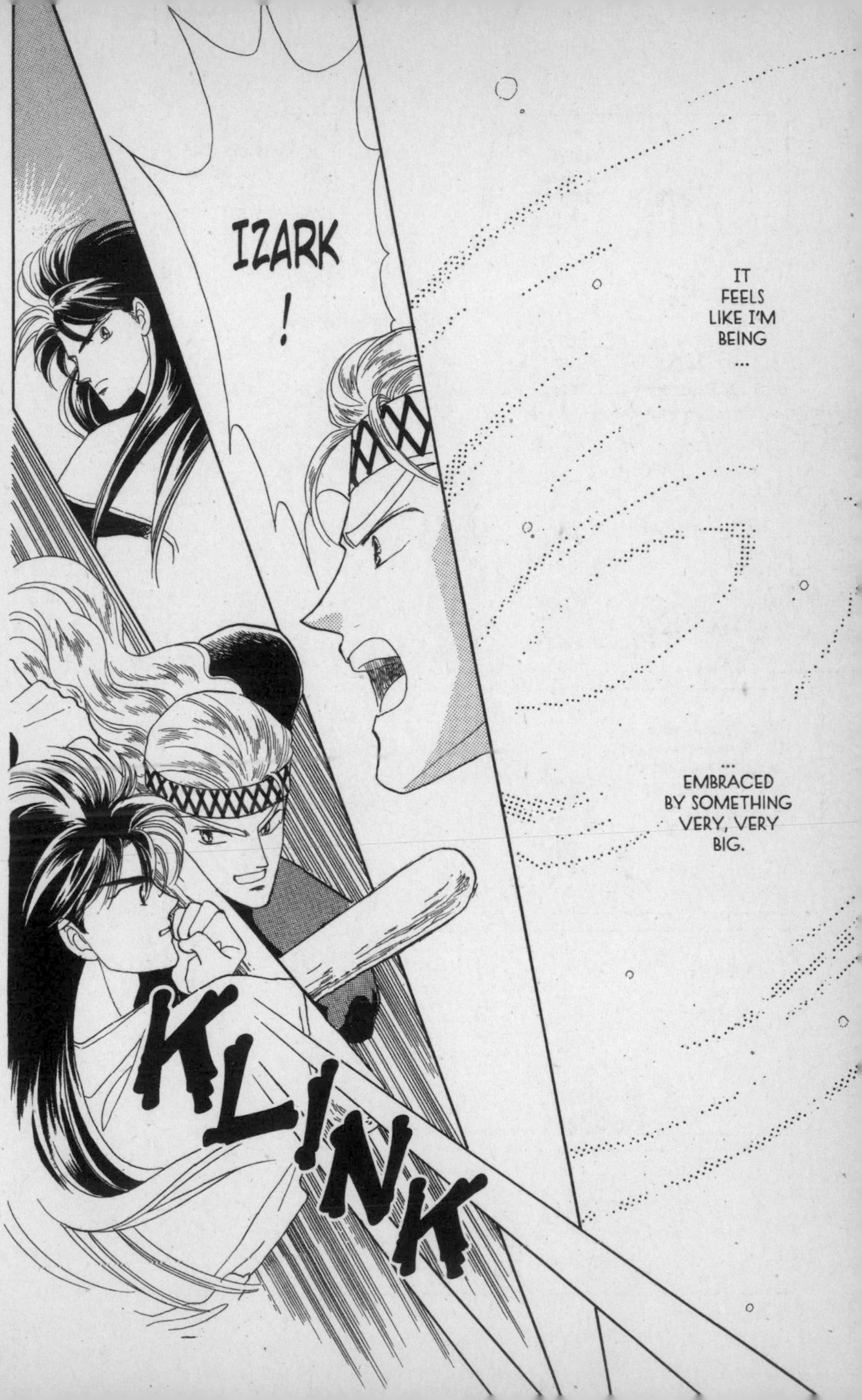
IT FEELS LIKE I'M BEING ...
... EMBRACED BY SOMETHING VERY, VERY BIG.
IZARK !
KLINK

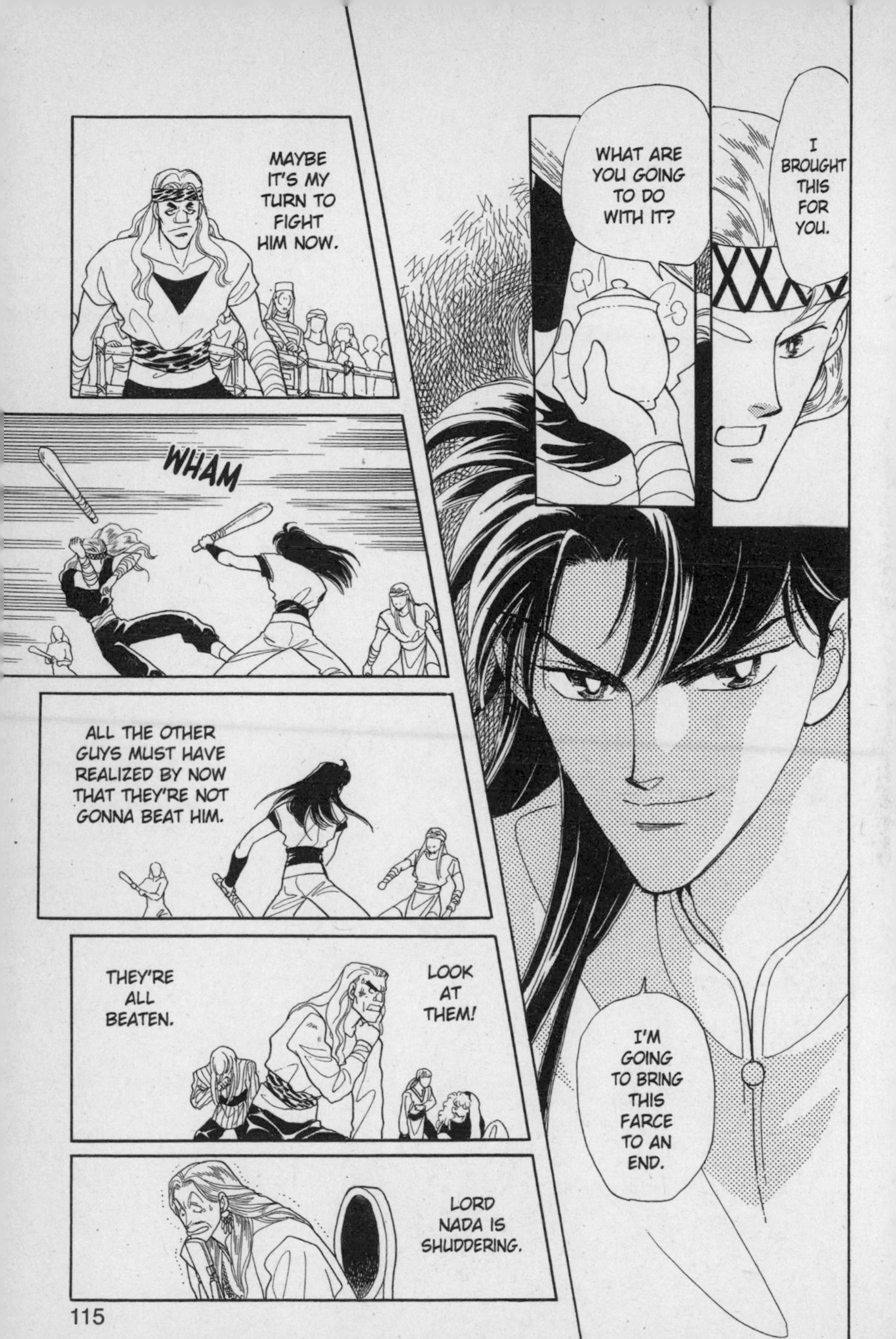
I BROUGHT THIS FOR YOU.
WHAT ARE YOU GOING TO DO WITH IT?
I'M GOING TO BRING THIS FARCE TO AN END.
MAYBE IT'S MY TURN TO FIGHT HIM NOW.
WHAM
ALL THE OTHER GUYS MUST HAVE REALIZED BY NOW THAT THEY'RE NOT GONNA BEAT HIM.
LOOK AT THEM!
THEY'RE ALL BEATEN.
LORD NADA IS SHUDDERING.

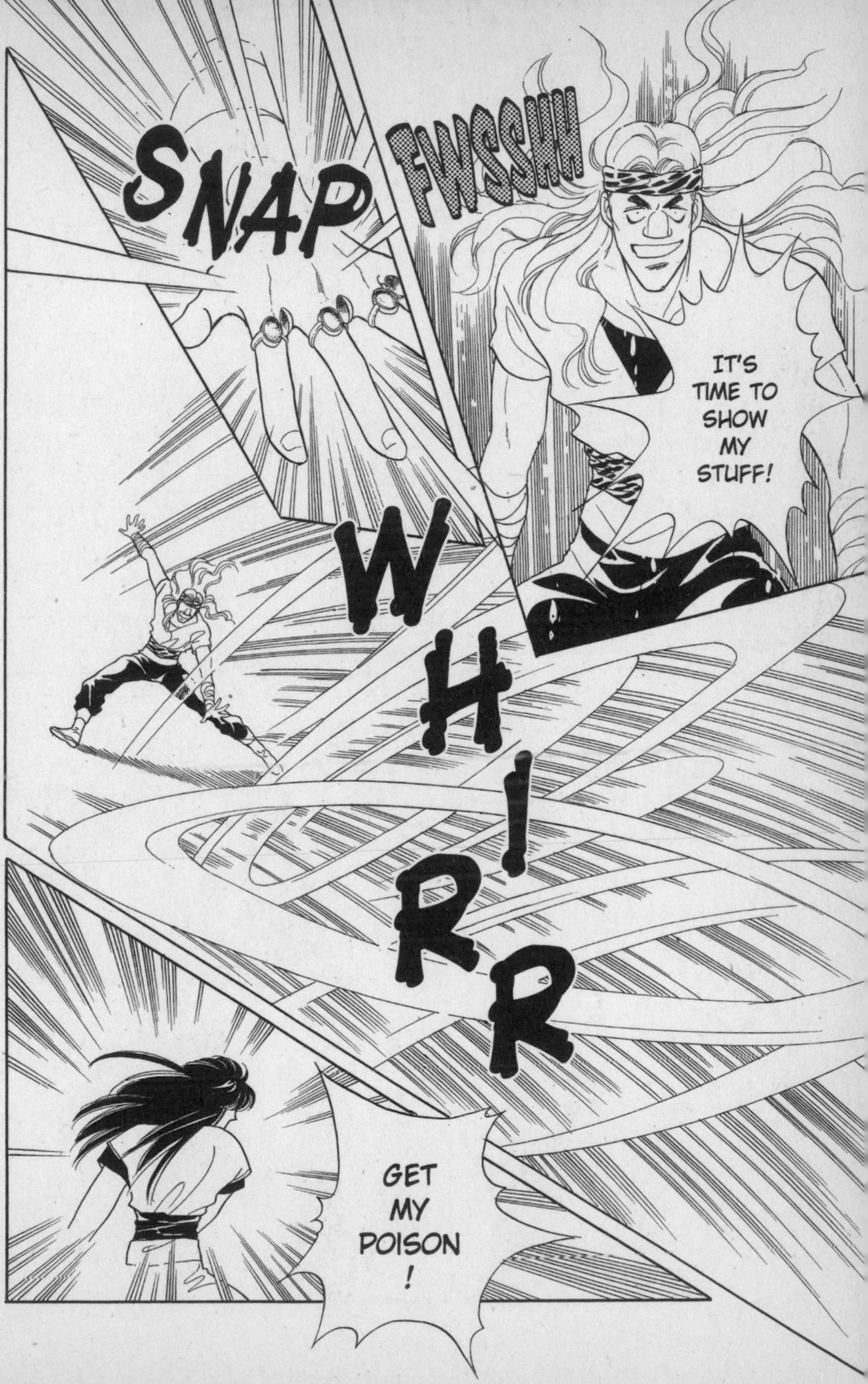
FWSSHH
IT'S TIME TO SHOW MY STUFF!
SNAP
WHIRR
GET MY POISON!

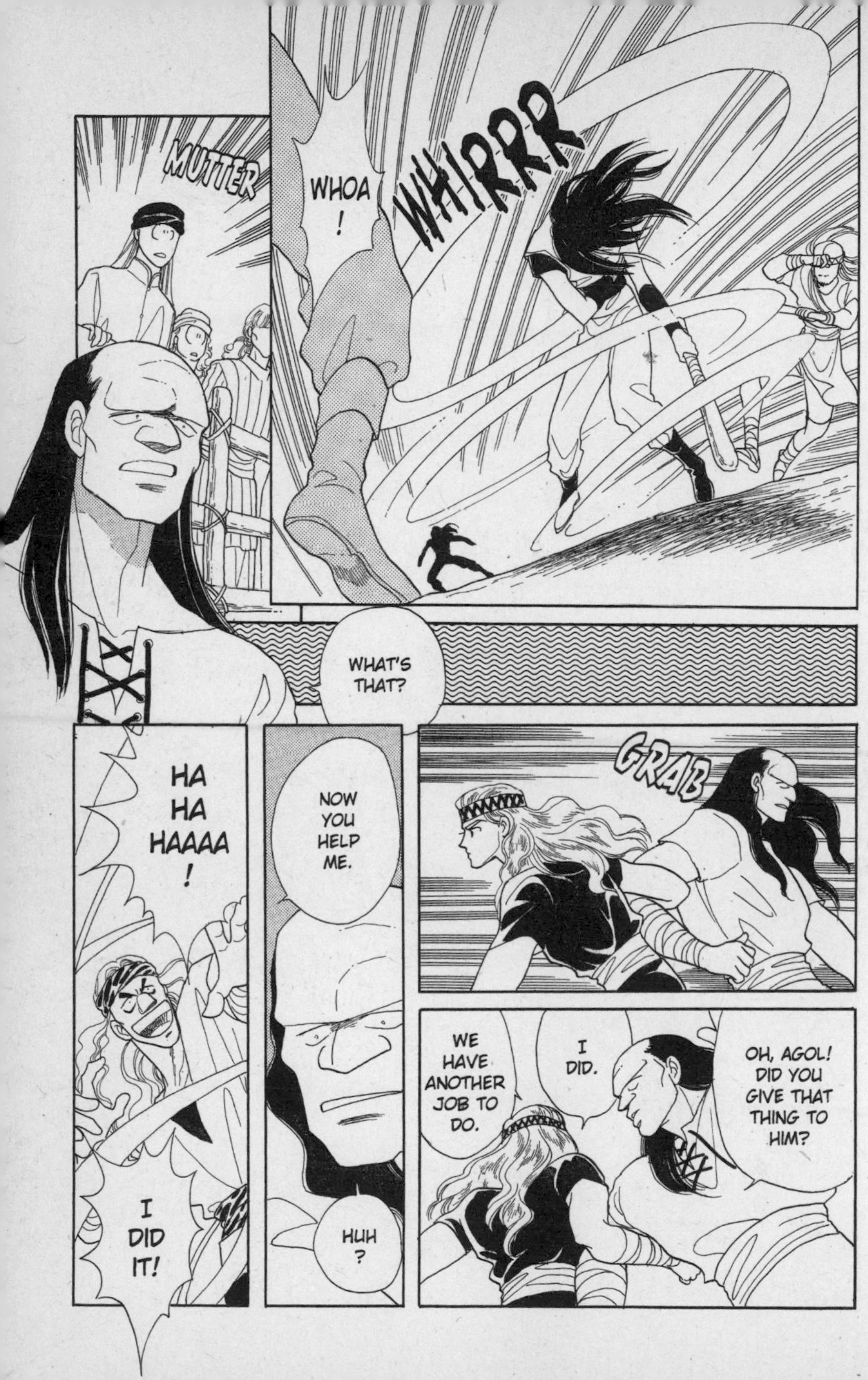
WHIRRR
WHOA!
MUTTER
WHAT'S THAT?
GRAB
OH, AGOL! DID YOU GIVE THAT THING TO HIM?
I DID.
WE HAVE ANOTHER JOB TO DO.
NOW YOU HELP ME.
HUH?
HA HA HAAAA!
I DID IT!

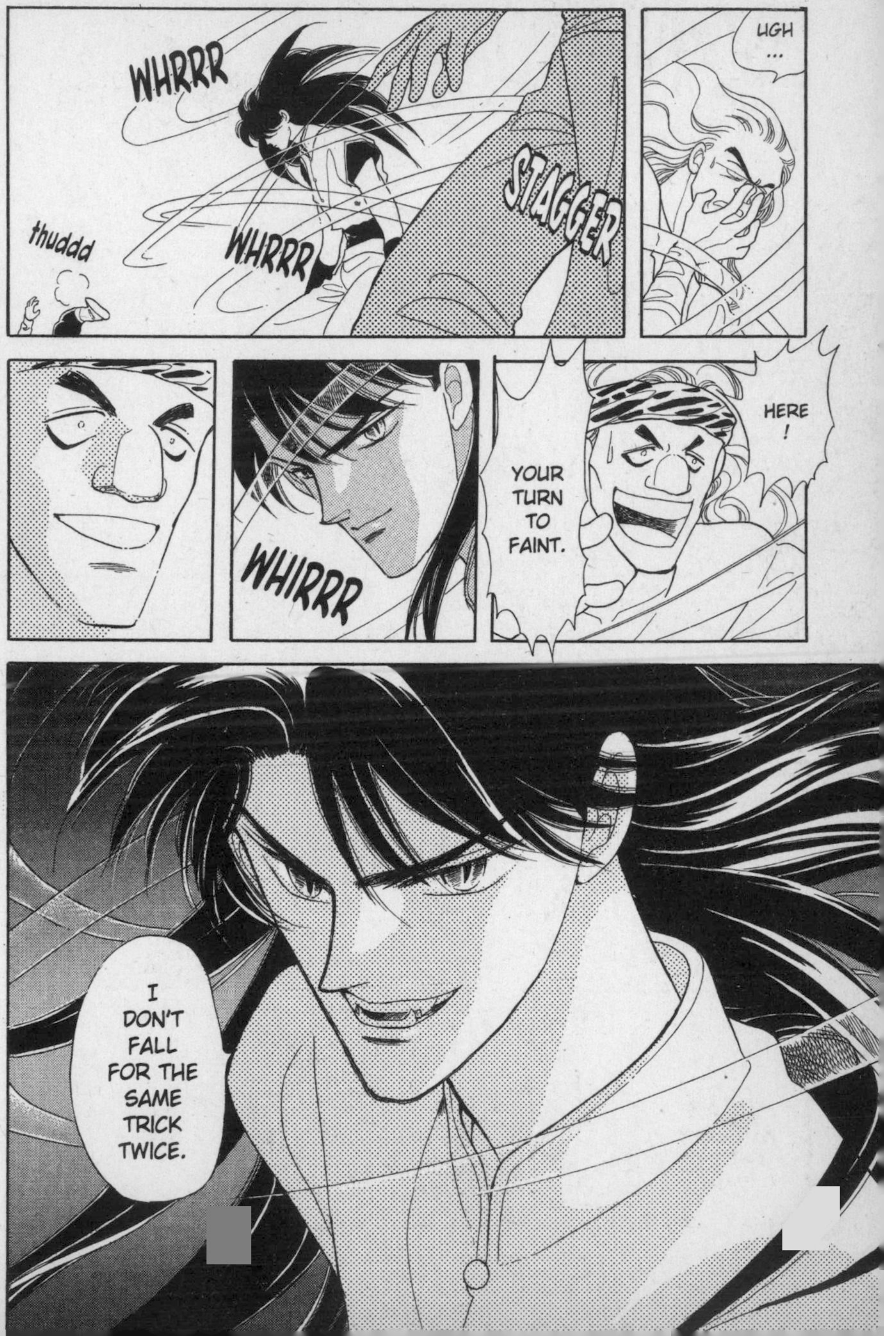
UGH ...
STAGGER
WHRRR
WHRRR
thuddd
HERE!
YOUR TURN TO FAINT.
WHIRRR
I DON'T FALL FOR THE SAME TRICK TWICE.

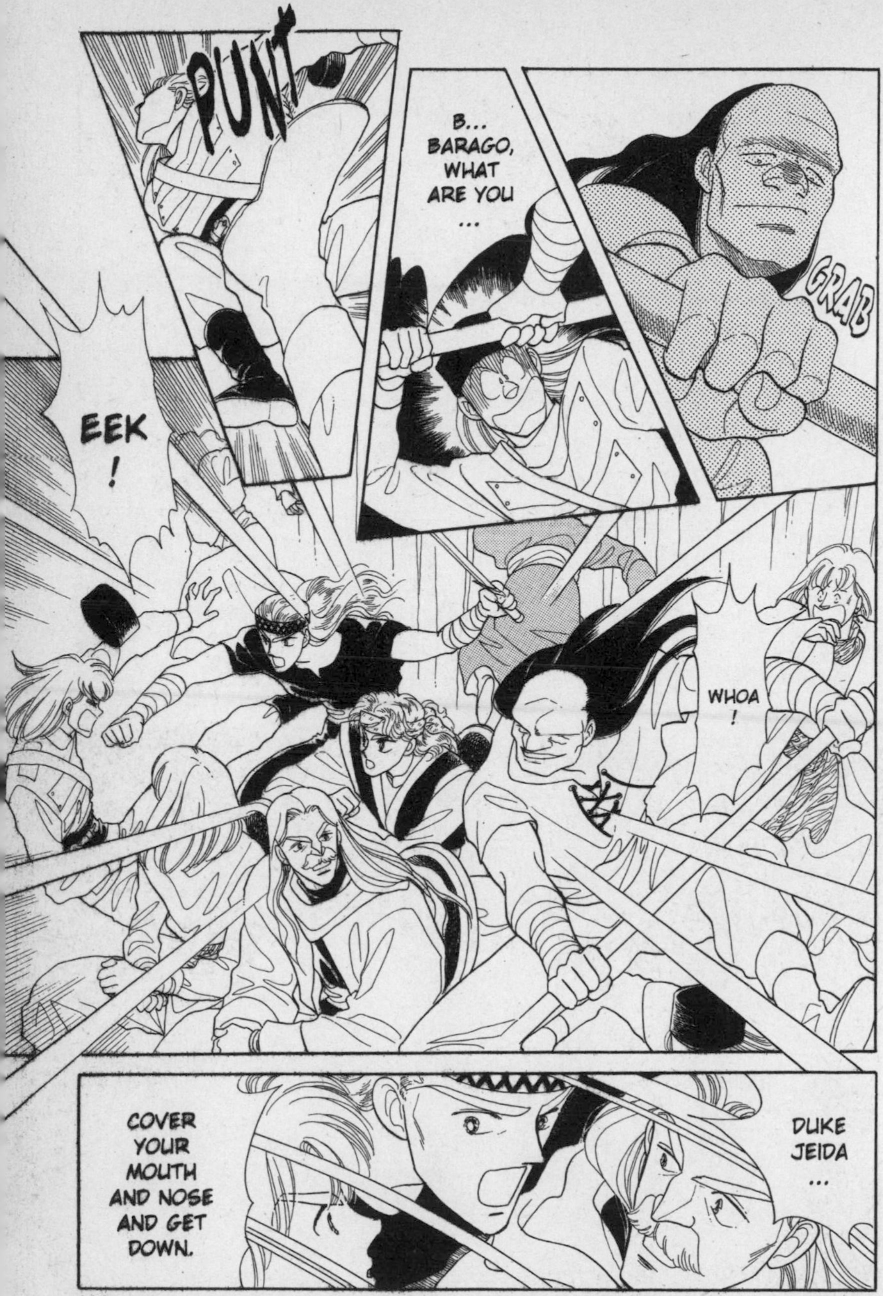
GRAB
B... BARAGO, WHAT ARE YOU ...
PUNT
WHOA!
EEK!
DUKE JEIDA ...
COVER YOUR MOUTH AND NOSE AND GET DOWN.

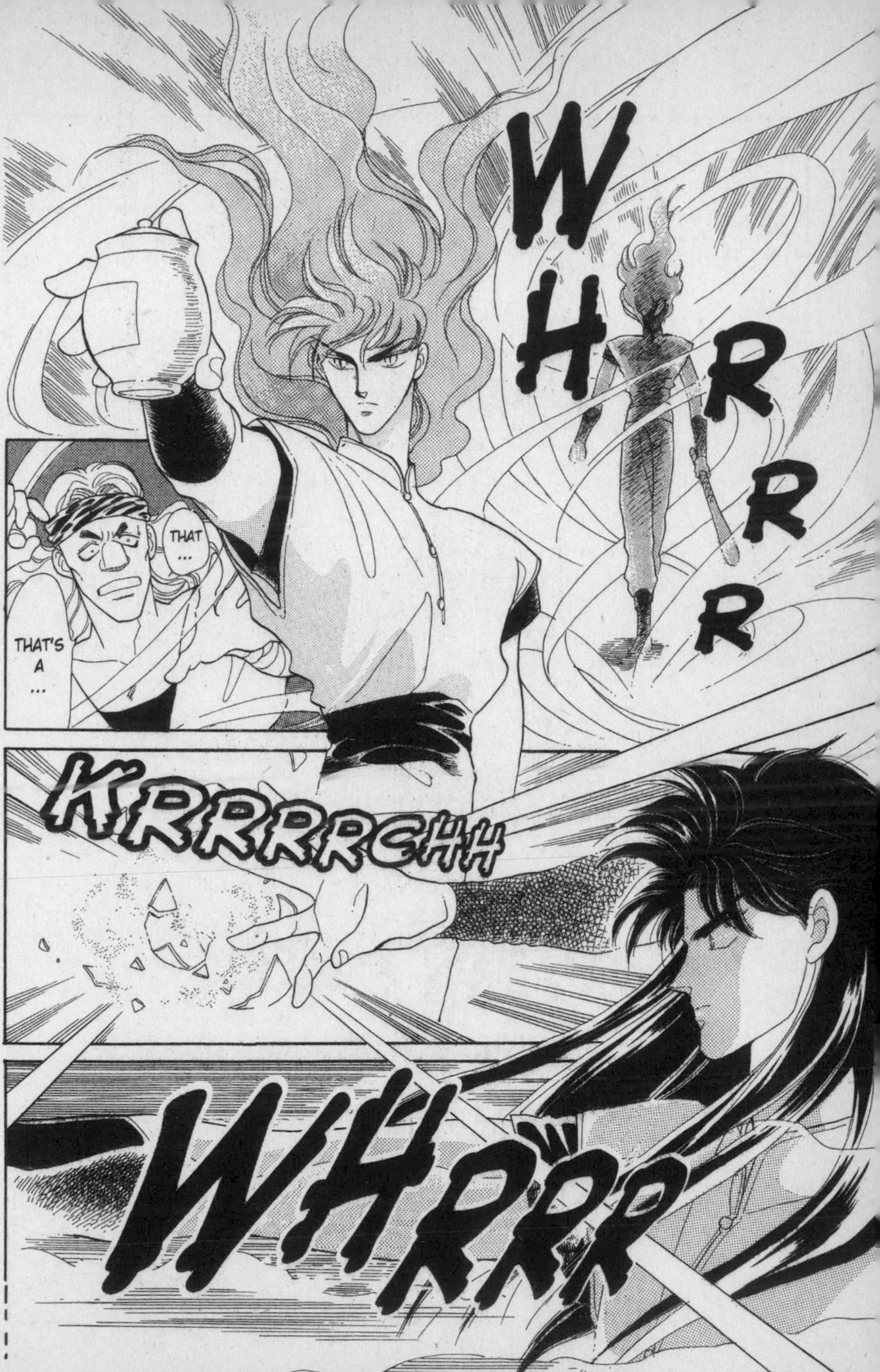
WHIRRR
THAT ...
THAT'S A ...
KRRRRRCHH
WHRRR

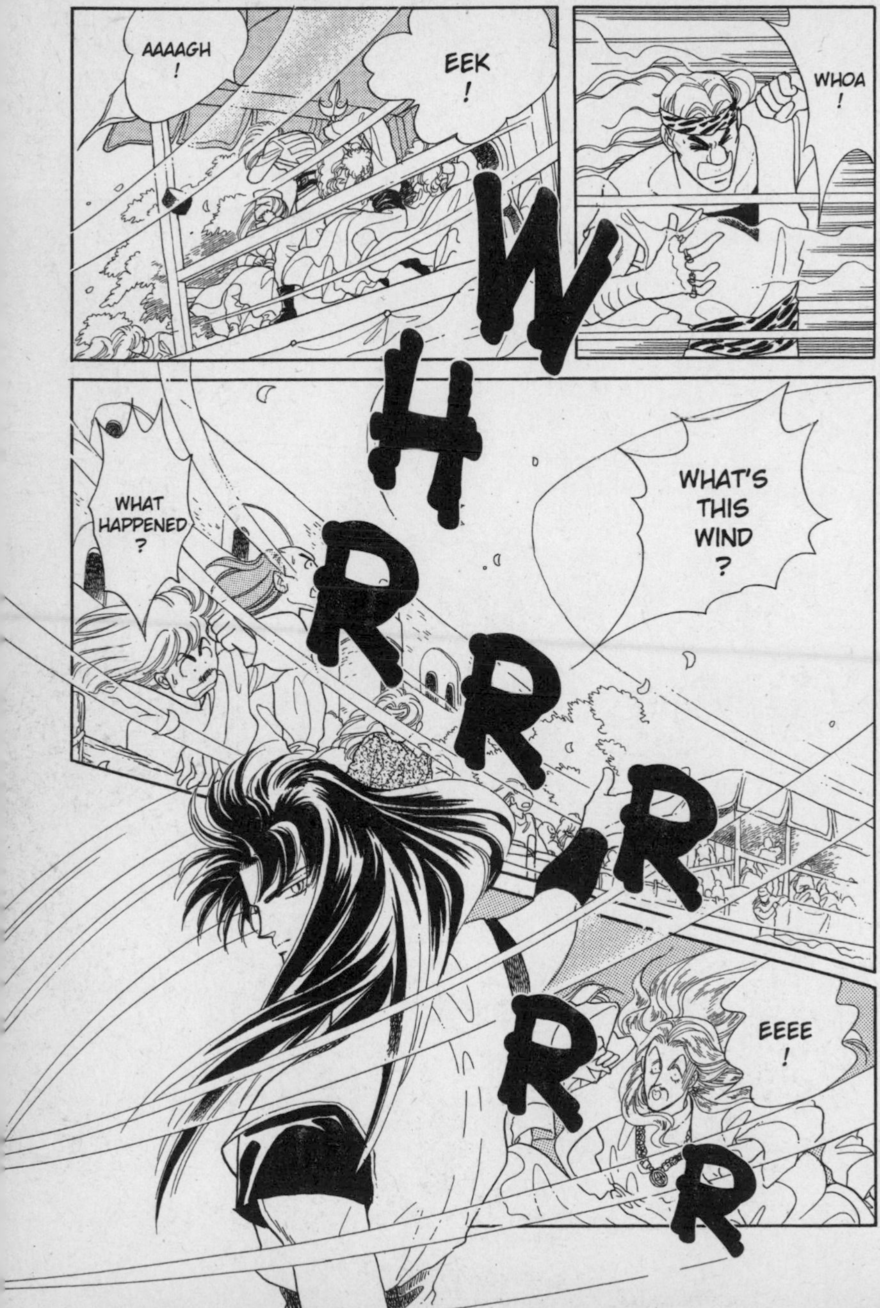
WHOA!
EEK!
AAAAGH!
WHRRRRRR
WHAT'S THIS WIND?
WHAT HAPPENED?
EEEE!

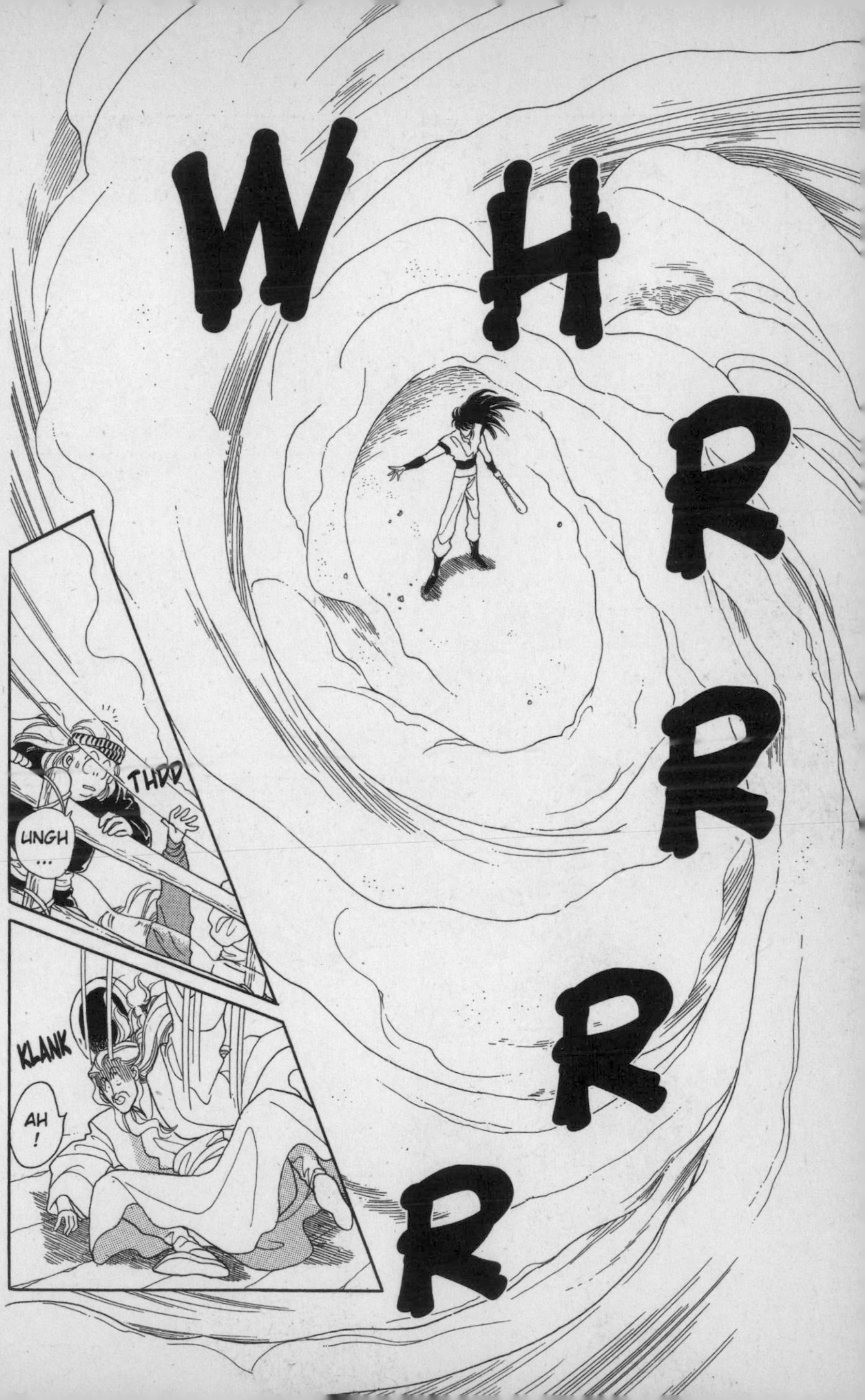
WHRRRR
THDD
UNGH ...
KLANK
AH !

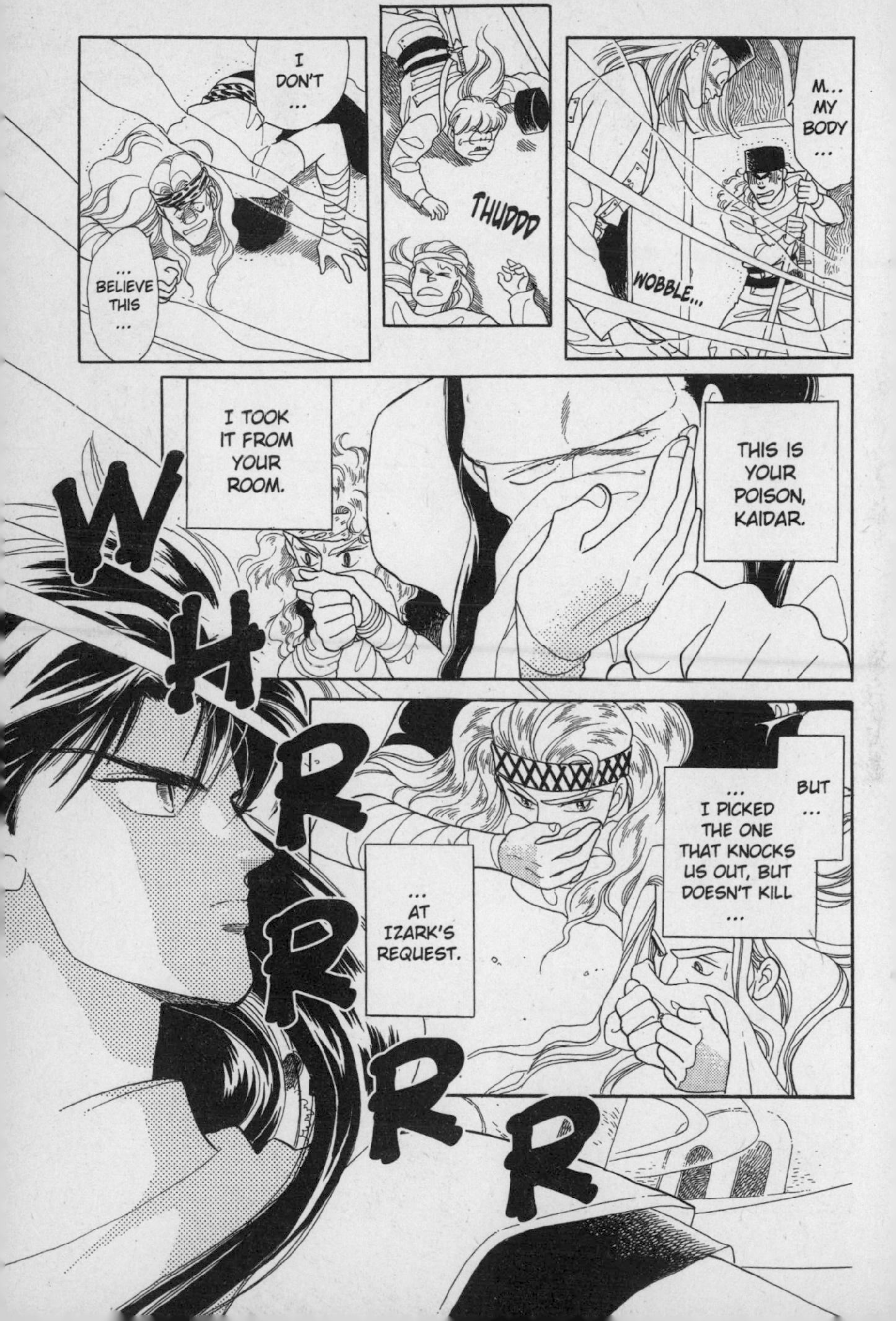
M... MY BODY ...
WOBBLE...
THUDDD
I DON'T ...
... BELIEVE THIS ...
THIS IS YOUR POISON, KAIDAR.
I TOOK IT FROM YOUR ROOM.
BUT ...
... I PICKED THE ONE THAT KNOCKS US OUT, BUT DOESN'T KILL ...
... AT IZARK'S REQUEST.
WHRRRR

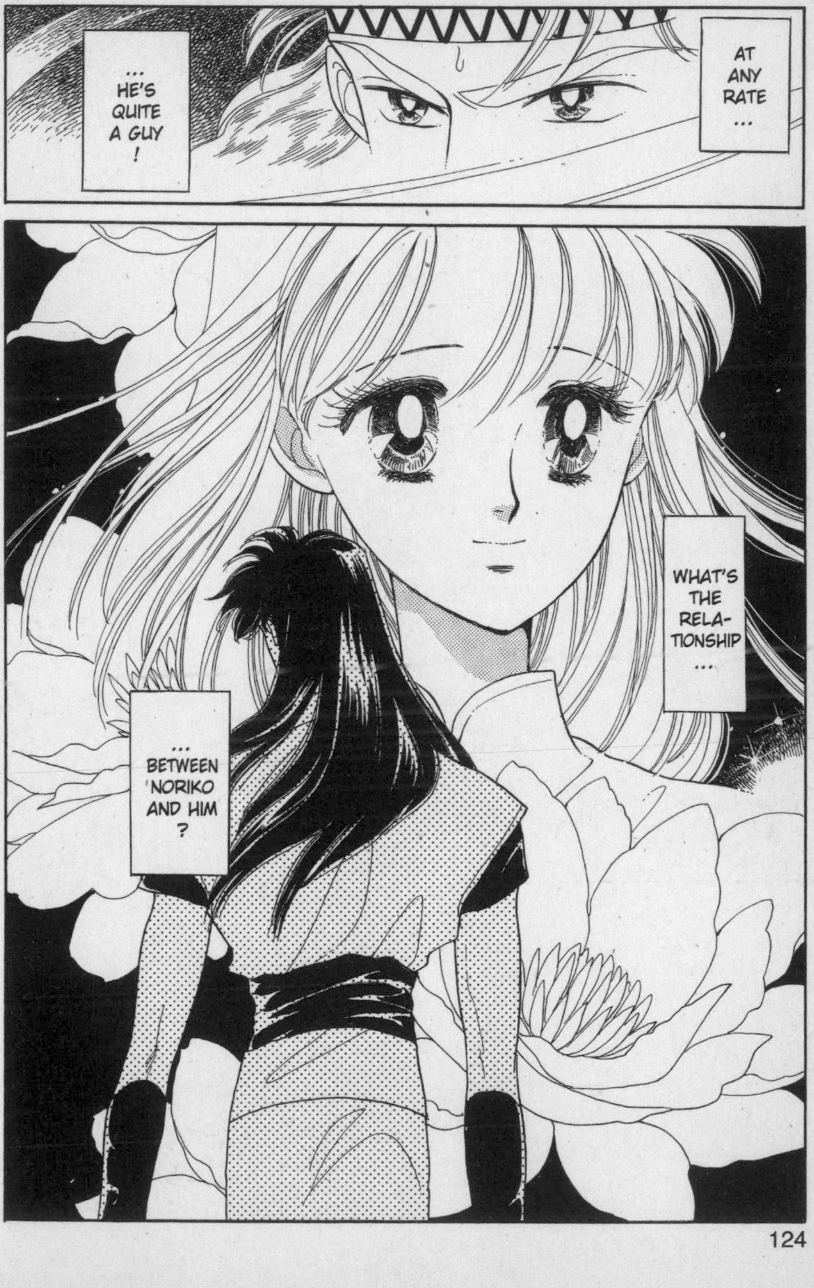
AT ANY RATE ...
... HE'S QUITE A GUY !
WHAT'S THE RELA-TIONSHIP ...
... BETWEEN NORIKO AND HIM ?

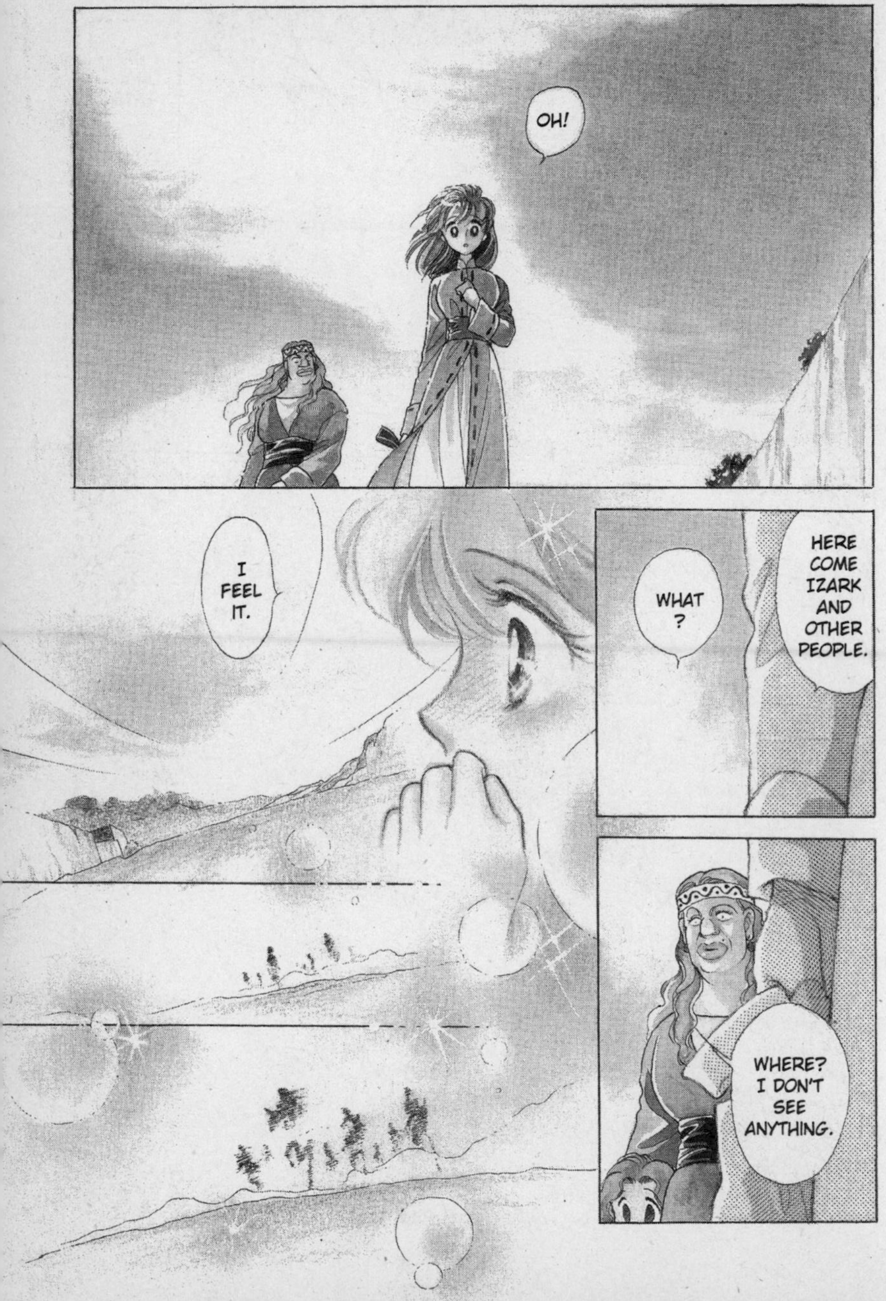
OH!
HERE COME IZARK AND OTHER PEOPLE.
WHAT?
WHERE? I DON'T SEE ANYTHING.
I FEEL IT.

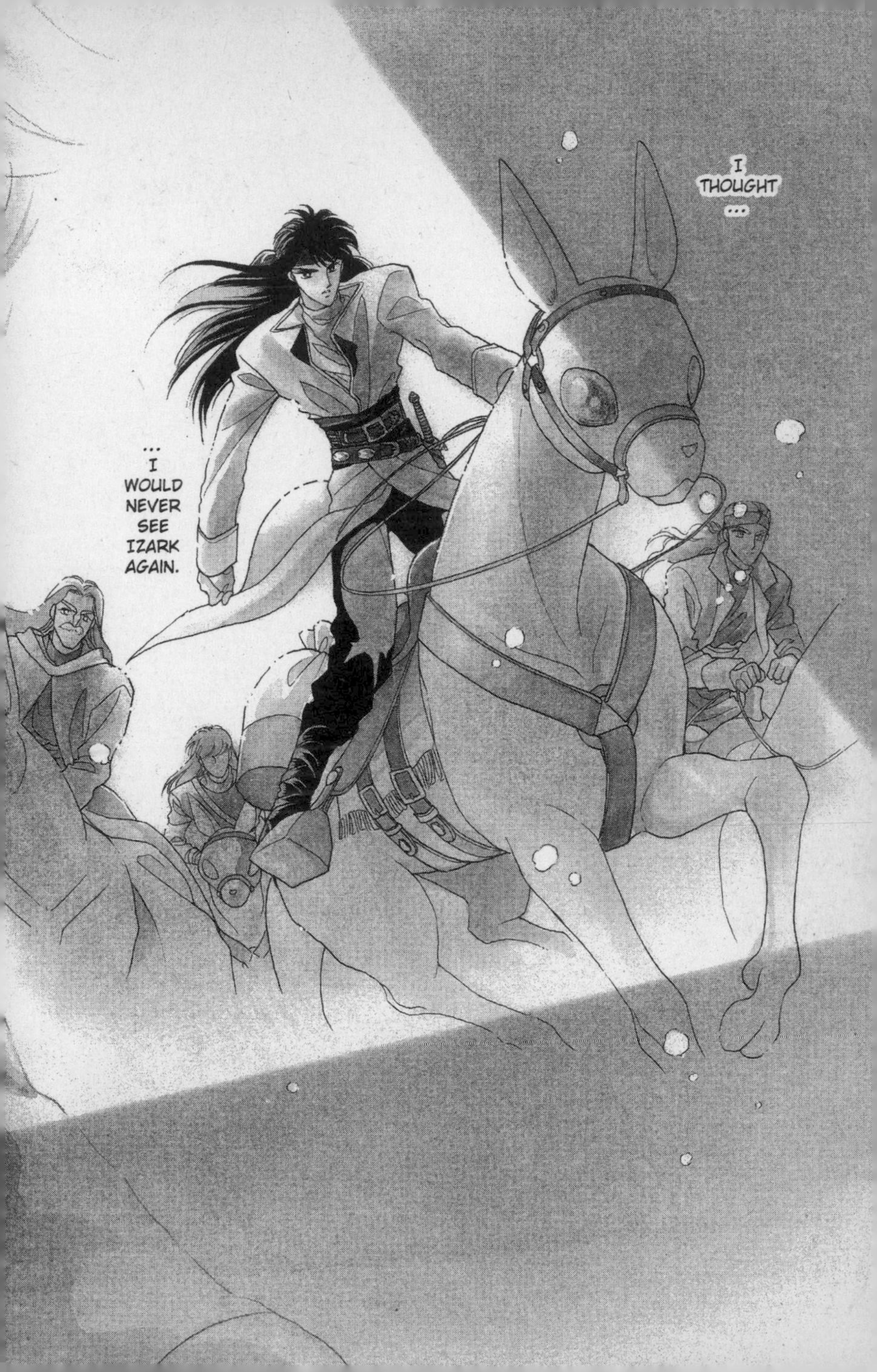
I THOUGHT ...
... I WOULD NEVER SEE IZARK AGAIN.

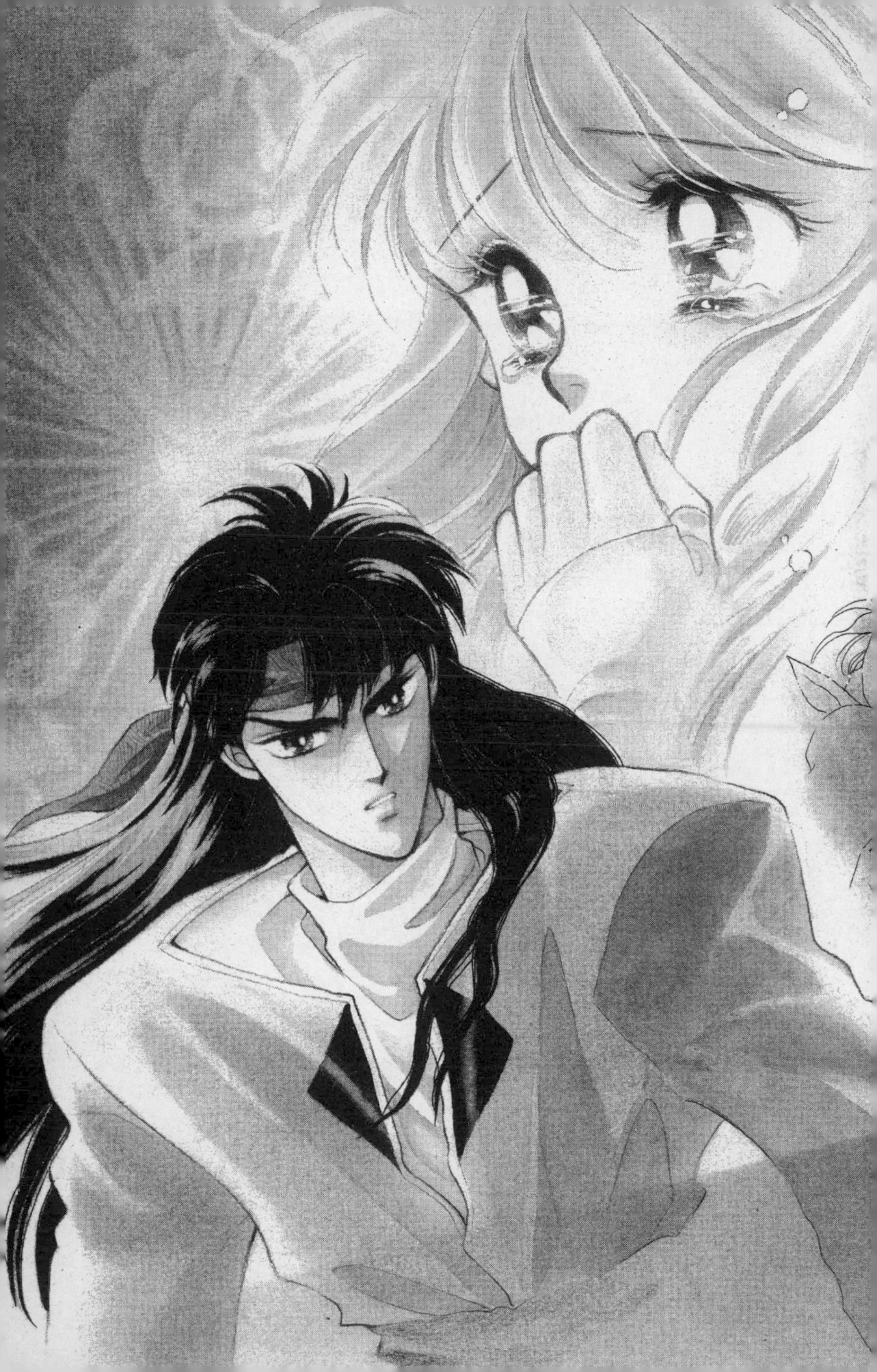

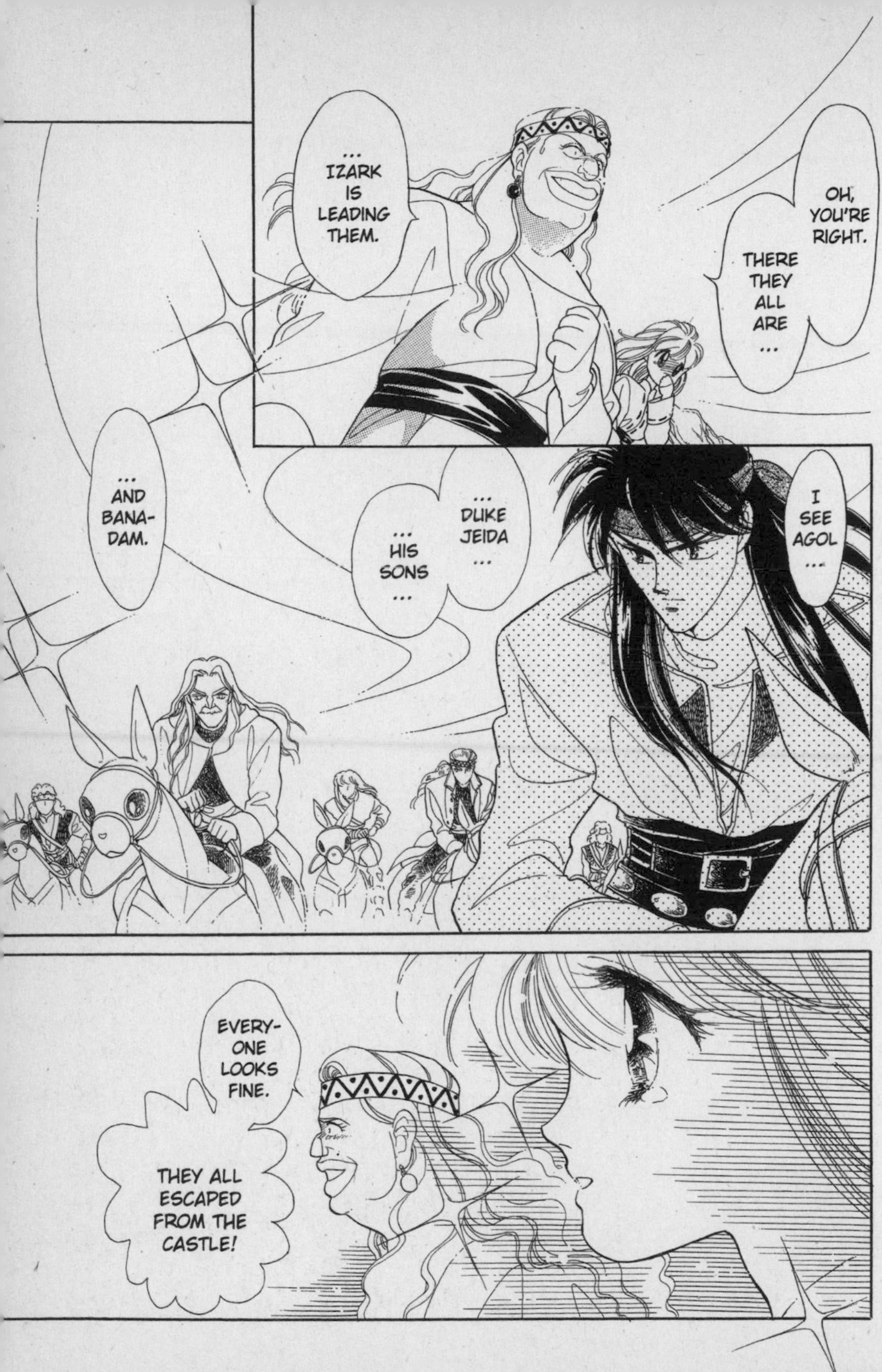
OH, YOU'RE RIGHT. THERE THEY ALL ARE ...
... IZARK IS LEADING THEM.
I SEE AGOL ...
... DUKE JEIDA ...
... HIS SONS ...
... AND BANA-DAM.
EVERY-ONE LOOKS FINE.
THEY ALL ESCAPED FROM THE CASTLE!

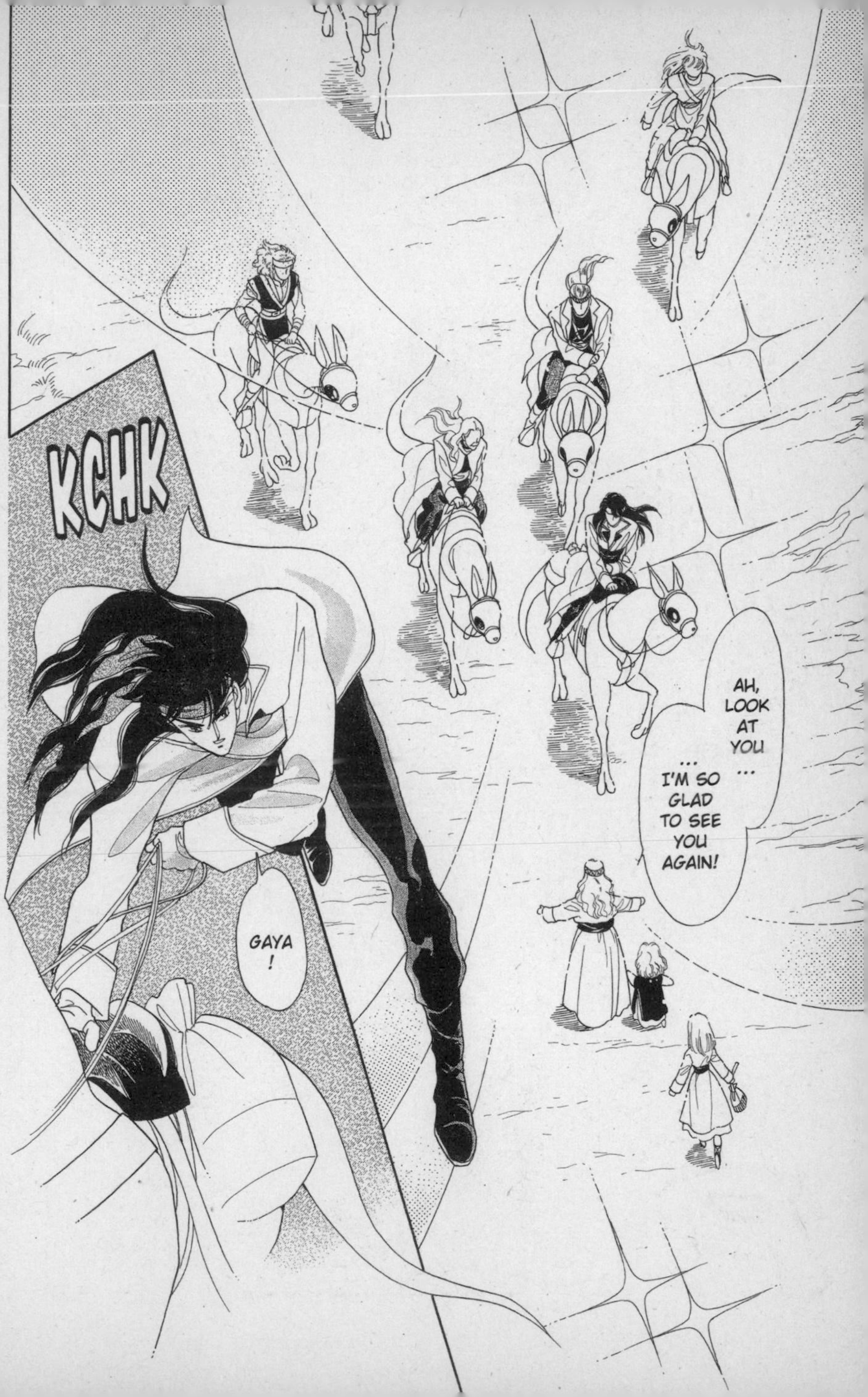
AH, LOOK AT YOU ...
... I'M SO GLAD TO SEE YOU AGAIN!
KCHK
GAYA!

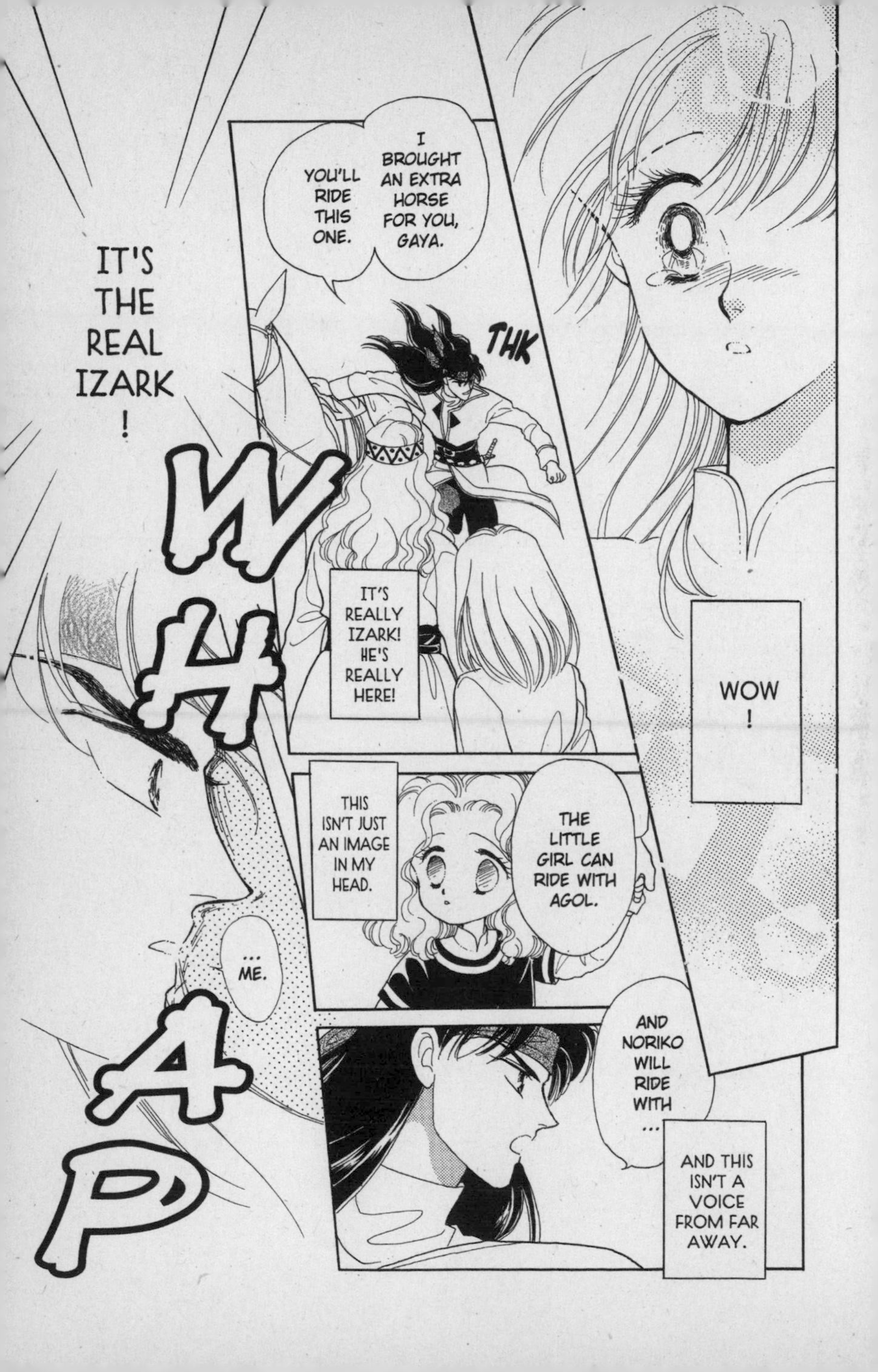
WOW!
I BROUGHT AN EXTRA HORSE FOR YOU, GAYA.
YOU'LL RIDE THIS ONE.
THK
IT'S REALLY IZARK! HE'S REALLY HERE!
IT'S THE REAL IZARK!
THE LITTLE GIRL CAN RIDE WITH AGOL.
THIS ISN'T JUST AN IMAGE IN MY HEAD.
AND NORIKO WILL RIDE WITH ...
AND THIS ISN'T A VOICE FROM FAR AWAY.
... ME.
WHAP

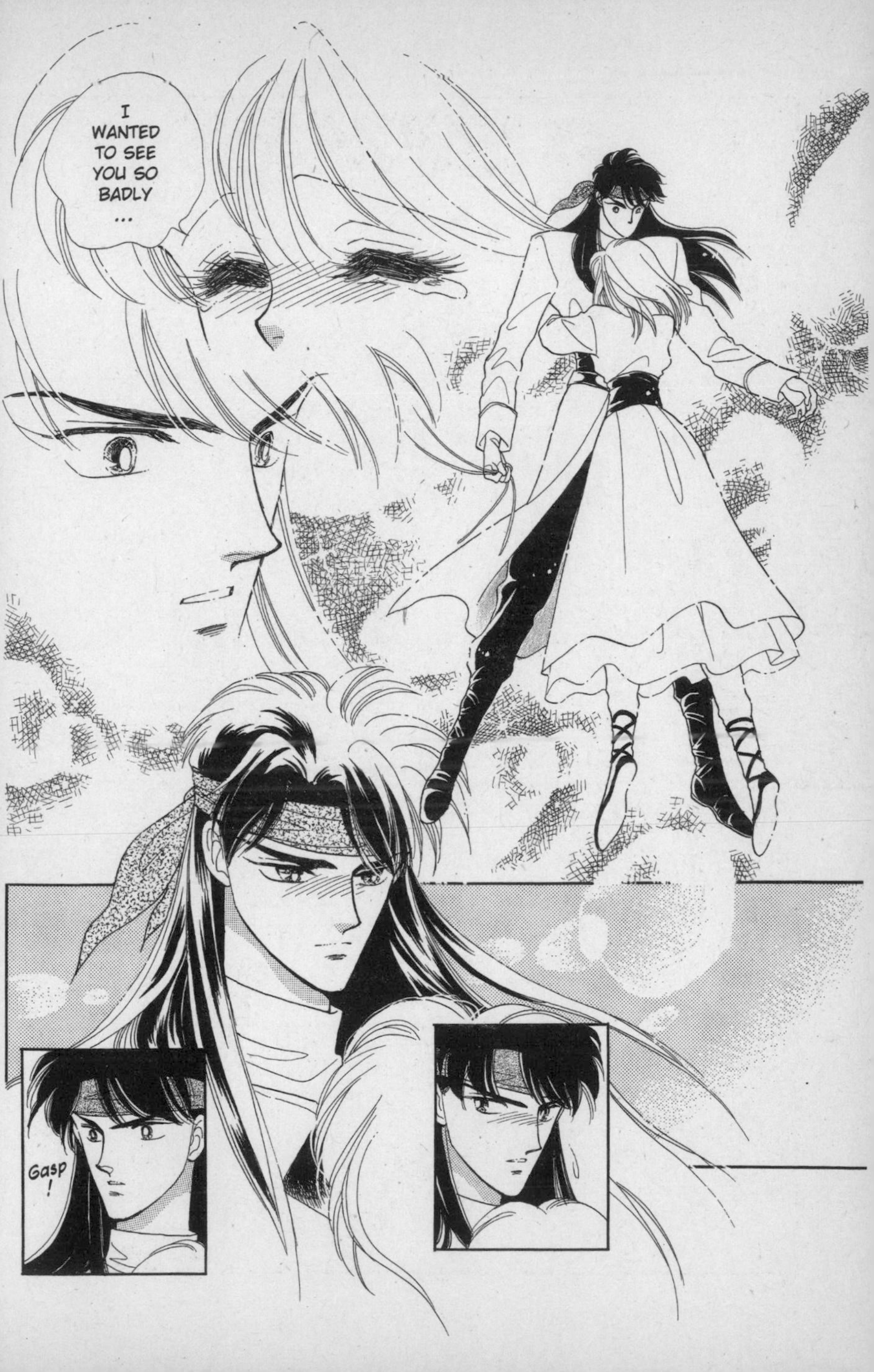
I WANTED TO SEE YOU SO BADLY ...
Gasp !

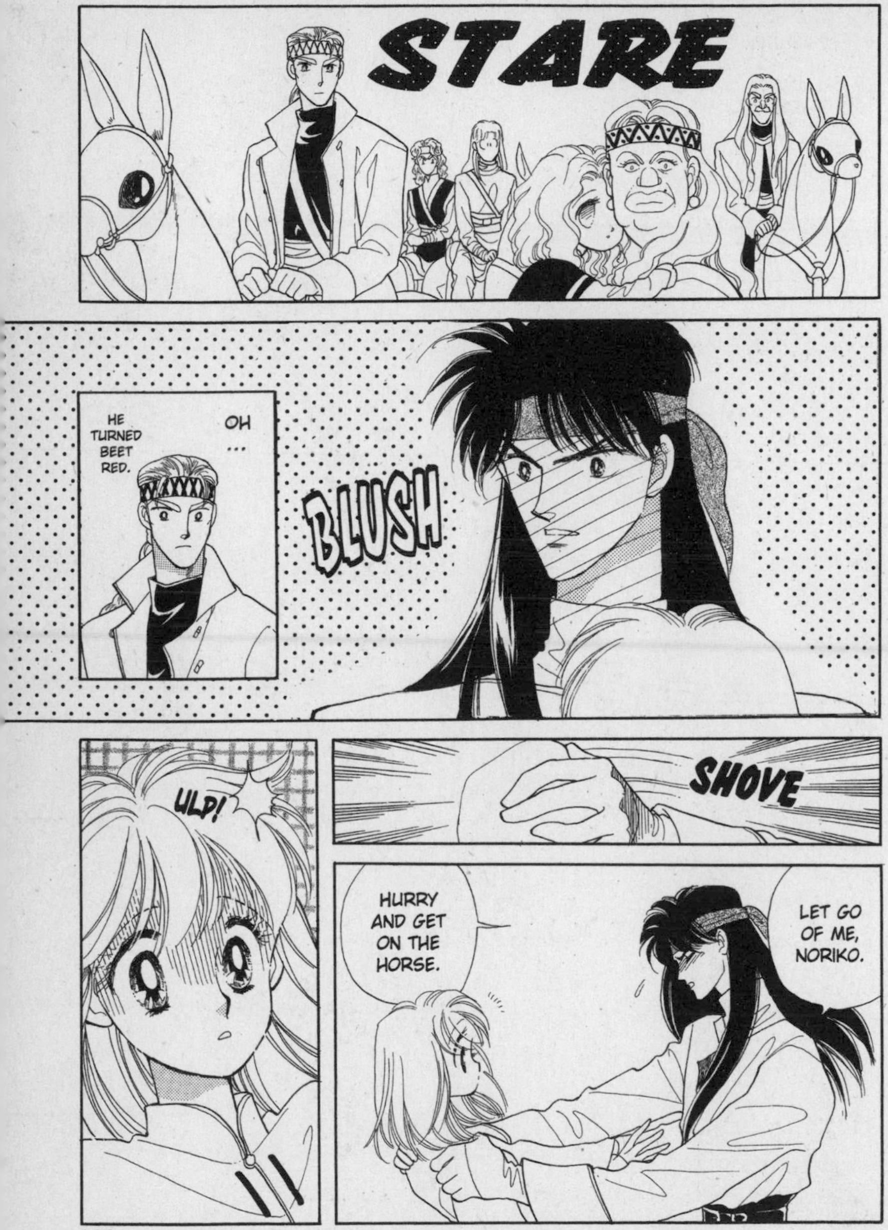
STARE
BLUSH
OH ...
HE TURNED BEET RED.
SHOVE
LET GO OF ME, NORIKO.
HURRY AND GET ON THE HORSE.
ULP!

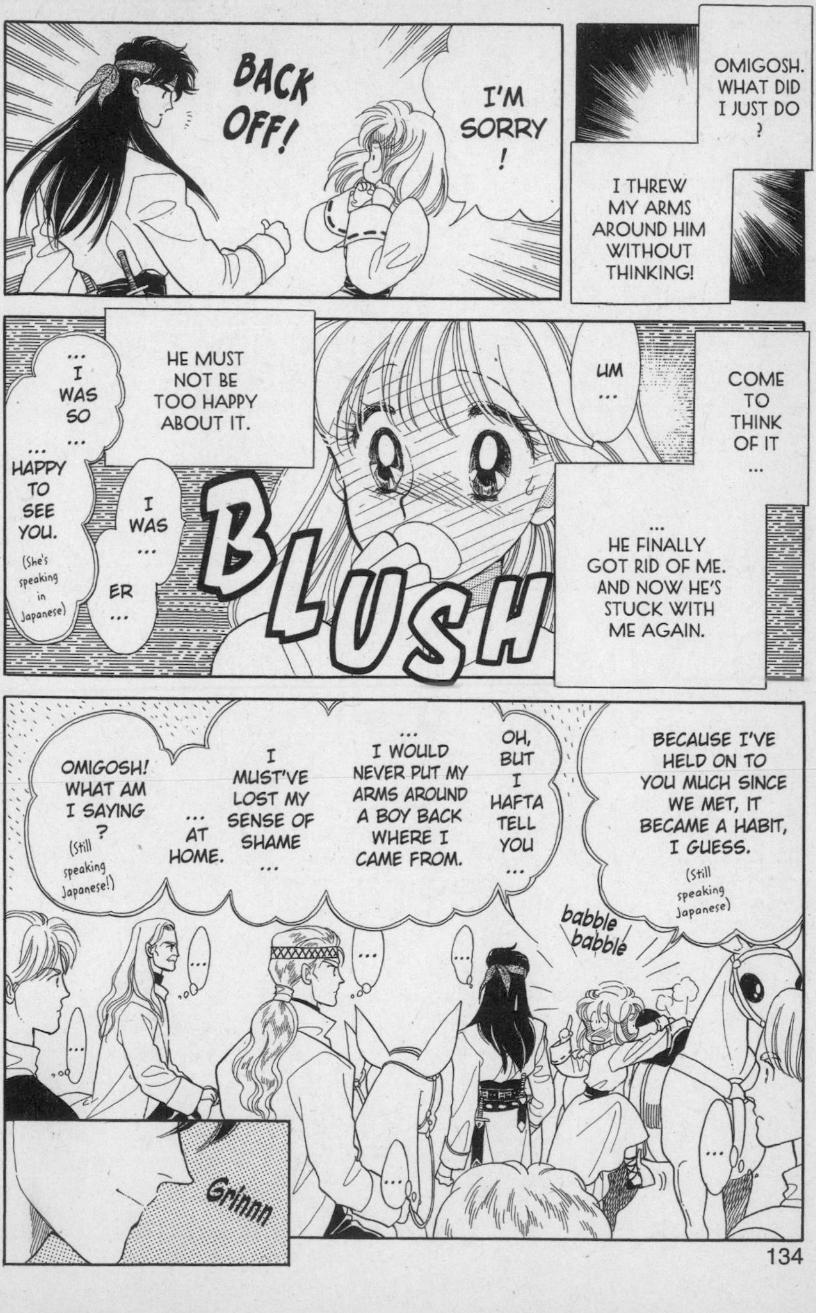
OMIGOSH. WHAT DID I JUST DO ?
I THREW MY ARMS AROUND HIM WITHOUT THINKING!
I'M SORRY !
BACK OFF!
COME TO THINK OF IT ...
... HE FINALLY GOT RID OF ME. AND NOW HE'S STUCK WITH ME AGAIN.
UM ...
HE MUST NOT BE TOO HAPPY ABOUT IT.
BLUSH
I WAS ... ER ...
... I WAS SO ... ... HAPPY TO SEE YOU.
(She's speaking in Japanese)
BECAUSE I'VE HELD ON TO YOU MUCH SINCE WE MET, IT BECAME A HABIT, I GUESS.
(Still speaking Japanese)
OH, BUT I HAFTA TELL YOU ...
... I WOULD NEVER PUT MY ARMS AROUND A BOY BACK WHERE I CAME FROM.
I MUST'VE LOST MY SENSE OF SHAME ...
... AT HOME.
OMIGOSH! WHAT AM I SAYING ?
(Still speaking Japanese!)
babble babble
...
...
...
...
...
...
Grinnn

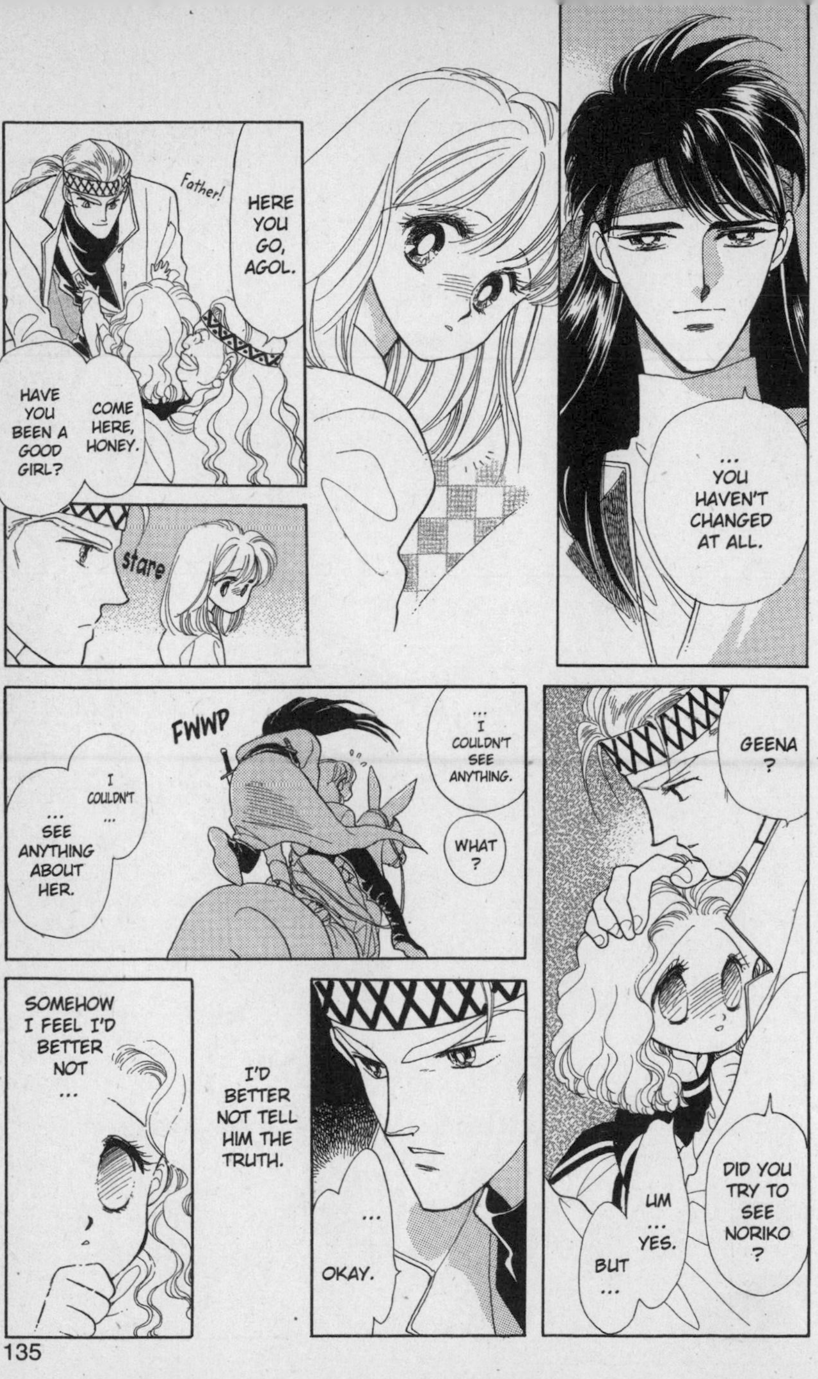
... YOU HAVEN'T CHANGED AT ALL.
HERE YOU GO, AGOL.
Father!
COME HERE, HONEY.
HAVE YOU BEEN A GOOD GIRL?
stare
GEENA ?
DID YOU TRY TO SEE NORIKO ?
UM ... YES.
BUT ...
... I COULDN'T SEE ANYTHING.
WHAT ?
FWWP
I COULDN'T ...
... SEE ANYTHING ABOUT HER.
I'D BETTER NOT TELL HIM THE TRUTH.
...
OKAY.
SOMEHOW I FEEL I'D BETTER NOT ...

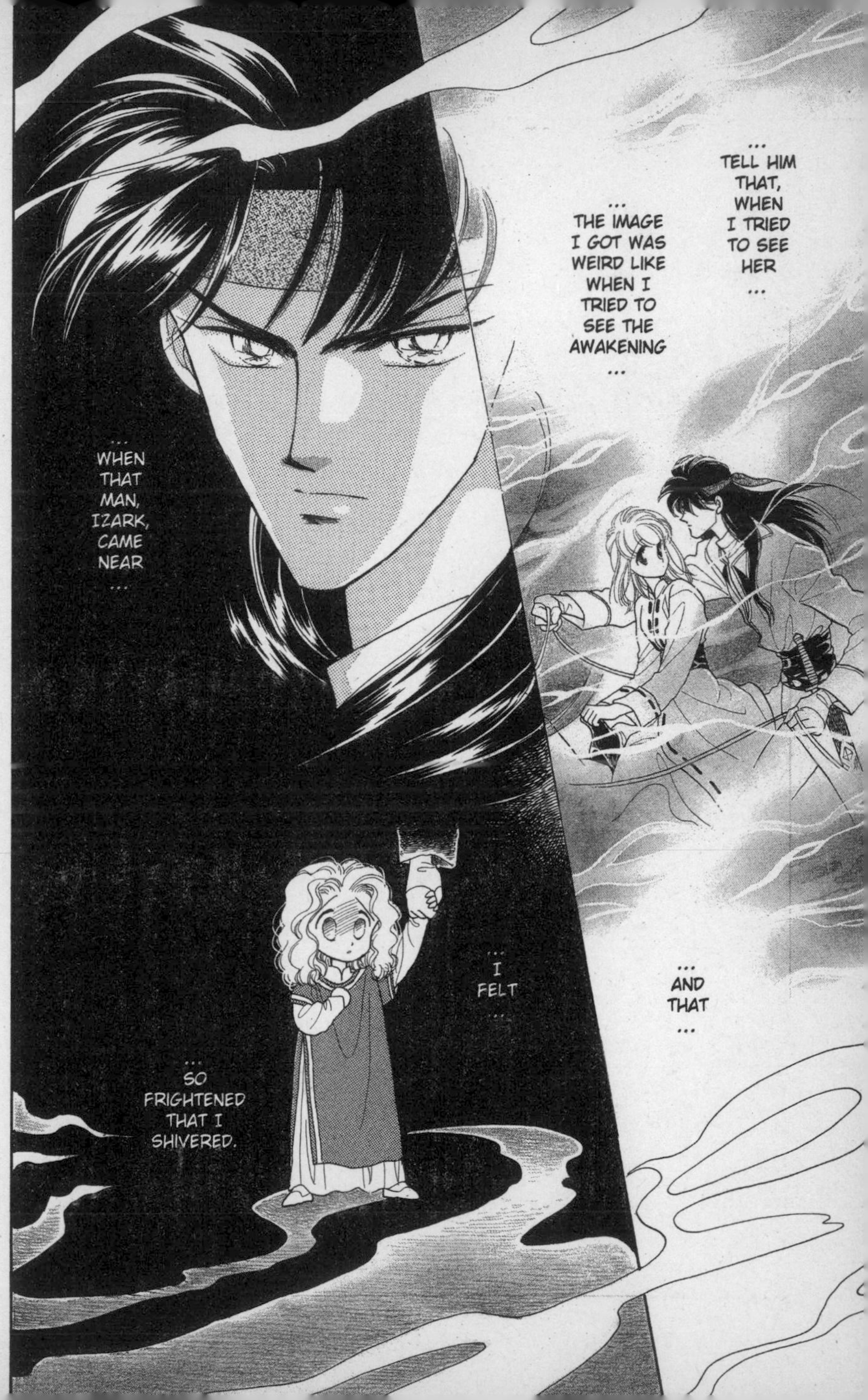
... TELL HIM THAT, WHEN I TRIED TO SEE HER ...
... THE IMAGE I GOT WAS WEIRD LIKE WHEN I TRIED TO SEE THE AWAKENING ...
... AND THAT ...
... WHEN THAT MAN, IZARK, CAME NEAR ...
... I FELT ...
... SO FRIGHTENED THAT I SHIVERED.

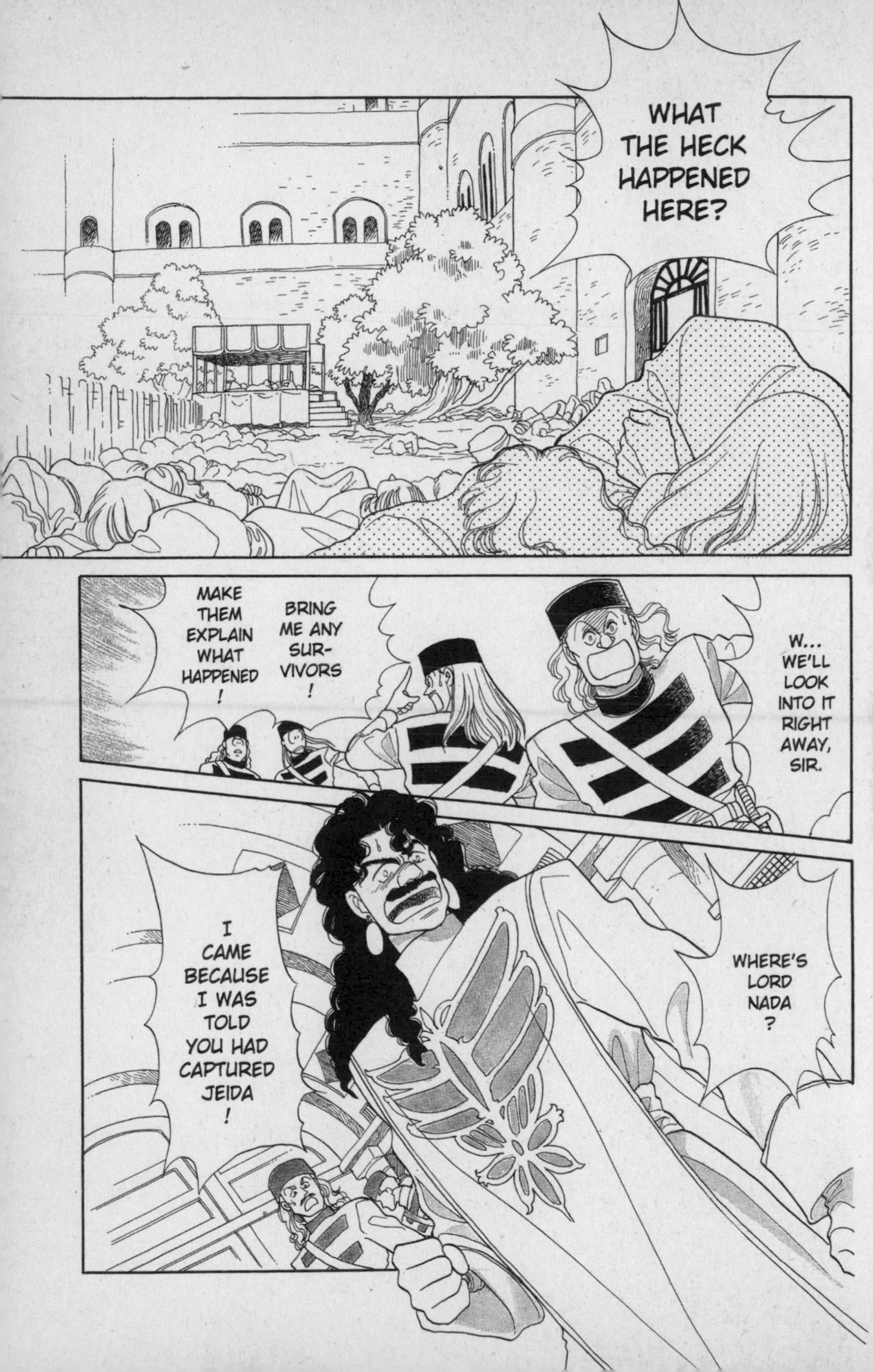
WHAT THE HECK HAPPENED HERE?
W... WE'LL LOOK INTO IT RIGHT AWAY, SIR.
BRING ME ANY SUR-VIVORS!
MAKE THEM EXPLAIN WHAT HAPPENED!
WHERE'S LORD NADA?
I CAME BECAUSE I WAS TOLD YOU HAD CAPTURED JEIDA!

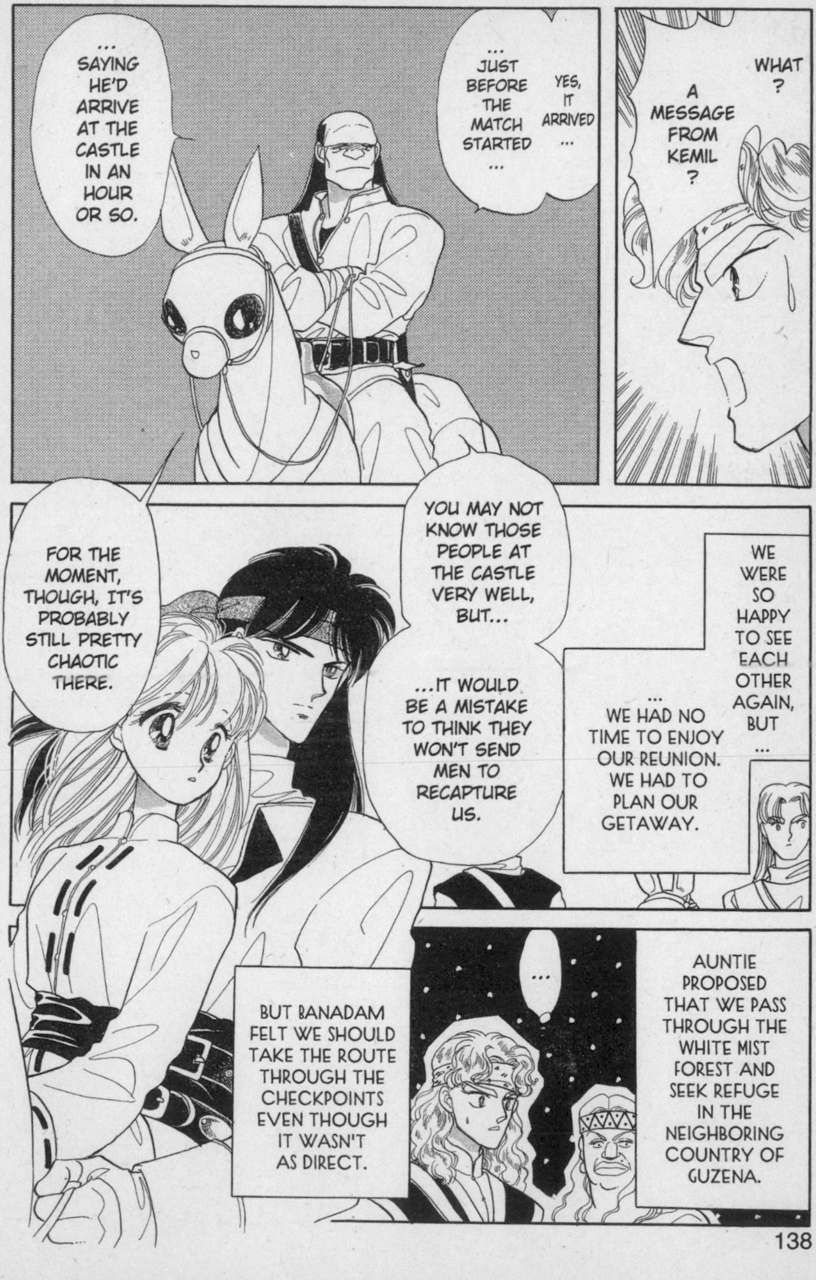
WHAT?
A MESSAGE FROM KEMIL?
YES, IT ARRIVED...
...JUST BEFORE THE MATCH STARTED...
...SAYING HE'D ARRIVE AT THE CASTLE IN AN HOUR OR SO.
WE WERE SO HAPPY TO SEE EACH OTHER AGAIN, BUT...
...WE HAD NO TIME TO ENJOY OUR REUNION. WE HAD TO PLAN OUR GETAWAY.
YOU MAY NOT KNOW THOSE PEOPLE AT THE CASTLE VERY WELL, BUT...
...IT WOULD BE A MISTAKE TO THINK THEY WON'T SEND MEN TO RECAPTURE US.
FOR THE MOMENT, THOUGH, IT'S PROBABLY STILL PRETTY CHAOTIC THERE.
AUNTIE PROPOSED THAT WE PASS THROUGH THE WHITE MIST FOREST AND SEEK REFUGE IN THE NEIGHBORING COUNTRY OF GUZENA.
...
BUT BANADAM FELT WE SHOULD TAKE THE ROUTE THROUGH THE CHECKPOINTS EVEN THOUGH IT WASN'T AS DIRECT.

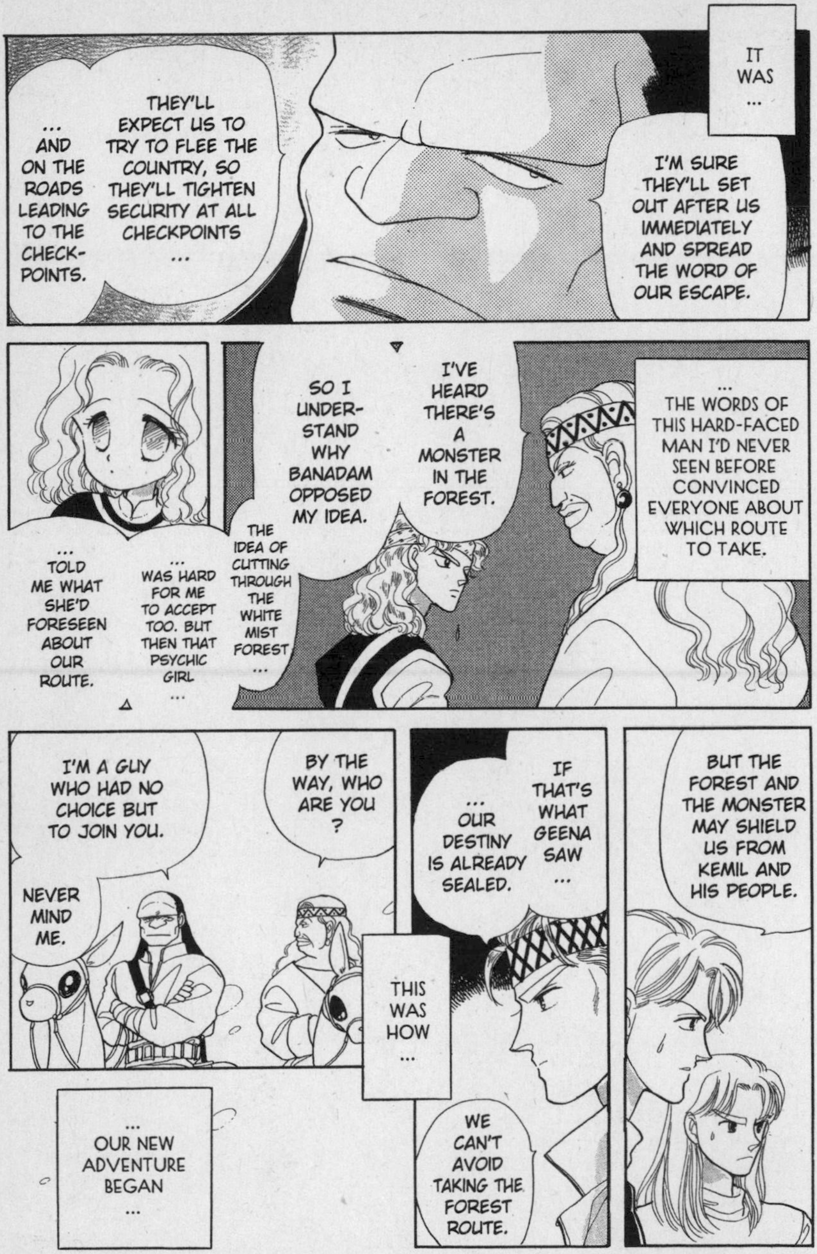
IT WAS ...
I'M SURE THEY'LL SET OUT AFTER US IMMEDIATELY AND SPREAD THE WORD OF OUR ESCAPE.
THEY'LL EXPECT US TO TRY TO FLEE THE COUNTRY, SO THEY'LL TIGHTEN SECURITY AT ALL CHECKPOINTS ...
... AND ON THE ROADS LEADING TO THE CHECK-POINTS.
... THE WORDS OF THIS HARD-FACED MAN I'D NEVER SEEN BEFORE CONVINCED EVERYONE ABOUT WHICH ROUTE TO TAKE.
I'VE HEARD THERE'S A MONSTER IN THE FOREST.
SO I UNDER-STAND WHY BANADAM OPPOSED MY IDEA.
THE IDEA OF CUTTING THROUGH THE WHITE MIST FOREST ...
... WAS HARD FOR ME TO ACCEPT TOO. BUT THEN THAT PSYCHIC GIRL ...
... TOLD ME WHAT SHE'D FORESEEN ABOUT OUR ROUTE.
BUT THE FOREST AND THE MONSTER MAY SHIELD US FROM KEMIL AND HIS PEOPLE.
IF THAT'S WHAT GEENA SAW ...
... OUR DESTINY IS ALREADY SEALED.
WE CAN'T AVOID TAKING THE FOREST ROUTE.
BY THE WAY, WHO ARE YOU ?
I'M A GUY WHO HAD NO CHOICE BUT TO JOIN YOU.
NEVER MIND ME.
THIS WAS HOW ...
... OUR NEW ADVENTURE BEGAN ...

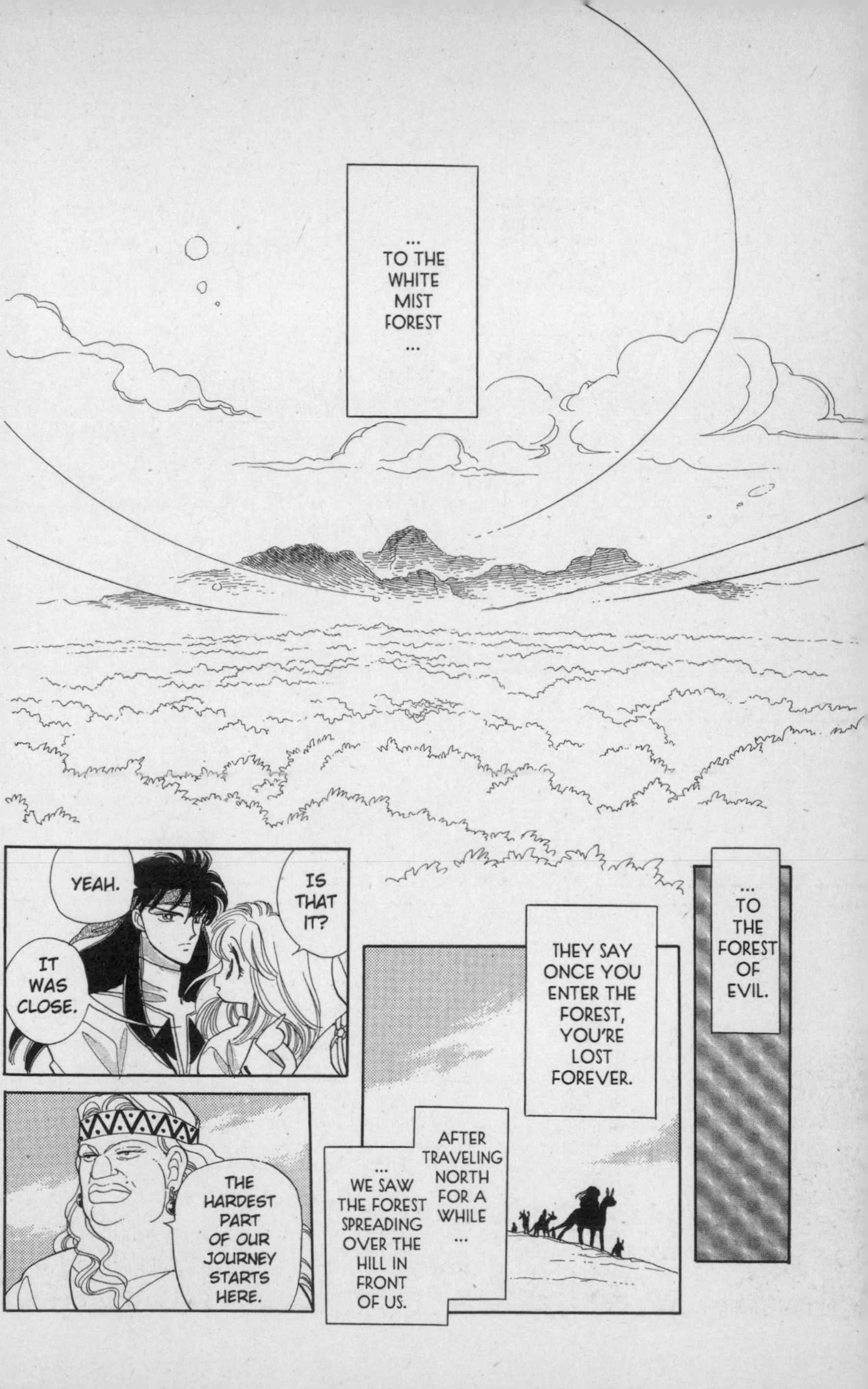

... TO THE WHITE MIST FOREST ...
... TO THE FOREST OF EVIL.
THEY SAY ONCE YOU ENTER THE FOREST, YOU'RE LOST FOREVER.
AFTER TRAVELING NORTH FOR A WHILE ...
... WE SAW THE FOREST SPREADING OVER THE HILL IN FRONT OF US.
IS THAT IT?
YEAH.
IT WAS CLOSE.
THE HARDEST PART OF OUR JOURNEY STARTS HERE.

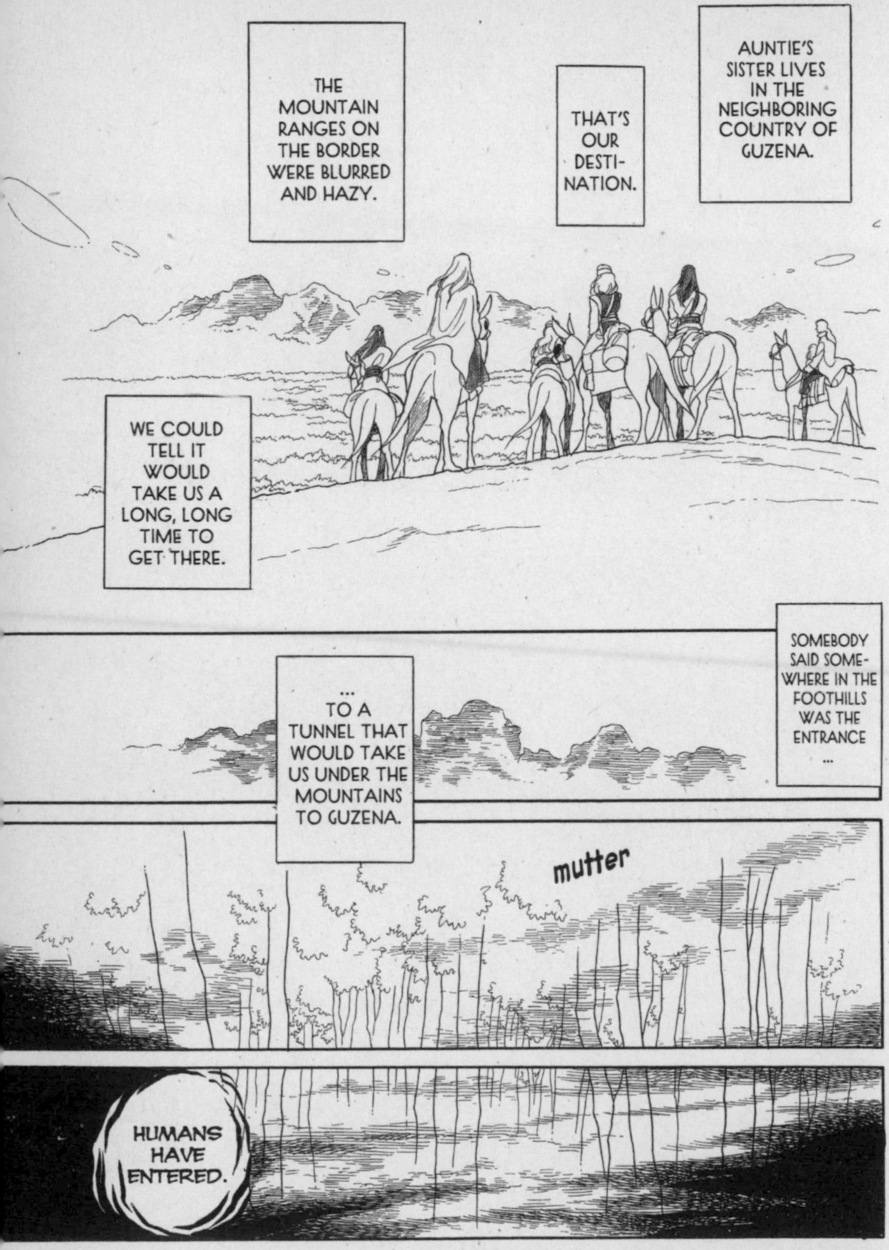
AUNTIE'S SISTER LIVES IN THE NEIGHBORING COUNTRY OF GUZENA.
THAT'S OUR DESTI- NATION.
THE MOUNTAIN RANGES ON THE BORDER WERE BLURRED AND HAZY.
WE COULD TELL IT WOULD TAKE US A LONG, LONG TIME TO GET THERE.
SOMEBODY SAID SOME- WHERE IN THE FOOTHILLS WAS THE ENTRANCE ...
... TO A TUNNEL THAT WOULD TAKE US UNDER THE MOUNTAINS TO GUZENA.
mutter
HUMANS HAVE ENTERED.

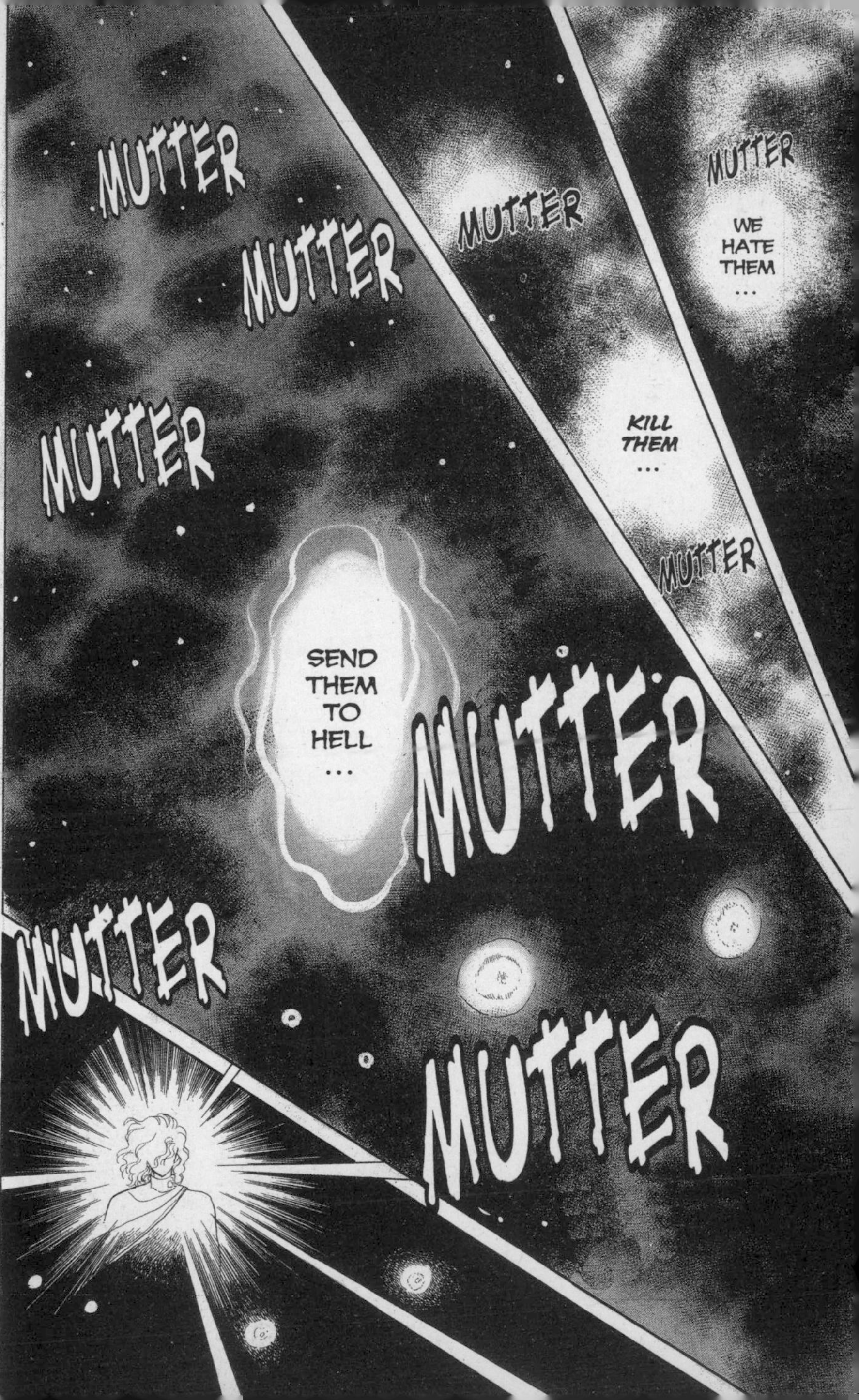
MUTTER
WE HATE THEM ...
KILL THEM ...
MUTTER
MUTTER
MUTTER
MUTTER
MUTTER
SEND THEM TO HELL ...
MUTTER
MUTTER
MUTTER

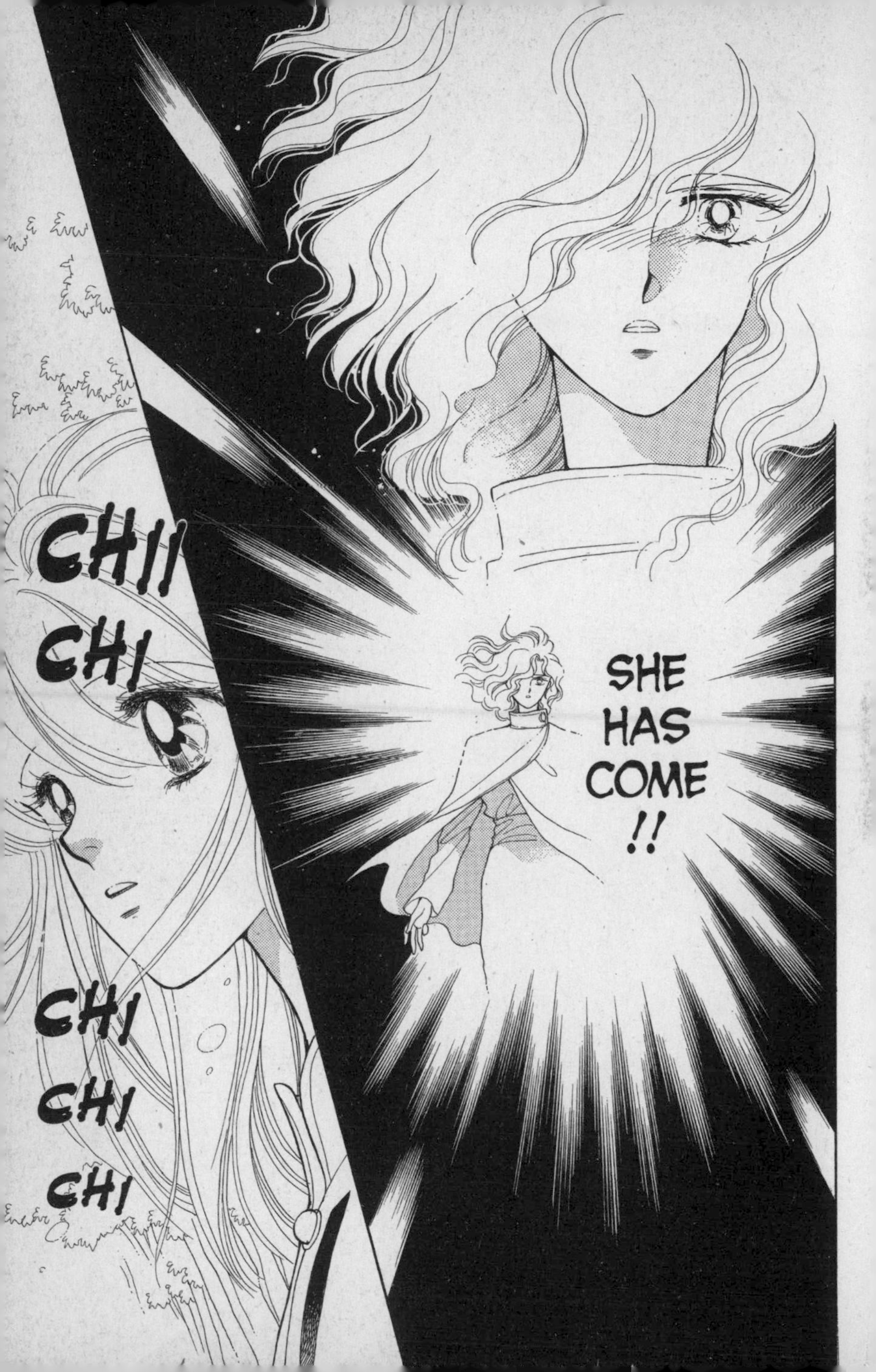
SHE HAS COME !!
CHII
CHI
CHI
CHI
CHI

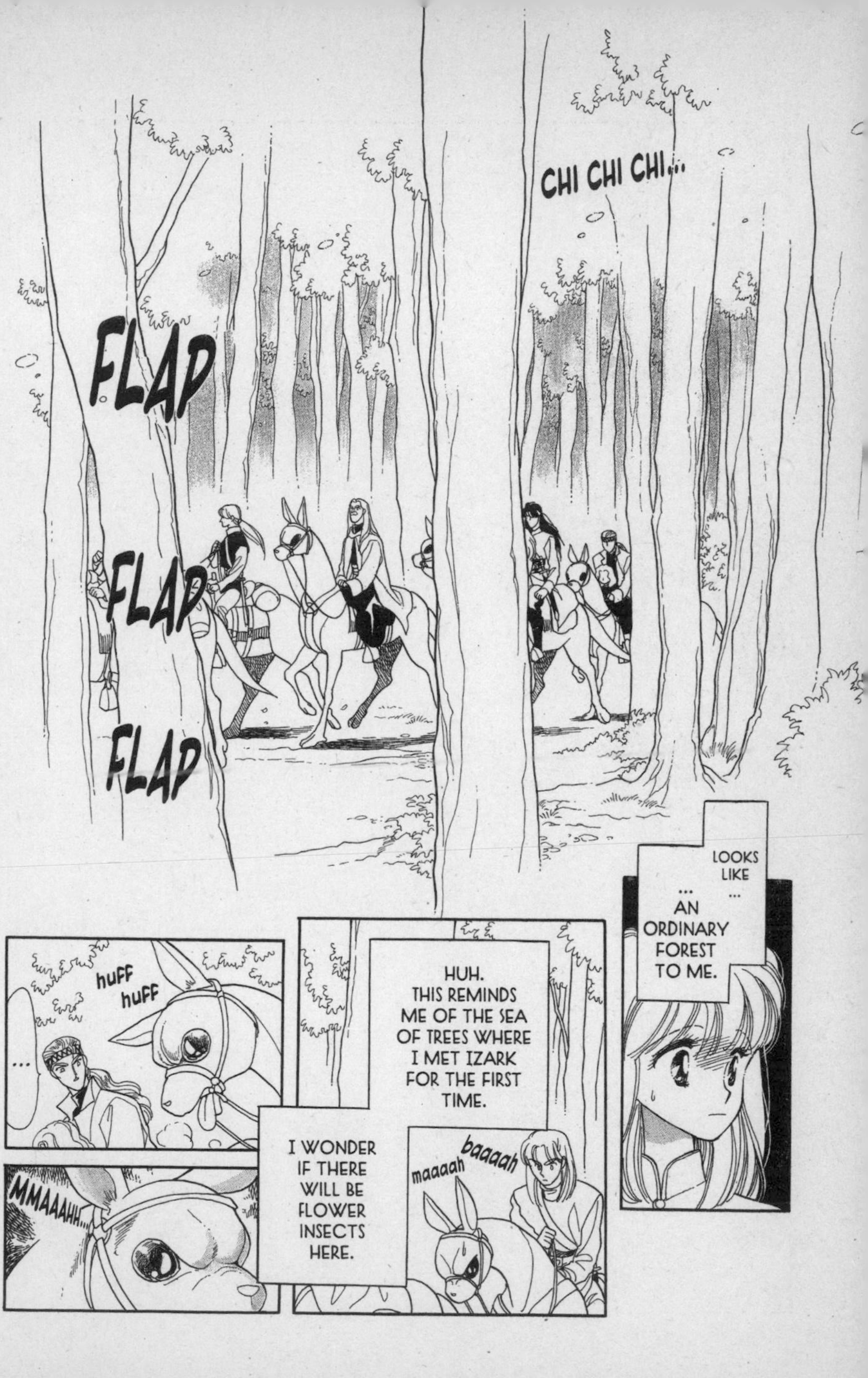
CHI CHI CHI...
FLAP
FLAP
FLAP
LOOKS LIKE ... ... AN ORDINARY FOREST TO ME.
HUH. THIS REMINDS ME OF THE SEA OF TREES WHERE I MET IZARK FOR THE FIRST TIME.
I WONDER IF THERE WILL BE FLOWER INSECTS HERE.
baaaah
maaaah
huff huff
...
MMAAAHH...

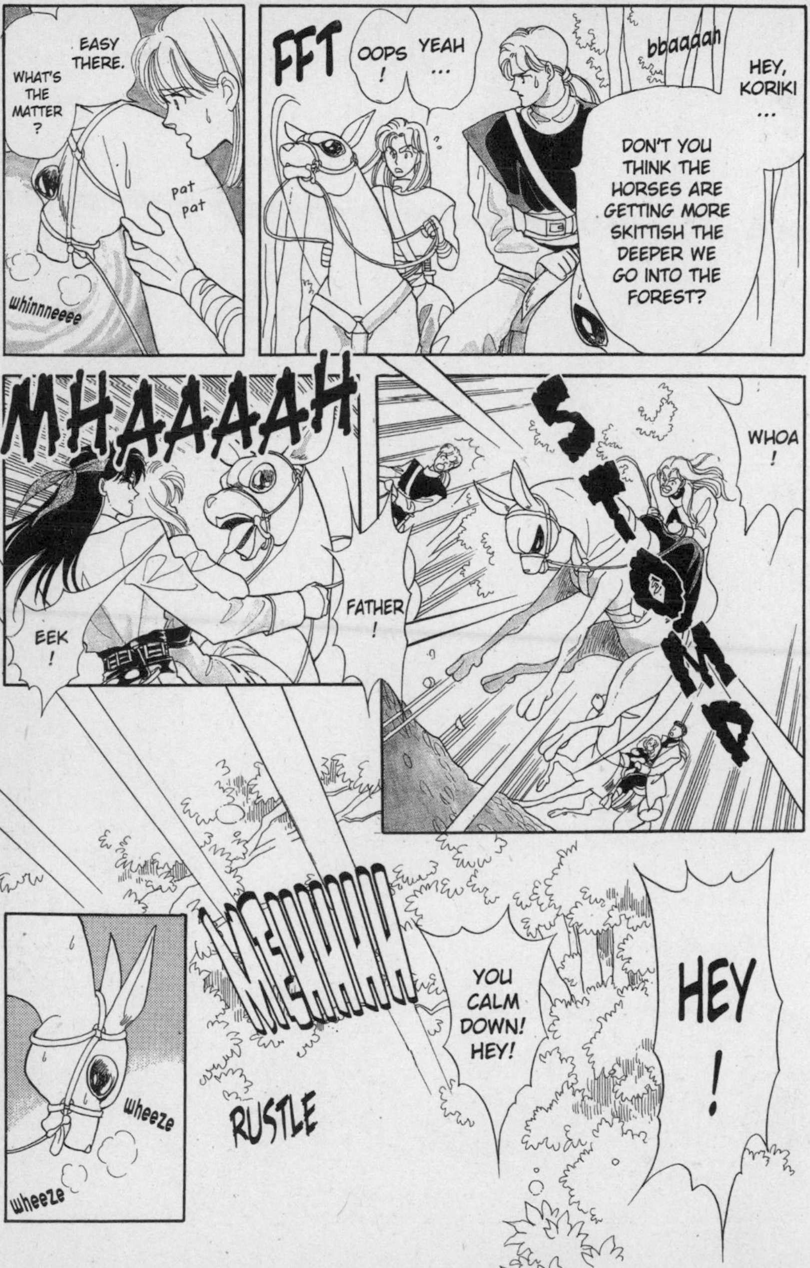
bbaaaah
HEY, KORIKI ...
DON'T YOU THINK THE HORSES ARE GETTING MORE SKITTISH THE DEEPER WE GO INTO THE FOREST?
YEAH ...
OOPS !
FFT
EASY THERE.
WHAT'S THE MATTER ?
pat pat
whinnneeee
STOMP
WHOA !
MHAAAAH
FATHER !
EEK !
HEY !
YOU CALM DOWN! HEY!
RUSTLE
wheeze
wheeze

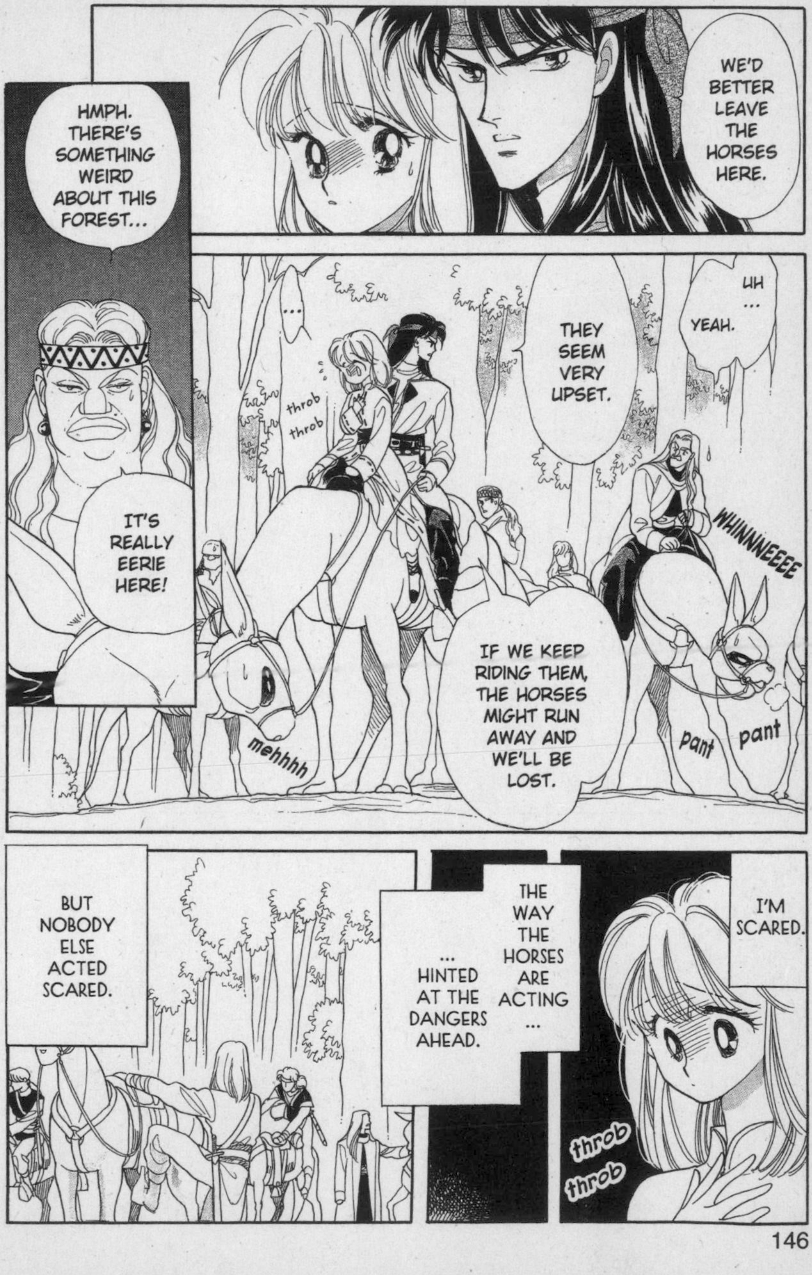
WE'D BETTER LEAVE THE HORSES HERE.
HMPH. THERE'S SOMETHING WEIRD ABOUT THIS FOREST...
IT'S REALLY EERIE HERE!
UH ... YEAH.
THEY SEEM VERY UPSET.
WHINNNEEEE
...
throb throb
IF WE KEEP RIDING THEM, THE HORSES MIGHT RUN AWAY AND WE'LL BE LOST.
pant pant
mehhhh
I'M SCARED.
throb throb
THE WAY THE HORSES ARE ACTING ...
... HINTED AT THE DANGERS AHEAD.
BUT NOBODY ELSE ACTED SCARED.

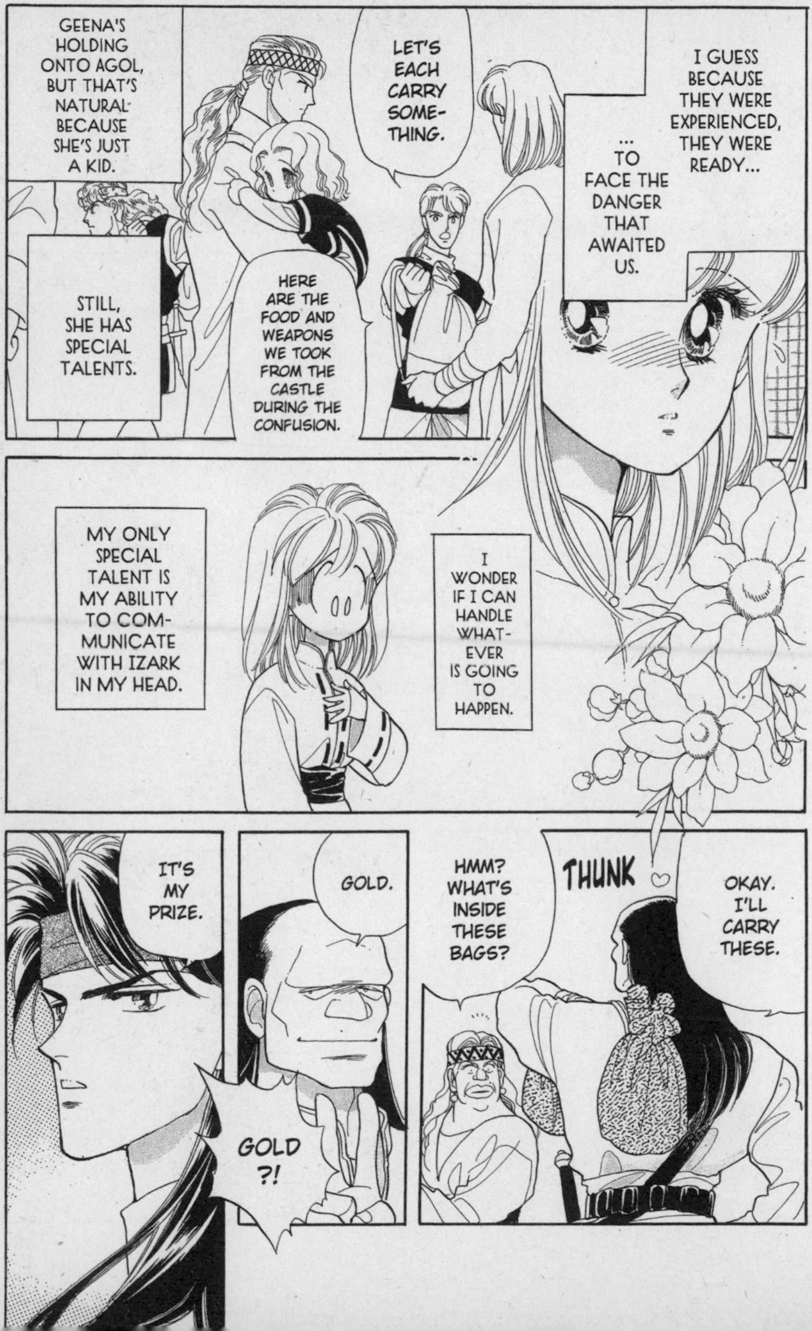
I GUESS BECAUSE THEY WERE EXPERIENCED, THEY WERE READY...
... TO FACE THE DANGER THAT AWAITED US.
LET'S EACH CARRY SOME-THING.
HERE ARE THE FOOD AND WEAPONS WE TOOK FROM THE CASTLE DURING THE CONFUSION.
GEENA'S HOLDING ONTO AGOL, BUT THAT'S NATURAL BECAUSE SHE'S JUST A KID.
STILL, SHE HAS SPECIAL TALENTS.
I WONDER IF I CAN HANDLE WHAT-EVER IS GOING TO HAPPEN.
MY ONLY SPECIAL TALENT IS MY ABILITY TO COM-MUNICATE WITH IZARK IN MY HEAD.
OKAY. I'LL CARRY THESE.
THUNK
HMM? WHAT'S INSIDE THESE BAGS?
GOLD.
GOLD ?!
IT'S MY PRIZE.

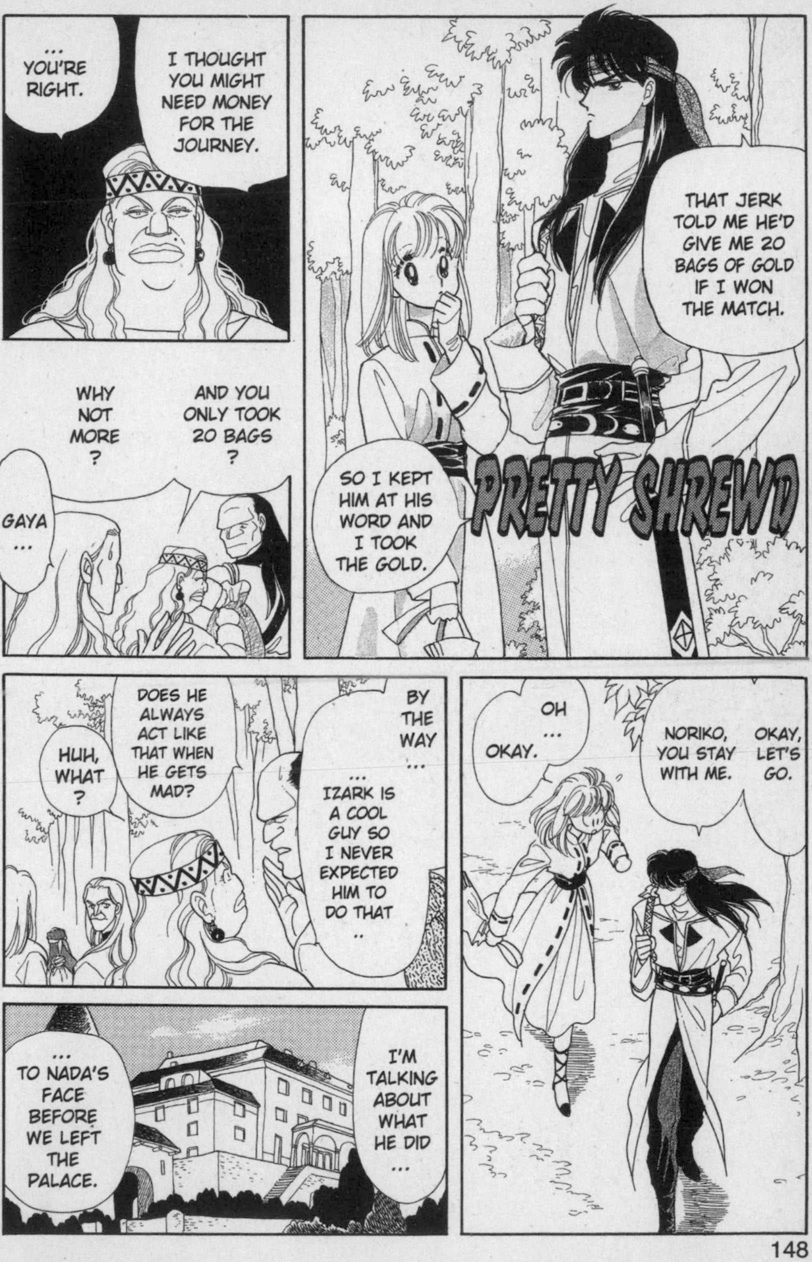
THAT JERK TOLD ME HE'D GIVE ME 20 BAGS OF GOLD IF I WON THE MATCH.
SO I KEPT HIM AT HIS WORD AND I TOOK THE GOLD.
PRETTY SHREWD
I THOUGHT YOU MIGHT NEED MONEY FOR THE JOURNEY.
... YOU'RE RIGHT.
AND YOU ONLY TOOK 20 BAGS ?
WHY NOT MORE ?
GAYA ...
OKAY, LET'S GO.
NORIKO, YOU STAY WITH ME.
OH ... OKAY.
BY THE WAY ...
... IZARK IS A COOL GUY SO I NEVER EXPECTED HIM TO DO THAT ..
DOES HE ALWAYS ACT LIKE THAT WHEN HE GETS MAD?
HUH, WHAT ?
I'M TALKING ABOUT WHAT HE DID ...
... TO NADA'S FACE BEFORE WE LEFT THE PALACE.

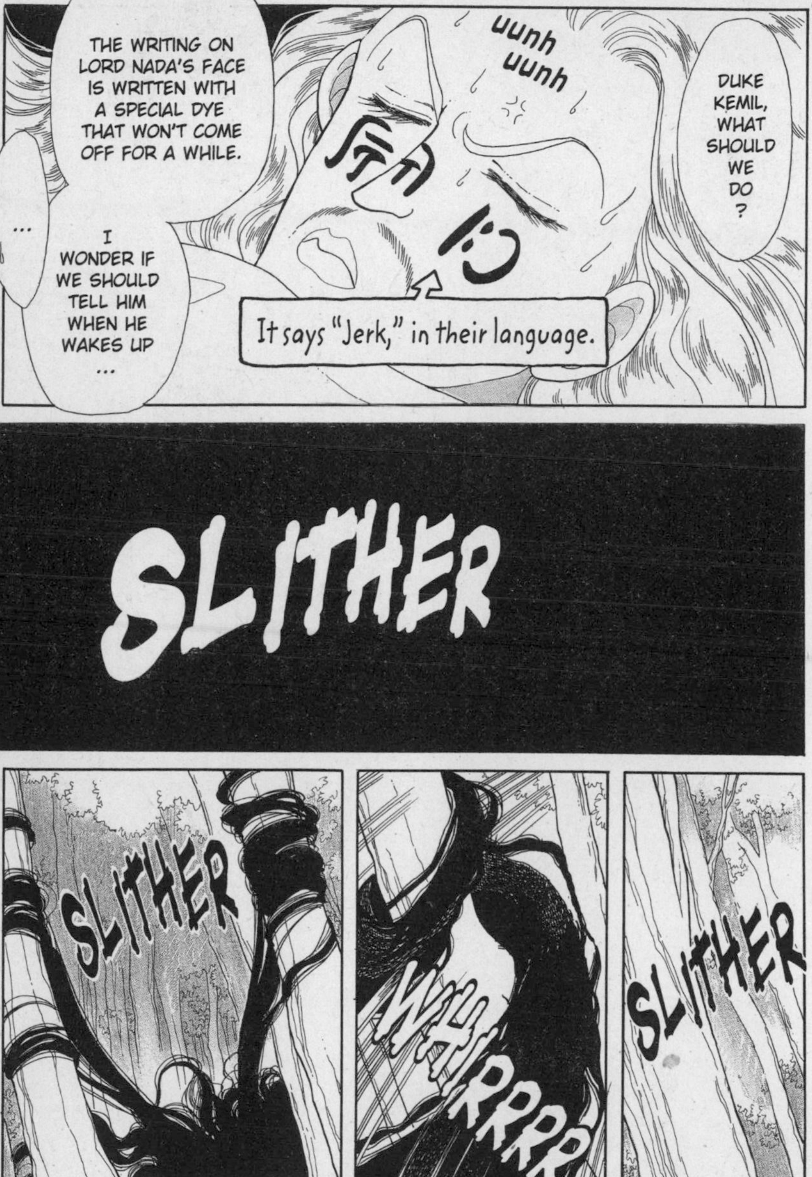
DUKE KEMIL, WHAT SHOULD WE DO?
uunh uunh
It says "Jerk," in their language.
THE WRITING ON LORD NADA'S FACE IS WRITTEN WITH A SPECIAL DYE THAT WON'T COME OFF FOR A WHILE.
...
I WONDER IF WE SHOULD TELL HIM WHEN HE WAKES UP ...
SLITHER
SLITHER
WHIRRRR
SLITHER

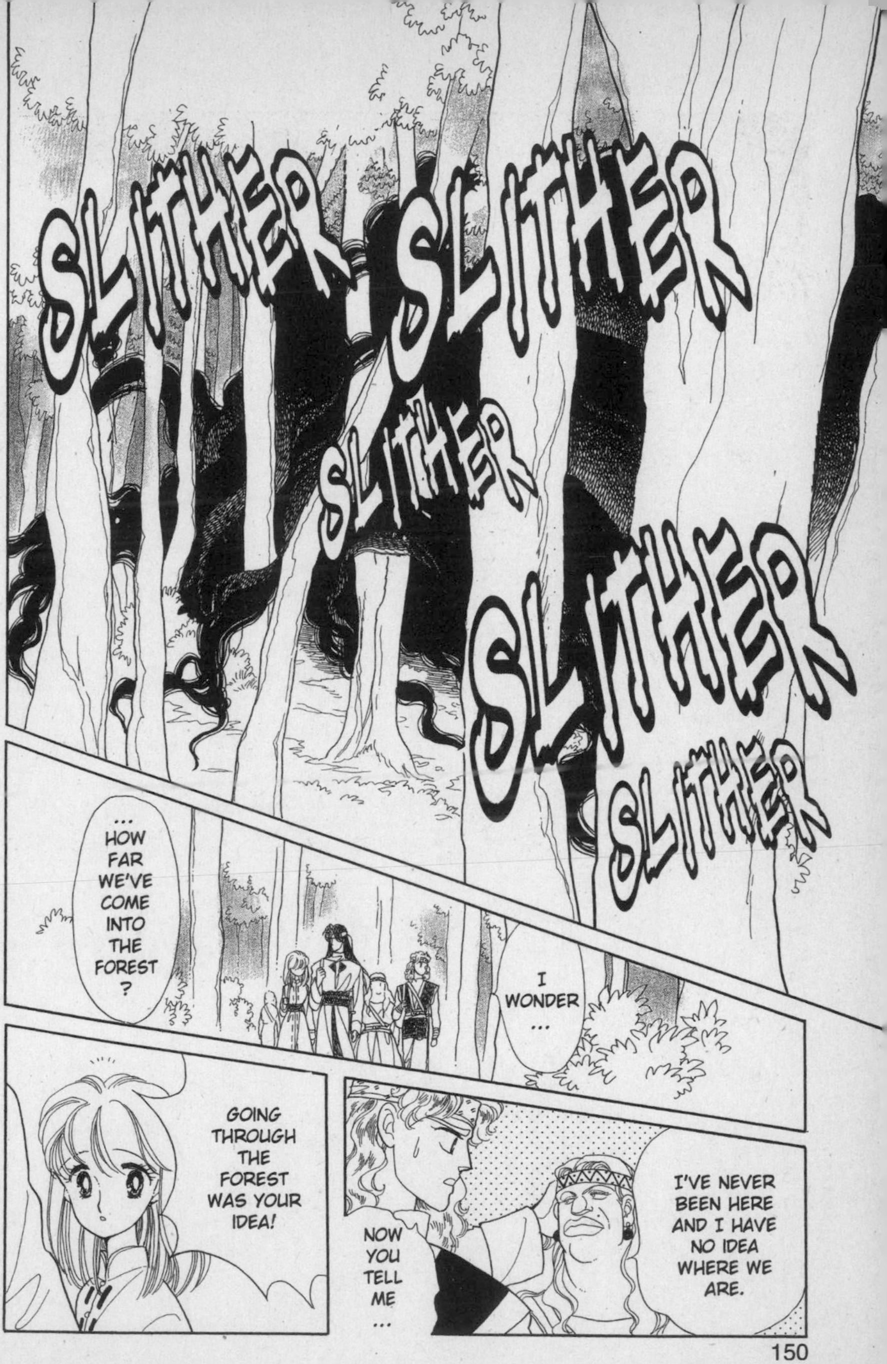
SLITHER
SLITHER
SLITHER
SLITHER
SLITHER
I WONDER ...
... HOW FAR WE'VE COME INTO THE FOREST ?
I'VE NEVER BEEN HERE AND I HAVE NO IDEA WHERE WE ARE.
NOW YOU TELL ME ...
GOING THROUGH THE FOREST WAS YOUR IDEA!

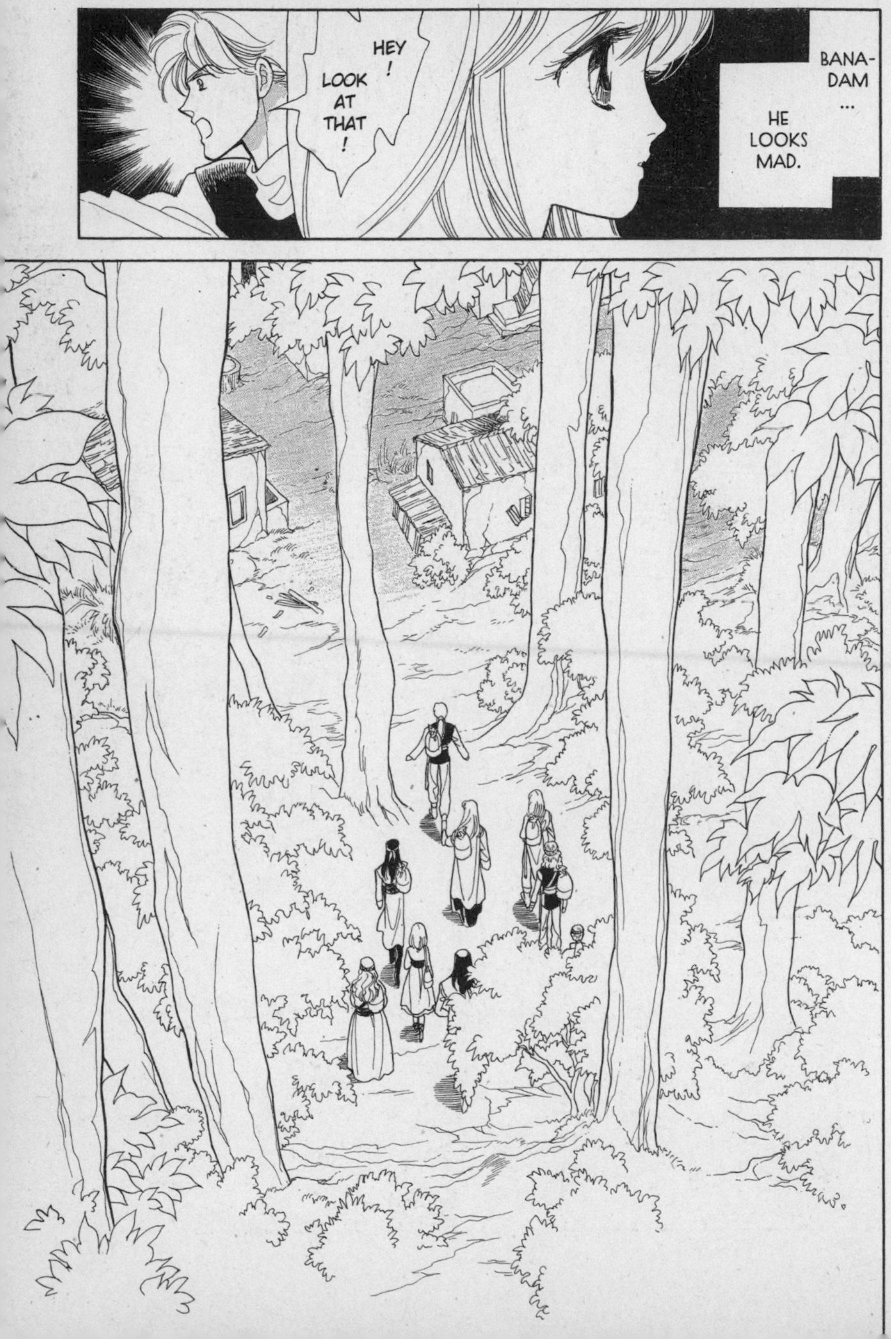
BANA-DAM ...
HE LOOKS MAD.
HEY!
LOOK AT THAT!

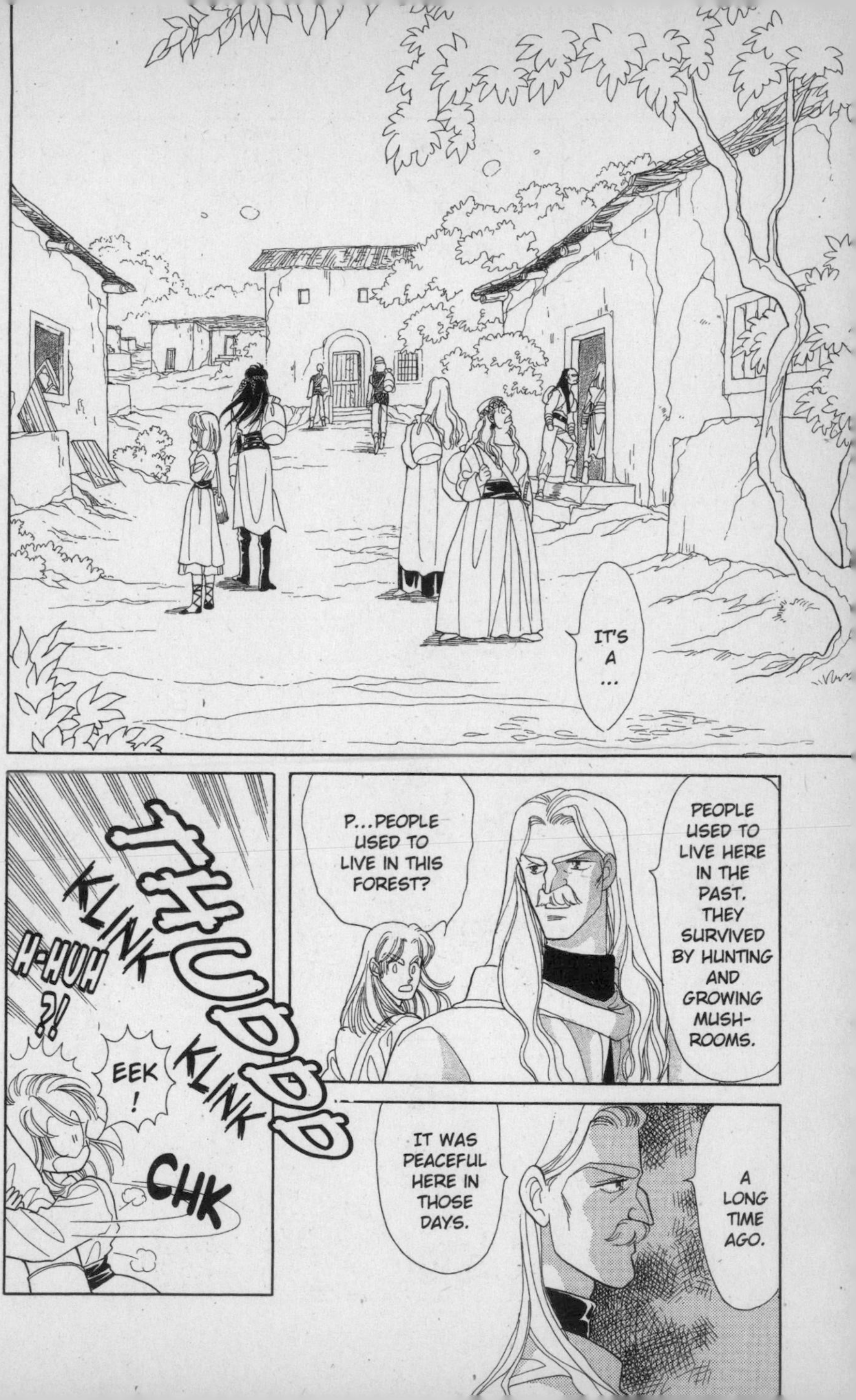
IT'S A ...
PEOPLE USED TO LIVE HERE IN THE PAST. THEY SURVIVED BY HUNTING AND GROWING MUSH-ROOMS.
P...PEOPLE USED TO LIVE IN THIS FOREST?
A LONG TIME AGO.
IT WAS PEACEFUL HERE IN THOSE DAYS.
THUDDD
KLINK KLINK
H-HUH ?!
EEK !
CHK

Sometimes I misspell Noriko as Iriko.

Iriko is dried sardines!

I might keep doing so until this series ends.

Noriko eating iriko.

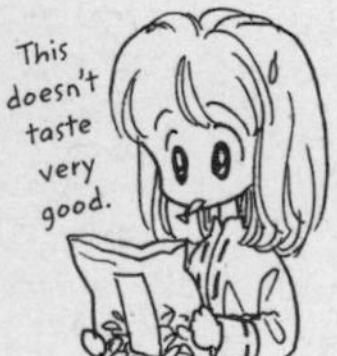
This doesn't taste very good.

Iriko is usually used to making broth...

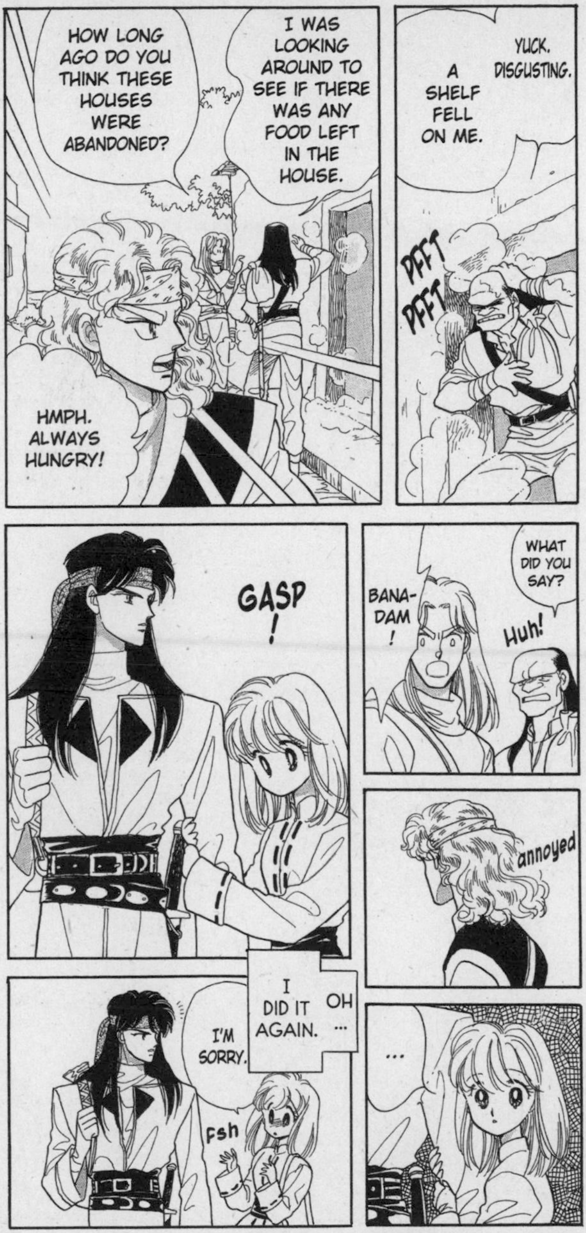
YUCK. DISGUSTING.
A SHELF FELL ON ME.
PFFT PFFT
I WAS LOOKING AROUND TO SEE IF THERE WAS ANY FOOD LEFT IN THE HOUSE.
HOW LONG AGO DO YOU THINK THESE HOUSES WERE ABANDONED?
HMPH. ALWAYS HUNGRY!
WHAT DID YOU SAY?
BANADAM!
Huh!
annoyed
GASP!
...
OH ...
I DID IT AGAIN.
I'M SORRY.
Fsh

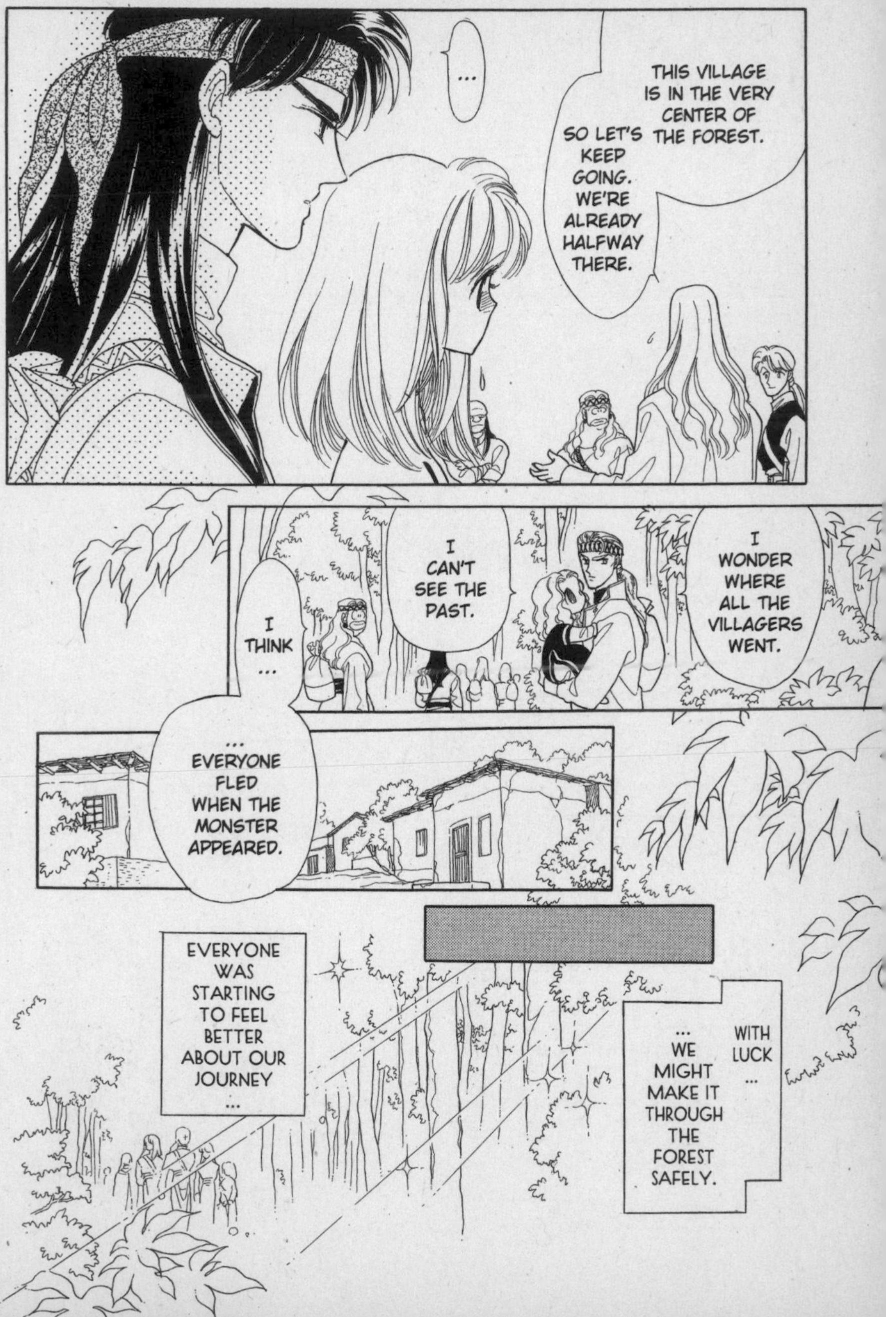
THIS VILLAGE IS IN THE VERY CENTER OF THE FOREST.
SO LET'S KEEP GOING. WE'RE ALREADY HALFWAY THERE.
...
I WONDER WHERE ALL THE VILLAGERS WENT.
I CAN'T SEE THE PAST.
I THINK ...
... EVERYONE FLED WHEN THE MONSTER APPEARED.
WITH LUCK ...
... WE MIGHT MAKE IT THROUGH THE FOREST SAFELY.
EVERYONE WAS STARTING TO FEEL BETTER ABOUT OUR JOURNEY ...

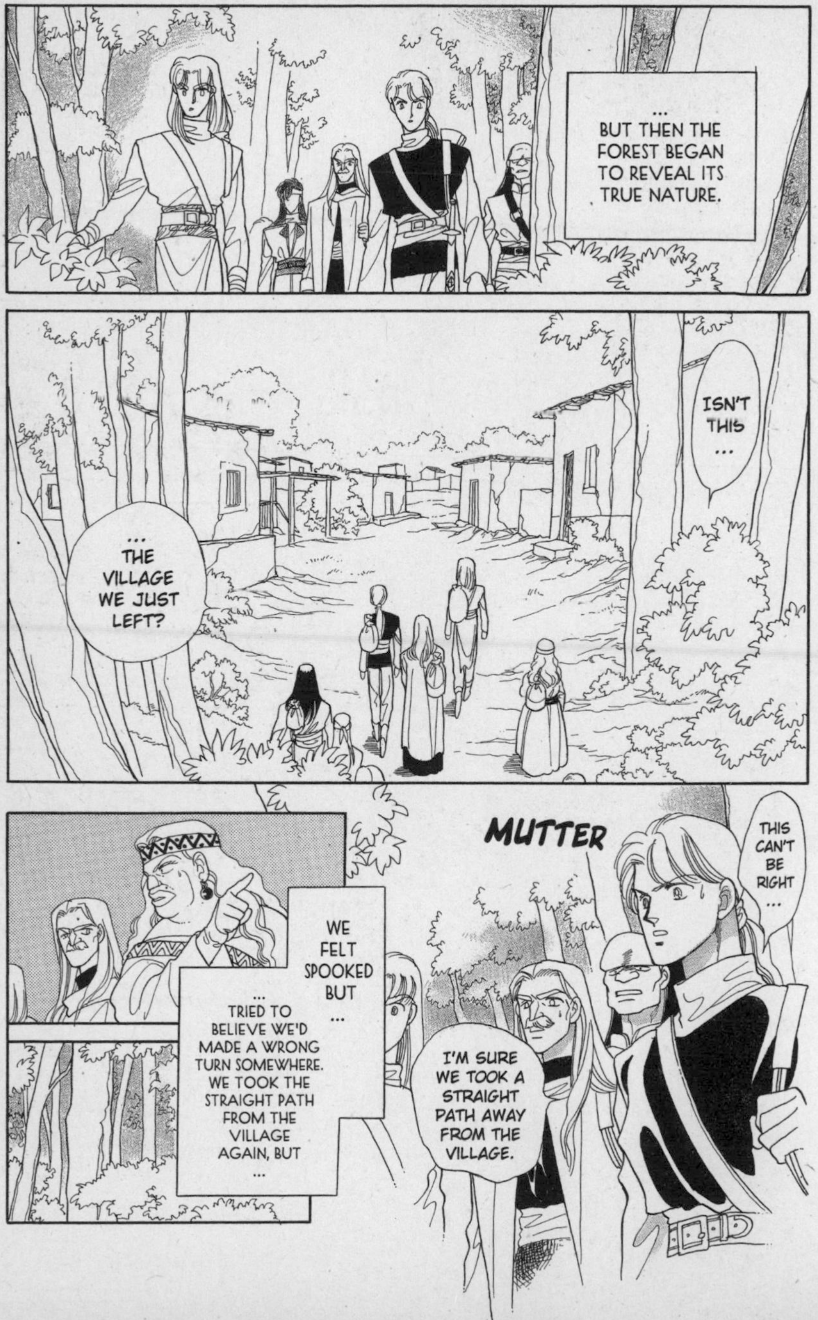
... BUT THEN THE FOREST BEGAN TO REVEAL ITS TRUE NATURE.
ISN'T THIS ...
... THE VILLAGE WE JUST LEFT?
MUTTER
THIS CAN'T BE RIGHT ...
I'M SURE WE TOOK A STRAIGHT PATH AWAY FROM THE VILLAGE.
WE FELT SPOOKED BUT ...
... TRIED TO BELIEVE WE'D MADE A WRONG TURN SOMEWHERE. WE TOOK THE STRAIGHT PATH FROM THE VILLAGE AGAIN, BUT ...

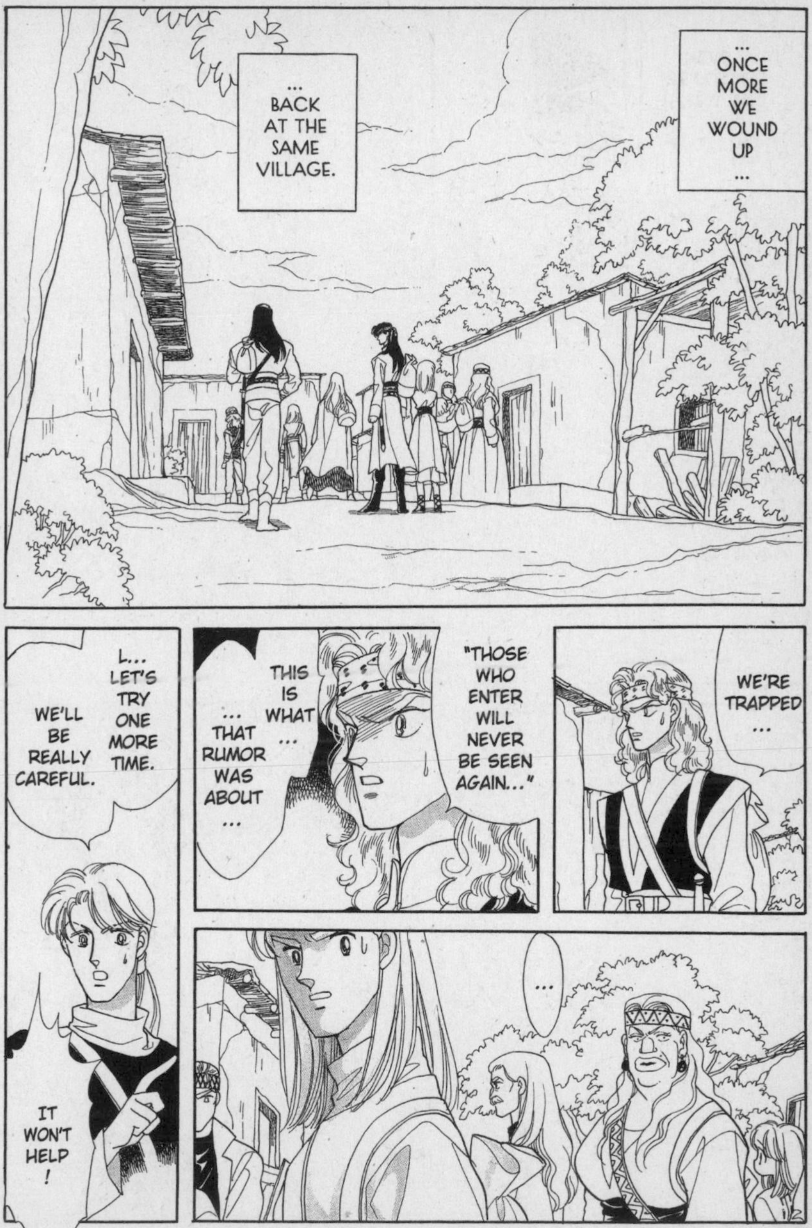
... ONCE MORE WE WOUND UP ...
... BACK AT THE SAME VILLAGE.
WE'RE TRAPPED ...
"THOSE WHO ENTER WILL NEVER BE SEEN AGAIN..."
THIS IS WHAT ...
... THAT RUMOR WAS ABOUT ...
...
L... LET'S TRY ONE MORE TIME.
WE'LL BE REALLY CAREFUL.
IT WON'T HELP !

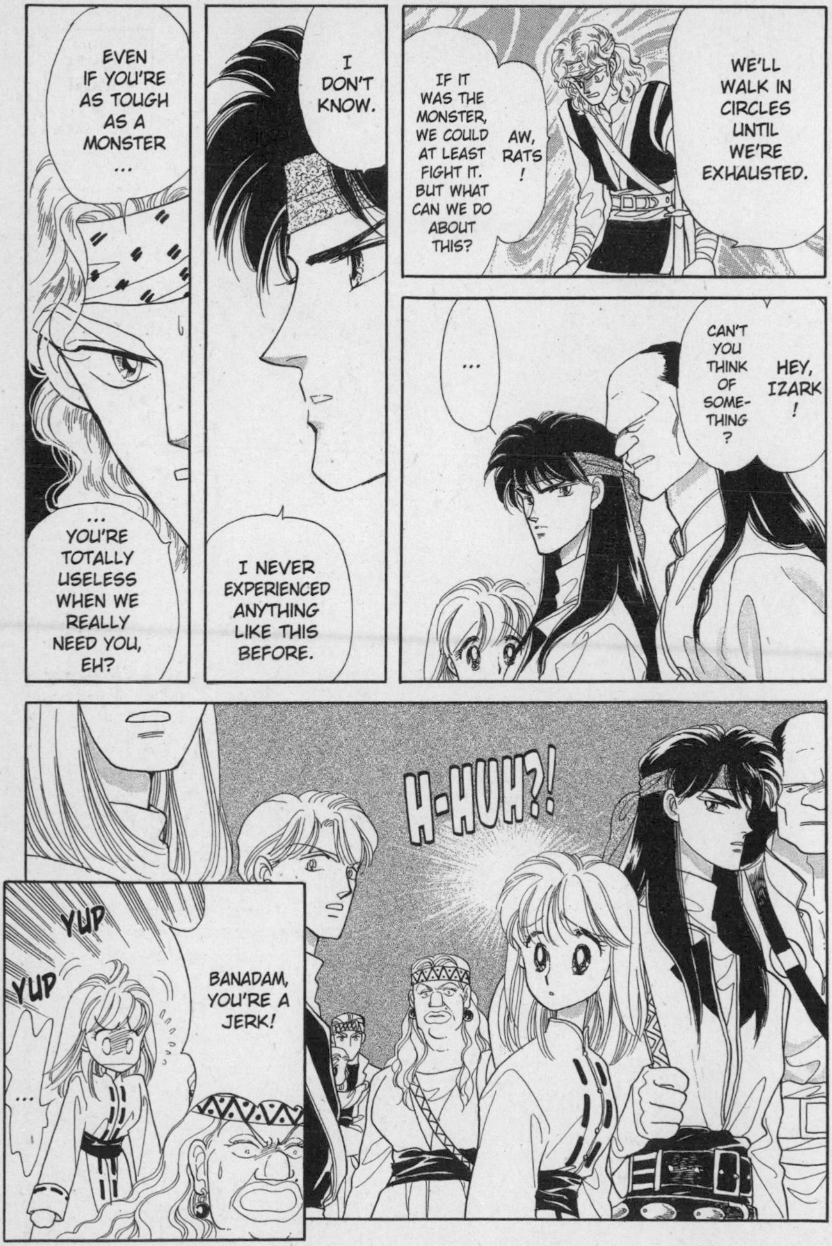
WE'LL WALK IN CIRCLES UNTIL WE'RE EXHAUSTED.
AW, RATS!
IF IT WAS THE MONSTER, WE COULD AT LEAST FIGHT IT. BUT WHAT CAN WE DO ABOUT THIS?
HEY, IZARK!
CAN'T YOU THINK OF SOME-THING?
...
I DON'T KNOW.
I NEVER EXPERIENCED ANYTHING LIKE THIS BEFORE.
EVEN IF YOU'RE AS TOUGH AS A MONSTER ...
... YOU'RE TOTALLY USELESS WHEN WE REALLY NEED YOU, EH?
H-HUH?!
YUP
YUP
BANADAM, YOU'RE A JERK!
...

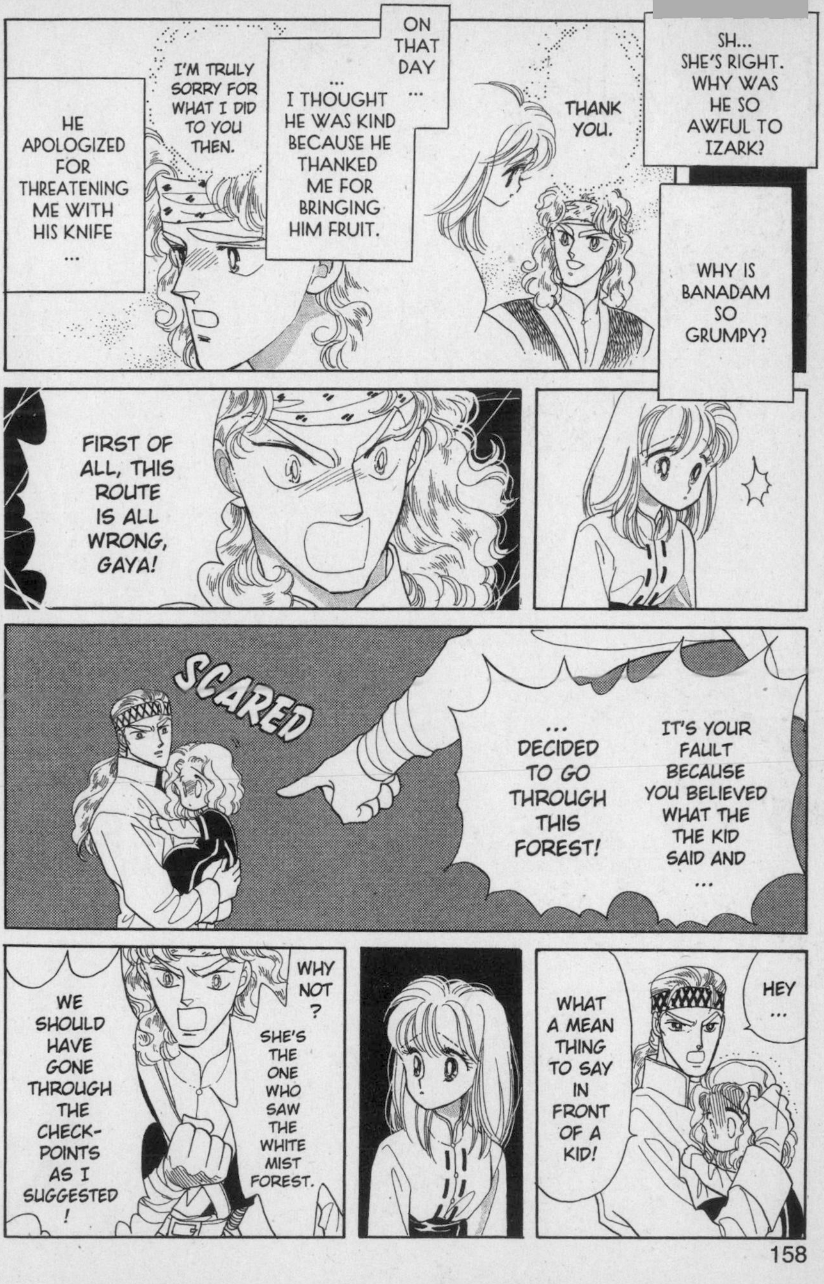
SH... SHE'S RIGHT. WHY WAS HE SO AWFUL TO IZARK?
WHY IS BANADAM SO GRUMPY?
THANK YOU.
ON THAT DAY ...
... I THOUGHT HE WAS KIND BECAUSE HE THANKED ME FOR BRINGING HIM FRUIT.
I'M TRULY SORRY FOR WHAT I DID TO YOU THEN.
HE APOLOGIZED FOR THREATENING ME WITH HIS KNIFE ...
FIRST OF ALL, THIS ROUTE IS ALL WRONG, GAYA!
IT'S YOUR FAULT BECAUSE YOU BELIEVED WHAT THE THE KID SAID AND ...
... DECIDED TO GO THROUGH THIS FOREST!
SCARED
HEY ...
WHAT A MEAN THING TO SAY IN FRONT OF A KID!
WHY NOT ?
SHE'S THE ONE WHO SAW THE WHITE MIST FOREST.
WE SHOULD HAVE GONE THROUGH THE CHECK-POINTS AS I SUGGESTED !

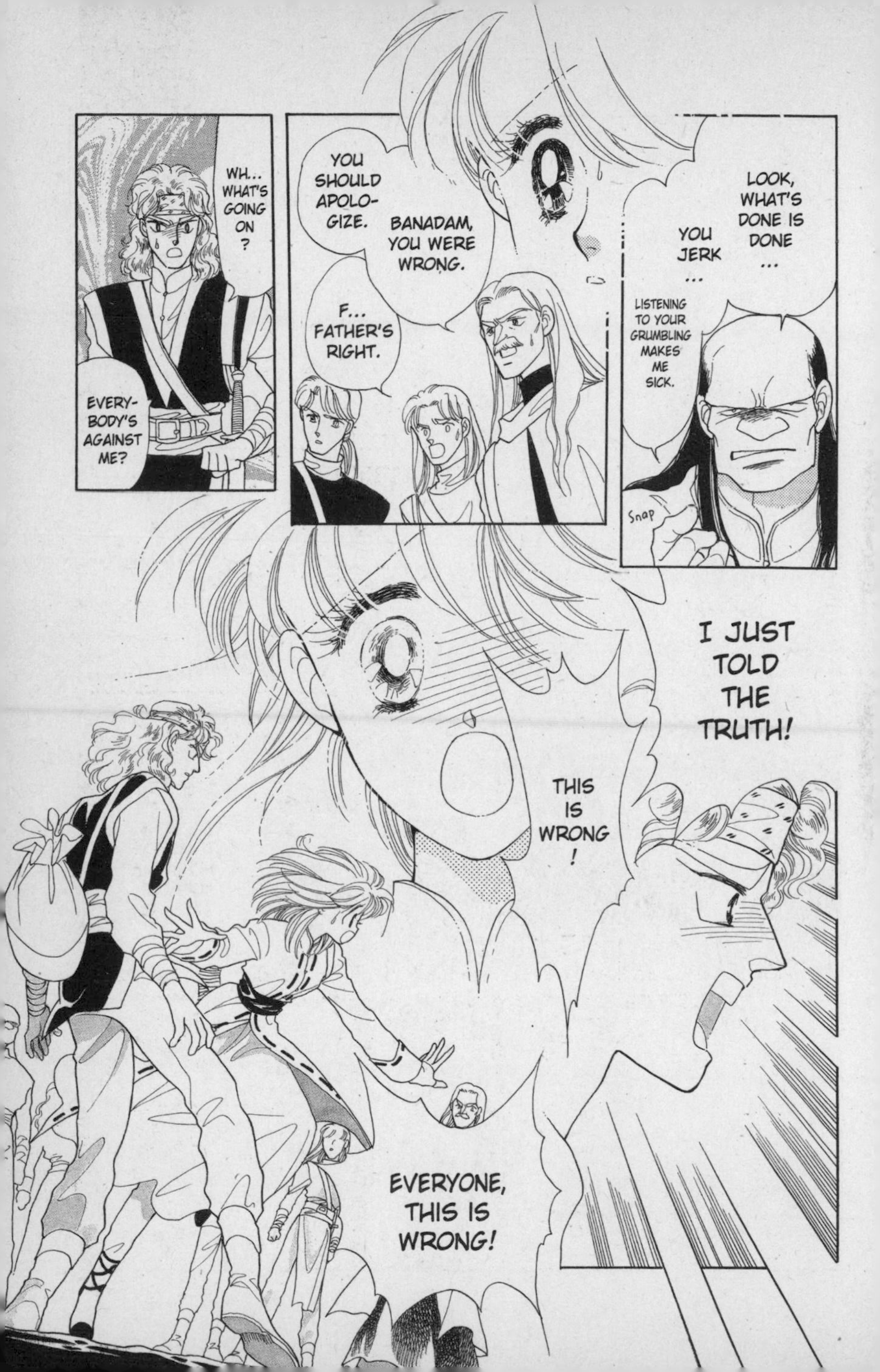
LOOK, WHAT'S DONE IS DONE ...
YOU JERK ...
LISTENING TO YOUR GRUMBLING MAKES ME SICK.
Snap
BANADAM, YOU WERE WRONG.
YOU SHOULD APOLO-GIZE.
F... FATHER'S RIGHT.
WH... WHAT'S GOING ON ?
EVERY-BODY'S AGAINST ME?
I JUST TOLD THE TRUTH!
THIS IS WRONG !
EVERYONE, THIS IS WRONG!

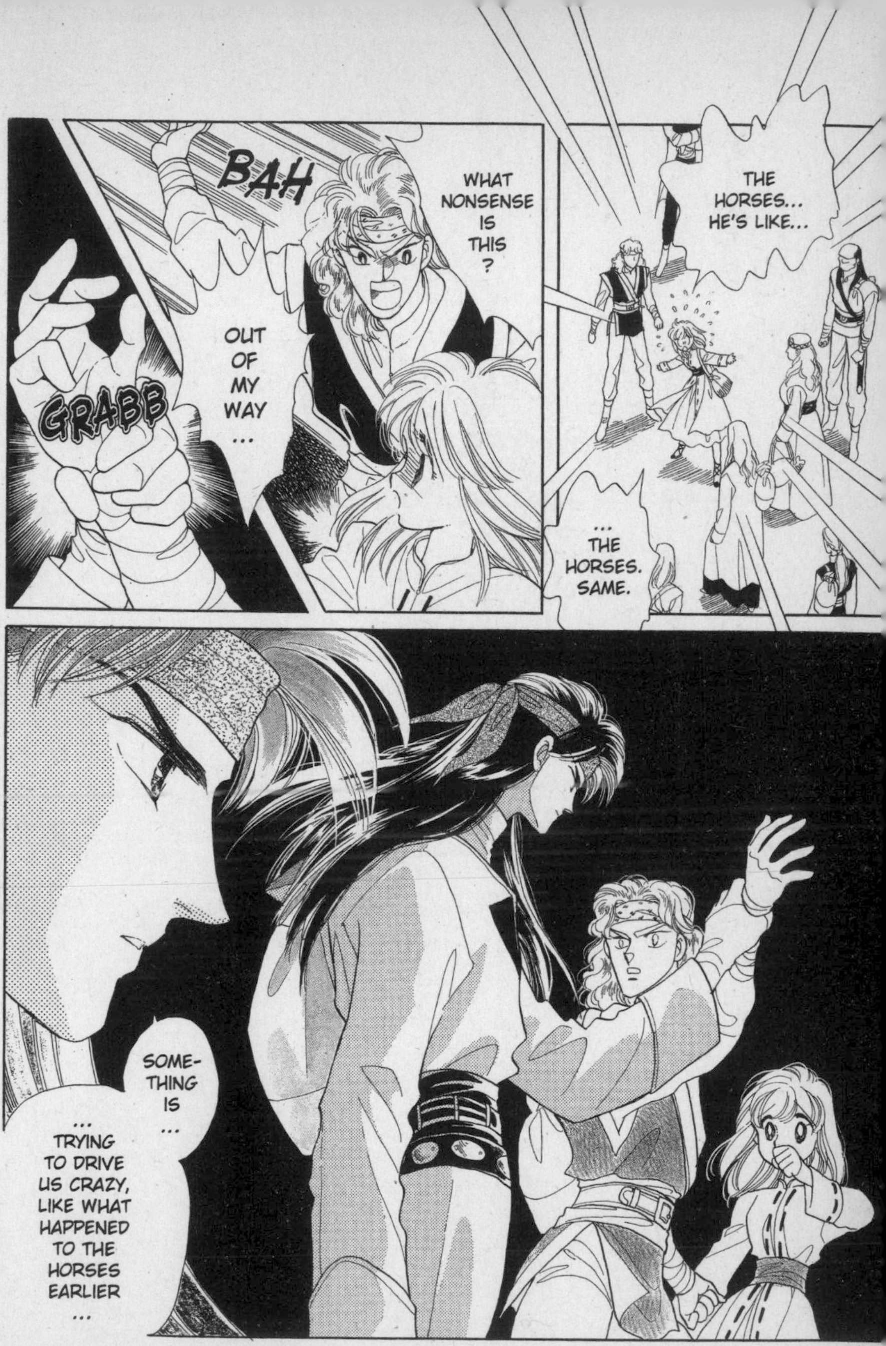
THE HORSES... HE'S LIKE...
... THE HORSES. SAME.
WHAT NONSENSE IS THIS ?
BAH
OUT OF MY WAY ...
GRABB
SOME-THING IS ...
... TRYING TO DRIVE US CRAZY, LIKE WHAT HAPPENED TO THE HORSES EARLIER ...

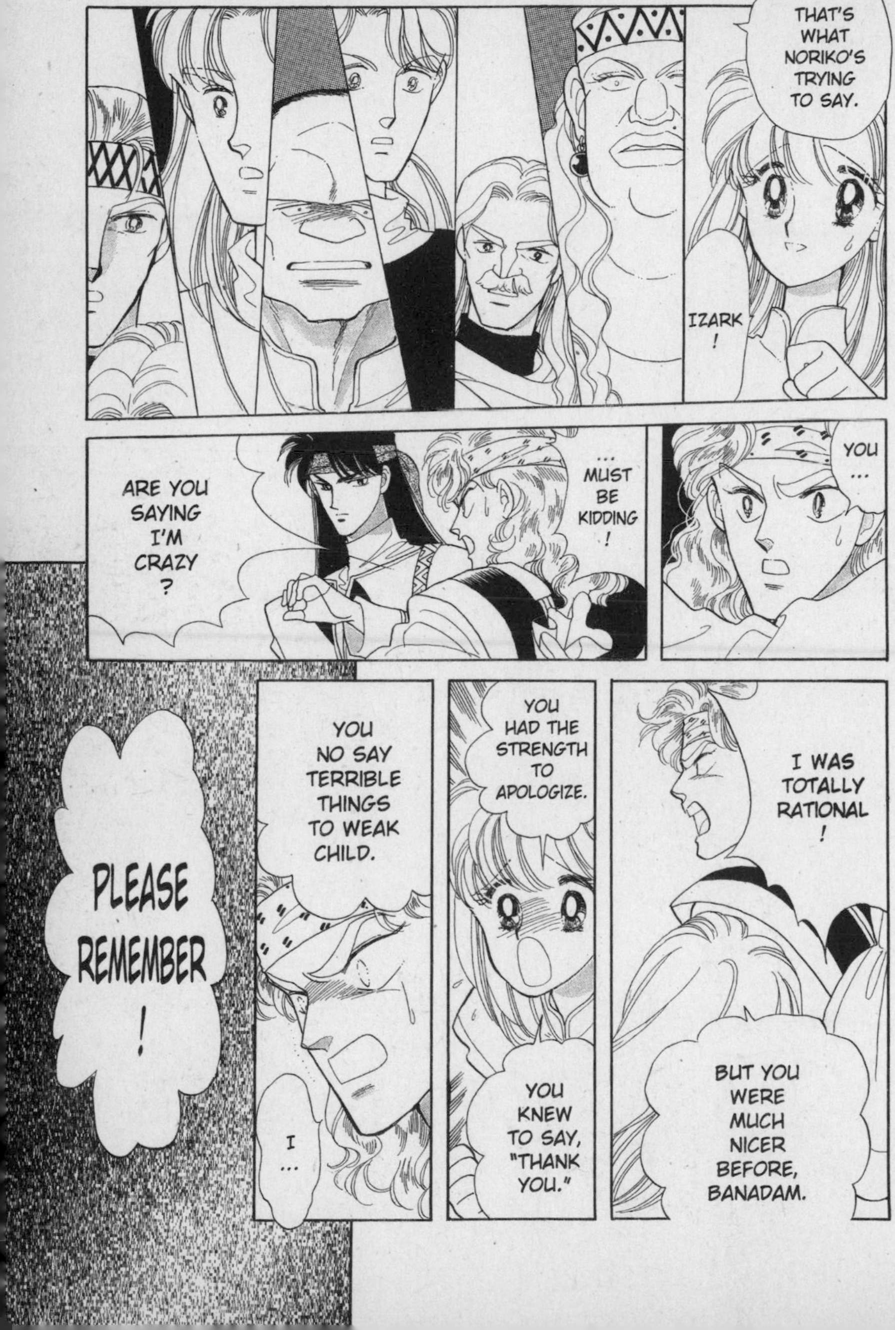
THAT'S WHAT NORIKO'S TRYING TO SAY.
IZARK !
YOU ...
... MUST BE KIDDING !
ARE YOU SAYING I'M CRAZY ?
I WAS TOTALLY RATIONAL !
BUT YOU WERE MUCH NICER BEFORE, BANADAM.
YOU HAD THE STRENGTH TO APOLOGIZE.
YOU KNEW TO SAY, "THANK YOU."
YOU NO SAY TERRIBLE THINGS TO WEAK CHILD.
I ...
PLEASE REMEMBER !

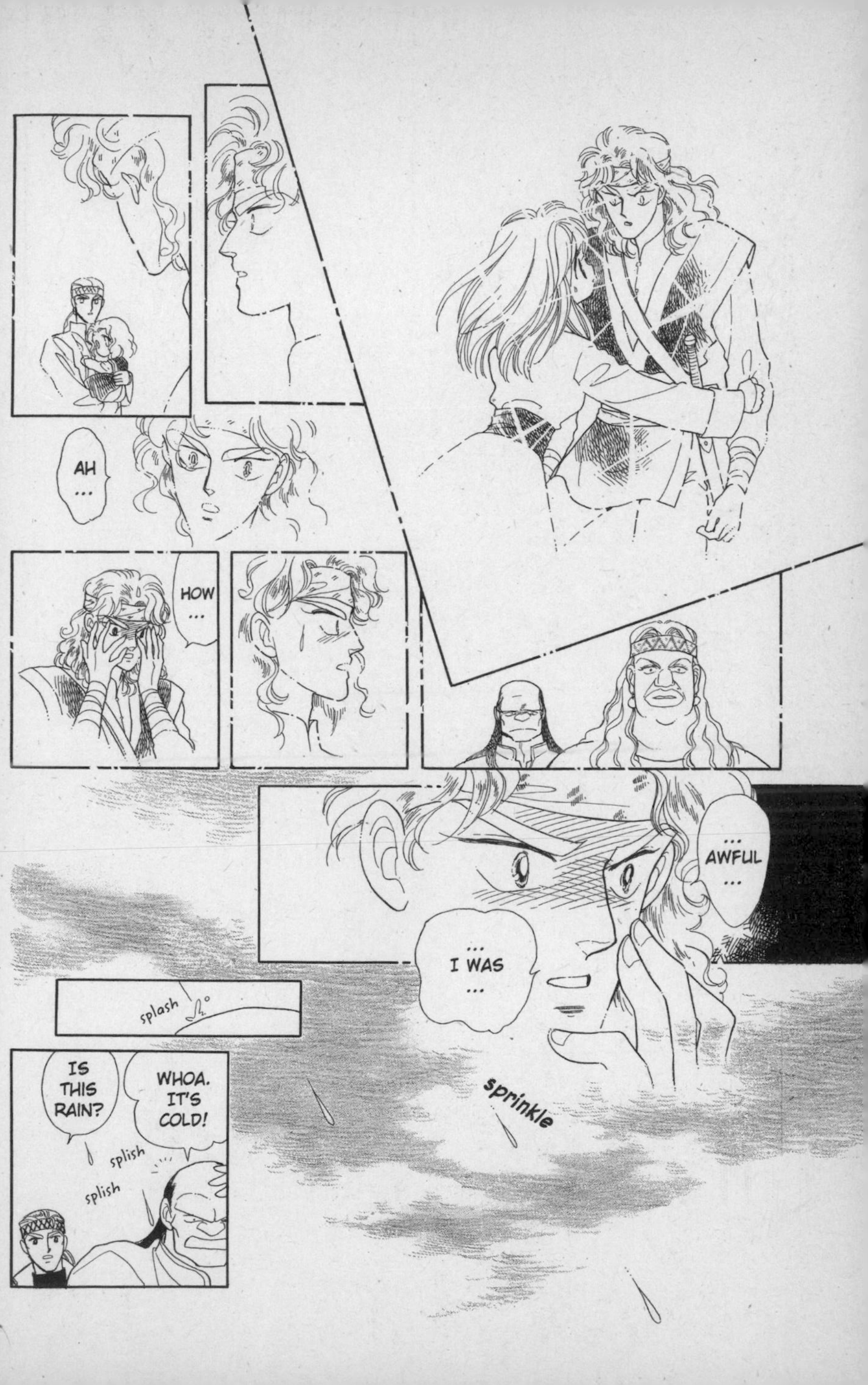
AH ...
HOW ...
... AWFUL ...
... I WAS ...
splash
sprinkle
WHOA. IT'S COLD!
IS THIS RAIN?
splish
splish

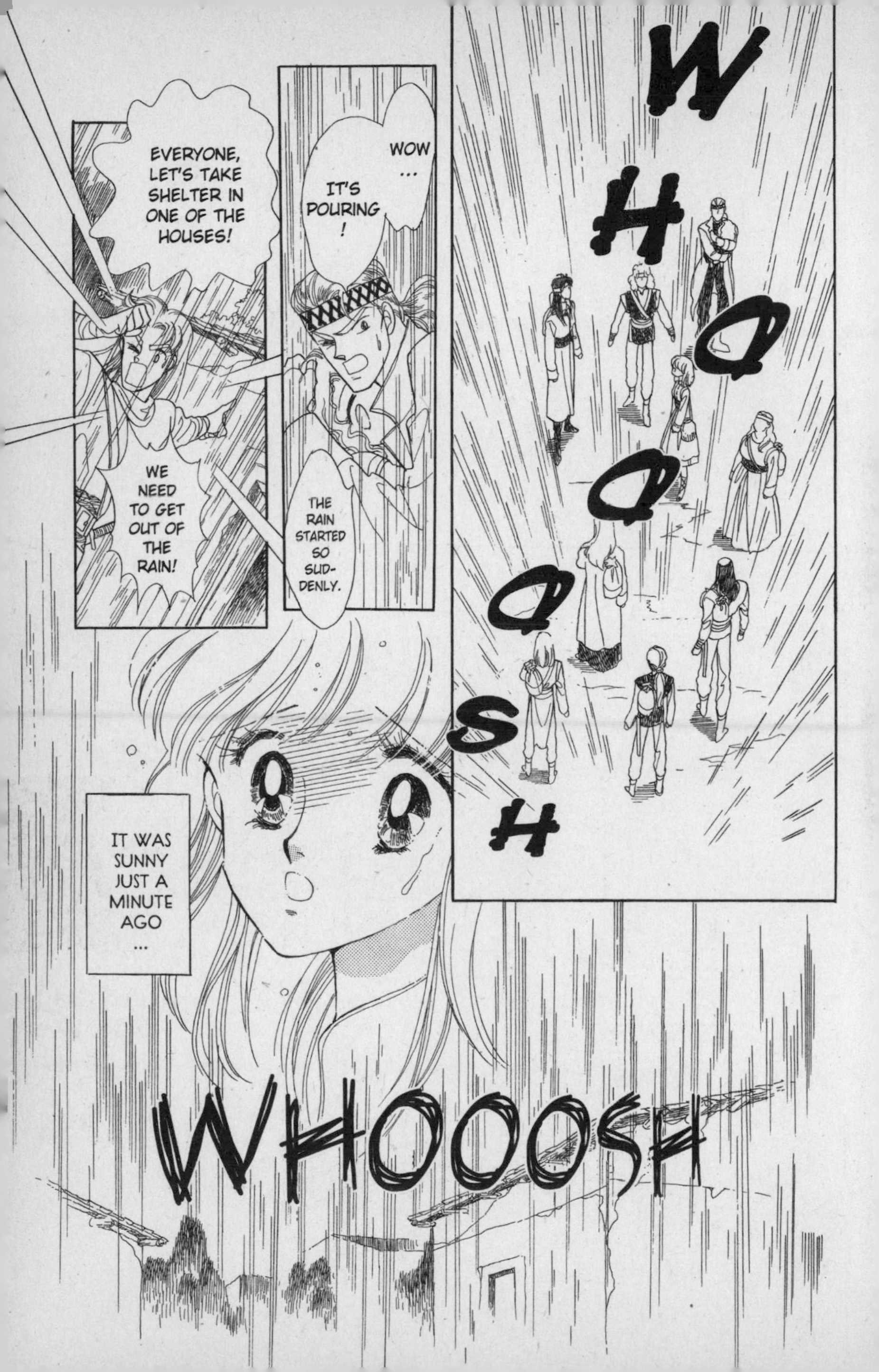
WHOOOSH
WOW ...
IT'S POURING !
THE RAIN STARTED SO SUD-DENLY.
EVERYONE, LET'S TAKE SHELTER IN ONE OF THE HOUSES!
WE NEED TO GET OUT OF THE RAIN!
IT WAS SUNNY JUST A MINUTE AGO ...
WHOOOSH

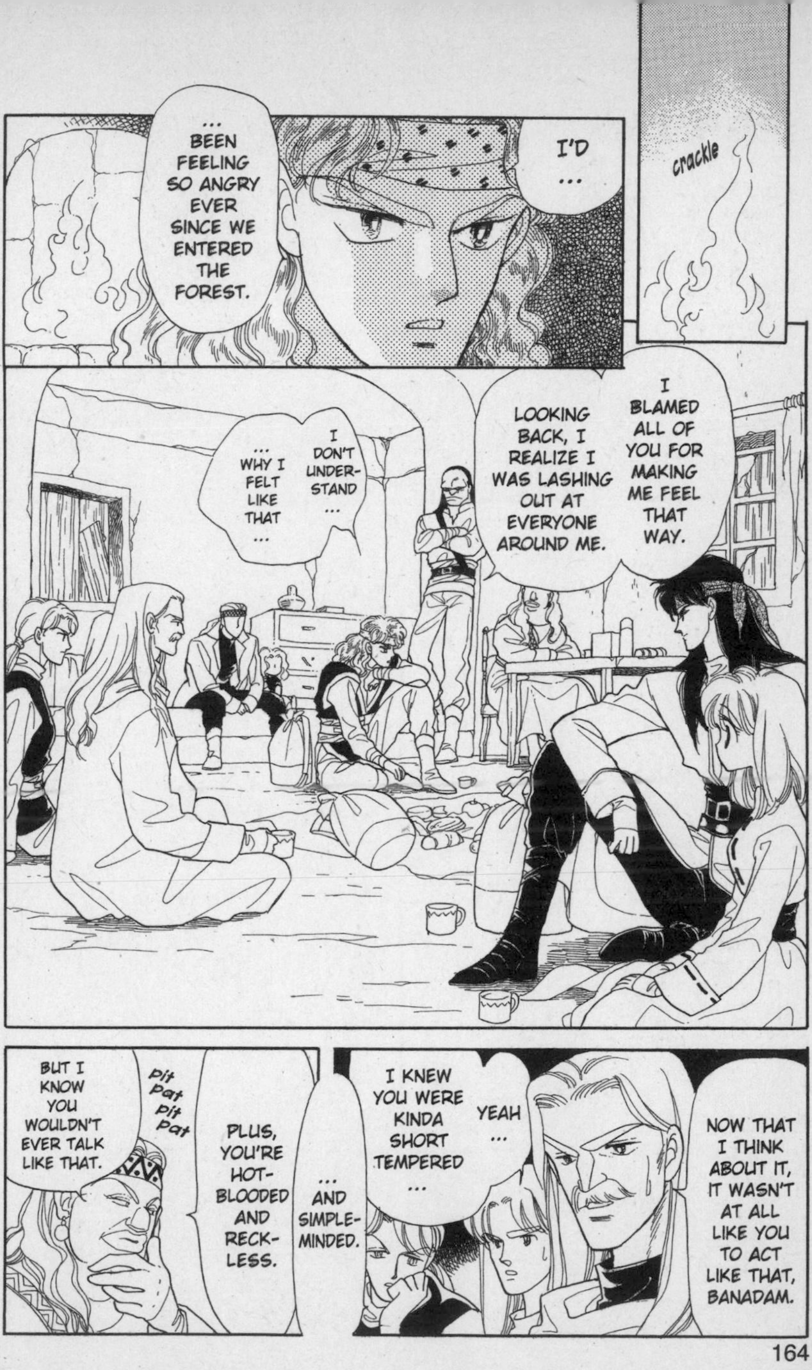
crackle
I'D ...
... BEEN FEELING SO ANGRY EVER SINCE WE ENTERED THE FOREST.
I BLAMED ALL OF YOU FOR MAKING ME FEEL THAT WAY.
LOOKING BACK, I REALIZE I WAS LASHING OUT AT EVERYONE AROUND ME.
I DON'T UNDER-STAND ...
... WHY I FELT LIKE THAT ...
NOW THAT I THINK ABOUT IT, IT WASN'T AT ALL LIKE YOU TO ACT LIKE THAT, BANADAM.
YEAH ...
I KNEW YOU WERE KINDA SHORT TEMPERED ...
... AND SIMPLE-MINDED.
PLUS, YOU'RE HOT-BLOODED AND RECK-LESS.
pit pat pit pat
BUT I KNOW YOU WOULDN'T EVER TALK LIKE THAT.

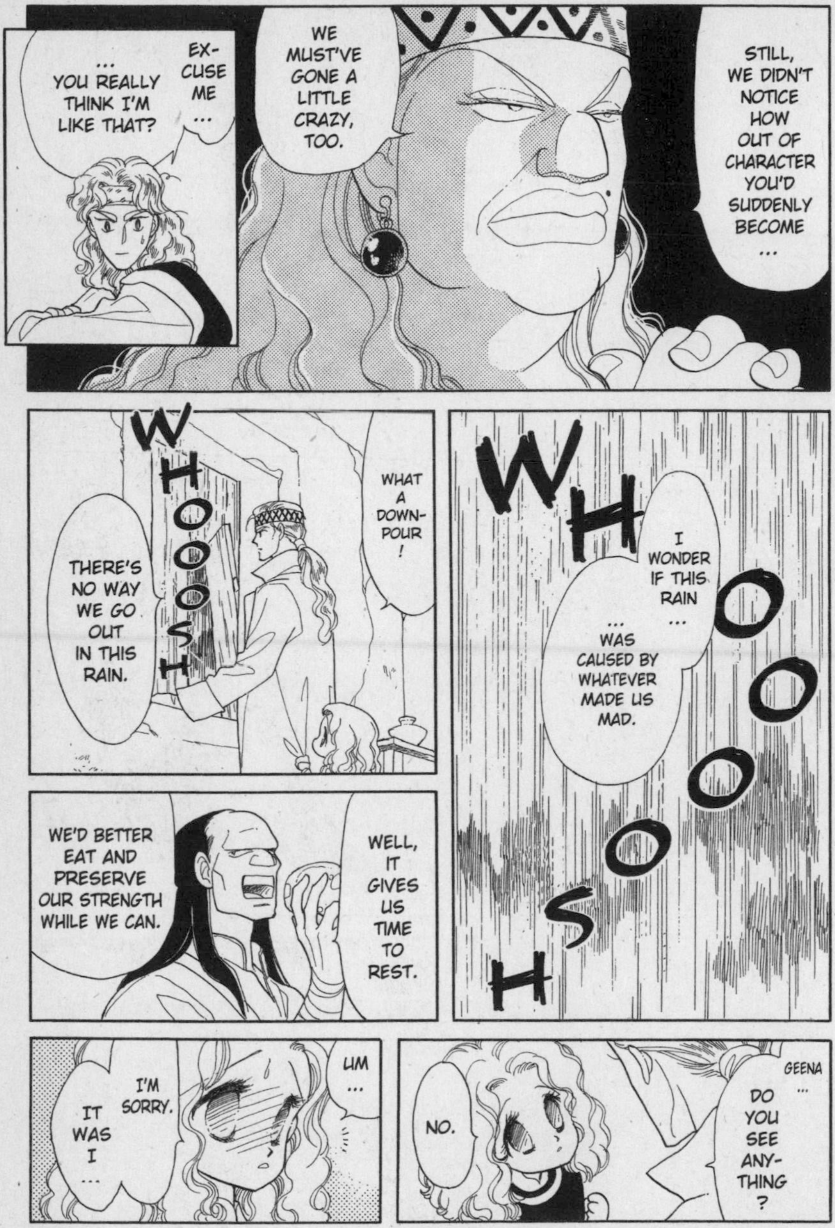
STILL, WE DIDN'T NOTICE HOW OUT OF CHARACTER YOU'D SUDDENLY BECOME ...
WE MUST'VE GONE A LITTLE CRAZY, TOO.
EX-CUSE ME ...
... YOU REALLY THINK I'M LIKE THAT?
WHOOOOSH
I WONDER IF THIS RAIN ...
... WAS CAUSED BY WHATEVER MADE US MAD.
WHAT A DOWN-POUR!
WHOOOSH
THERE'S NO WAY WE GO OUT IN THIS RAIN.
WELL, IT GIVES US TIME TO REST.
WE'D BETTER EAT AND PRESERVE OUR STRENGTH WHILE WE CAN.
GEENA ...
DO YOU SEE ANY-THING?
NO.
UM ...
I'M SORRY.
IT WAS I ...

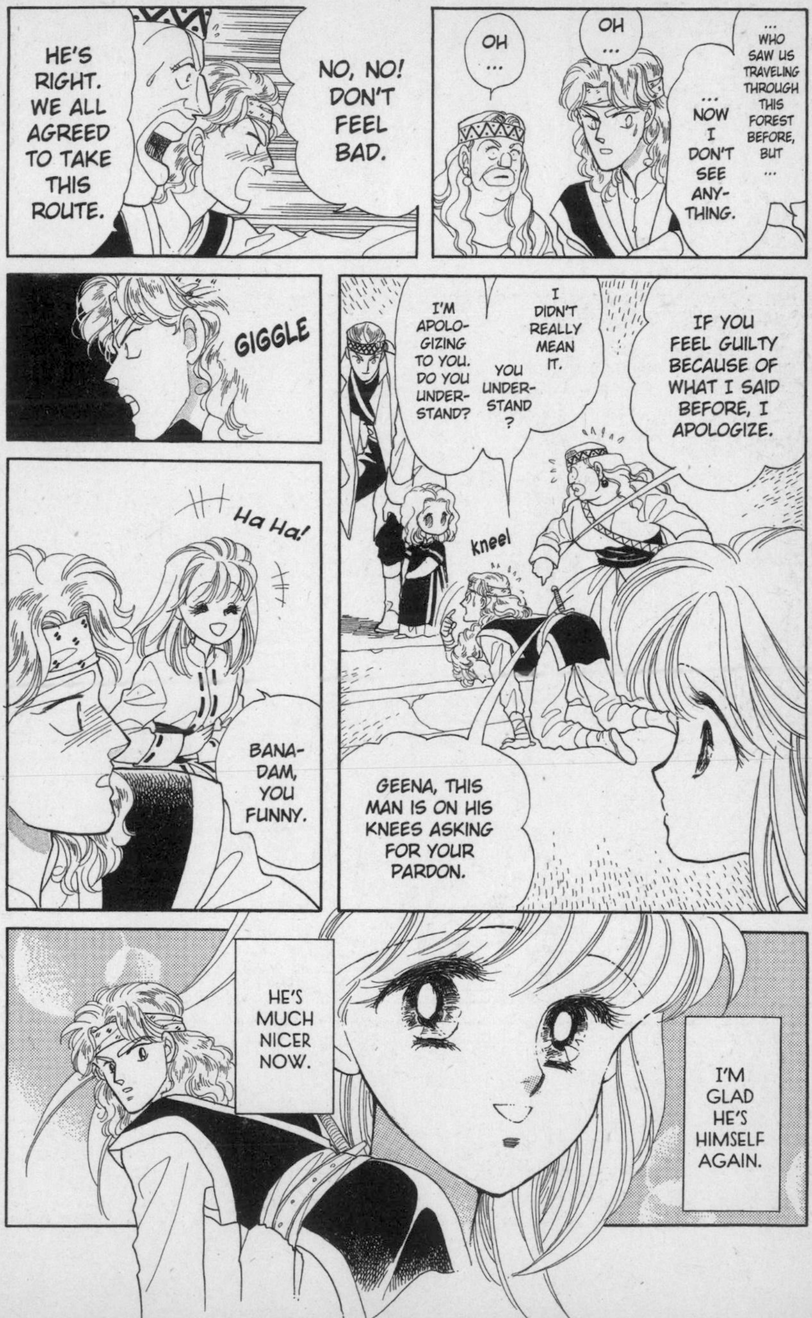
... WHO SAW US TRAVELING THROUGH THIS FOREST BEFORE, BUT ...
... NOW I DON'T SEE ANYTHING.
OH ...
OH ...
NO, NO! DON'T FEEL BAD.
HE'S RIGHT. WE ALL AGREED TO TAKE THIS ROUTE.
IF YOU FEEL GUILTY BECAUSE OF WHAT I SAID BEFORE, I APOLOGIZE.
I DIDN'T REALLY MEAN IT.
YOU UNDERSTAND?
I'M APOLOGIZING TO YOU. DO YOU UNDERSTAND?
kneel
GEENA, THIS MAN IS ON HIS KNEES ASKING FOR YOUR PARDON.
GIGGLE
Ha Ha!
BANADAM, YOU FUNNY.
I'M GLAD HE'S HIMSELF AGAIN.
HE'S MUCH NICER NOW.

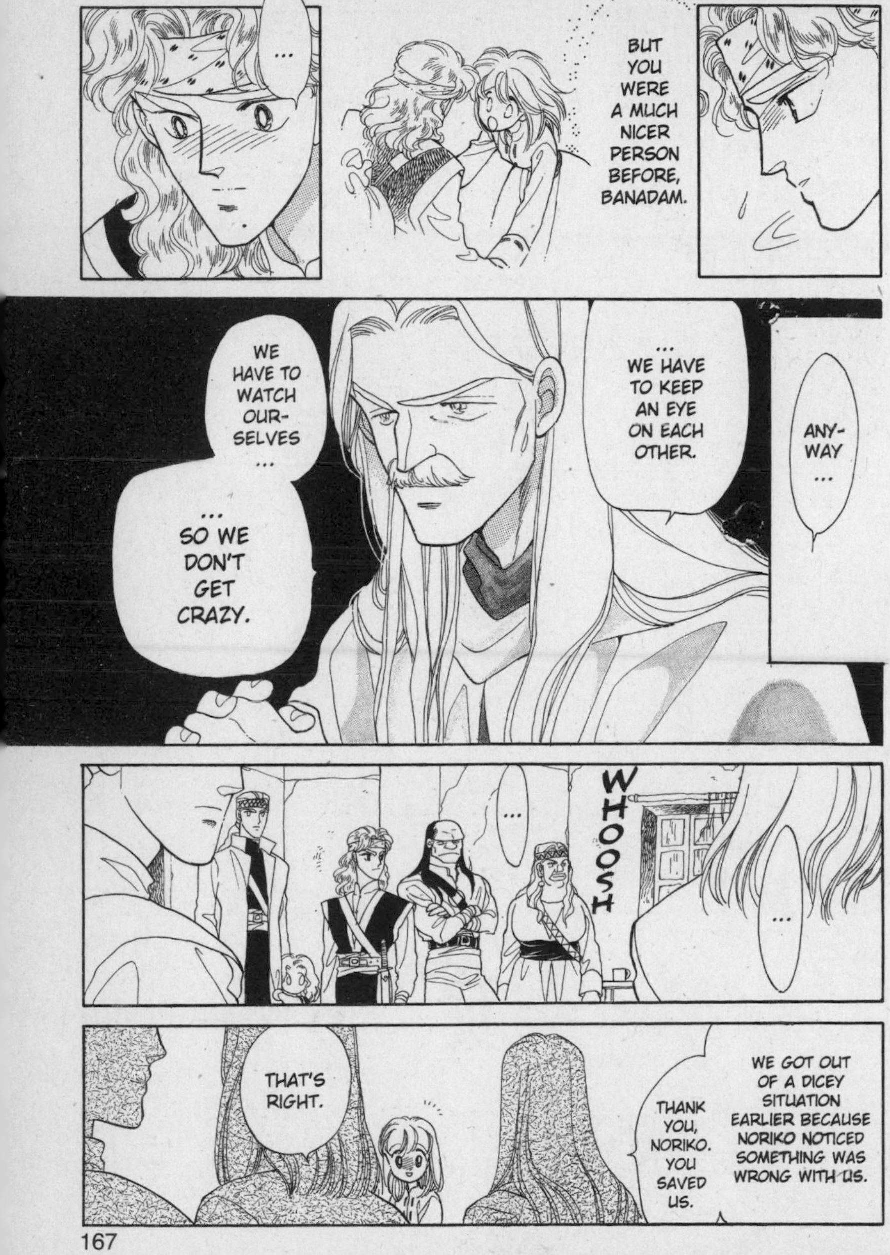

BUT YOU WERE A MUCH NICER PERSON BEFORE, BANADAM.
...
ANY-WAY ...
... WE HAVE TO KEEP AN EYE ON EACH OTHER.
WE HAVE TO WATCH OUR-SELVES ...
... SO WE DON'T GET CRAZY.
...
WHOOSH
...
WE GOT OUT OF A DICEY SITUATION EARLIER BECAUSE NORIKO NOTICED SOMETHING WAS WRONG WITH US.
THANK YOU, NORIKO. YOU SAVED US.
THAT'S RIGHT.

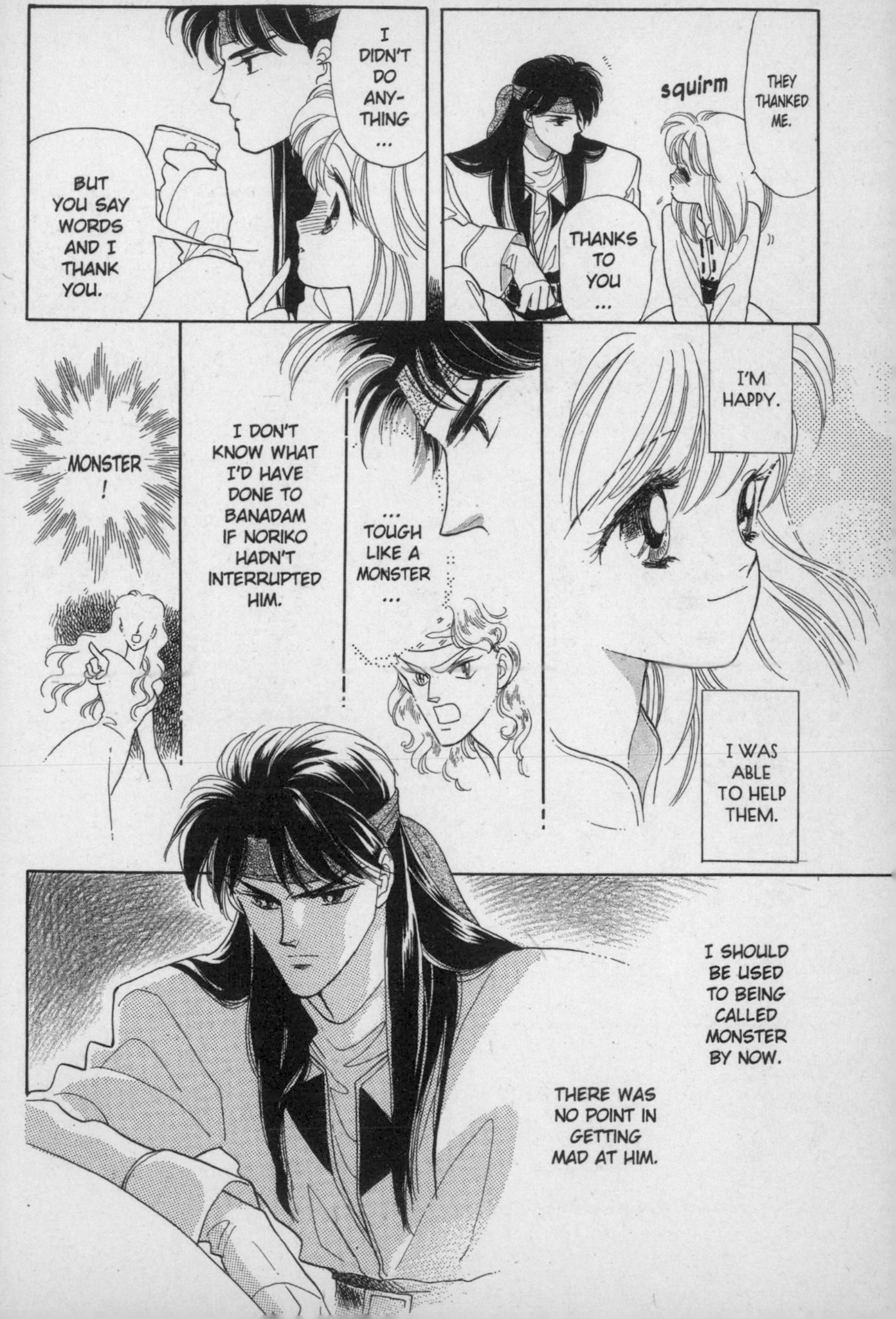
THEY THANKED ME.
squirm
THANKS TO YOU ...
I DIDN'T DO ANY-THING ...
BUT YOU SAY WORDS AND I THANK YOU.
I'M HAPPY.
I WAS ABLE TO HELP THEM.
... TOUGH LIKE A MONSTER ...
I DON'T KNOW WHAT I'D HAVE DONE TO BANADAM IF NORIKO HADN'T INTERRUPTED HIM.
MONSTER !
I SHOULD BE USED TO BEING CALLED MONSTER BY NOW.
THERE WAS NO POINT IN GETTING MAD AT HIM.

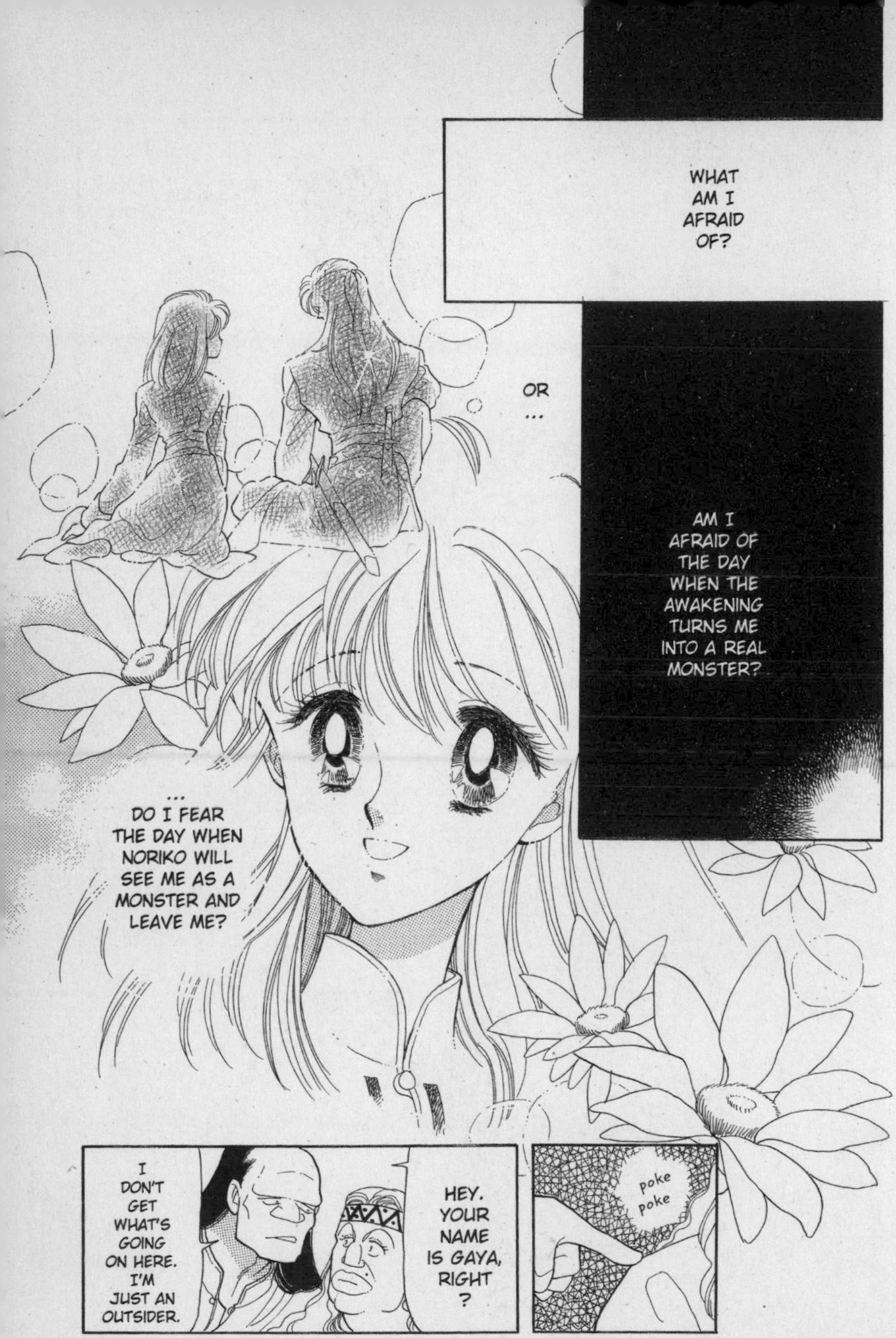
WHAT AM I AFRAID OF?
OR ...
AM I AFRAID OF THE DAY WHEN THE AWAKENING TURNS ME INTO A REAL MONSTER?
... DO I FEAR THE DAY WHEN NORIKO WILL SEE ME AS A MONSTER AND LEAVE ME?
poke poke
HEY. YOUR NAME IS GAYA, RIGHT?
I DON'T GET WHAT'S GOING ON HERE. I'M JUST AN OUTSIDER.

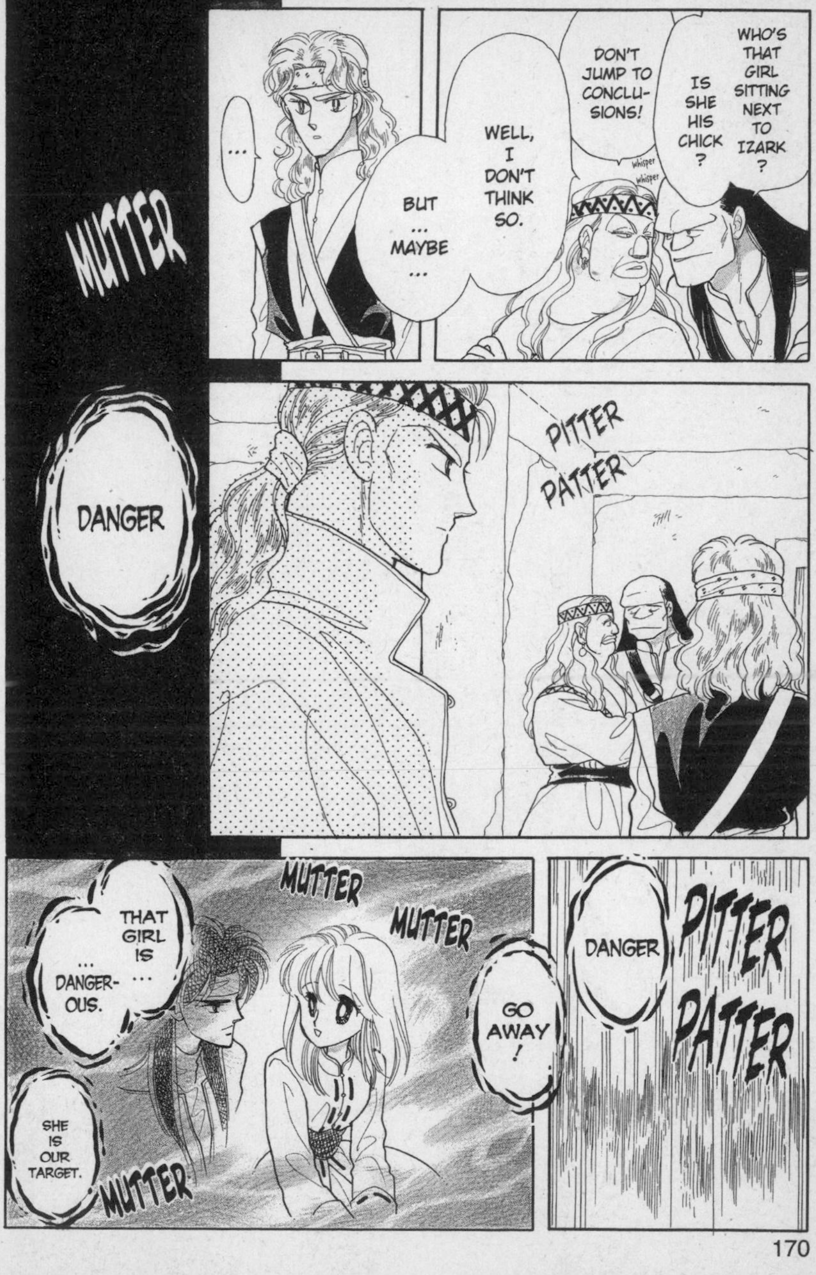
WHO'S THAT GIRL SITTING NEXT TO IZARK?
IS SHE HIS CHICK?
DON'T JUMP TO CONCLUSIONS!
whisper whisper
WELL, I DON'T THINK SO.
BUT ... MAYBE ...
...
MUTTER
PITTER PATTER
DANGER
PITTER PATTER
DANGER
GO AWAY!
MUTTER
MUTTER
THAT GIRL IS ... DANGER-OUS.
SHE IS OUR TARGET.
MUTTER

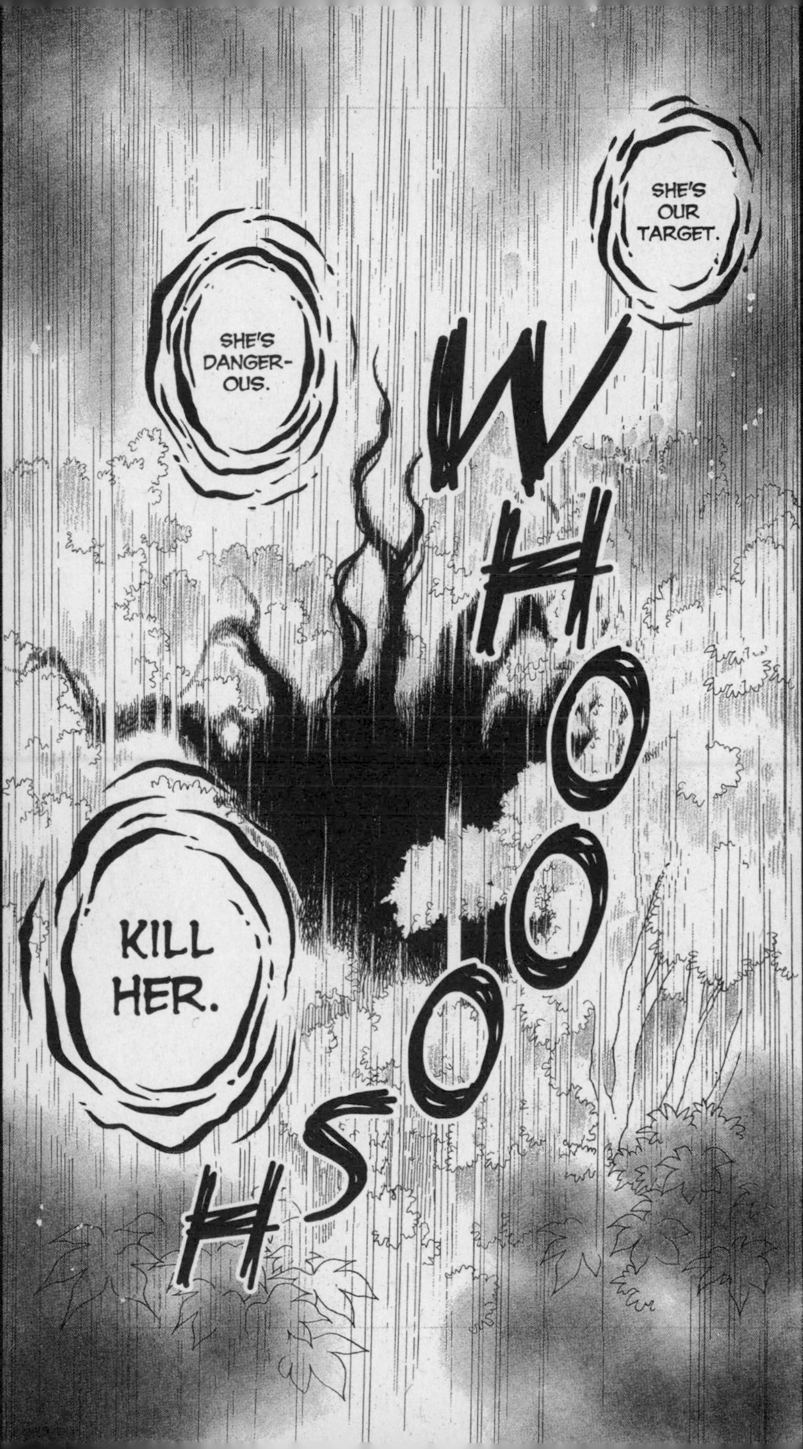
SHE'S OUR TARGET.
SHE'S DANGER-OUS.
WHOOOSH
KILL HER.

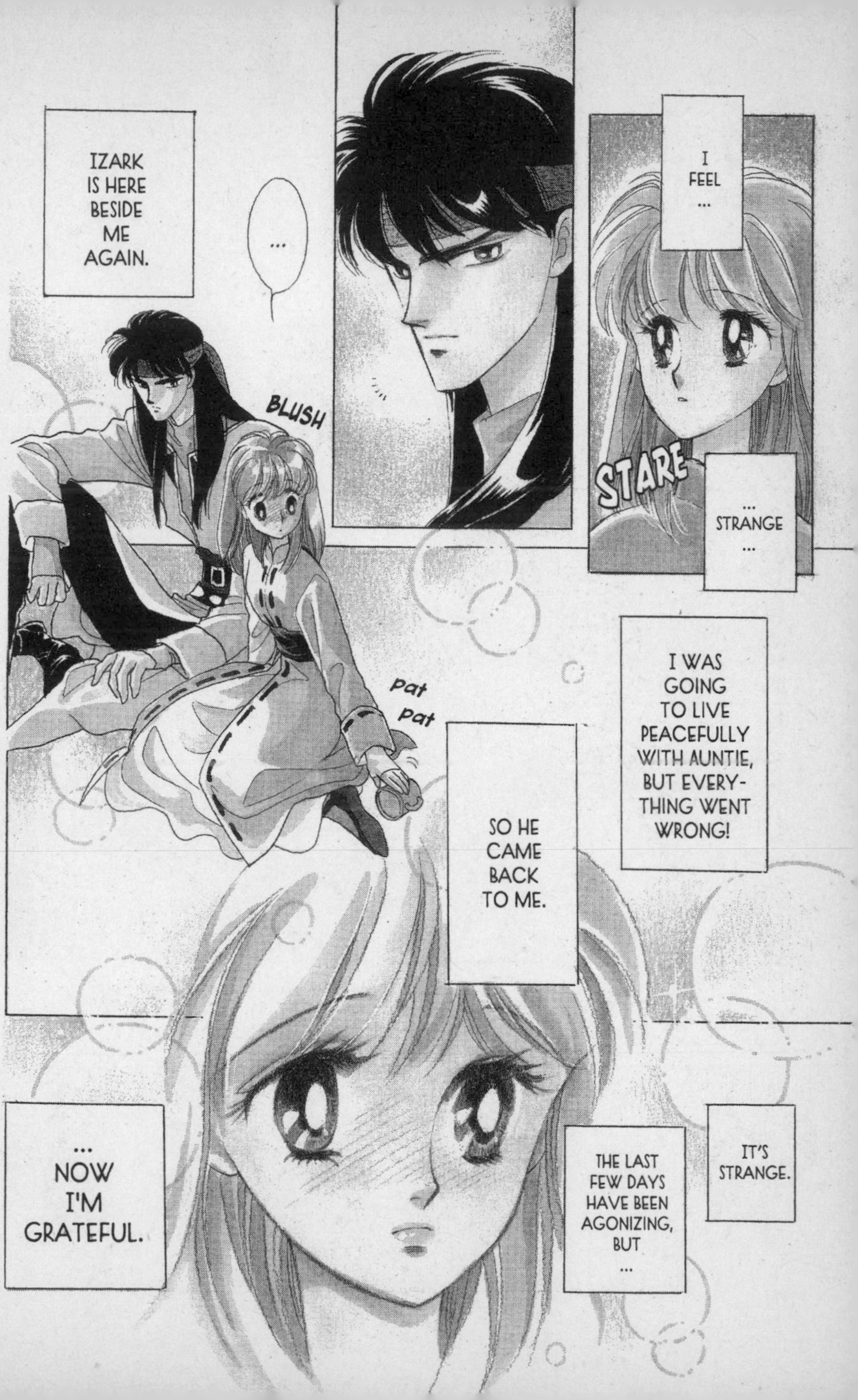
I FEEL ...
STARE
... STRANGE ...
IZARK IS HERE BESIDE ME AGAIN.
...
BLUSH
pat pat
I WAS GOING TO LIVE PEACEFULLY WITH AUNTIE, BUT EVERY-THING WENT WRONG!
SO HE CAME BACK TO ME.
IT'S STRANGE.
THE LAST FEW DAYS HAVE BEEN AGONIZING, BUT ...
... NOW I'M GRATEFUL.

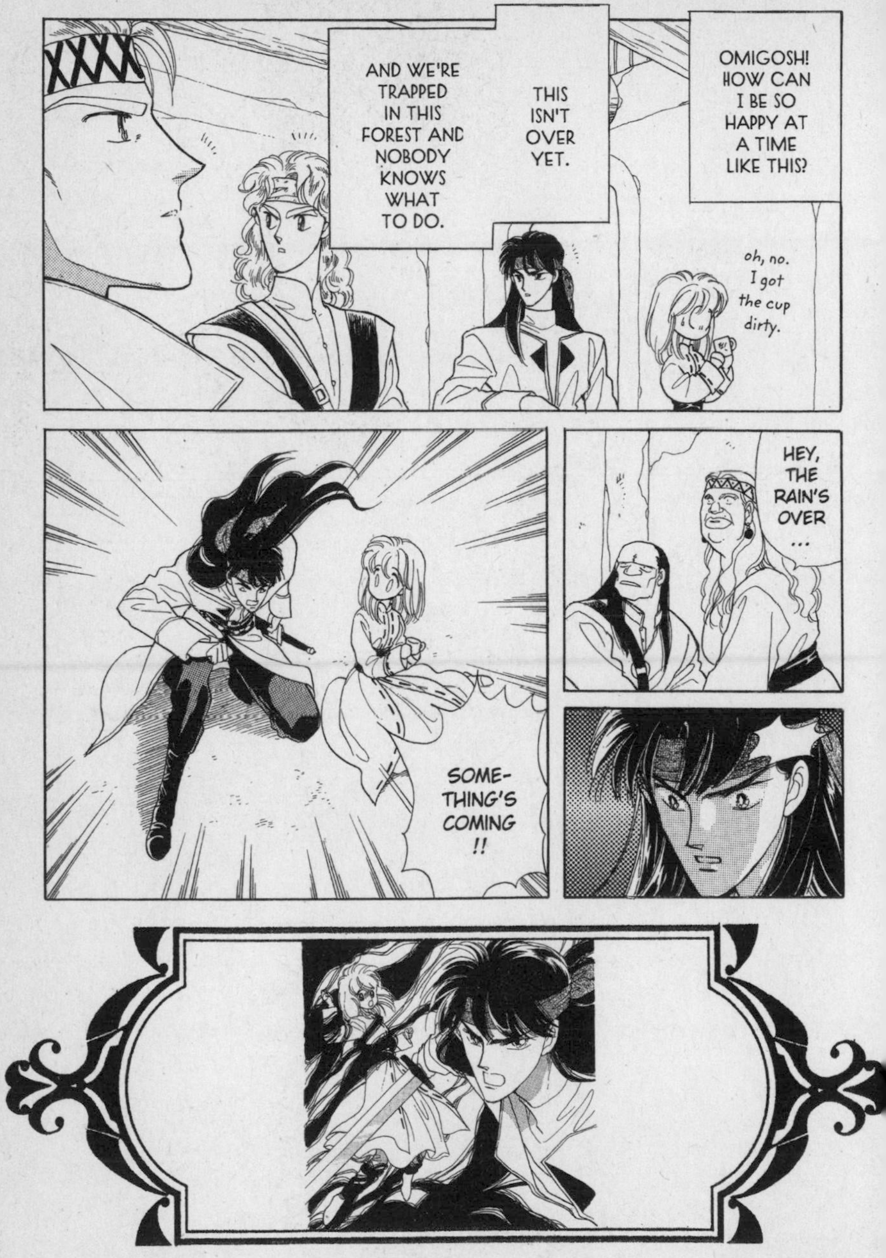
OMIGOSH! HOW CAN I BE SO HAPPY AT A TIME LIKE THIS?
THIS ISN'T OVER YET.
AND WE'RE TRAPPED IN THIS FOREST AND NOBODY KNOWS WHAT TO DO.
oh, no. I got the cup dirty.
HEY, THE RAIN'S OVER ...
SOME-THING'S COMING !!

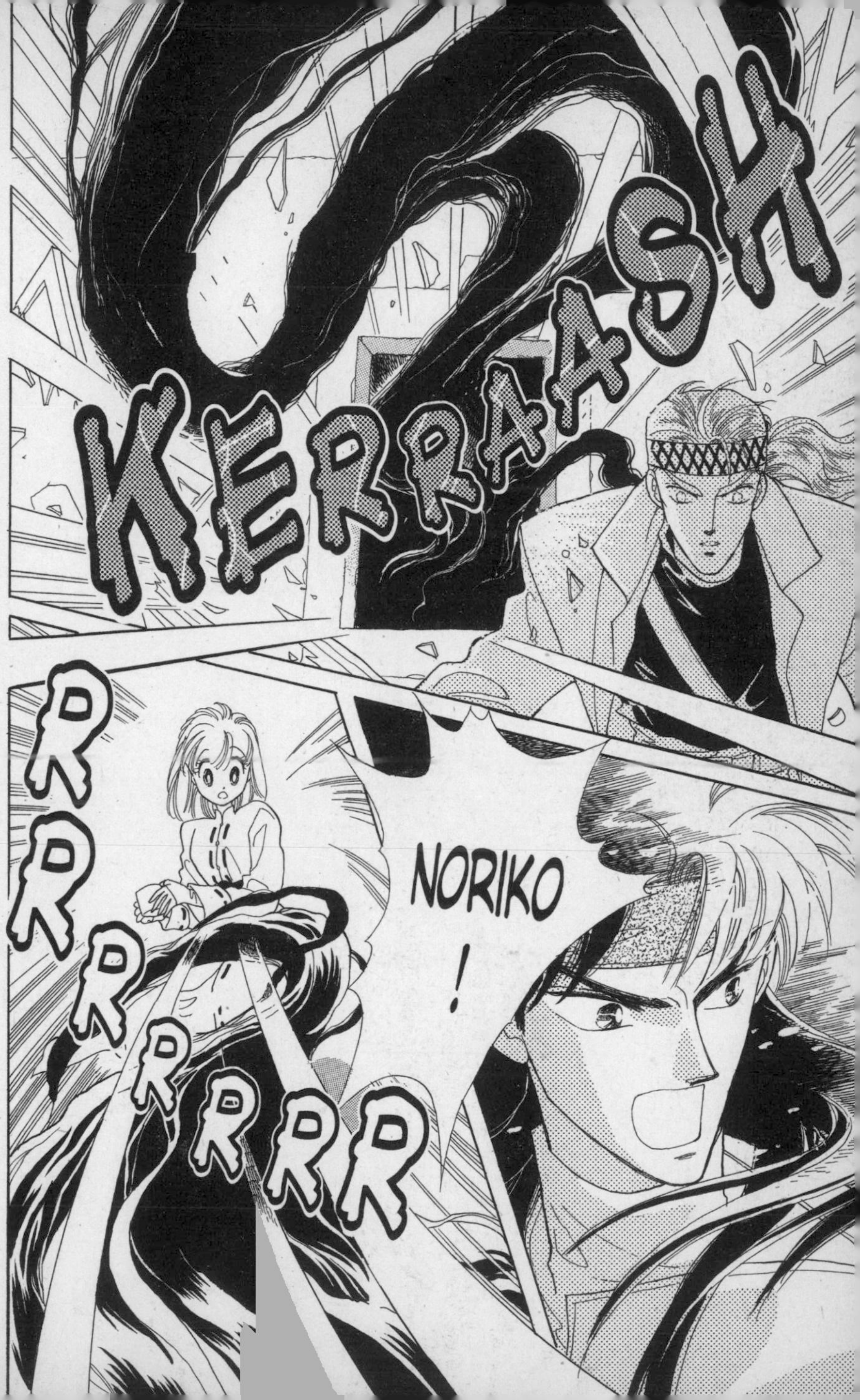
KERRAASH
NORIKO!
RRRRRRR

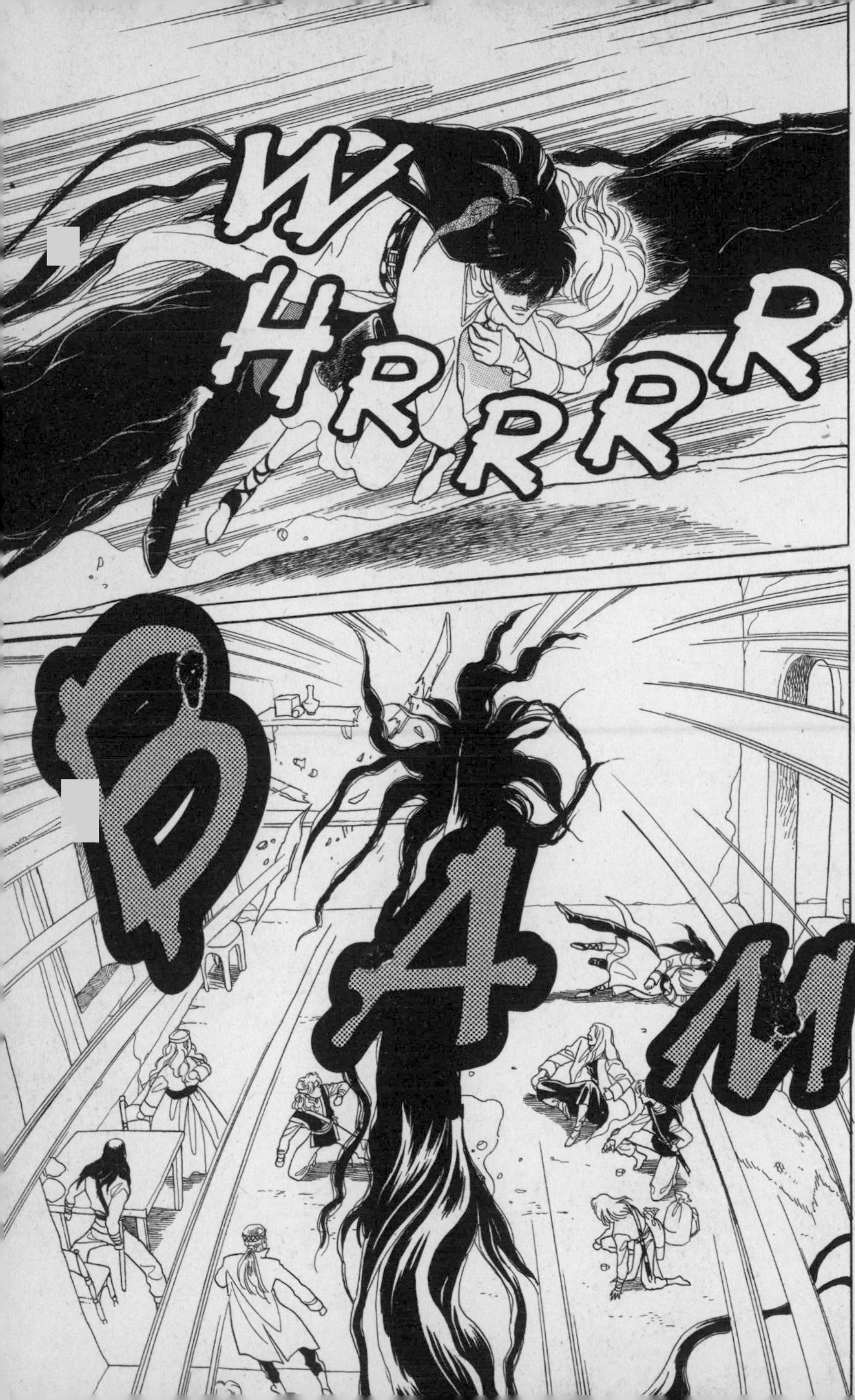
WHRRRR

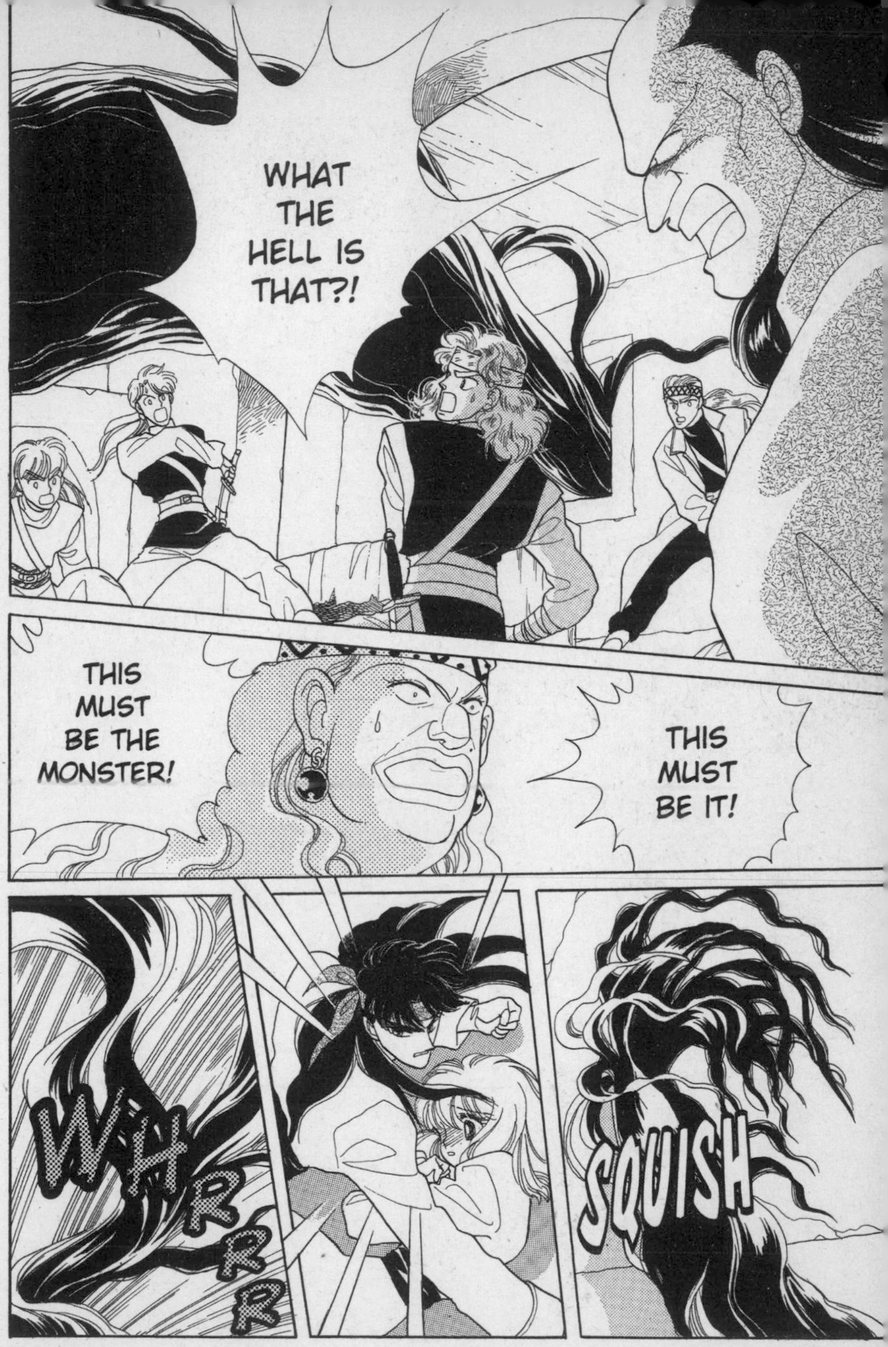
WHAT THE HELL IS THAT?!
THIS MUST BE IT!
THIS MUST BE THE MONSTER!
SQUISH
WHRRR

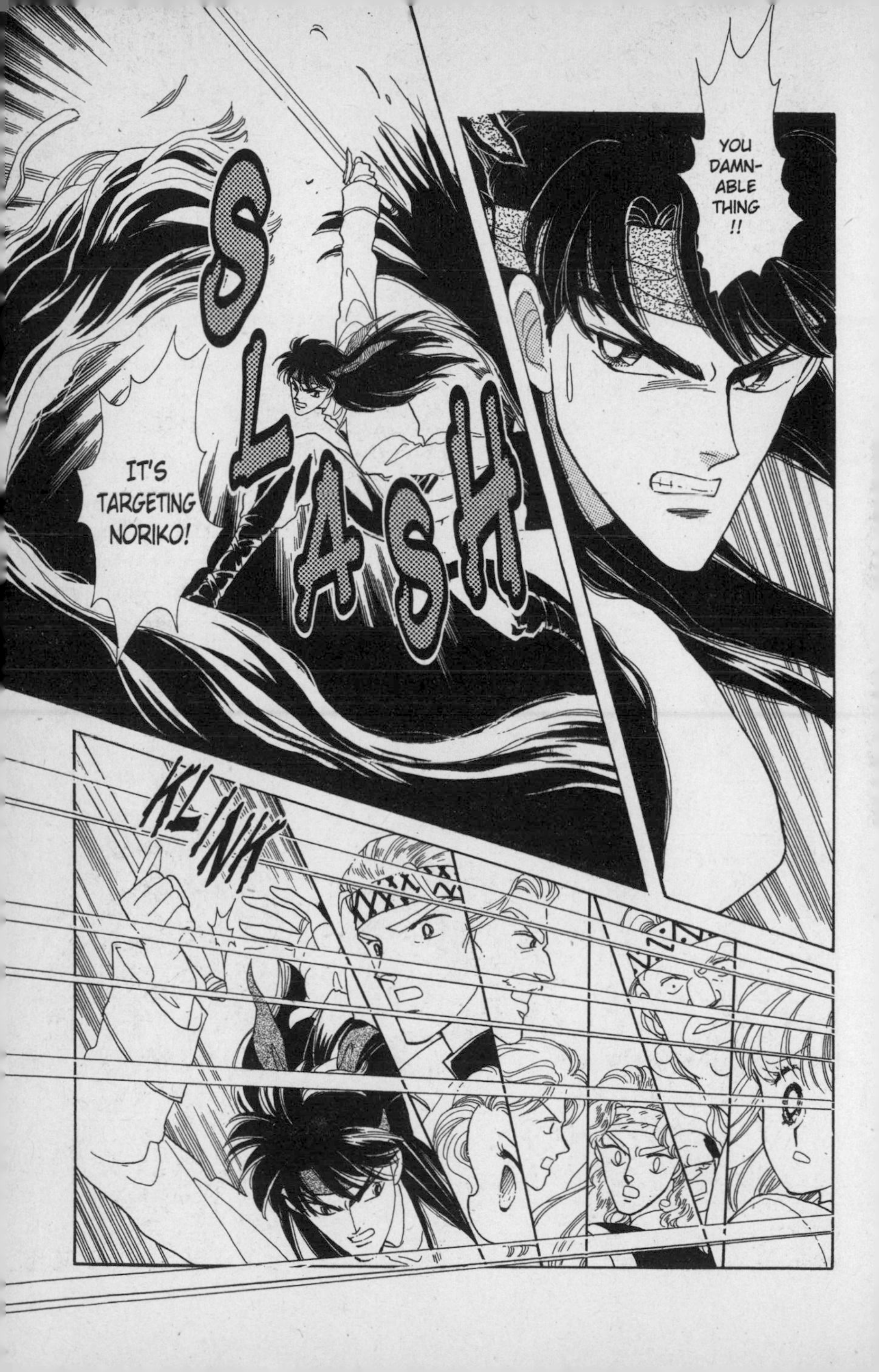
YOU DAMN-ABLE THING !!
SLASH
IT'S TARGETING NORIKO!
KLINK

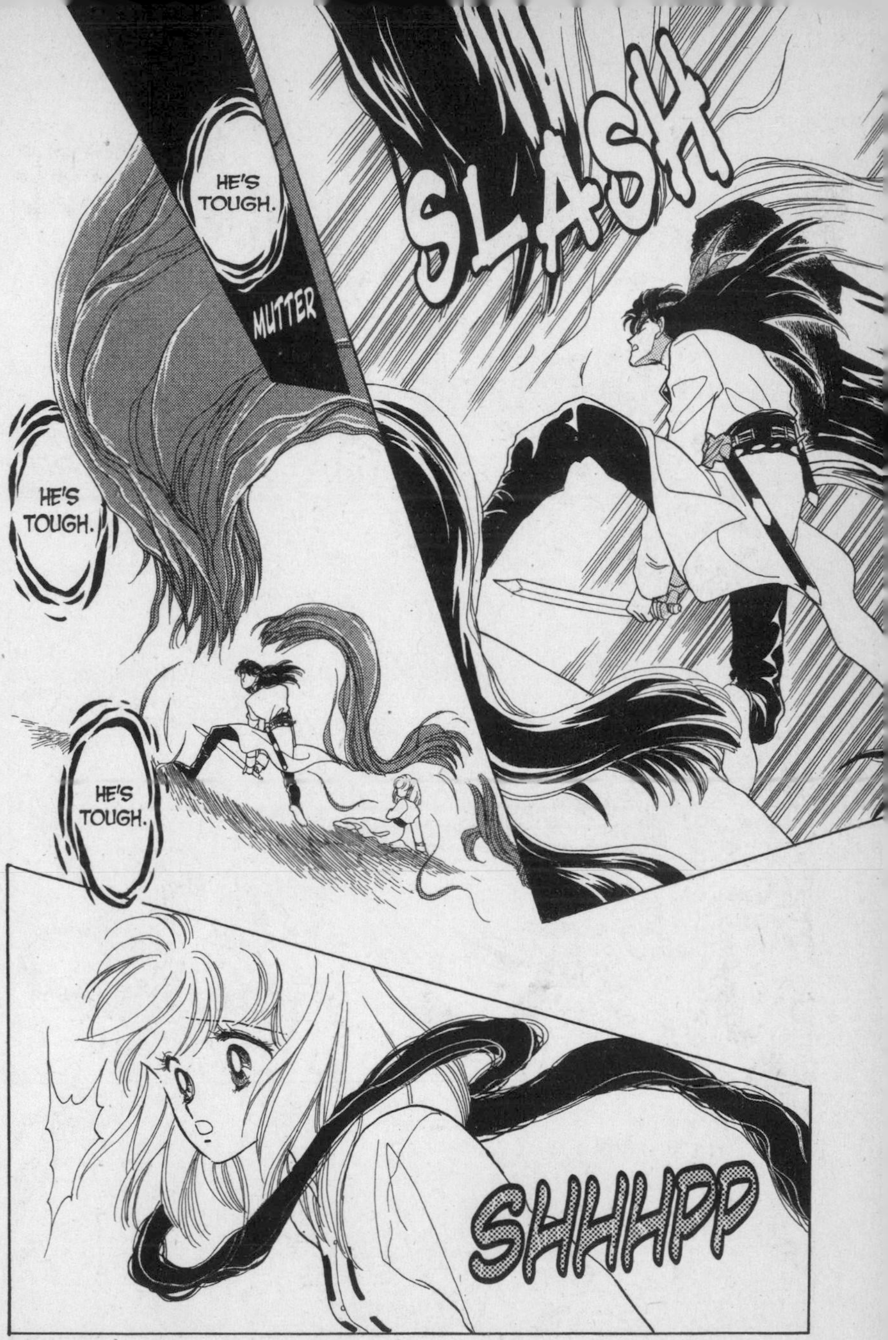
SLASH
HE'S TOUGH.
MUTTER
HE'S TOUGH.
HE'S TOUGH.
SHHHPP

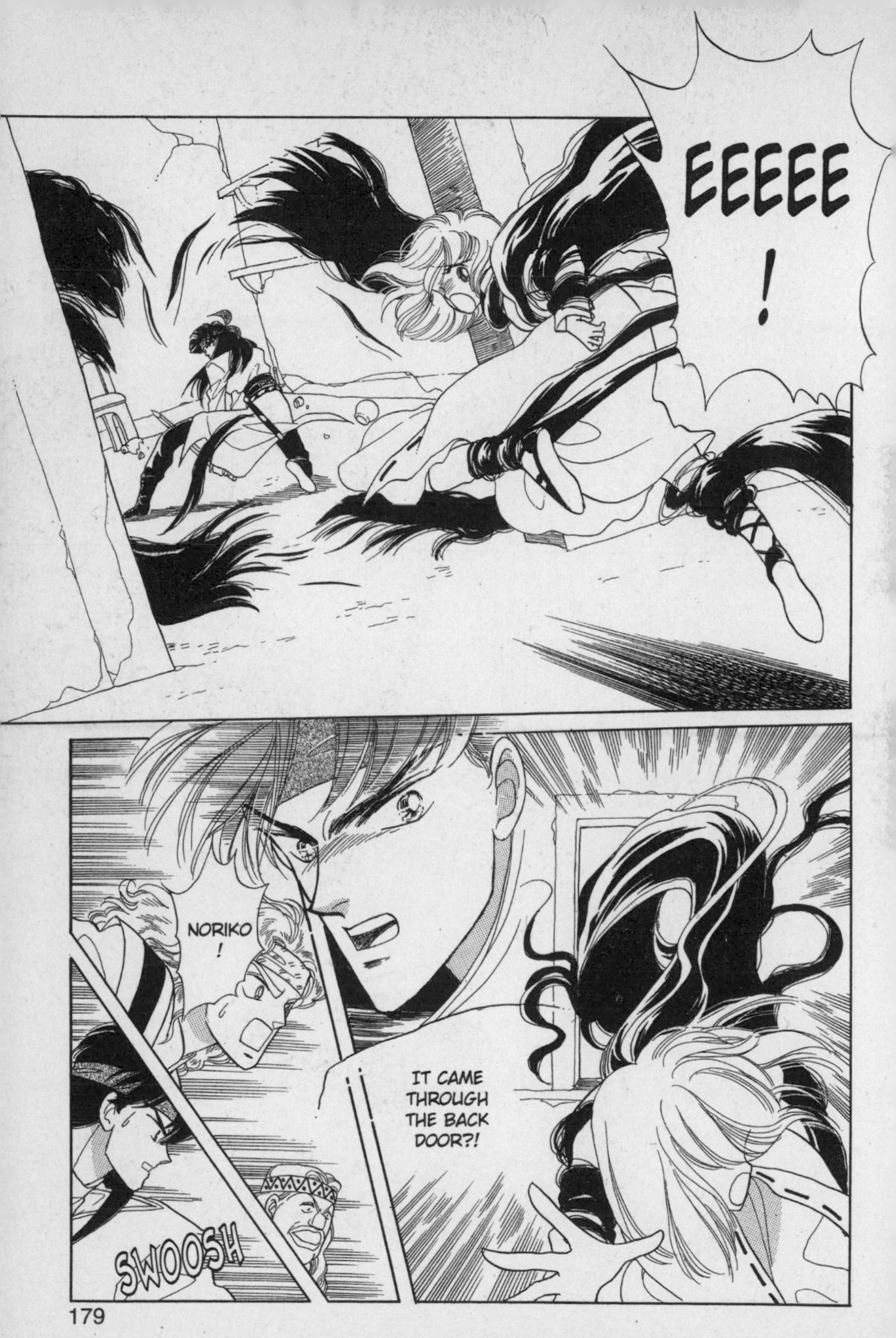
EEEEE
!
IT CAME THROUGH THE BACK DOOR?!
NORIKO
!
SWOOSH

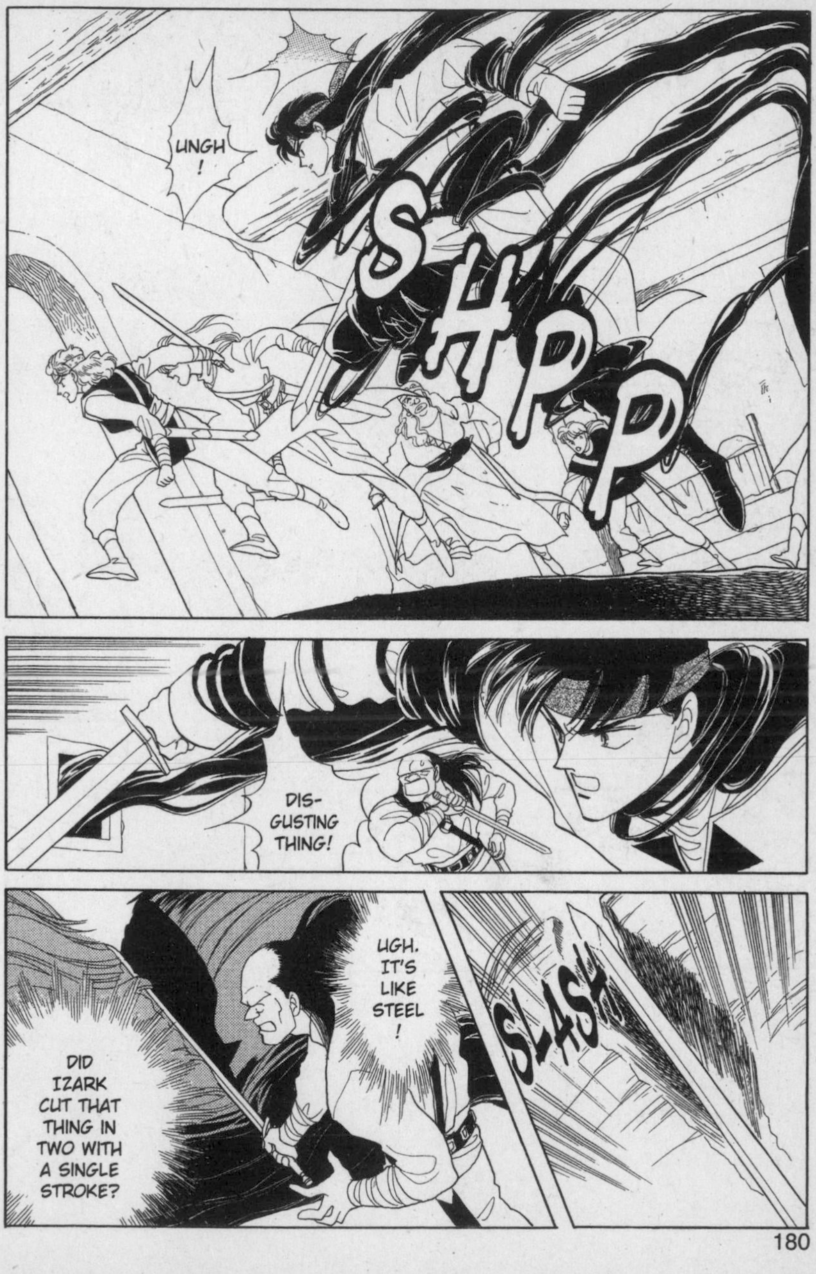
UNGH!
SHPP
DIS-GUSTING THING!
SLASH
UGH. IT'S LIKE STEEL!
DID IZARK CUT THAT THING IN TWO WITH A SINGLE STROKE?

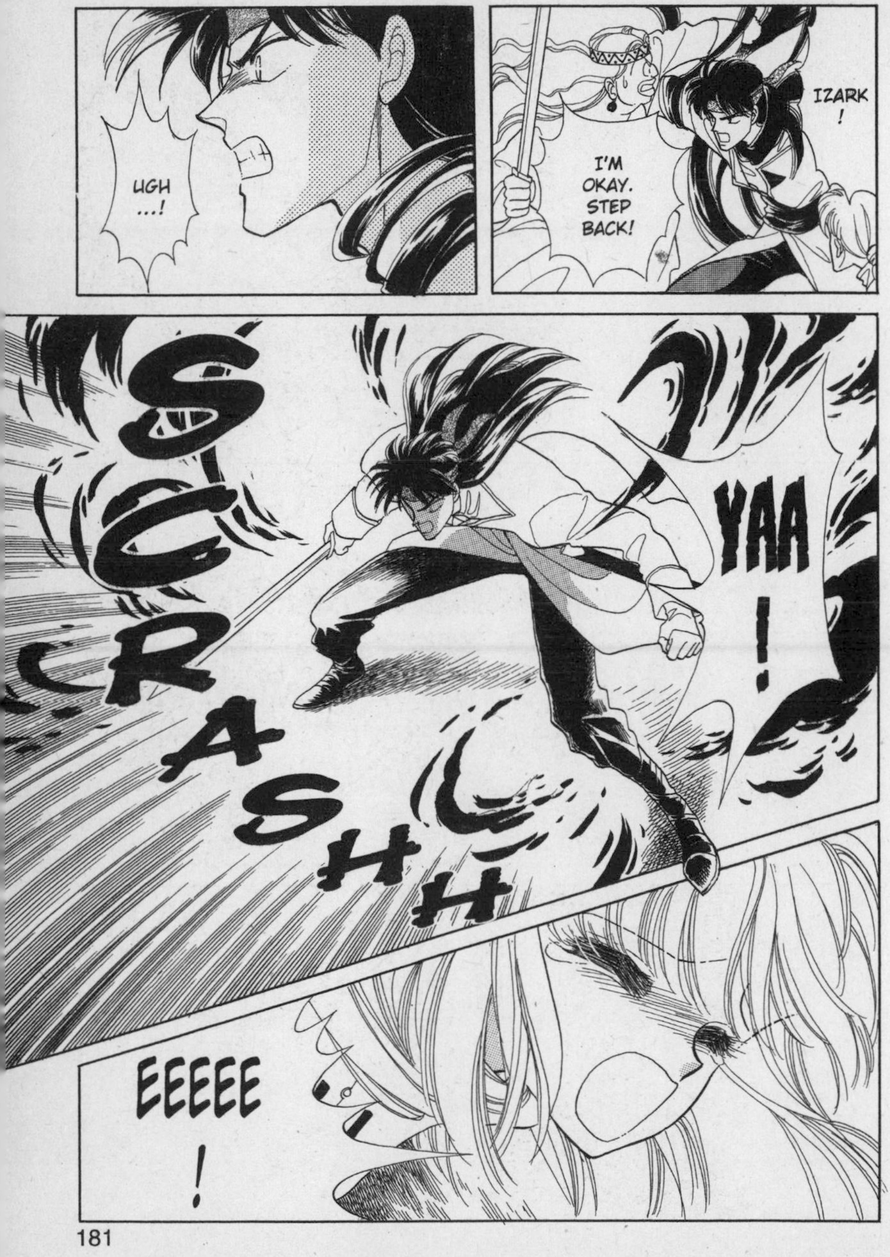
IZARK!
I'M OKAY. STEP BACK!
UGH ...!
YAA!
SCRASHH
EEEEE!

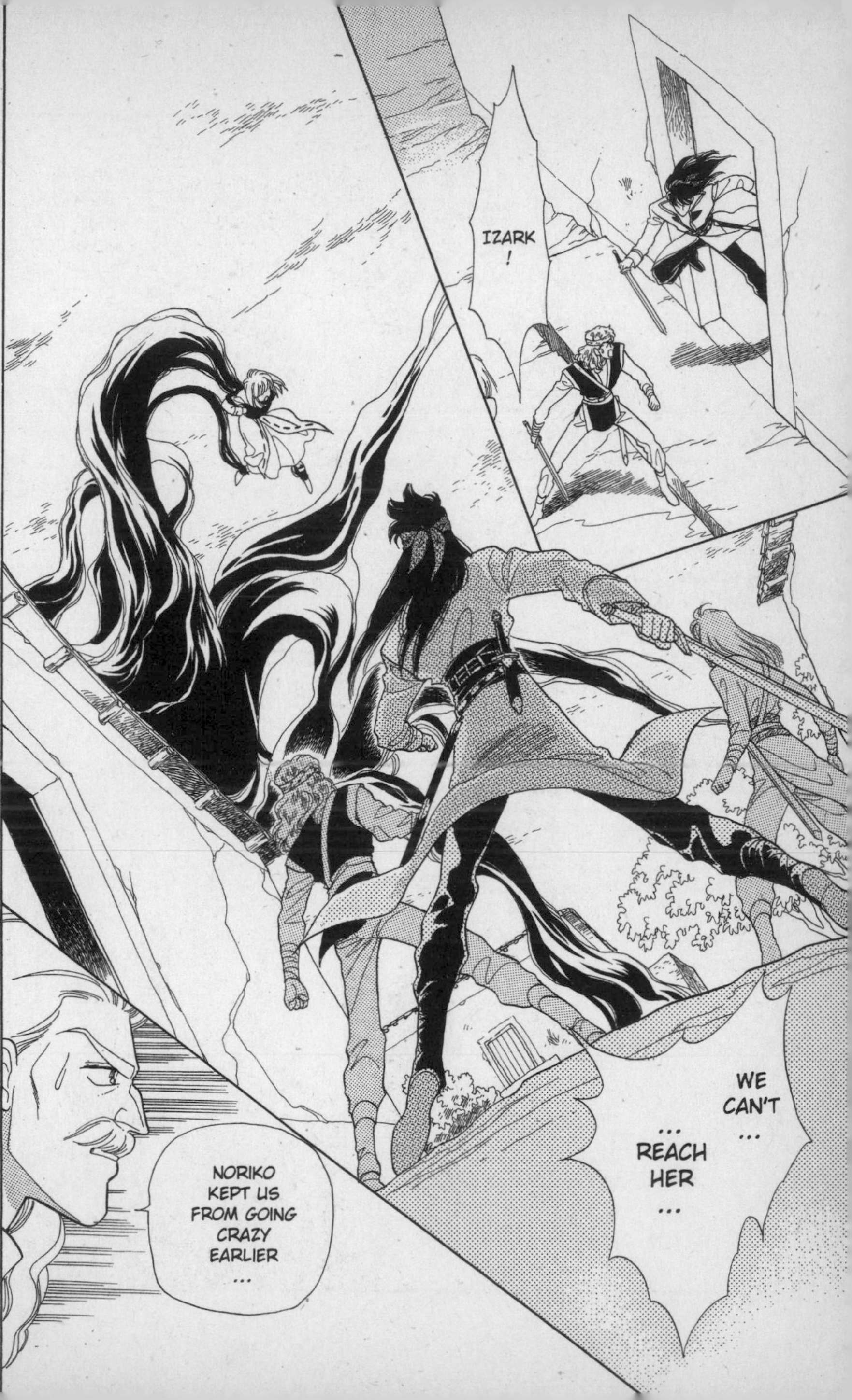
IZARK !
WE CAN'T ... ... REACH HER ...
NORIKO KEPT US FROM GOING CRAZY EARLIER ...

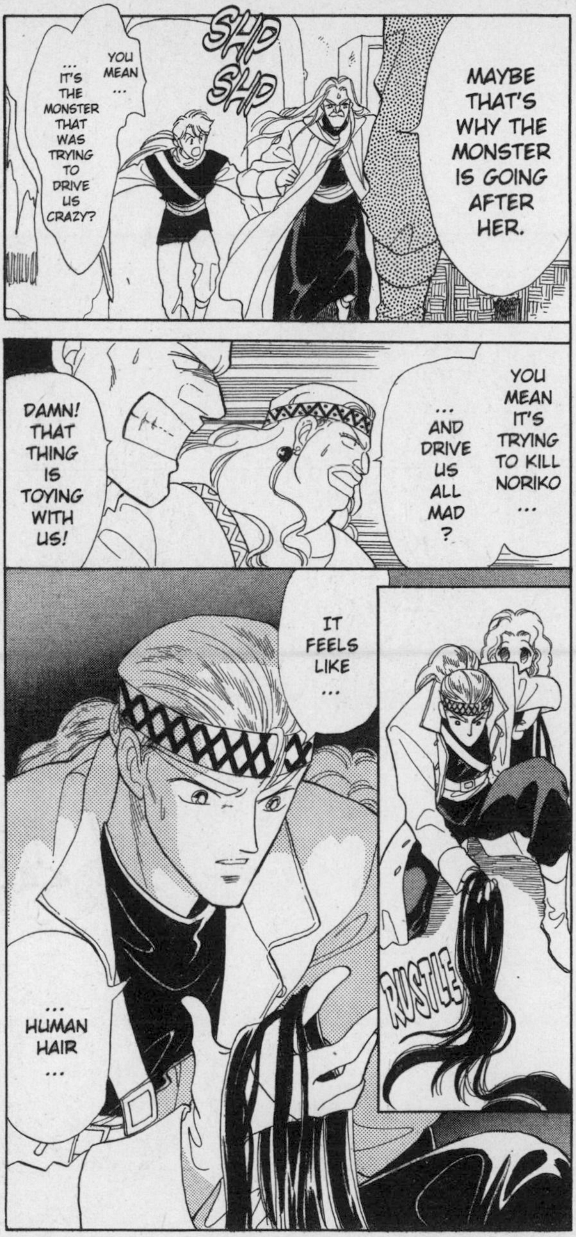
MAYBE THAT'S WHY THE MONSTER IS GOING AFTER HER.
SHP SHP
YOU MEAN ...
... IT'S THE MONSTER THAT WAS TRYING TO DRIVE US CRAZY?
YOU MEAN IT'S TRYING TO KILL NORIKO ...
... AND DRIVE US ALL MAD?
DAMN! THAT THING IS TOYING WITH US!
RUSTLE
IT FEELS LIKE ...
... HUMAN HAIR ...

Thank you for your fan letters. ♡♡

I apologize for not being able to write back to you.

But I read every one of the letters I receive. ♡♡♡

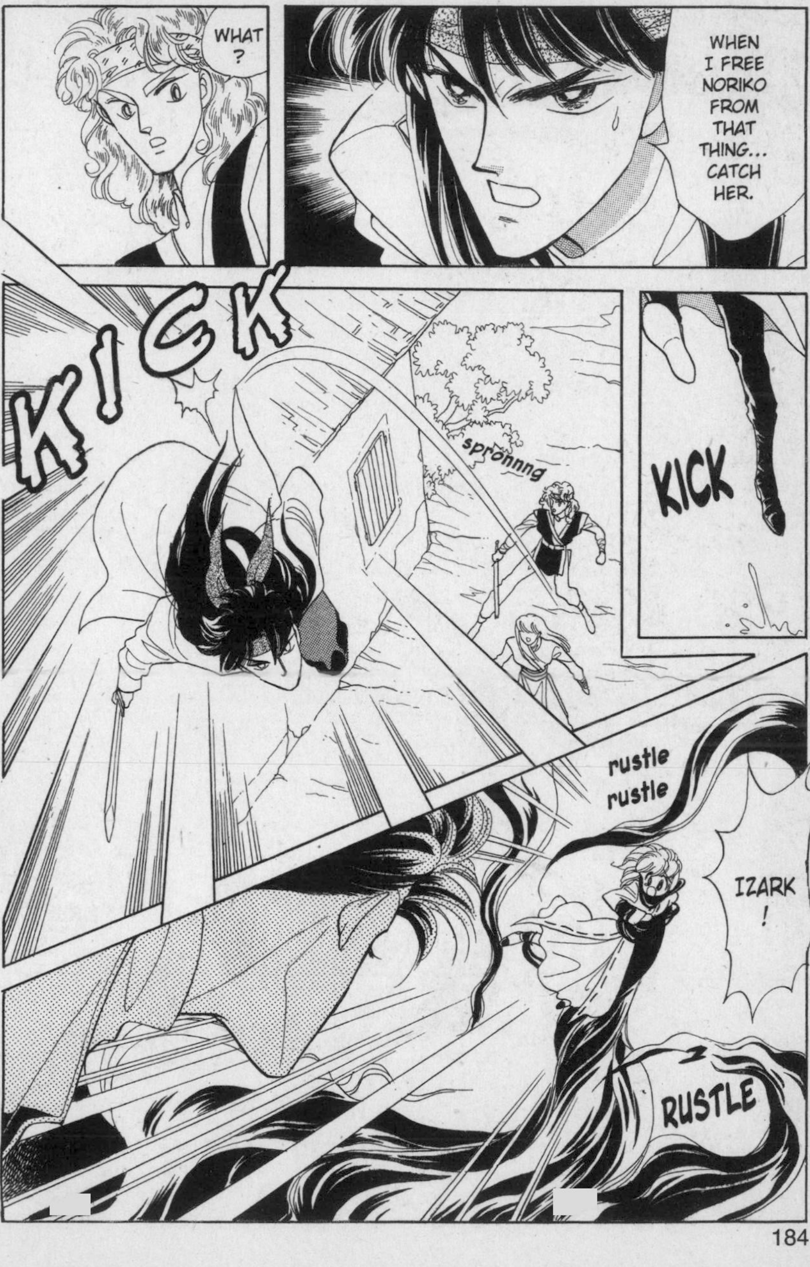
WHEN I FREE NORIKO FROM THAT THING... CATCH HER.
WHAT?
KICK
KICK
spronnng
rustle rustle
IZARK!
RUSTLE

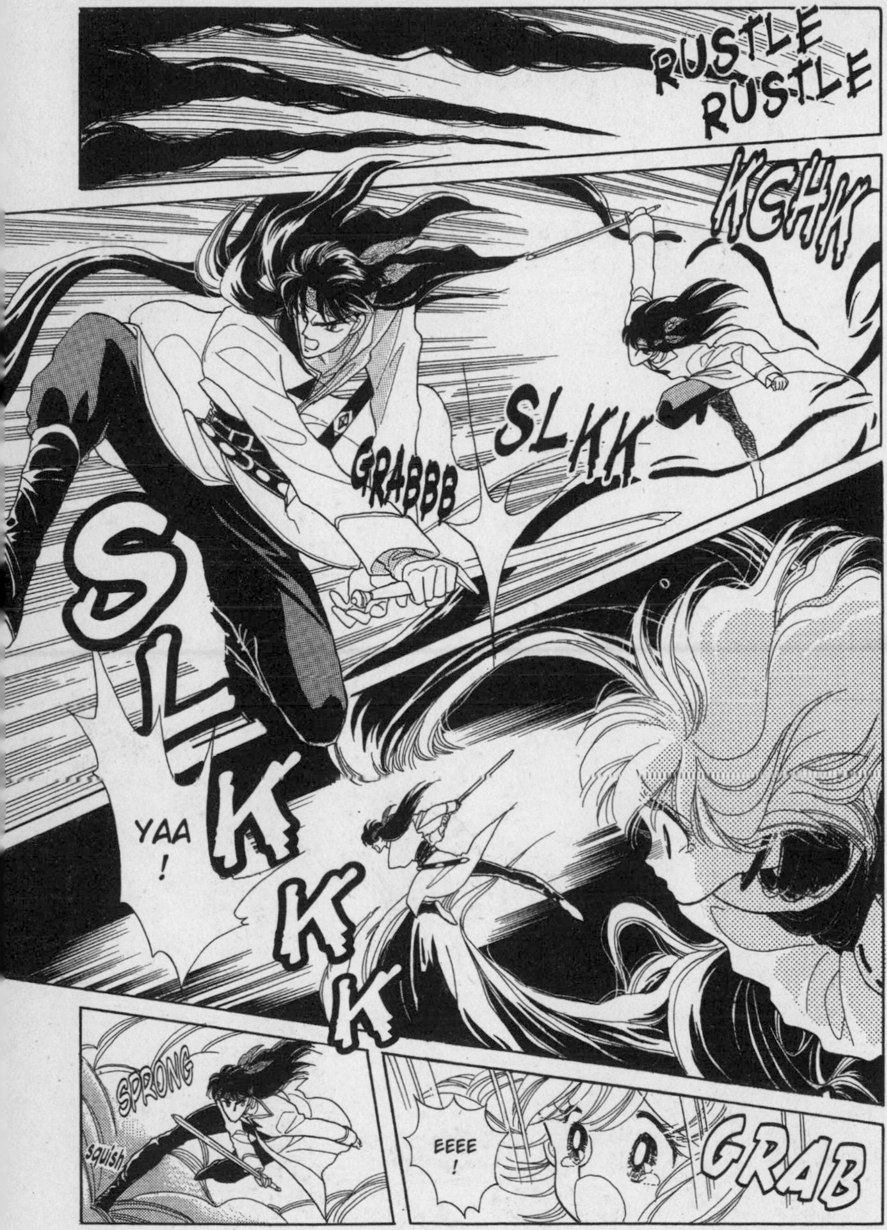
RUSTLE
RUSTLE
KCHK
SLKK
GRABBB
SLKKK
YAA!
GRAB
EEEE!
SPRONG
squish

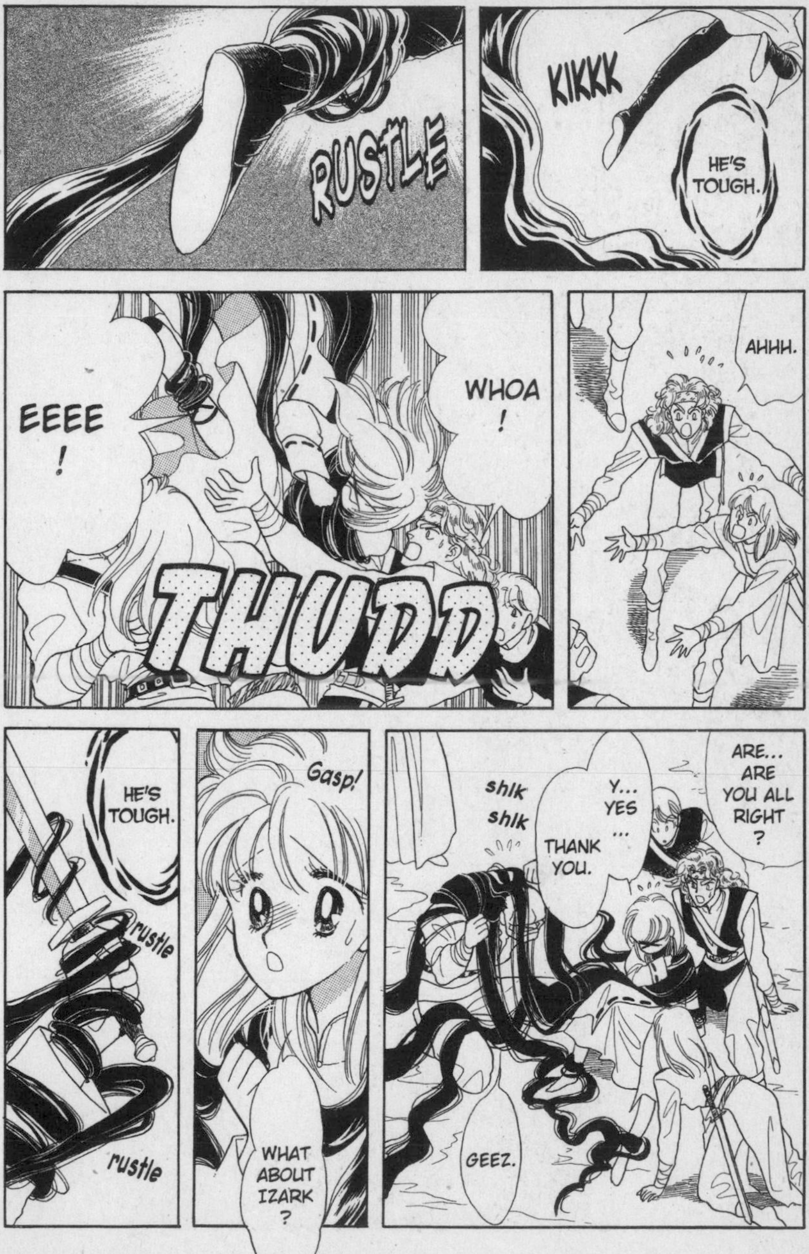
KIKKK
HE'S TOUGH.
RUSTLE
AHHH.
WHOA!
EEEE!
THUDD
ARE... ARE YOU ALL RIGHT?
Y... YES... THANK YOU.
shlk shlk
GEEZ.
Gasp!
WHAT ABOUT IZARK?
HE'S TOUGH.
rustle
rustle

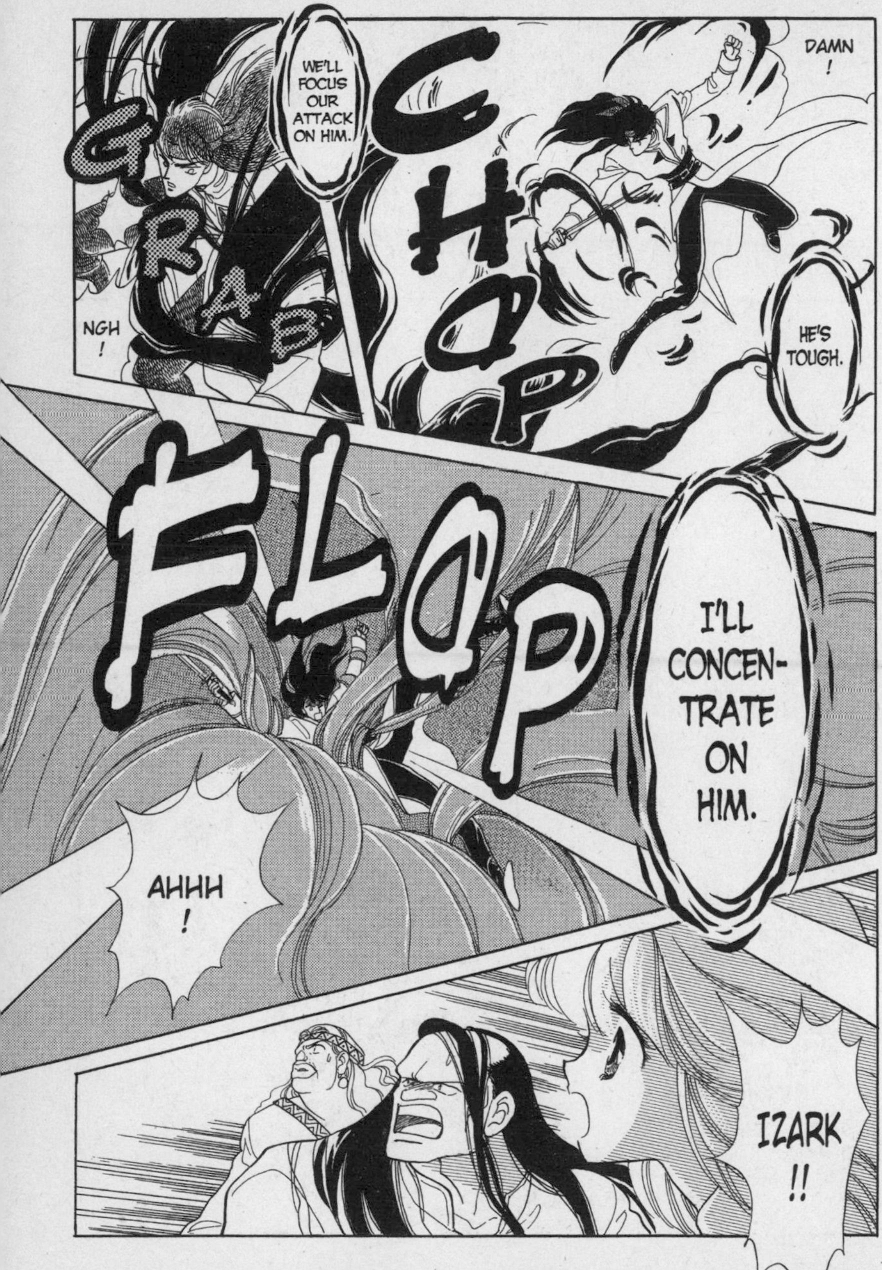
DAMN!
CHOP
HE'S TOUGH.
WE'LL FOCUS OUR ATTACK ON HIM.
GRAB
NGH!
I'LL CONCENTRATE ON HIM.
FLOP
AHHH!
IZARK!!

From Far Away
Vol. 4
Shôjo Edition

Story and Art by
Kyoko Hikawa

English Adaptation/Trina Robbins
Translation/Yuko Sawada
Touch-Up Art & Lettering/Walden Wong
Cover & Graphic Design/Andrea Rice
Editor/Eric Searleman

Managing Editor/Annette Roman
Director of Production/Noboru Watanabe
Editorial Director/Alvin Lu
Sr. Director of Acquisitions/Rika Inouye
Vice President of Sales & Marketing/Liza Coppola
Executive Vice President/Hyoe Narita
Publisher/Seiji Horibuchi

Printed in the U.S.A.

Published by VIZ, LLC
P.O. Box 77010
San Francisco, CA 94107

Shôjo Edition
10 9 8 7 6 5 4 3 2 1
First printing, April 2005

www.viz.com

store.viz.com

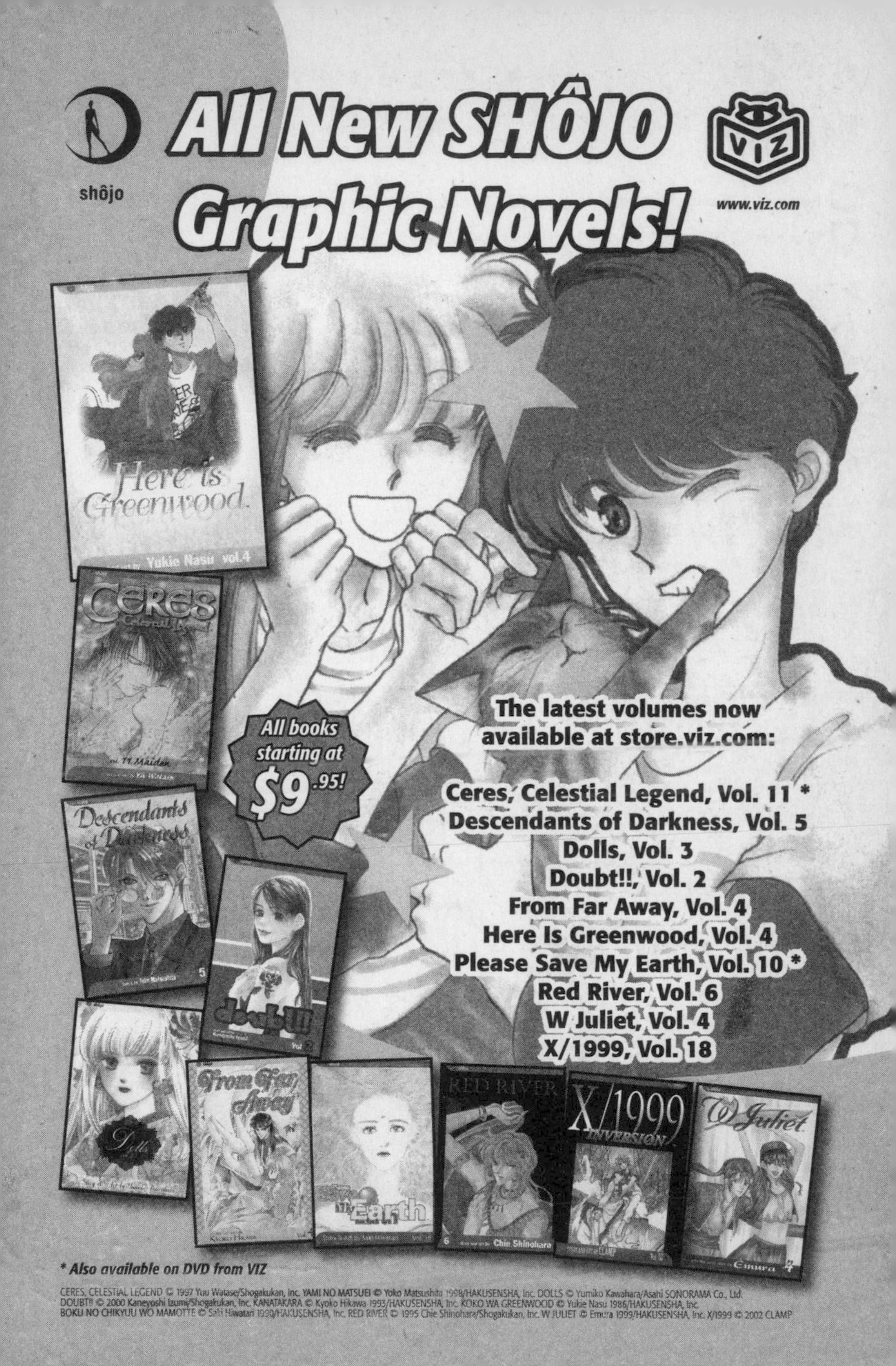
shôjo
All New SHÔJO
Graphic Novels!
VIZ
www.viz.com
Here is Greenwood
Yukie Nasu vol.4
Ceres Celestial Legend
Descendants of Darkness
doubt!!
Dolls
From Far Away
My Earth
RED RIVER
Chie Shinohara
X/1999 INVERSION
CLAMP
W Juliet
Emura
All books starting at $9.95!
The latest volumes now available at store.viz.com:
Ceres, Celestial Legend, Vol. 11 *
Descendants of Darkness, Vol. 5
Dolls, Vol. 3
Doubt!!, Vol. 2
From Far Away, Vol. 4
Here Is Greenwood, Vol. 4
Please Save My Earth, Vol. 10 *
Red River, Vol. 6
W Juliet, Vol. 4
X/1999, Vol. 18
* Also available on DVD from VIZ
CERES, CELESTIAL LEGEND © 1997 Yuu Watase/Shogakukan, Inc. YAMI NO MATSUEI © Yoko Matsushita 1998/HAKUSENSHA, Inc. DOLLS © Yumiko Kawahara/Asahi SONORAMA Co., Ltd. DOUBT!! © 2000 Kaneyoshi Izumi/Shogakukan, Inc. KANATAKARA © Kyoko Hikawa 1993/HAKUSENSHA, Inc. KOKO WA GREENWOOD © Yukie Nasu 1986/HAKUSENSHA, Inc. BOKU NO CHIKYUU WO MAMOTTE © Saki Hiwatari 1990/HAKUSENSHA, Inc. RED RIVER © 1995 Chie Shinohara/Shogakukan, Inc. W JULIET © Emura 1999/HAKUSENSHA, Inc. X/1999 © 2002 CLAMP

COMPLETE OUR SURVEY AND LET US KNOW WHAT YOU THINK!

☐ Please do NOT send me information about VIZ products, news and events, special offers, or other information.

☐ Please do NOT send me information from VIZ's trusted business partners.

Name: _____

Address: _____

City: _____ **State:** _____ **Zip:** _____

E-mail: _____

☐ **Male** ☐ **Female**   **Date of Birth** (mm/dd/yyyy): ___ / ___ / _____   (Under 13? Parental consent required)

What race/ethnicity do you consider yourself? (please check one)

☐ Asian/Pacific Islander   ☐ Black/African American   ☐ Hispanic/Latino

☐ Native American/Alaskan Native ☐ White/Caucasian   ☐ Other: _____

What VIZ product did you purchase? (check all that apply and indicate title purchased)

☐ DVD/VHS _____

☐ Graphic Novel _____

☐ Magazines _____

☐ Merchandise _____

Reason for purchase: (check all that apply)

☐ Special offer   ☐ Favorite title   ☐ Gift

☐ Recommendation   ☐ Other _____

Where did you make your purchase? (please check one)

☐ Comic store   ☐ Bookstore   ☐ Mass/Grocery Store

☐ Newsstand   ☐ Video/Video Game Store ☐ Other: _____

☐ Online (site: _____)

What other VIZ properties have you purchased/own? _____

_____

How many anime and/or manga titles have you purchased in the last year? How many were VIZ titles? (please check one from each column)

ANIME
- ☐ None
- ☐ 1-4
- ☐ 5-10
- ☐ 11+

MANGA
- ☐ None
- ☐ 1-4
- ☐ 5-10
- ☐ 11+

VIZ
- ☐ None
- ☐ 1-4
- ☐ 5-10
- ☐ 11+

I find the pricing of VIZ products to be: (please check one)

☐ Cheap   ☐ Reasonable   ☐ Expensive

What genre of manga and anime would you like to see from VIZ? (please check two)

☐ Adventure   ☐ Comic Strip   ☐ Science Fiction   ☐ Fighting

☐ Horror   ☐ Romance   ☐ Fantasy   ☐ Sports

What do you think of VIZ's new look?

☐ Love It   ☐ It's OK   ☐ Hate It   ☐ Didn't Notice   ☐ No Opinion

Which do you prefer? (please check one)

☐ Reading right-to-left

☐ Reading left-to-right

Which do you prefer? (please check one)

☐ Sound effects in English

☐ Sound effects in Japanese with English captions

☐ Sound effects in Japanese only with a glossary at the back

THANK YOU! Please send the completed form to:

NJW Research
42 Catharine St.
Poughkeepsie, NY 12601

All information provided will be used for internal purposes only. We promise not to sell or otherwise divulge your information.